TO PRAY AS

A JEW

Books by the Same Author

BEYOND THYSELF

SUKKOT

TO BE A JEW
A Guide to Jewish Observance in Contemporary Life

TO RAISE A JEWISH CHILD
A Guide for Parents

TO ❧ PRAY ❧ AS ❧ A JEW

A Guide to the Prayer Book and the Synagogue Service

RABBI HAYIM HALEVY DONIN

BasicBooks
A Member of the Perseus Books Group

The Hebrew text used in this book is from the *Rinat Yisrael Siddur*, edited by Shlomo Tal and published by Moreshet Publishing Co., Jerusalem.

Library of Congress Cataloging-in-Publication Data

Donin, Hayim.
To pray as a Jew.

Includes indexes.
1. Jews. Liturgy and ritual. Daily prayers—
Commentaries. 2. Jews—Rites and ceremonies.
3. Prayer (Judaism) I. Title.
BM675.D3Z75   296.4   80-50554
ISBN: 0-465-08628-4 (cloth)
ISBN: 0-465-08633-0 (paper)

01 RRD-H   30 29 28 27 26 25 24 23 22

Dedicated to my father and mother
—of blessed memory—
Max Dolnansky (1892–1960)
(Mordechai ben Moshe Halevy)
and
Eva Dolnansky (1900–1974)
(Rivka bat David Tzvi)

ת נ צ ב ״ ה

CONTENTS

INTRODUCTION   3

Chapter 1

THE QUEST FOR SPIRITUALITY   9

Chapter 2

TO FEEL AT HOME IN THE SYNAGOGUE: KNOWING WHAT TO DO 23

Chapter 3

THE SHEMONEH ESREI: THE AMIDAH OF "EIGHTEEN" BLESSINGS 69

Chapter 4

THE AMIDAH FOR THE SABBATH AND FESTIVALS

Chapter 5

KEDUSHAH AND OTHER ADDITIONS TO THE AMIDAH

Chapter 6

THE SHEMA AND ITS BLESSINGS

CONTENTS

Chapter 7

THE VERSES OF SONG—PESUKEI d'ZIMRA
(THE INTRODUCTORY PRAYERS)   167

Chapter 8

THE MORNING BLESSINGS—BIRKHOT
HASHAHAR (THE PRELIMINARY PRAYERS) 183

Chapter 9

SUPPLICATIONS AND OTHER SUPPLEMENTARY PRAYERS   202

Chapter 10

THE KADDISH   216

Chapter 11

RESPONSES IN PRAYER   227

Chapter 12

THE TORAH READING SERVICE 231

Chapter 13

WELCOMING THE SABBATH: KABBALAT SHABBAT 256

Chapter 14

PRAYERS FOR SPECIAL OCCASIONS 264

Chapter 15

THE GRACE AFTER MEALS: BIRKAT HAMAZON   284

Chapter 16

THE BLESSINGS BEFORE EATING: BIRKHOT HANEHENIN   305

Chapter 17

HOME PRAYERS FOR SABBATHS AND FESTIVALS 319

Chapter 18

RULES RELATING TO THE PRAYER SERVICE 337

Epilogue

THE ETHICAL DIMENSION OF JEWISH PRAYER 357

Appendix

PREFACE

THERE IS hardly a Jew who does not at some time in his life hold a Jewish prayer book, a *siddur* (pl. *siddurim**) in his hands. In most Jewish schools, the siddur is the standard text used for the practice of reading once the child has learned the letters of the Hebrew alphabet. Thus, even a child exposed only to the most meager religious training is likely to have had contact with the siddur. So would a person who suffers the loss of a loved one and comes into a synagogue, if only to say the *Kaddish.* If a Jewish home has any Hebrew religious texts at all, the siddur, if only one for the High Holy Days,** is sure to be among them. Indeed, it may be the only one.

The siddur is the Jewish religious text in widest circulation, surpassing even the Hebrew Bible. It is published in many countries by dozens of publishers in countless editions. The siddur has been translated into many languages. In the English language alone, at least half a dozen different translations are in use. These translations are usually printed opposite or below the Hebrew text. Many commentaries on the siddur have been written by great scholars, and some editions of the siddur appear with a commentary on the page.

The siddur deserves all this attention because it is more than just a book of prayers. I take the liberty of quoting a short passage from my book *To Be a Jew.*§

* The full Hebrew title for the Jewish prayer book is *Siddur Tefilah* or *Seder Tefilah,* which means the Order of Prayer. But one hardly ever hears it called by its full name. Instead, it is simply called *siddur* ("order") and that is how I shall refer to it throughout this book. (Most Jews are familiar with the other form of the same word, *seder,* which, when used alone, refers to the ritual order that is followed on the first two nights of Passover.)

** A siddur intended specifically for use on one of the holidays is called a *mahzor,* which means a cycle, because some of the prayers in it are said only periodically or cyclically.

§ New York: Basic Books, 1972, pp. 179–180.

[The siddur is] a vast repository of all the principles of Jewish faith, a record of both the great victories and tragic defeats Israel has known in its long history. It is a testimony of the aspirations and hopes of the Jewish people throughout time. It is witness to the ethical and moral heights to which Jewry aspired and attained. It is a reminder of laughter and gaiety, of celebration and rejoicing, as well as of sorrow and grief, of mourning and bemoaning that takes place in the life of the individual as in the life of an entire people. [The siddur] provides insights into daily Jewish living as well as into all the special occasions and festivals in the Jewish calendar. It contains Biblical passages that date as far back as 3300 years; prayers composed by the Sages as long as 2500 years ago. While most of the prayers are hallowed by their Biblical and Talmudic origins, there will also be found some that have been written since.

The Siddur is study as well as prayer. It is moral instruction and ethical guidance as well as pleas for personal needs. It emphasizes *man's duties* as well as his *rights*. It is the record *par excellence* of Israel's relationship with God.

I have become convinced that throughout most of Jewish history, it has been the siddur, or rather the prayers themselves, that have been the most popular vehicle for conveying to the masses the basic principles of the Jewish faith. The doctrinal lessons that the sages wished to emphasize in their struggle against sectarian heresies found their way into the prayers. The prayers thus became a most effective "textbook" for teaching, instilling, and perpetuating Jewish values and faith.

Franz Rosenzweig once wrote, "The sum and substance of the whole of historical Judaism, its handbook and its memorial tablet, will ever be the Prayer Book: the Daily and the Festival, the Siddur and the Maḥzor. He to whom these volumes are not a sealed book has more than grasped 'the essence of Judaism.' He is informed with it as with life itself; he has within him 'a Jewish world'."*

It is therefore ironic that in our times the siddur, though in widespread use, is perhaps the least understood, the least studied, and the least appreciated of all Jewish religious texts. Relatively few are able to see its beauty or to be inspired by its contents.

---

* Nahum M. Glatzer, *Franz Rosenzweig: His Life and Thought* (Philadelphia: Jewish Publication Society, 1953), p. 251.

People unfamiliar with the siddur see it as a forest of words in which they feel lost, encountering page after page of endless, seemingly repetitive passages. If this is not enough to frighten someone who lacks the compass of a Jewish education, certainly it can bore and make one feel deeply uncomfortable in the synagogue. There are surely countless Jews who stay away from the synagogue only because they feel so utterly lost when they get there, neither knowing what to do with the book in their hands nor being able to follow the ritual of the service. Many who would *like* to pray simply don't know how. Unfamiliarity in this case may even encourage a display of indifference or the flaunting of disbelief.

On the other hand, there are people who know exactly what prayers to say and where in the siddur to find them. These are people who can easily read the Hebrew text and who feel quite at home in any synagogue. It is likely that they have prayed regularly all or most of their lives. Yet a great many in this group also have a problem, though they may hesitate to admit it or may be entirely unaware of it: either they do not understand the Hebrew; or if they do, the words say nothing to them. While they speed through the forest of words, they see only the trunks of the trees and catch no glimpse of the light, beauty, and splendor of the whole. For such people, familiarity has dulled the awe and excitement that the siddur should generate. It is taken too much for granted, regarded as too elementary, and unworthy of serious study. The siddur has become for them exactly what the sages cautioned us against: a source of routine prayer—words that flow from the lips but not from the heart.

I hope that this book will answer the needs of both these groups. It should help the relatively well informed to gain a much better understanding of the inner structure of the siddur and a greater appreciation of the spiritual richness embedded in the words that they have for so long been accustomed to say. At the same time, I have tried to keep in mind the people for whom the prayer service is still confusing. Many of the sections in Chapter 2 have been included mainly for their benefit, as have numerous details throughout the book.

What I have done is to present a mixture of *halakha* and history, *midrash* and philosophy, in an attempt to explain the contents of the siddur and the structure of the service in such a way as to help make the siddur come alive, to make it more exciting and more meaningful. It is not my purpose to convince anyone to pray or of the need to pray. I leave that task to others, perhaps even to the reader himself. But if one is moved to pray, or feels committed to prayer as a religious duty, or simply wishes better to understand the substance of Jewish prayer, then this book is intended to show the way, to enlighten, and hopefully to inspire.

I touch but do not dwell on the differences between the Sephardic and the Ashkenazic rites; I touch even less on the differences that are sometimes found in different siddurim within each of the traditional rites. For the differences are relatively minor, while the general structure of the service is the same. If one is familiar with one siddur and one rite, one will be comfortable with another.

The English translations of the Hebrew prayers used in this book are my own. I found it difficult to choose from among the many existing translations. While some are better than others, I was not completely satisfied with any of them. I do not know whether my translation will prove to be more satisfactory than the others. When translating, we tread a fine line. The Talmud cautions that "he who translates a verse with strict literalness is a falsifier, and he who makes additions to it is a blasphemer" (Tosefta Megillah [Vilna Shas] 3:21). Therefore I have sought a translation that tries to balance contemporary usage, traditional interpretation, and literal meaning. I also wish to note that all italics in the quotations from Biblical and other sources, unless otherwise indicated, are my own.

I have decided to retain the use of "Thou," "Thee," and "Thy" in all passages that address themselves directly to God. The more contemporary "You" and "Your," which I had at first considered using, made me uncomfortable in some instances, although I find it difficult to explain why this should be so. The Hebrew *atah* (and the Yiddish *du*) reflects the familiar and the intimate approach to God with which I am comfortable. Still, English seems to demand, at least in some places, the more reverent "Thou" and "Thy."

The English transliteration does not strictly follow the accepted convention to which Jewish scholarly writings subscribe. My purpose is to have the Latin characters read as easily as possible and for the transliterated words to sound as close as possible to the Hebrew. The transliteration follows the Sephardic pronunciation, the dialect spoken in Israel. Those who are able to read the Hebrew can of course use the pronunciation or dialect with which they are most comfortable.

One final word of explanation. Almost everyone who saw the manuscript raised the question: "Why do you start with the *Shemoneh Esrei?*" Most books on the subject follow the order of the siddur. Those that do not at least give precedence to the *Shema*, which is the older of the two, and whose degree of sanctity is higher as its source is the Torah. The primary reason for my approach is that I find it easier to convey an understanding of the entire structure of the prayer service by starting with the *Shemoneh Esrei*, which is the core of every service, and then to build around it.

So much more could have been written about prayer in general and about prayers in particular. But every book reaches an optimal size for its purposes. The problem I had to weigh and consider was what to omit rather than what else to include. I hope that I have achieved a happy balance.

I wish to express my gratitude to Moreshet Publishing Ltd., Jerusalem, for permission to use portions of the *Rinat Yisrael Siddur*, edited by Shlomo Tal. Apart from its beautiful and elegantly distinctive typeface, the Hebrew text in this siddur contains several features found in no other prayer book. One feature assists the reader to accent the words correctly. The symbol ‷ over the last letter of a word indicates that the accent is on the last syllable. The symbol ‹ over a word indicates the accent either on the first or second syllable.

Another feature assists the reader who wishes to read in the Sephardic dialect. Not every ָ vowel (pronounced *aw* in Ashkenazic) is pronounced *ah* in Sephardic. The vowel signs in this siddur distinguish between the vowel ָ (*kamatz gadol*), which is pronounced *ah* in the Sephardic dialect, and the less common *kamatz katan*, which is shown as ׇ and which has an *aw* sound even in the Sephardic pronunciation.

It should be noted that God's name appears in this siddur as יהוה—as it does in the Torah and in all printed Hebrew Bibles, as well as in older siddurim. In all other prayer books, God's name is abbreviated to יְיָ . Both are read in exactly the same way: Adonai (in Sephardic), Ådonoi (in Ashkenazic).

I am deeply indebted to those who critically read the entire manuscript. They include Rabbi Dr. Martin L. Gordon, Rabbi

PREFACE

Leonard Oschry, Rabbi Uziel Weingarten, Dr. Naomi G. Cohen, Professor Marvin Fox, and Dr. Sara Reguer. Their insights, criticism, and suggestions contributed immeasurably to the quality of this book. And I am most grateful to Rabbi Avraham Kroll and Rabbi Moshe Hershler for their guidance on the many fine halakhic points that needed to be clarified and resolved for this book.

My thanks are also extended to several friends who read the manuscript in its various stages and whose comments were very helpful. They are Morris L. Green, Dr. Martin Norton, Yale Roeh, Dr. Mark Segal and Joyce Segal, Miriam Soller, and my wife Tzivia. Sound advice also came from George Greenfield of Harper and Row, Publishers, Inc., and I wish to express my appreciation to him. I also wish to pay tribute to my typist, Haya Raphael, whose devotion and superb skill made my work so much easier. To Sidney Eisenshtat, for his precious counsel, special thank you.

I am most grateful to Erwin A. Glikes, my friend of many years and formerly my editor and publisher, whose keen insights once again found expression in the pages of this book; to Midge Decter who enthusiastically completed the editorial work on the manuscript and carefully guided it through all its subsequent stages; and to Arthur Krystal whose thoughtful copy editing contributed much to the refinement of this book.

Finally, I thank Almighty God for having kept me alive, sustained me, and enabled me to reach this season.

HAYIM HALEVY DONIN

CHRONOLOGY OF AGES
IN JEWISH HISTORY

wwwwwwwwwwwwwwwwwwwwwwwwwwwwwwwwwwwwwwwwwwwwwwwwwwwwwwwwwwwwwwwwwwww

To PROVIDE the reader with some historical perspective to different periods mentioned in the book, I offer the following outline:

Period of the Patriarchs: 2000–1700 B.C.E.

The Exodus from Egypt: circa 1280 B.C.E.

The Period of King David: 1005–965 B.C.E.

Period of the First Temple: 928–586 B.C.E.

Period of the Second Temple: 515 B.C.E.–70 C.E.

Period of the Mishnah (Tannaitic Period): From the beginning of the first century C.E. until about 220 C.E. I refer to this period as the early Talmudic period.

Period of the Gemara (Amoraic Period): From the beginning of the third century C.E. until 500 C.E. I refer to this period as the later Talmudic period.

Post-Talmudic Period [Savoraim]: 500–640 C.E.

Period of the Geonim [the heads of the Talmudic academies]: From 640 C.E.–1038 C.E.

Period of the Early [Rabbinic] Authorities (*Rishonim*): From the beginning of the eleventh century C.E. till the end of the fifteenth century.

Period of Latter-day [Rabbinic] Authorities (*Aḥaronim*): From the beginning of the sixteenth century C.E. until the present day.

KEY TO ABBREVIATIONS AND ACRONYMS USED IN CITATIONS

~~~~~~

Torah—The Five Books of Moses

Gen.	Genesis	(*Bereshit*)
Exod.	Exodus	(*Shemot*)
Lev.	Leviticus	(*Vayikra*)
Num.	Numbers	(*Bamidbar*)
Deut.	Deuteronomy	(*Devarim*)

Neviim and Ketubim—The Prophets and Writings

Josh.	Joshua	(*Yehoshua*)
Sam.	Samuel	(*Shemuel*)
Is.	Isaiah	(*Yeshayahu*)
Jer.	Jeremiah	(*Yirmiyahu*)
Ez.	Ezekiel	(*Yehezkel*)
Hos.	Hosea	(*Hoshea*)
Neh.	Nehemiah	(*Nehemiah*)
Ps.	Psalms	(*Tehillim*)
Prov.	Proverbs	(*Mishlei*)
Esth.	Esther	(*Ester*)
Chron.	Chronicles	(*Divrei Hayamim*)

Talmudic Sources

The name of a Talmudic tractate is always spelled out. If followed by a number such as 31a or 31b, reference is to the page in the Babylonian Talmud. If followed by a number such as 7:4, reference is to the Mishnah, the numerals indicating chapter and section. If the name of a tractate is preceded by Yer. (Yerushalmi), reference is to the Jerusalem or Palestinian Talmud; the numerals that follow refer to chapter and section.

Codes and Commentaries

OH   *Orah Hayim,* one of the four sections of the *Shulhan Arukh,* the code of Jewish law compiled by Rabbi Joseph Karo (1488–1575).

YD   *Yoreh Deah,* one of the four sections of the Shulhan Arukh.

MA   *Magen Avraham,* a halakhic commentary on Orah Hayim by Rabbi Avraham ben Hayim Halevy Gumbiner (1637–1683).

MB   *Mishnah Berurah,* a halakhic commentary on Orah Hayim by Rabbi Israel Meir HaKohen, known as the Chafetz Chayim (1838–1933). A parallel commentary, also cited, is called *Biur Halakha.*

AH   *Arukh HaShulhan,* an eight-volume compendium of Jewish law by Rabbi Yehiel Michael Epstein (1829–1908). It follows the order of the Shulhan Arukh.

Rashi   *Rabbi Shelomo Yitzhaki* (1040–1105), a commentary upon the Bible and Talmud.

Tos.   *Tosafot.* Commentary on the Talmud by twelfth and thirteenth century C.E. talmudists.

Maim.   *Maimonides* (1135–1204). Citations refer to the *Mishneh Torah,* his code of Jewish law. The Hebrew acronym of his name is *Rambam.*

Rema   *Rabbi Moses Isserles* (circa 1525–1572). His halakhic notes on the Shulhan Arukh are incorporated into the latter work.

CONTEMPORARY WORKS MENTIONED IN CITATIONS

~~~~~~

Igrot Moshe, Oraḥ Ḥayim. Two volumes of responsa by Rabbi Moshe Feinstein. Published in New York, 1959–1963.

Mekor Ḥayim HaShalem. A five-volume code of Jewish law by the Chief Rabbi of Tel Aviv-Jaffe, Rabbi Hayim David Halevy. He is the author of three volumes of responsa, *Asei Lekha Rav*, which is also cited.

Netiv Binah. A five-volume work on prayer by Rabbi Issachar Jacobson. Published in Tel Aviv, 1968–1978.

Olat Re'iyah. A two-volume commentary on the prayer book by Rabbi Abraham Isaac HaKohen Kook (1865–1935). Published in Jerusalem, 1962.

Yesodei Yeshurun. A six-volume halakhic compendium by Rabbi Gedalia Felder. Published in Toronto, 1954–1970.

KEY TO PRONUNCIATION
OF TRANSLITERATED
WORDS

ei as in *say*
ai as in *my*
e as in *red*
i as in *key*
u as in *moon*
a as in *llama*
o as in *law* (for Sephardic pronunciation);
   as in *cold* (for Ashkenazic pronunciation)
kh is used instead of ch for the guttural sound of the letter כ or ך,
   as in *barukh*
ḥ is used instead of ch for the softer guttural sound of the letter ח,
   as in *l'ḥayim*.

---

* Accepted spellings for certain common words, such as "Amen" or "Hallel," have been retained.

TO PRAY AS
A JEW

Introduction

IT IS TRUE that at times I pray only because it is my duty to obey the Jewish law that requires me to pray. But there are also times that I pray because I sincerely want to pray. These are the times when I want to reach out and talk to my Father in Heaven, to my Maker, the Holy One, blessed be He. These are the times when I want to cry out to the Supreme Being, to communicate with Him in a way that I can communicate with no one else. I cannot see Him, but He is real. He is there!

Such moments come to me only occasionally, but they come. Sometimes it is when I am in distress or when I feel lonely and isolated from all the world. Sometimes it is when I feel anxious about the safety or health of loved ones, or when my people are being threatened. At such moments my cry is likely to be accompanied by a shed tear, a pained heart, a feeling of despair. Sometimes it is when a great sense of relief comes over me, or when truly joyous news exhilarates me and makes me ecstatic. Then my cry is apt to be accompanied by a sense of exuberance and by a feeling of gratefulness. Whether God will accept my prayers and affirmatively respond to them, I do not know. That He hears my prayers, I firmly believe!

If I did not regularly pray out of a sense of obligation to pray, I do not think that I could really pray at those times when I truly want to do so.

I remember when as a young boy I watched my father, of blessed memory, recite his prayers. Sometimes, particularly on the High Holy Days, tears flowed from his eyes. I remember feeling embarrassed. I did not understand what made him cry. I wanted him to stop. I looked away. I still do not know what his thoughts were at those times, but now I understand. I was watching a most intimate communication between him and his Maker. Now I, too, sometimes communicate with my Maker.

We live in an age when it is not fashionable to pray. Even among those who join synagogues, only a small percentage pray daily or even weekly. Those who do not worship regularly put on an air that they are somehow beyond that stage, that they do not need to pray. Their reason for affiliating with a synagogue is to identify with the Jewish people and the Jewish community, and perhaps even with the Jewish faith. But not for the purpose of prayer.

Some consider the spiritual arrogance of contemporary man to be a stumbling block to prayer. Since prayer requires the capacity to be in awe and to feel thankful, the immodest and arrogant personality simply cannot pray because he has no sense of awe or gratitude. He puts too much faith in his own ability to do wonders and ascribes all achievements to his own powers. He lacks the necessary measure of humility.

While this may be true for some individuals, it is perhaps skepticism and doubt that make it difficult for other people to engage God in conversation. It is not that they are atheists or even agnostics; it is simply that they waver between faith and doubt. Even of Noah, who is described in the Bible as a "righteous man" who "walked with God," it is said that "he believed and didn't believe," for he lacked the faith to move immediately into the ark that he was commanded to build, and did not move in until the very last moment (Rashi, Gen. 7:7). Our generation, too, often appears to be precariously balanced between believing and not believing, sometimes leaning in one direction, sometimes in the other.

Or perhaps the reason for the unfashionability of prayer is simply that most people don't know how to pray. They were never properly taught. Yet prayer is more commonplace than most people realize *if* we do not think of it as taking place only within a structured religious service and only through the medium of prescribed and sanctioned words. *"Dear God, make her well"* is as simple and classic a prayer as there can be. Moses said this prayer for his sister Miriam when she was stricken with leprosy (Num. 12:13). In one form or another this prayer is recited by countless mothers and fathers, husbands and wives, brothers and sisters, children, friends, and lovers. Or consider the sigh of relief, *"Thank God!"* that comes after going through a period of intense anxiety in the wake of a serious accident or a dangerous illness or a fateful mission, or when loved ones seem suspended between life and death or between success and ruin. This, too, is a prayer and is just as likely to be said by people who think that they never pray as by those who pray with deliberate and conscious regularity. Or consider the feeling of awe and admiration that wells up in one's heart when coming upon great natural scenes: vast oceans, breathtaking mountains, stunning deserts. King David summed it up saying, "O Lord, how great are Thy works!" Is this not a prayer, even though it may come out simply as *"Magnificent!"* by those with less poetic talent than the author of the Book of Psalms? But if they believe these phenomena to be God's handiwork and mean to praise Him, then this word, too, constitutes a prayer. Or consider the person who has qualms of conscience about some wrongdoing and in the privacy of his own thoughts says, *"How truly sorry I am!"* This, too, is a prayer, especially if the words "forgive me" are added.

These examples are universal; they are also the four types of prayer that make up the content of the siddur. The prayer of petition, which most people think of as the nature and purpose of all prayer, is just one of four types of prayer. The other three types of prayer consist of thanksgiving, of praise of God, and of prayers that are basically self-searching and confessional. The Hebrew word for "to pray" (*l'hitpalel*) does not mean "to ask" or "to petition" God. It is derived from a stem, *pll*, that is closest in meaning to the last of these four types of prayer. It means to judge; therefore l'hitpalel, ("to pray"), could also be translated as "to judge oneself." Here lies a clue to the real purpose for engaging in prayer. Whether we petition God to give us what we need, or thank Him for whatever good was granted, or extol Him for His awesome attributes, all prayer is intended to help make us into better human beings.

While Jews who choose to live their lives in accordance with the commandments and the traditions of Judaism will engage in daily prayer as part of their religious commitment, even Jews who have moved away from traditional observance and from the habit of fixed regular prayer still find many occasions when they not only utter sincere, heartfelt words of prayer but consciously wish to participate in the more formal prayer services.

While spontaneous prayer may on some occasions come easily to one's lips, it usually poses a great challenge. For one who is not trained to pray, it is not easy to pray. "What do I say?" and "How do I say it?"—are questions that arise. It may be quite acceptable in Judaism to ask a saintly or religious person to pray on one's behalf on the assumption that his added prayers might carry more weight. (Berakhot 34b). But "Pray for me, Rabbi" is usually meant as a request that the Rabbi substitute (rather than supplement) his own prayers for that of another's. In the final analysis, we believe that every person has the same right and duty to approach God. And to do so might well be more meaningful than to seek out intercessors.

Our sages understood the problem. They realized that few people possess the ability to express their innermost feelings and thoughts. And so they provided us with prayers composed by master liturgists, and set up a formal structure within which we could give expression to the vast range of human moods, to our personal hopes and fears, to our national aspirations and experiences, to our simplest material needs, and to our highest spiritual yearnings that transcend history and reach into the infinite. This also served to teach us what to ask for and to educate us in the aspirations we should have. The classical prayers and the structured services have withstood the test of time. Jews in every generation have continued to find ever meaningful and ever relevant the words composed as long ago as three thousand years. And why not? Technology may have advanced, cultures may have changed, but human nature and the human condition have remained constant. Jewish prayer has proven itself to be both timely and timeless.

Prayer does not belong exclusively to the followers of any one faith. All people who believe in God are moved at one time or another to utter a heartfelt prayer to Him. And sometimes confirmed nonbelievers are equally moved. But if prayer is common to people of all faiths, what makes Jewish prayer Jewish?

6

Introduction

Jewish prayer is prayer that uses the idiom of the Hebrew Bible and reflects the Jewish soul. It is prayer that expresses the basic values of the Jewish people and affirms the central articles of Jewish faith. It is prayer that reflects our historical experience and gives expression to our future aspirations. When the prayer of a Jewish person does not reflect one of these components, he may be praying, but it cannot be said that he is praying as a Jew.

A Jew may choose his own words when praying to God; but when he uses the words of the siddur, he becomes part of a people. He identifies with Jews everywhere who use the same words and express the same thoughts. He affirms the principal of mutual responsibility and concern. He takes his place at the dawn of history as he binds himself to Abraham, Isaac, and Jacob. He asserts his rights to a Jewish future in this world and to personal redemption in the world-to-come.

Whatever is special about Jewish theology, whatever is special about Jewish values, whatever is special about Jewish history—is also special about Jewish prayer.

One final thought. Attending synagogue services and praying are often thought of as one and the same. It is assumed that a person who does one also does the other. This assumption should be valid, but it is not, especially today. One may pray, and pray daily, but do so privately, outside the framework of the synagogue. On the other hand, there are those who come to the synagogue to attend the services but do not engage in prayer. They come in response to an invitation by a host family to join it in celebrating a *Bar-Mitzvah* or some other event. They come to watch, not to pray. There is hardly a rabbi who has not at one time experienced the empty feeling of having a packed synagogue consisting mostly of people who sit politely and quietly, watching services, sometimes not even bothering to open a prayer book. These people may be "attending services," but they are not participating in prayer. Being a spectator at a Jewish worship service is not the same as being a worshiper. To be a worshiper requires a certain involvement, if only to answer "Amen" at certain points, if only for the heart to feel that it wants to be a part of what is being said.

The situation I have described is pathetic because it is not caused by lack of belief or unwillingness to pray. It is the estrangement from the synagogue and its ritual, from the prayer book and its contents, which make those present uncertain about even the minimal measure of involvement that the sages provided for.

It is my hope that as a result of reading or studying this volume, spectators will learn how to become worshipers, and worshipers will be encouraged to become more inspired participants in the prayer experience. If it is true, as Judah Halevi said, that "prayer is for the soul what nourishment is for the body" (Kuzari III:5), then they can only become the richer and healthier for it.

The Lord is near to all who call upon Him, to all who call upon Him in truth.

(Psalms 145:18)

www

The Quest for Spirituality

IN THE BEGINNING

FROM the dawn of human history, the sacrificial offering was the basis of divine worship. It was not until Abraham made his covenant with God that there arose a people who broke away from pagan idols, multiple deities, and human sacrifice—turning to worship One God, the spiritual Supreme Being. Although the act of sacrifice still remained for them the accepted way to express thanks, to celebrate holy days, and to gain Divine pardon, the worship of God was not confined to the bringing of sacrifices. Pure prayers, independent of any sacrificial offerings, were also said by the Patriarchs of Israel. The Torah records many such instances of prayer. When "Abraham prayed to God" (Gen. 20:17) and when he pleaded with God on behalf of the inhabitants of Sodom (Gen. 18:23), he set precedents followed by his descendants after him. Prayer also embellished and accompanied the sacrificial rites. Individuals who brought sin offerings to the Temple in Jerusalem were required to say confessional prayers (Lev. 5:5; Num. 5:7). Special prayers were said by those who brought the offering of the first fruits and the tithe (Deut. 26:5–10; 13–15). Levites in the Temple sang verses from the Book of Psalms, and the priests regularly said the Priestly Blessing, as well as other prayers, and recited Scriptural readings that included the Shema and the Ten

Commandments. Lay representatives of the people who were present in the Temple courtyard joined in with various prayer responses. (See pp. 12–13.) And though the Talmud states that prayer is a rabbinical ordinance (Berakhot 21a), Maimonides explains that it is only the times of prayer, the contents of prayer, and the number of prayer services that are of rabbinic origin; the basic obligation to pray is a Torah requirement (Hil. Tefilah 1:1). He bases his view on the Oral Tradition's interpretation of the Biblical verse: "You shall serve the Lord your God with all your heart" (Deut. 11:13). How does one serve with the heart? By praying (Taanit 2a). The founder of the Ḥasidic Ḥabad sect (Lubavitch), Reb Shneur Zalman of Lyady, supported the view of Maimonides when he said that "the idea of prayer is the foundation of the whole Torah."

Until the time of the Second Temple, there were no fixed prayers and no set times for prayer. Each person prayed whenever he wanted, saying as much or as little as he wished. The contents of his prayers were entirely up to him. Prayer was spontaneous, a spiritual reaction to personal experiences. Some prayed once daily, others prayed many times a day. Some dwelled at length on their prayers, others were concise. There were no set rules (Maim. Hil. Tefilah 1:3). Only the twice-daily recitation of the Shema is a Biblical duty whose fixed time framework is also of Biblical origin.

It was Ezra, the Scribe, and the 120 Men of the Great Assembly, who in the early period of the Second Temple (about 485 B.C.E.) first fixed the number of daily services, composed the general outline of the basic prayers, and set the times for saying them. Almost twenty-five hundred years ago, they established three daily worship services—for morning, afternoon, and evening. Thrice-daily prayer seems to have been an old Israelite tradition among the pious. Reference to it is found in Psalms (55:18) and in the book of Daniel (6:11). This practice is said to have been inspired by the three Patriarchs: Abraham, Isaac, and Jacob. According to aggadic interpretation of the verses (Berakhot 26b), the Torah tells of Abraham praying in the morning (Gen. 19:27), of Isaac praying towards dusk (Gen. 24:63), and of Jacob praying at night (Gen. 28:10).

One Talmudic source associates the tradition of praying three times a day with the daily changes in nature and the desire to pay homage to God as the power that makes them happen (Yer. Berakhot

4:1). The changes between day and night are clear; the most obvious change in nature that takes place in the afternoon is the shift of the sun from east to west. But there is also a less obvious change mentioned in Genesis 3:8: the onset of the "winds of the day," associated with the late afternoon.* This phenomenon is clearly felt in Jerusalem and in other parts of Israel where a sudden change in temperature and gusting winds occur in the late afternoons, in summer and in winter.

But it is also true that when thrice-daily prayer was formally established by Ezra, it was meant to correspond to the communal sacrifices (the *korban tamid*) that were then offered daily in the Temple. The Talmud confirms this. "Said Rabbi Joshua ben Levi, 'The prayers were instituted to correspond to the daily [Temple] offerings: The morning prayer corresponds to the daily morning (shaharit) offering; the afternoon prayer corresponds to the late afternoon (minha) offering; and the evening prayer (arvit or maariv) corresponds to the nighttime burning on the altar of all the fat and organs of the daily offerings" (Berakhot 26b). Certainly the additional prayer (musaf) said on Sabbaths and all Biblical holidays corresponds to the additional offering that the Torah prescribes for these days.

When the Second Temple was destroyed by the Romans in the year 70 C.E., ending all sacrifices, the sages declared prayer to be an acceptable substitute. Though prayer services had long since become an established practice, a Biblical text reassured the people that their prayers were as efficacious in gaining Divine pardon or meriting Divine reward as were their sacrifices. The prophet Hosea had already said, "We will render, instead of bulls, [the offering of] our lips" (14:3). The sages understood this to mean that our prayers will be as acceptable before the Holy One, blessed be He, as were the animals offered on the altar (Yoma 86b).

And since the times for prayer were synchronized with the biblically fixed times for the sacrificial offerings, the spiritual link

---

* While *minha*, the term for the afternoon service is commonly explained to mean "a gift" and is identified with the afternoon offering in the Temple, Targum Onkelos, the ancient Aramaic translation of the Torah, uses the equivalent word *menah* (literally "the part of the day that is beginning to settle or rest") as a translation for "winds of the day." This suggests that the word "minha," in the sense of *menuhah* ("rest"), is a term that also refers to a time of the day, just as do the names of the other services, *shaharit*, from the word *shahar* ("morning"), and *arvit* or *maariv*, from the word *erev* ("evening").

between the two was strengthened. Faithful to a spirit in Judaism that was always striving for greater spirituality in man's relationship with God, one sage, Rabbi Elazar, declared rather unequivocally that "prayer is superior to sacrifices" (Berakhot 32b); and others taught that "if one is humble of spirit, the Torah credits him with having brought every offering to God" (Sanhedrin 43b).

MA'AMADOT: FORERUNNER OF THE
SYNAGOGUE SERVICE

Most scholars believe that the origin of the synagogue dates back to the Babylonian exile in the sixth century B.C.E., when an exiled nation, deprived of the Temple and its sacrificial worship, would gather on the Sabbaths and the holidays to say prayers and listen to the messages of their prophets and teachers. When these Jews returned from their Babylonian exile, they brought the tradition of these regular prayer assemblies back to Eretz Yisrael. Even when they rebuilt the Temple and reinstated the sacrificial system, they continued to conduct prayer services in the towns and villages, thereby establishing synagogues alongside the central Jerusalem Temple. Others, however, believe that the Sabbath prayer gatherings in Babylonia were based on earlier precedents, and that the synagogue may have had its unheralded and obscure beginnings in a system called *ma'amadot* that was devised, according to the Mishnah (Taanit 4:2) by the "early prophets" in the early days of the First Temple. Even scholars who are uncertain as to the exact historical beginnings of the ma'amadot still agree that they were the most important factor in the development of synagogue worship, inasmuch as it was through this system that prayer sacrifices were first set up on a regular basis in towns and villages throughout the land.

What were the ma'amadot? They made up a network by which the public-at-large was represented at the Temple during the offering of the daily sacrifices. Since the Torah states (Num. 28:1) that the sacrifices were to be brought by the people, it was necessary that the people be represented at the ritual even though they were not permitted to perform any of the priestly or levitical duties. "How can the offering of a person be brought [on the altar] and he not be present?" asks the Mishnah (Taanit 4:2). And so a system was devised to allow for public representation at the Temple's sacrificial ritual.

The priests and the Levites were divided into twenty-four watches or shifts of duty (*mishmarot*), each of which took its turn in officiating at the Temple sacrifices. Each *mishmar* was responsible for one week's tour of duty every six months. The country, likewise, was divided into twenty-four districts. Each district appointed a delegation of distinguished Israelites known for their piety to represent it at the public offerings. The men chosen to be part of this delegation were called *Anshei Ma'amad*, ("Men of Standing"), so called because they were delegated *to stand by* to observe the Temple ritual. Each district was attached to one of the twenty-four *mishmarot*. When each district's tour of duty came around, those district representatives who were able to travel went to Jerusalem with the priests and the Levites of the mishmar and personally stood by to observe the ritual proceedings. They also assembled to read from Genesis and to say prayers and supplications. The Anshei Ma'amad who were not able to travel to Jerusalem for the week desisted from their labors during that week and also gathered each day in a central place for prayer and scripture reading. Two of these daily prayer assemblies, one in the morning (Shaḥarit), the other in the afternoon (Minḥa), were timed to coincide with the two daily communal sacrifices. There was also an additional (Musaf) gathering at noon which was unrelated to any sacrifice, and a *Neilah* ("Closing of the Gates") prayer assembly at the end of each day. The prayers they said mostly corresponded to the psalms that were being said in the Temple at the same time. If a *kohen* ("priest") was present, he would conclude these daily prayer meetings with the recitation of the Priestly Blessing, just as was being done at the same hour in the Temple. The prayer gatherings of these delegations, both in the Temple and in their respective villages, were called *ma'amadot* (s. *ma'amad*) (Maim. Hil. Klei Hamikdash 6:1–6).

While these prayer assemblies were held in each location only two weeks a year, it was, "the first time in Jewish history that there took place prayer services that were held regularly and on a daily

13

basis."* And though at first only the Anshei Ma'amad participated, in the course of time the prayer assembles would attract large crowds who joined the Anshei Ma'amad in prayer.

The influence of the ma'amadot was felt long after the Second Temple was destroyed and the system disbanded. Pious men would linger in the synagogue after the daily services to read the scriptural portions from Genesis that were once read by the Anshei Ma'amad. To this day, some editions of the siddur carry a section called "Ma'-amadot," which consists of readings for the seven days of the week: verses from Genesis (as was once done), plus selected excerpts from the Bible, the Mishnah, and the Gemara. This little-known section is a legacy that points to the fact that the entire synagogue service may well go back to this ancient tradition of communal prayer.

THE MERIT OF COMMUNAL WORSHIP

One of the distinctive features of Jewish prayer from its earliest beginnings was this emphasis on communal or congregational worship (*tefilah b'tzibbur*). One may fulfill the *mitzvah* of prayer by praying privately, but there is special merit in praying with others as part of a congregation.

So much significance is still placed on communal worship that if one is unable to attend a communal service, he is advised that the next best thing to do is to pray privately *at the same time* as the congregation is praying. The sages taught that God listens more readily to the prayers of a congregation than He does to those of an individual. Psalm 69:14 is interpreted to mean that the "favorable time" for prayer (*eit ratzon*), the time when prayer is most welcomed by God, is "when the congregation is praying" (Berakhot 8a). Furthermore, the sages tell us that when ten or more pray together, the "Divine Presence" (*Shekhina*) is with them. For it says in the Psalms that

* Yitzhak Moshe Elbogen, *Hatefilah b'Yisrael b'Hitpathuta haHistorit* (Tel Aviv: Dvir Co. Ltd. 1972) p. 180.

"God standeth in the congregation of God" (82:1), and that an individual's prayer is more likely to be accepted if he says it while praying with the congregation (Berakhot 6a).

The emphasis on getting together to pray instead of praying separately and alone helped spur the growth of the synagogue as the "small sanctuary" for regular communal worship. And while an established place for worship, the synagogue, is the preferred place for prayer, the absence of a synagogue is not an impediment to communal worship. A quorum (*minyan*) can conduct a service almost any place.

Communal worship provided a cohesive influence in the Jewish community. It added meaning to the fact that most of the prayers were formulated in the plural and not in the singular—stressing the responsibility that Jews have for one another. It seemed to make the community more aware of and responsive to the needs of the individual.

Communal worship made it possible to note the major occasions of a person's life. An individual's grief was shared by the congregation. So were his joys. The communal service was even tailored in parts to reflect the special occasions of one's personal life. (See pp. 207–208.) Jews may have known much suffering, known too the empty feeling of being a people isolated in the world, but a Jew who regularly worshiped with a congregation was never alone.

The tradition of communal worship also made it possible to bring into the religious community those unable to pray because of insufficient background and learning. It must be remembered that until about the eighth century c.e. prayers were always said by heart. There had existed a fundamental resistance to writing down prayers (Shabbat 115b), just as there had been a tradition against writing down the Oral Torah. The prohibition was eventually lifted, but it was not until the eighth century that written prayer books came into use. The first formal siddur for year-round use, as we know it today, was compiled by Rav Amram Gaon (ninth century c.e.). Before then it was necessary to memorize the prescribed prayers in order to fulfill one's religious duty. Those unable to memorize would have been excluded from religious fellowship had it not been the established practice to gather together for worship. In this context, only one learned person with a good memory was required to recite aloud the main prayer in the service (the Amidah) to enable the untutored to discharge their prayer obligation by listening to the blessings being recited on their behalf and by responding with "Amen" (OH 124:3, MB:12).

The man leading the communal worship in this way was known as the Shaliaḥ Tzibbur ("Emissary of the Congregation"). At various times and places, this person has been called by different names: Shatz (the Hebrew acronym for Shaliaḥ Tzibbur), Ba'al Tefilah ("Master of Prayer"), and Ḥazzan ("Cantor"). The last title is now generally reserved for one who serves professionally in the capacity of shaliaḥ tzibbur. Actually, the "emissary of the congregation" need not be a professional cantor nor an ordained rabbi. Any adult male of the congregation may act in this capacity. The "emissary" is not an intermediary between the congregation and God; he is simply their agent, one who says the prayers on their behalf (Berakhot 5:5). In parts of the service, his role is only to provide the cue and thus co-ordinate the prayers of the congregation. By concluding the last verse or two of each prayer stanza, he sets a uniform pace for everyone to keep to. For my purposes, I shall call this person simply the "Prayer Leader."

HEBREW: THE PREFERRED LANGUAGE FOR JEWISH PRAYER

A legitimate question can be raised by those who do not understand Hebrew. How can one strive for spirituality in prayer if one does not understand the meaning of the words? Does not the Code of Jewish Law stress the importance of understanding the words of the prayers? Did not the sages themselves prescribe that a few prayers, like Kaddish, be said in the Aramaic vernacular of their day because a great many people did not understand Hebrew (Berakhot 3a; Tos. s.v. v'onin). Although Hebrew is the preferred language for Jewish prayer (mitzvah min hamuvḥar), the prayers need not be said in Hebrew. Indeed, the halakha rules that one may pray in any language that one understands (OH 101:4, 62:2, MB:3).

A Hasidic tale illustrates the spirit of this ruling. A boy from a small rural village where there were few Jews and no synagogue, one day accompanied his father to the city to do some marketing. While there, they went into a synagogue. The boy had never been in a synagogue before and he was impressed and moved by the sight of the congregation at prayer. He, too, wanted to pray. But he did not know how. His father had taught him only to say the letters of the Hebrew alphabet, but no more than that. So a thought occurred to him. He began to recite the alphabet over and over again. And then he said, "O Lord, You know what it is that I want to say. You put the letters together so they make the right words." That, too, was a Jewish prayer.

Thus, even in a synagogue, an individual is permitted to pray in any language he understands. However, it is important that the congregation itself pray collectively in Hebrew (OH 101, MB:13). There are several reasons why this distinction is made:

· A relatively uniform Hebrew service helps preserve and maintain the unity of the Jewish people throughout the world. Not only does it bind every Jew closer to the Holy Land, it enables a Jew to feel at home in synagogues around the world, even in countries where fellow Jews speak other languages and one is otherwise unable to communicate with them. If Jews everywhere were to conduct services in their respective vernaculars, and only an elite group of scholars retained the Hebrew, the resulting estrangement from the synagogues of fellow Jews would be a serious blow to Jewish unity.

· Estrangement from Hebrew also means to become estranged from the Torah·and all other classical sources. It means a loss in the understanding of Hebraic concepts and Jewish values, which in the final analysis are still best conveyed through the Hebrew idiom.

· By abandoning the Hebrew service, we would eliminate the most urgent reason for teaching Hebrew to the next generation. By providing an "easy" path to spiritually-meritorious desires, the community might well destroy the incentive of individuals without Hebrew training to invest the time and effort needed to learn, first, Hebrew reading and then, the meaning of the prayers.

· Finally, and most important, the severance of the organic bond with the Hebrew language by a Jewish community historically has led to the total assimilation and ultimate disappearance of that community.

17

What has been said thus far does not resolve the personal dilemma of the individual who wishes to understand what he or she is saying and finds it meaningless to pray in an unfamiliar language. Yet even for that individual, use of the vernacular, while permissible as a short-term solution, may not be the best way to attain the truly spiritual experience for which he yearns.

The importance of Hebrew as the language of Jewish prayer is not that it is the spoken, everyday tongue of Israel, but that it is the tongue of the prophets, the language of the Bible, "the sacred tongue" (*lashon hakodesh*) to countless generations of Jews, in both Eretz Yisrael and in the Diaspora. Hebrew is not only a tool of communication; it possesses innate spiritual significance as the repository of the Divine mystery. If one does not quite understand it, it is best to use a prayer book with a translation to which one can frequently refer. In due time, if one prays regularly, one will better understand the Hebrew words as well as the general meaning of each prayer.

Although Jewish prayer is not meditation, and words must be uttered, prayer does not consist only of words. Prayer also requires a mood, a feeling. That is why the pious ancients were known to spend a considerable amount of time just getting into the spirit of prayer. If a person recites prayers that he does not fully understand, yet his heart is humble before God and his thoughts are directed to his Father in Heaven, will his Father in Heaven not understand his intent or deem his prayers less worthy of consideration?

KAVANAH: IT'S THE SPIRIT THAT COUNTS

The next chapter of this book is devoted largely to the formal procedures and the mechanics involved in the ritual of worship. Lest anyone get the erroneous impression that Judaism is concerned only with the perfunctory recitation of words and with mechanical participation in ceremony or ritual, let us here and now place all of Jewish worship into its proper perspective.

Jewish law requires the worshiper to be aware that it is God who is being addressed, to "know before Whom you are standing" (Berakhot 28b). Reading from a prayer book does not mean that one is praying. One may read a prayer book as one reads any other kind of book—to find out what it says or to relish the beauty of the poetry. Such reading does not qualify as prayer. To transform reading into prayer, there must be at least a sense of standing in the presence of God and the intent to fulfill one of His commandments.

The Hebrew word for having such intent is *kavanah*. The Talmud teaches that "he who prays must direct his heart to heaven" (Berakhot 31a). This is the minimum level of kavanah in all prayer. Without it, it is not prayer. Kavanah in prayer is the very antithesis of the mechanical and perfunctory reading of words.

Kavanah can be defined in still other ways, with each definition representing ascending levels of kavanah, each one a challenge to the worshiper. The next level of kavanah is to know and understand what one is saying. The one following that is to free one's mind of all extraneous and interfering thoughts, so as to concentrate better on the prayers. At the highest level, kavanah also means to think about the deeper meaning of what one is saying, while praying with extraordinary devotion.

The laws of prayer actually forbid one to pray if one cannot attain the minimum level of kavanah. And though the *Shulḥan Arukh* appears resigned to the fact that Jews will pray even when they cannot attain kavanah, it nevertheless proceeds to put the rule on record: namely, that "one should *not* pray in a place where, or at such a time when, there is interference with kavanah" (OH 98:2).

The sages recognized that one cannot have the proper kavanah when one is in a mood of extreme anger or sorrow, or is distraught with problems, when one is extremely fatigued, or when there are external distractions. All such conditions must therefore be removed before one engages in prayer. "One stands up to pray only when in a reverent frame of mind," says the Talmud, in a ruling that sets the framework for prayer (Berakhot 5:1). "Reverent" is meant not to preclude prayers said in joy but to exclude frivolity.

Individuals, even those who pray with faithful regularity, may at times be accused of reciting their prayers in a most perfunctory manner. A far more serious problem exists in those congregations where idle talk and endless chatter in the midst of the prayer service indicates an obvious lack of kavanah and a total absence of spirituality.

The failure lies with individuals, not with Judaism or Jewish prayer. Such behavior is contrary to both the letter and the spirit of Jewish law. Those who are guilty of this transgression are condemned as "sinners." (OH124:7, MB:27; OH151:1) They may self-righteously view themselves as still engaged in a religious activity, yet their decidedly irreligious behavior makes a mockery of prayer and constitutes an affront to God and to the sanctity of the synagogue. In the same vein Jewish law cautions scholars against studying the holy books while the congregation is engaged in prayer. It causes others to sin by encouraging disrespect for prayer. (OH 124:4, MB:17).

If there is any mitzvah in which it is the spirit that counts, it is prayer. The Torah, the Talmud, the Midrash, the codes of law, are unanimously consistent about this point. And all the halakhic rules of prayer and of decorum were designed to intensify the spiritual quality of worship.

Should circumstances make it necessary for a person to choose between saying more prayers without kavanah and saying fewer prayers with kavanah, the fewer are clearly preferred (OH 1:4, MB: 12)—if the choice is kept within the framework of a schedule of priorities. (See pp. 342–344.) Says the Talmud: "The Holy One, blessed be He, desires the heart" (Sanhedrin 106b).

SONG: AN AID TO KAVANAH

The power of music to stir the heart, to arouse the emotions, to intensify the mood one wishes to attain, made it a factor in Jewish prayer from its earliest beginnings. "Sing unto the Lord with thanksgiving, sing praises upon the harp unto our God" (Psalms 147:7) points to a rich tradition of song, both vocal and instrumental among the early Israelites. The Talmud considers song to be a way by which to serve God in joy and gladness, a disposition that the Torah deems crucial to worship (Deut. 28:47; Arakhin 11a).

And while a nation immersed in grief after the destruction of the Second Temple in 70 C.E. set a ban on the use of instrumental music as a sign of mourning for the Temple (OH 560:3), vocal music remained an essential component of prayer and Scripture reading. Bible was not dryly read but was chanted in much the same way as it is in today's synagogue (Megillah 32a).

Rabbi Judah he-Ḥasid (circa 1150–1217 C.E.) wrote: "Say your prayers in a melody that is most pleasant and sweet to you. Then you shall pray with proper kavanah, because the melody will draw your heart after the words that come from your mouth. Supplicate in a melody that makes the heart weep, praise in a melody that makes the heart glad" (Sefer Ḥasidim:11).

The Talmud even requires being "skilled in chanting and having a pleasant voice" as one of the qualifications of a Prayer Leader (Taanit 16a).

Cantillations: The Scriptural Chant

Synagogue music can be divided into two general types, both with roots extending back into the Temple period. One type is the cantillations or the chant associated with Scriptural reading. The cantillations are governed by a series of musical notations called "trop" (*ta'amai ha-mikra*), which are found in the printed text of the Hebrew Bible either below or above each word. These are the notes that a Bar-Mitzvah boy learns to read in order to chant the Haftarah, (the reading from the Prophets). Although the melodies associated with the trop differ slightly for the reading of the Torah, for the Prophets, and for each of the five *Megillah* scrolls, they nevertheless share the same basic inflections. Correct rendition of the trop will automatically punctuate a sentence properly.

Nusaḥ: The Musical Motif

Another type of synagogue music is called *nusaḥ*, which is the musical motif that permeates different prayer services. The Sabbath, the festivals, the High Holy Days, all have their distinctive nusaḥ— and one who leads the services on these days should be thoroughly familiar with the proper nusaḥ. Although the wrong nusaḥ, or the lack of it, does not invalidate a service, it is part of the sacred tradition of the synagogue.

Since not every prayer was subject to a nusaḥ tradition, the professional Ḥazzan in European Ashkenazic communities, who came into his own during the Middle Ages, found sufficient leeway to compose other musical renditions for parts of the service. The *piyyut* (see pp. 280–283) especially provided opportunities for musical creativity. At times this leeway was carried to excess by those who introduced melodies from popular folk songs, who improperly repeated words or passages of a prayer so as to fit them to the music, and who unnecessarily prolonged services to the discomfiture of a congregation by lengthy "operatic" compositions. Religious authorities as early as the twelfth century condemned those who made the prayers secondary to the music, or whose purpose was to entertain a congregation rather than to lead it in prayer (OH 53:11, Sefer Ḥasidim:418).

The musical tradition of the different countries where Jews lived also affected the way the cantillations and the nusaḥ were sung. Because of the great difference in the tonal quality of the music sung in the European tradition and that sung in the Arab countries, the musical part of the synagogue service turned out to be the most striking difference between the services of the Ashkenazic Jewish communities of the West and the Sephardic communities of the Middle East. The Sephardic communities in the Spanish and Portuguese rite have their own distinctive chant, different from the others.

Song also became an important part of the Sabbath meals. These religious songs are called *zemirot*. While the words of these compositions are the same everywhere, the music to which they are sung varies depending on local or family tradition. New melodies are in fact constantly being composed for them, and popular melodies are often adapted to them.

And though the prayers were said for a long time (even on Sabbaths and holidays) with a minimum of joyous song and without the assistance of congregational singing, the view of Rabbi Judah he-Ḥasid that we use melody to enhance prayer and deepen kavanah has become widely shared.

Ḥasidism, a religious movement which arose in Poland about two hundred years ago, was the first in modern times to once again emphasize song as a way of serving God in joy. It has had a strong impact on many non-Ḥasidic congregations. Congregational singing has reestablished itself as an integral element in contemporary worship, particularly on Sabbaths and festivals, just as the Psalmist advised almost three thousand years ago: "Serve the Lord with gladness, come before His presence with singing" (Psalms 100:2).

CHAPTER
2

To Feel at Home in the Synagogue: Knowing What To Do

I SUSPECT that countless Jews would have returned to the synagogue long ago if they did not fear that their unfamiliarity with the ritual would embarrass them. Some, who do attend some services, would like nothing better than to be called upon to receive an honor during the service, yet reject all such overtures on the part of synagogue officials. They do so not because they are overly modest or feel humbly undeserving of the honor, but because they do not know what to do. There is no reason that any Jew should be so uninformed when he steps into what should be his second home. Where else if not the synagogue should a Jew feel at home and be at ease? So before embarking on this guide to the prayer book, I should like to explain the procedure and ritual of the synagogue. In this way, perhaps, I can help remove one of the barriers (i.e., the embarrassment of an obvious ignorance of the basics) for those who would like to find their way back to the synagogue, to the siddur, and to Jewish prayer.

WHEN ENTERING A SYNAGOGUE

Every Jew may enter any synagogue with confidence. Even if one is a stranger passing through town, the synagogue is there for him as much as it is for the townspeople. Some people may feel awkward about attending a synagogue with which they are not affiliated, but the feeling is unwarranted. If the synagogue is small or if only a handful of people are present, it is only natural that those in attendance might turn to stare for a moment at a stranger. If you are that stranger, try not to feel self-conscious. You can acknowledge those who look your way with a slight nod. That usually suffices to normalize the relationship. If they are friendly people, and the service has not yet begun, someone may even approach to welcome and greet you; it may be the rabbi or the sexton or just one of the worshipers. If no one does, it may be that they are just as shy as you. If it is a large synagogue and many worshipers are in attendance, the likelihood is that no one will even notice your presence. If you are the type who is glad to be unnoticed and left alone, that should suit you. If you are the type who feels that you should be noted and greeted, you may be disappointed and somewhat irked. Whatever the reception, you should know that as a Jew you belong and are welcome in any synagogue throughout the world. Some of my fondest recollections and most memorable experiences are associated with stopping to attend prayer services at synagogues in strange cities and foreign countries.

PROPER DRESS FOR A SYNAGOGUE

A male should not enter a synagogue without a headcovering. Any hat will do. Because it is convenient and light, the yarmulke or skullcap (*kippah*) has become the preferred headgear in most places. Most synagogues in North America keep a supply of such caps near the entrance to the sanctuary or chapel for the benefit of those who arrive without one. The skullcap itself has no intrinsic religious sanctity, but the wearing of a head covering, especially in a holy place and when saying prayers, is an ancient Jewish form of respect for God.

The Talmud makes several references to the covering of one's head as a sign of both respect and humility before God. "Rav Huna did not walk four *amot* ["six feet"] bareheaded; he would say, 'The Shekhina ["Divine Presence"] is above my head' " (Kiddushin 31a). The sages said, "Cover your head so that reverence for God be upon you" (Shabbat 156b). And while no direct Biblical reference requires the wearing of a head covering at any time, the Torah did require the priests to wear a head covering while they were engaged in the Temple service. The head covering was part of the sacred vestments that were to be worn as a sign of respect and glory before God (*lekavod uletiferet*) (Exod. 28:2,4).

The mere suggestion in the Torah of its attitude toward the head covering—even if only indicated for the priests—may have been sufficient for its transformation to a universally accepted custom by a people who had been commanded to become "a kingdom of priests and a holy nation" (Exod. 19:6).

The custom is that a woman wears a head covering only if she is married.

As for general dress, much depends on local custom. In North America, a tie and jacket for a man is the norm. In warmer climates and vacation areas, the rule is generally relaxed to allow open collars and no tie. During the Israeli summer, it is acceptable to attend services there without a jacket, in an open-collared shirt. For a woman, a sleeveless, bare back or low-cut garment is definitely out as are mini skirts and slacks. The latest fashion, perhaps suitable for a festive social occasion, may not always be appropriate for the synagogue. One should be guided by good taste and common sense. Modest attire is the rule.

What has been said till now applies to every occasion, weekdays as well as Sabbaths and festivals. On Sabbaths and festivals, however, proper dress for the synagogue should further take into consideration the traditional Jewish view that requires one to dress for the Sabbath. (Shabbat 113a). And while the daily work clothes of a farmer or laborer may be appropriate for synagogue wear during the weekday, they are inappropriate on the Sabbath and festivals. In the world of white-collar work, there may be less of a distinction between what one wears during the working week and when dressing in honor of the Sabbath. Still, the distinction between "work" and "dress" clothes should be borne in mind. A pair of jeans, suitable perhaps for weekday wear in the synagogue, is unsuitable for the Sabbath.

This is perhaps an appropriate place to add a word about how to conduct oneself in general when attending services. One should not smoke (even on a weekday), eat, chew gum, or act in a frivolous manner in a synagogue. Any behavior that could be regarded as disrespectful when in the presence of royalty is surely out of place before the King of Kings.

FINDING A SEAT

One may feel free to take any vacant seat, except on the High Holy Days when reserved seats are assigned to worshipers. In synagogues with separate seating sections for men and women—as is typical of the Orthodox synagogue—one should be careful to select his or her seat in the appropriate section.

It might happen, especially on a Sabbath, that one or more rows of seats are held in reserve for a visiting group that is expected to arrive. Should that occur, and one of the officials of the synagogue asks you to change your seat, do so as casually as you can. He will be indebted to you for cooperating.

Regular worshipers in a synagogue will often make it their practice to take the same seat every time they come to pray. Some do so as a matter of course, as a result of habit; others because they knowingly wish to abide by the ruling in the Shulḥan Arukh that requires one "to fix a place for one's prayers" (OH 90:19). The ruling is based on the dictum of a Talmudic sage who credits Abraham with having set the precedent for it (Berakhot 6b).

If you therefore come into a synagogue and take a seat and then have the uneasy feeling that someone who came in after you is eyeing your seat, do not hesitate to inquire, "Did I take your seat?" and offer to move to another one. In all likelihood, the offer will be rejected. Even if the regular worshiper has "a fixed place" where he sits all the time, the ruling is that any seat within an area of approximately six feet ("four amot") of his own still qualifies as being within the parameter of "his fixed place" (OH 90, MB:60).

GETTING A PRAYER BOOK (SIDDUR) AND BIBLE (ḤUMASH)

In some synagogues, a siddur and a Ḥumash (the Five Books of Moses) are placed in a rack before every seat. In other synagogues, siddurim and Ḥumashim will be found on a table near the entrance to the sanctuary or chapel. On a Sabbath or holiday morning (and whenever else the Torah is read) (see p. 50), take both a siddur and a Ḥumash and proceed to your seat. At all other times, one need take only a siddur. A quick glance inside the cover should help you distinguish one from the other. Some editions of the siddur include a section containing the brief Torah portions that are read on a weekday morning or on a Sabbath afternoon; the siddur alone suffices for these times.

FINDING ONE'S WAY IN THE SIDDUR: HOW THE SERVICES ARE ARRANGED

The key to finding one's place in the siddur is no different than for any other book. First one must know what one is looking for. There is usually a table of contents which can guide one, if not to the exact page, then to the general section that one wants. Also, one should become familiar with the Hebrew headings at the top of each page and develop the habit of glancing at them. They identify the service on the page and often the particular section in the service. As one leafs through the siddur, these headings provide constant guidance.

The general arrangement of the services in most siddurim intended for daily year-round use and their identifying Hebrew headings are as follows:

The first part of the siddur is reserved for the weekday services. These are arranged in the following order:

- The Morning Weekday Service   תפלת שחרית לחול
- The Afternoon Weekday Service   תפלת מנחה לחול
- The Evening Weekday Service   תפלת ערבית לחול

The next part of the siddur is reserved for the Sabbath services. These are usually arranged in the following order:

- Welcoming the Sabbath   קבלת שבת
- Evening Service for Sabbaths and Festivals   ערבית לשבת וליום טוב
- Morning Service for Sabbaths and Festivals   שחרית לשבת וליום טוב
- Additional Service for Sabbath   מוסף לשבת
- Afternoon Service for Sabbath   מנחה לשבת

The heading for the Sabbath evening and morning service invariably includes the words: "And Festivals," (וליום טוב) because except for the *Amidah* prayer, there is almost no difference between the Sabbath and the festival services.

Blessings for the Sabbath candles will usually be found at the beginning of the Sabbath section. Kiddush for the Sabbath and the zemirot will be found following the evening and morning Sabbath services. In most siddurim, an entire book of the Mishnah known as *Pirkei Avot*, ("Ethics of the Fathers,") is found following the Sabbath afternoon service.

The evening service that concludes the Sabbath day is found in some prayer books in its entirety following the Sabbath afternoon service. Most prayer books, however, expect you to turn to the weekday section for the Saturday night service inasmuch as they are almost identical. Only those supplementary prayers that are unique to the Saturday night service will be found at the very end of the Sabbath section.

After the Sabbath services, the third part of the siddur is reserved for prayers said *only* on the holidays. A breakdown of this section in most prayer books would be as follows:

- Hallel, Psalms of Praise   הלל
- Additional Amidah for Rosh Ḥodesh   מוסף לראש חדש
- Amidah for Festivals   עמידה לשלש רגלים
- Additional Amidah for Festivals   תפלת מוסף לשלש רגלים

Just before or just after the Musaf Amidah for the festivals, there is usually a whole series of prayers said only on holidays: the Kiddush for the Festivals, the Priestly Blessing, the blessings for Sukkot (the blessing for the *lulav* and the *Hoshanot* ritual), the special prayers for dew and rain, the Simḥat Torah service, the Yizkor memorial service, the blessings and prayers connected with Counting the Omer.

The very last part of the daily siddur varies much more widely from one edition to the next in respect to what else is included. Some siddurim contain such prayers as the Grace after Meals, the various blessings for food, the Marriage Ceremony, the Circumcision Service, the Ceremony for the Redemption of the First Born, prayers for the sick, and prayers said in a house of mourning. Other siddurim may contain the text of the brief Torah portions read in the synagogue on Monday and Thursday mornings, on Sabbath afternoons, and on such other weekday occasions as Rosh Ḥodesh and Ḥanukkah. Still other siddurim have the entire Book of Psalms appended to it.

If one regularly uses a particular siddur, one will soon become familiar with its full contents and its distinctive features. If your siddur lacks any of these particular sets of prayers or texts, you can acquire a siddur containing them at a local Hebrew book dealer.

PUTTING ON A TALLIT

The *tallit*, commonly referred to in English as a "prayer shawl," is a four-cornered garment or cloak to whose corners fringes (*tzitzit*) are affixed. These endow the garment with its religious significance. The tzitzit are attached to the corners as a reminder of the Lord's commandments. This is in keeping with the Biblical passage from Numbers 15:37-41, which is read as the third paragraph of the Shema. (See p. 155 for the full text.)

Although four-cornered garments were common in ancient times, changing styles could have rendered this mitzvah obsolete. To prevent the total disappearance of a mitzvah that possessed such great symbolic significance, that was, in fact, a reminder of all other mitzvot, the sages encouraged the wearing of a specially-made, four-cornered garment. It became especially noteworthy to do so during times of prayer (Maim. Hil. Tzitzit 3:11).

The tallit is worn by Jewish males at every morning service, Sabbaths and weekdays (except on Tisha b'Av). The tallit is not worn at either afternoon or evening services, except at the afternoon service on Tisha b'Av and on the night of Yom Kippur.

Those who own their own tallit generally bring it to the synagogue, especially on weekdays. However, many synagogues provide the worshiper with a tallit just as they provide him with a yarmulke and a siddur. (This is not so in Israeli synagogues where only prayer books are provided, and where one is expected to bring his own tallit and yarmulke.) If you therefore arrive at a synagogue without your own tallit, check to see if any are available for your use. If so, take one and return it after the service.

If you should find yourself in a synagogue and see young men worshiping without a tallit, you can safely assume that they are not married (unless they happen to be non-Jewish visitors). In some Orthodox congregations it is the custom for a young man not to wear a tallit until after his wedding day. If he happens to be called to the Torah for an *aliyah* or is asked to lead the service, he will put a tallit on for those occasions.

The custom of not wearing a tallit before marriage was explained and justified by Rabbi Jacob Möllen (1356-1427), known as Maharil. He based his opinion on the proximity of two Biblical verses. One, (Deut. 22:12), reaffirms the commandment of wearing tzitzit (a tallit is in conformance with that mitzvah); the very next passage deals with marriage and begins with the words: "If a man taketh a wife . . ." (Deut. 22:13). Most halakhic authorities, however, deny the validity of drawing such a conclusion from the mere proximity of these verses and find no justification at all for this custom, for it involves nullifying the observance of an important mitzvah. The wearing of a *tallit katan* is not regarded as an adequate substitute. The Shulḥan Arukh clearly rules that "one should take care to don tzitzit (a tallit) at the time of prayer". This is *in addition to the tallit katan* that one would wear under one's garments (OH 24:1, MB:3). The Mishnah Berurah sums up the objection of most authorities to the custom of not wearing a tallit before marriage, and expresses amazement at Maharil for having defended it: "It is most surprising. Should one sit by and not keep the mitzvah of tzitzit (tallit) until one marries?" (OH 17:3, MB:10).

It is therefore proper that every male over thirteen, married or unmarried, wear a tallit. In addition to the halakhic considerations, it also adds visual inspiration to a congregation at worship. For educational reasons, wearing a tallit should be encouraged even among children under the age of thirteen.

Instructions for Putting on a Tallit

· Spread open the tallit and hold it in both hands.
· Recite the following blessing:

בָּרוּךְ אַתָּה יהוה אֱלֹהֵינוּ מֶלֶךְ הָעוֹלָם, אֲשֶׁר
קִדְּשָׁנוּ בְּמִצְוֹתָיו וְצִוָּנוּ לְהִתְעַטֵּף בַּצִּיצִית.

Barukh atah Adonai eloheinu melekh ha-olam, asher kidshanu b'mitzvotav, v'tzivanu l'hitatef b'tzitzit.

Blessed be Thou, Lord our God, King of the universe, who sanctified us with His commandments, and commanded us to wrap ourselves in the tzitzit.

· Throw the tallit over your shoulders in much the same way as you would a cape.
· Before adjusting the tallit so that it rests comfortably on the shoulders, it is customary momentarily to wrap the tallit around one's head immediately following the above blessing (OH 8:2).

31

(1)

(2)

(3)

(4)

(1) A tallit worn fully over back and shoulders. (2) Folding the tallit over the shoulders. (3) A tallit folded back over the shoulders —a side view. (4) A front view.

Some worshipers wear the tallit over the head to reduce distraction and to permit greater concentration.

If one borrows a tallit that belongs to the synagogue, one may recite the blessing over the tallit even if it is to be worn for only a short period.

If one borrows a tallit from another worshiper for a short part of the service, one should *not* recite the blessing over it. The person from whom the tallit is borrowed does *not* recite the blessing again when it is returned and he puts it back on.

A tallit must not be taken into a lavatory. If one needs to use these facilities during the services, one should remove the tallit before entering and leave it outside. There is no need to repeat the blessing when one puts the tallit back on.

PUTTING ON TEFILLIN

Tefillin, one for the hand and one for the head, are worn by adult male Jews at weekday morning services in conformance with the Biblical injunction to "bind them for a sign upon your hand and for frontlets between your eyes" (Deut. 6:8). They are not worn on Sabbaths or on the festivals. The reason is that the tefillin were intended to serve as a symbol, as a reminder of the commandments on days when one is occupied by multiple burdens. At such times, the tefillin is also a spiritual adornment. But the Sabbath and the entire period of the festivals (including ḥol hamoed) are also symbols of the covenant between God and Israel, vivid reminders of God's Presence and of all His commandments. They are themselves an adornment to the life of the Jew. To add the observance of tefillin to the grandeur of the Sabbath or the festival would be superfluous. (Those in the diaspora who put on tefillin during the intermediate days of the festival justify this practice because they work on these days, and while the work may be permissible, it nevertheless endows these days with a weekday quality.)

Every Jew should own his own pair of tefillin to use at home and in the synagogue. Unlike the tallit, tefillin are not put on until shortly before one's Bar-Mitzvah. Since tefillin are relatively costly, and head tefillin need to be adjusted to size, most synagogues do not provide tefillin as they do a yarmulke, a siddur, and even a tallit. Nevertheless, several pairs may be kept in reserve by the rabbi or sexton, and made available on request.*

The tallit is always put on before the tefillin in accordance with the principle of always ascending in holiness (*maalin bakodesh*). First we *cover* ourselves with a tallit, and then move on to *bind* ourselves with the symbols of holiness (OH 25:1, Biur Halakha). The tallit is given priority also because of the general rule: That which is observed more often precedes that which is observed less often (Zevaḥim 89a). In this case, a tallit is worn all seven days of the week, while tefillin are worn only on weekdays.

At the end of the service, the procedure is reversed. The tefillin are removed first, and the tallit is taken off last. The rule to remember: first on, last off!

Instructions for Putting on Tefillin

The next few pages are a detailed, step-by-step guide for putting on tefillin; these instructions may be of interest to those not familiar with the procedure. Others may find that they offer a response to questions that are sometimes asked about tefillin.

೩೬ One should stand while putting on or taking off tefillin.

೩೬ While putting on the tefillin, one should not engage in conversation or allow one's attention to be diverted. One neither answers "Amen" nor responds to the Kaddish nor joins in Kedushah. If one is in the midst of putting on one's tefillin and hears either Kaddish or Kedushah being recited, one should merely stop to listen without joining in the responses.

೩೬ Take out the hand tefillin (*shel yad*) from the bag, unwind the leather straps (*retzuot*), and remove the ornamental case.

---

* If one comes to a weekday synagogue service without a pair of tefillin, and no spare pair is available to borrow, it is preferable to wait and borrow a pair from another worshiper after the service is completed rather than to say the Shema and Shemoneh Esrei without tefillin. There is no objection to reciting the preliminary parts of the service (the Morning Blessings and the Verses of Song) without either tallit or tefillin.

ঌ Place the hand tefillin on the left arm. A left-handed person puts tefillin on his right arm. One reason for the practice is based on the juxtaposition of the verses "And you shall bind them on your hands . . ." and "You shall write them on the doorposts . . ." (Deut. 6:8–9). The lesson inferred is that the hand that writes is also the hand that does the binding. Therefore a left-handed person who writes with his right hand puts tefillin on his left arm, as do all right-handed people. Although this question was a matter of serious dispute among the Early Authorities and was never clearly resolved, this answer is based on the tradition passed on by my own teachers.

ঌ The hand tefillin is set on the biceps of the arm in such a way that the broad side of the lip or edge is set toward the top of the arm and not the bottom.

ঌ Before tightening the strap around the biceps, check to make sure that the knot is adjacent to the box and has not slid away.

ঌ Recite the following blessing:

בָּרוּךְ אַתָּה יהוה אֱלֹהֵינוּ מֶלֶךְ הָעוֹלָם, אֲשֶׁר קִדְּשָׁנוּ בְּמִצְוֹתָיו וְצִוָּנוּ לְהָנִיחַ תְּפִלִּין.

Barukh atah Adonai eloheinu melekh ha-olam, asher kidshanu b'mitzvotav, v'tzivanu l'hani-ah tefillin.

Blessed be Thou, Lord our God, King of the universe, who sanctified us with His commandments, and commanded us to put on tefillin.

ঌ Tighten the strap and wind it seven times around the forearm below the elbow with a counter-clockwise motion.* Make sure that the black side of the leather strap is on the outside. Then wrap the remaining length of strap around the palm of the hand.

---

* This accords with Ashkenazic practice. In the Ḥassidic-Sephardic tradition, the knot on the hand tefillin faces away from the person, so that the strap must be wound around the arm with an outward clockwise motion.

&? Take out the head tefillin (*shel rosh*) from the bag. Unwind the straps, remove the ornamental case, and place the tefillin upon the head.

&? Tefillin must come in direct contact with the body—on the head as well as on the arm—without any intervening materials (OH 27:4, 5).

&? Before adjusting the tefillin on the head, recite the following blessing and declaration:

בָּרוּךְ אַתָּה יהוה אֱלֹהֵינוּ מֶלֶךְ הָעוֹלָם, אֲשֶׁר קִדְּשָׁנוּ בְּמִצְוֹתָיו וְצִוָּנוּ עַל מִצְוַת תְּפִלִּין. בָּרוּךְ שֵׁם כְּבוֹד מַלְכוּתוֹ לְעוֹלָם וָעֶד.

Barukh atah Adonai eloheinu melekh ha-olam, asher kidshanu b'mitzvotav, v'tzivanu al mitzvat tefillin.
Barukh shem kvod malkhuto l'olam va-ed.

Blessed art Thou, Lord our God, King of the universe, who has sanctified us with His commandments, and commanded us concerning the mitzvah of tefillin.
Blessed is the name of His Glorious Majesty forever and ever.

&? Adjust the tefillin to rest comfortably and correctly on the head as illustrated. The head tefillin should be placed above the forehead in such a way that it lies above the hairline and is centered between the eyes. The knot on the headstrap should be centered behind the head at the base of the skull. The straps are brought forward and allowed to hang loosely in front of the chest.

&? Unwrap the strap from around the palm and wind it three times around the middle finger: once around the middle part of the finger and twice around the lower part closest to the knuckle. The remainder of the strap is then carried around the ring finger and rewound around the palm. While doing this, or immediately thereafter, say the following:

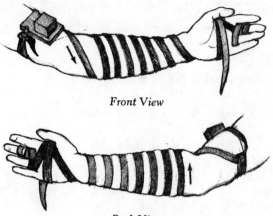

Front View

Back View

Correct Tefillin Position on Hand

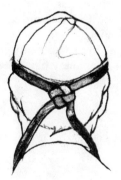

Back View

Side View

Correct Tefillin Position on Head

וְאֵרַשְׂתִּיךְ לִי לְעוֹלָם, וְאֵרַשְׂתִּיךְ לִי בְּצֶדֶק וּבְמִשְׁפָּט וּבְחֶסֶד
וּבְרַחֲמִים: וְאֵרַשְׂתִּיךְ לִי בֶּאֱמוּנָה, וְיָדַעַתְּ אֶת יהוה:

I will betroth you to me forever; I will betroth you to me in righteousness and justice, in kindness and mercy; I will betroth you to me in faithfulness; and you shall know the Lord (Hosea 2:21–22).

When removing the tefillin, reverse the procedure:

&❧ Unwind the strap around the fingers, rewinding it about the palm.

&❧ Remove the head tefillin and wrap it up neatly.

&❧ Unwind the strap around the palm and the forearm and slip off the hand tefillin. Wrap it up neatly.

There are various ways to wrap up tefillin—as long as the straps are wound around the lip of the tefillin that extends on all sides of the square box containing the parchment and not around the box itself. There is no religious significance to these methods. Use whichever is easiest and most suited to the size tefillin you have.

On Rosh Ḥodesh, tefillin are removed just before the Musaf Amidah and not at the end of the service. On ḥol hamoed, if tefillin are worn, they are removed just before Hallel.

Even more so than with a tallit, one must never enter a lavatory while wearing tefillin. It is customary to kiss the tefillin when taking them out of their bag and before putting them back in.

POSTURES AT PRAYER: SITTING, STANDING, BOWING, PROSTRATING, SWAYING

The most important thing about assuming the correct posture during a prayer service is to do it naturally. If the congregation changes from sitting to standing or vice versa, and you suddenly find yourself in a posture different from that of everyone else, don't jump! Casually change posture. You may also notice that a knowledgeable worshiper, who is at a different point in his own prayers from the rest of the congregation, does not hesitate to stand while everyone else is sitting, or, with the exceptions to be noted in the next paragraph, to sit while everyone else is standing.

Standing

To stand in prayer before God is the normally correct posture for Jewish prayer. Therefore, when we address Him directly or say a passage in which we sanctify His Name, or which has some special significance, we stand. As a mark of respect, we stand before the Holy Ark when it is open and also whenever the Torah is carried through the synagogue (Maim. Hil. Sefer Torah 10:9).

Since, as we shall see, the complete prayer service includes many preliminary and introductory passages, and involves listening to the Prayer Leader or to the Torah Reader, it is permissible to sit during a greater part of the service. For historical reasons, we also sit when reciting the Shema. (See pp. 147–148.)

Generally one need stand only when actually saying those prayers that traditionally require standing.* These include the Amidah; Kaddish; Aleinu; Hallel; Barukh She'amar, the opening blessing of the Pesukei d'Zimra; from Vayevarekh David through Yishtabaḥ, the closing blessing; Mizmor l'Todah, a psalm in the weekday Pesukei d'Zimra; the prayer for the new month; and special memorial prayers such as Yizkor.

It is proper that everyone in the synagogue stand:

· When the Prayer Leader says the passage of Borkhu
· When the Kedushah is said during the repetition of the Amidah
· When the Ark is open
· When the Torah is in motion, being carried to or from the Ark

In some congregations, it is customary for everyone to stand when Kaddish is said, either by the Prayer Leader or by mourners.

Bowing

Bowing occurs rarely during Jewish prayer. It is done four times during the Amidah or Shemoneh Esrei (see pp. 77, 102); once more

---

* An invalid in a chair, or a sick person who may not get off the bed, may say the Amidah and all other prayers that are traditionally said standing while sitting or lying down.

during the concluding meditation (see p. 72); once during the Aleinu prayer (see p. 213); and once when responding to the Prayer Leader's declaration of Borkhu (see p. 166). In the latter three instances, a simple bow at the waist is sufficient.

To execute the proper bow in the Amidah, slightly bend the knee when saying *barukh*, and bow from the waist when saying *atah*. One resumes an erect posture when saying *Adonai*.

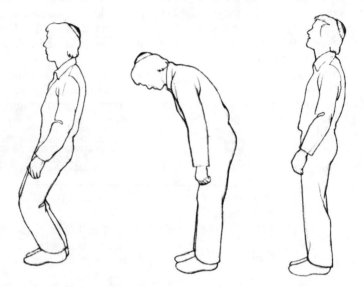

One who finds it physically difficult to execute a bow in the prescribed way may simply bow his head or bend slightly forward.

Falling Prostrate

A rare posture, once commonly practiced, is that of falling prostrate. (See pp. 204–205.) Kneeling is totally absent from Jewish prayer except as a step in falling prostrate. This takes place today only during the High Holy Days, once on Rosh Hashanah and four times on Yom Kippur. On both of these holy days it is done when the Aleinu prayer is said in the repetition of the Musaf Amidah, and it is done three more times on Yom Kippur when the Avodah (the description of the Temple service) is read.

In most contemporary congregations very few people keep to the tradition of falling prostrate. Sometimes it is only the Prayer Leader and the rabbi who does so. In more traditional congregations, however, some worshipers, men and women, will join the Prayer Leader and rabbi in the act of prostrating themselves. In Israeli synagogues, the practice is more widespread than in synagogues elsewhere. Since this is a position that we are unaccustomed to, one who has never done this before might very well demur. But once accomplished, the experience provides such a spiritual uplift that one looks forward to repeating it. Those willing to try this ancient ritual form on the rare occasions that call for it might welcome the following diagrams of the correct procedure.

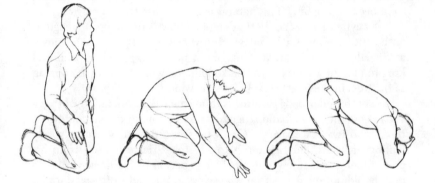

Swaying

Swaying is surely the most widespread and most typical movement associated with Jewish prayer, yet it is not imperative in Jewish law or even a universally recommended custom. There are those who sway slightly while they pray. Others do so with greatly exaggerated and rapid movements of the body. And still others, great and pious scholars among them, say their prayers with hardly a trace of movement.

One will notice swaying most often among those standing in prayer, but some worshipers sway even when they are seated. Abudarham explains swaying as symbolizing a verse in Psalms: "All my limbs shall declare, 'O Lord, who is like unto Thee' " (Psalms 35:10). When one sways to and fro, it is as though the entire body is caught up in prayer.

Swaying during prayer, however, is primarily a matter of habit and the result of early training rather than a matter of religious symbolism.

Rabbi Judah Halevi, in his classic twelfth-century text "The Kuzari" (II, 80), suggests a totally different reason for the development of swaying among Jews. When books were rare, he writes, it was the practice for people studying Torah to gather about in a circle to read from the same volume. "Each would take a turn to bend down to read a passage resulting in a continual bending and sitting up. Those who observed such groups tended to imitate the practice, which then became a habit." This habit was later transferred to prayer.

Swaying has been both defended and criticized by religious authorities. Rabbi Isaiah Halevy Horowitz (circa 1565–1630), known as Shelah, wrote: "Can you imagine a person approaching a mortal king to present a petition and make requests while his body is swaying as the trees in the forest sway before the wind?"

The founder of Ḥasidism, Rabbi Israel Baal Shem Tov (1700–1768), on the other hand, suggests a sympathetic understanding of those who sway excessively. "One who sees a drowning person wildly flailing his arms and twisting his body to extricate himself from his predicament, will surely not mock that person or his movements. So one should not mock a person who sways in the midst of prayer, for he is engaged in saving himself from the torrent of extraneous and improper thoughts that threaten to engulf him and prevent him from properly concentrating on his prayers."

According to the halakha, the question of whether or not to sway should be determined by how it affects prayer. For some people, swaying is an aid to concentration. For others, it is a definite disturbance and interferes with concentration. Whatever helps one concentrate on the prayers is the correct thing to do (OH 48, MB:5; MA:4).

KISSING: AN ACT OF RELIGIOUS DEVOTION

Kissing is a universal sign of affection. It is an act of love, an expression of endearment, not only between man and woman, parents and children, but is also the expression of one's feelings for the ritual objects and the religious duties associated with them.

There are no religious laws that require us to kiss a ritual or holy object. There is only the force of custom as it develops through the ages. In varying degrees kissing has become an optional commonplace among Jews as an expression of religious devotion at the following times:

ৈ The tallit is kissed just before putting it on.

ৈ The tefillin are kissed when taking them out of their bag and before replacing them in the bag.

ৈ The tzitzit are kissed at the end of Barukh She'amar and during the recitation of the Shema.

ৈ The *mezuzah* on the doorpost is sometimes kissed upon entering or leaving a house. It is done by touching the mezuzah with one's hand and kissing the fingers that made contact with the mezuzah.

ৈ The Torah is kissed when it passes by in the synagogue. Here, too, it is often done by extending a hand to touch the Torah mantle and then kissing the hand. Some touch the Torah with the edge of a tallit and then kiss the tallit.

ৈ The Torah is also kissed before one recites the blessings over it. Here it is done by taking the edge of one's tallit or the sash that is used to tie the scroll together, touching the outside of the scroll with it, and then kissing the tallit or the sash. Many people place the tallit or sash to the very words where the reading is about to begin. The sages advised against doing this as it may hasten a wearing away or erasure of the letters. At best, they recommend touching only the margin area near the line where the reading is about to begin. In all instances, one should not touch the Torah parchment with one's bare hand. The custom of not doing so derives from a special edict issued by the sages prohibiting such contact (Shabbat 14a; OH 147:1).

43

ह‍ॐ The curtain on the Ark (*parokhet*) is kissed before one opens it, or after closing it when the Torah is put away.

ह‍ॐ A siddur and Ḥumash are kissed before putting them away. These holy books are also kissed if they are accidentally dropped on the floor.

THE CHARITY BOX AT DAILY SERVICES

The sages were the first to set a personal example in the daily giving of alms. The Talmud tells about Rabbi Elazar who would always give a coin to a poor man before saying his prayers (Bava Batra 10a). He based his action on a verse in Psalms (17:15): "I shall behold Thy face in *righteousness*," which may also be read as "*with charity*." The act of charity, even a modest one, was seen as the key of admission to the Divine Presence. Maimonides tells us that many great sages performed a charitable act before praying (Hil. Aniyim 10:15), and the Shulḥan Arukh suggests that it is a desirable practice for everyone to follow in preparation for prayer (OH 92:10). This is the background for the almost universal practice of passing around a charity (*tzedakah*) box during weekday services into which worshipers drop one or more coins.

In larger synagogues, the sexton will go up and down the aisles with the charity box (*pushke* in Yiddish) either during the preliminary service or during the repetition of the Amidah. In smaller synagogues, the charity box is kept in some conspicuous place and worshipers simply go up to it either at the very start of the services or at some convenient moment.

The purpose is not so much to raise significant sums for some important cause as it is to provide the worshiper with the opportunity to engage in an act that is traditionally associated with meaningful prayer.

Collecting charity or giving alms is, of course, never done on Sabbaths and holidays since it is forbidden to handle money on these days. However, one may pledge to charity, and the opportunity to do so is often provided by the synagogue especially on the High Holy days.

The charity box is a daily reminder of the ethical dimension inherent in prayer, about which more will be said in the concluding chapter of this book.

WHAT TO DO WHEN ASKED
TO OPEN THE ARK

The worship service among Jews does not require an established or ordained clergy. Any qualified layman who possesses the necessary knowledge may conduct any part of the service. But even in modern congregations, where a professional religious leadership—rabbi, cantor, and sexton—is engaged to conduct most aspects of the service, there are still roles reserved for and assigned to the men of the congregation. Some of these roles are relatively simple to perform; others require a little knowledge and perhaps the experience of having watched someone else do it first.

It is only to be expected that being called upon to participate in any part of the synagogue ritual should have come to be regarded as a distinct honor (*kibud*) among synagogue-goers. It means a chance of doing something that has religious merit; it also means being acknowledged by the congregation as a person who merits recognition. Among the honors in the service are opening and closing the Ark, carrying a Torah, being called to recite blessings over the Torah (*aliyah*), raising and dressing the Torah scroll, and reading from the Prophets (Haftarah).

Yet there may be individuals who, though they would feel honored to be called upon to participate, hesitate about accepting an honor even when it is offered. They may feel uncertain about their ability to properly perform the task. Or they may be gripped by the understandable awe of participating in a sacred task. Or the hesitation may be nothing more serious than the fear of appearing solo in public —the "stage-fright" phenomenon. Whatever the case, the instructions in this and subsequent sections should provide the necessary confidence for one to accept any of the synagogue honors that may be offered to him.

Whenever the Torah is read at a service, it is first removed from the Ark in a ceremonial manner and carried to the bimah in a procession. The honor of participating in this ceremony is extended to one or more worshipers. The honor is called *pesiḥa* (Ashkenazic pronunciation) or *petiḥa* (Sephardic pronunciation). It means "opening" and refers to the first act in the ceremony—the opening of the Ark. It is sometimes also called *hotza'ah*, which refers to the task of taking the Torah out of the Ark.

There are times when the pesiḥa honor is independent of removing a Torah scroll. Some prayers are traditionally said before an open Ark. At such times, which occur frequently at High Holy Day services, one simply opens the Ark, stands aside to say the prayer with the congregation, and then closes it at the prayer's conclusion.

Taking Out the Torah Scroll

Should you be honored with taking out the Torah scroll, walk up to the Ark when the Torah Reading portion of the service is reached. On the Sabbath, this begins with the passage *Av Haraḥamim*. Wait until the Prayer Leader begins the very next passage: *Vayehi Binsoa*. At that point, pull aside the parokhet and open the doors of the Ark. If it is a weekday, reach in immediately and take out a Torah scroll. If it is a Sabbath or holiday, step back a little and wait until the congregation and the Prayer Leader complete the prayer that is said after Vayehi Binsoa: *Brikh Shmei*. If you remembered to take your siddur with you, open the siddur and join in the prayer. If not, wait patiently until they finish. The Prayer Leader will then approach the Ark. At that point, reach into the Ark and take out the Torah scroll. If the gabbai or sexton wants you to take out a specific Torah scroll, he will signal you which one to take. Hand the Torah to the Prayer Leader. There is a knack to doing this smoothly.

As you remove the Torah from the Ark, the front of the scroll is facing you. With the front still facing you, place the Torah scroll directly into the hands of the Prayer Leader. (Do not try to turn it around and rest it on your shoulders before giving it to the Prayer Leader. That will only complicate the matter.) Follow the diagrams.

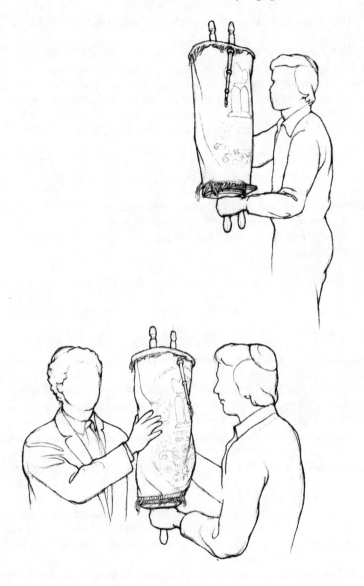

Turn back to close the doors of the Ark and to draw the parokhet back over it.

There are days when two Torah scrolls are taken out. Two persons are then sent up for the honor. One person follows the described procedure, except that he takes out two scrolls instead of one. The task of the second person is to carry the second Torah scroll. So after handing the first scroll to the Prayer Leader, one takes out a second Torah scroll and gives it to the other person honored with *pesiḥa*.

Some congregations follow the custom of always sending up two people for pesiḥa even when only one Torah scroll is taken out. Where this is done, the two share the opening of the Ark doors. After one pulls the parokhet aside, each one then opens one of the two doors of the Ark. All else remains the same, except that a quick decision has to be reached between the two honorees as to who will reach in to take out the Torah.

Procedure on the Bimah

The Prayer Leader, holding the Torah, now faces the congregation. You do the same. Stand discreetly behind him and somewhat to the side. If there is another person carrying a second Torah, he too faces the congregation, standing immediately to the side of the Prayer Leader, who begins to chant several passages which, on Sabbaths and holidays, begin with the words *Shema Yisrael* ("Hear O Israel, the Lord our God, the Lord is One!"). On weekdays, it begins with *Gadlu*. Join in the congregational response. When the Prayer Leader is finished, he walks down the steps (if there are any) and proceeds in a procession either around the *bimah* (from where the Torah is read) or around the synagogue. If there is a second Torah scroll, the person holding it walks immediately behind the Prayer Leader. Follow whoever is carrying the scroll almost all the way back to the bimah and then walk back to your seat.

If the rabbi and other synagogue dignitaries join in the procession, as they do on Sabbaths and holidays, permit them to fall in immediately behind the Prayer Leader or behind the one carrying the second Torah, as the case may be, while you take up the rear.

When holding or carrying a Torah, one does so with the right hand, with the Torah resting on the right shoulder. This practice was inspired by two Biblical verses. One describes God as having given the Torah with "His right hand" (Deut. 33:2). The other describes embracing the object of one's love, "his right hand should embrace me" (Song of Songs 8:3). One who is visibly handicapped, may carry the Torah in his left arm. (OH 134:2, Rema, MB:12).

Returning the Torah Scroll

The honor of pesiḥa, unless there are specific instructions to the contrary, involves opening the Ark for the return of the Torah. This duty is called *hakhnasah*. While the Prayer Leader is carrying the Torah back to the Ark, the one so-honored should step up ahead and open the Ark. The precise moment for doing so is when the passage *Uvnuho Yomar* is reached.

If two Torah scrolls are taken out, the one who carried the second scroll should go up to the bimah when the Prayer Leader is ready for the return procession, and carry a Torah back to the Ark.

As the Prayer Leader approaches the Ark, take the Torah from him and put it back in the Ark. If there are two scrolls, take them both. In taking the Torah scroll from him, the front of the Torah scroll should be facing you, and should remain so as you return it to its niche in the Ark. Wait a moment until everyone completes the Uvnuḥoh Yomar prayer. If the congregation and the Prayer Leader chant it slowly, as they are likely to do on a Sabbath or a festival, step back and wait until they finish. Then close the Ark, kiss the parokhet if you wish, leave the Ark area, and return to your seat.

WHAT TO DO WHEN CALLED UP
FOR AN ALIYAH

The honor of reciting the blessings over the Torah is called an *aliyah*, which means "going up"; it refers to the fact that the person so honored ascends or goes up to the bimah where the Torah is read. The word also connotes that participating in this ritual represents a spiritual ascent.

There are a number of occasions in life when tradition entitles a person to receive an aliyah. These occasions, made more significant by this honor, are as follows: when a boy turns thirteen years of age (Bar-Mitzvah), before he gets married (*aufruf*, a Yiddish word that means "to be called up" [to the Torah]), when naming a baby daughter, and on the Sabbath before one observes a *yahrzeit* (the anniversary of a parent's death). One can also request an aliyah to mark a birthday, an anniversary, the recovery from a sickness, or when one wants to recite the *gomel* blessing. (See pp. 249–251.) Synagogue officials generally try to be accommodating. (See pp. 350–351 for list of priorities.)

On Monday and Thursday mornings, on Sabbath and Yom Kippur afternoons, as well as on the holidays of Ḥanukkah, Purim, and all the fast days, the Torah reading is divided into three portions, and only three persons are called up for an aliyah. On Rosh Ḥodesh and on the intermediate days of Pesaḥ and Sukkot (ḥol hamoed), four people are called up. On the festival days of Pesaḥ, Shavuot and Sukkot, and on Rosh Hashanah, the Torah reading is divided into five portions, and five aliyot are distributed. On Yom Kippur morning, there are six aliyot. But on the Sabbath day, the Torah reading is divided into seven portions, allowing seven aliyot. It is not permissible to call up fewer than the prescribed number; and except for the Sabbath (and Simḥat Torah), it is not permissible to add to the prescribed number (Megillah 4:1–2). Since Jewish law permits calling up more than seven persons on thc Sabbath,* some congregations take advantage of this leniency to divide the Torah reading into more than seven portions, providing one or more additional aliyot for the worshipers. Other congregations look askance at the practice because it lengthens the service, and they insist on limiting the number of aliyot to the prescribed number.

The first aliyah is always given to a kohen (one of priestly descent), if such a person is present in the congregation. The Mishnah cites the "ways of peace" as the reason for this practice. But the sages ascribed the practice as also in keeping with the Torah requirement "to sanctify him" (Lev. 21:8), which they understood as a mandate that in all sacred matters the kohen be given priority (Gitin 59a, b; OH 135:3, MB:9).

---

* Except when the portion of Haazinu is read so as not to arbitrarily interrupt the Song and when a Sabbath coincides with a festival because the reading is very short.

The second aliyah is then given to a Levite. The remaining aliyot are distributed among the rest of the congregation, who are classified as "Israelites."

The names of the other aliyot are really the Hebrew words for the ordinal numbers. They are as follows: *Shlishi* ("third"), *Revi'i* ("fourth"), *Ḥamishi* ("fifth"), *Shishi* ("sixth"), *Shvi'i* ("seventh").

If only one aliyah is added to the seven prescribed ones, the additional one is called *aharon*, which means "last." If more than one aliyah is added, then each additional aliyah is called *hosafah*, which means "an addition"; and only the very last hosafah is called "aharon."

The Procedure in the Aliyah

No matter which aliyah you are given, the procedure is the same. Step up to the Torah. The Torah Reader will point to the word or line where he will begin to read. Take the edge of your tallit, touch it to the outside of the scroll or the margin area that is closest to where the reading is to begin, and place it lightly to your lips. Stand directly in front of the scroll and place both hands on the two handles projecting from the bottom of the scroll. They are each called an *eitz ḥayim* ("a tree of life"), the name having been inspired by a verse describing the Torah as "a tree of life to them who take hold of it" (Proverbs 3:18). One also grasps the Torah in this manner in keeping with the practice of always taking hold of the object over which a blessing is being recited (OH 206:4; 139:11).

Keep the scroll open and say:

בָּרְכוּ אֶת יהוה הַמְבֹרָךְ.

Barkhu et Adonai hamvorakh.

Bless the Lord who is blessed.

The congregation makes the following response and you repeat it:

בָּרוּךְ יהוה הַמְבֹרָךְ לְעוֹלָם וָעֶד.

Barukh Adonai hamvorakh l'olam va-ed.

Blessed is the Lord who is forever blessed.

You then say the first Torah blessing:

בָּרוּךְ אַתָּה יהוה אֱלֹהֵינוּ מֶלֶךְ הָעוֹלָם, אֲשֶׁר
בָּחַר־בָּנוּ מִכָּל־הָעַמִּים, וְנָתַן־לָנוּ אֶת־תּוֹרָתוֹ.
בָּרוּךְ אַתָּה יהוה, נוֹתֵן הַתּוֹרָה.

Barukh atah Adonai eloheinu melekh ha-olam, asher bahar banu mikol ha-amim, v'natan lanu et Torato. Barukh atah Adonai, notein ha-Torah.

Blessed art Thou, Lord our God, King of the universe, who has chosen us from among the nations and has given us His Torah. Blessed art Thou, Lord, who gives the Torah.

After completing the blessing, release the left *eitz ḥayim* to allow the Torah Reader to take hold of it, and move slightly to the right. Keep your right hand on the right eitz ḥayim throughout the reading.

When the Reader completes reading your Torah portion, take hold of the left eitz ḥayim, roll the two sides of the scroll together, and recite the second blessing:

בָּרוּךְ אַתָּה יהוה אֱלֹהֵינוּ מֶלֶךְ הָעוֹלָם, אֲשֶׁר
נָתַן־לָנוּ תּוֹרַת־אֱמֶת וְחַיֵּי עוֹלָם נָטַע בְּתוֹכֵנוּ.
בָּרוּךְ אַתָּה יהוה, נוֹתֵן הַתּוֹרָה.

Barukh atah Adonai eloheinu melekh ha-alom, asher natan lanu Torat emet, v'ḥayei olam nata b'tokheinu. Barukh atah Adonai, notein ha-Torah.

Blessed art Thou, Lord our God, King of the universe, who gave us a Torah of truth, and planted within us eternal life. Blessed art Thou, Lord, who gives the Torah.

52

After you complete the second blessing, another person is called up to the Torah. You are then asked for your name so that the sexton or the gabbai can recite a personalized blessing on your behalf at this point.

That blessing is called *Mi She'beirakh*. (See pp. 251–252.) Whenever you are asked for your name, which may be now or before being called up, give your Hebrew name and your father's Hebrew name. For example, if your name is Moshe and your father's name is Yitzḥak, say, "Moshe *ben* ("son of") Yitzḥak." An adopted son may use the name of his adoptive father if the latter raised him (Yesodei Yeshurun II, pp. 188–191).

You may at this time request that a special Mi She'beirakh prayer be recited for a sick person. You should be prepared to provide the Hebrew name of the sick person and that of his or her *mother*. When praying for the sick, as in every prayer of entreaty (*tehinah*), we use not the name of the father but that of the mother. This practice is based on a verse from the Psalms where David beseeches God and says, "I am Thy servant, the son of Thy maidservant" (Psalms 116:16). Apparently, a mother's prayer is felt to be more sincere and more likely to be favorably received. If the prayer is for a male whose name is Yaakov and whose mother's name is Rivka, say, "Yaakov ben Rivka." If it is for a female whose name is Shoshana and whose mother's name is Rivka, say, "Shoshana *bat* ("daughter of") Rivka." If the mother's name is not known, the father's name may be used.

Remain on the bimah until the person who receives the aliyah after you completes the second blessing. Now is the proper time to step down from the bimah and return to your seat.

There is a custom to ascend the bimah from the right side and to descend from the left side. This is reminiscent of Temple practice where the ascent to the altar was from the right and the descent was from the left (Zevaḥim 63a, b). Also, the entrance to the Temple Mount was from the right side (Middot 2:2). With such precedent, the right side became the preferred side for all entrances.

A parallel tradition is to take the shortest possible route from one's seat to the bimah, regardless of whether it means going up by left or right, and to return to one's seat by taking the longer route. This is to show respect for the Torah: the shortest route symbolizes the eagerness with which one wishes to thank God for the Torah, and the longer route symbolizes the hesitation with which one takes leave of the Torah.

If one is seated so that one must choose between the two traditions, priority is given to the shorter route, even if it means ascending from the left (OH 141:7). The common denominator in both traditions is to leave or descend from the side other than the one used in going up.

THE MAFTIR ALIYAH

A special aliyah is *Maftir*. This aliyah not only involves the recitation of the two Torah blessings, but it also calls for the recitation of the five blessings which precede and follow the reading of a portion from the Prophets, which is said following the Torah reading on all Sabbaths and holidays. The person receiving this honor is generally expected to recite these blessings and also to chant the Prophetic selection in the appropriate melody. The selection from the Prophets is called the Haftarah. This is the aliyah that is usually reserved for a Bar-Mitzvah, or for a person whom the congregation wishes to specially honor, or for a person celebrating a special occasion in his life. The person who receives this honor is usually notified in advance so that he may prepare himself. Whether notice is given an hour, a day, or a week in advance will depend on the congregation and on the person who is to receive it. (See pp. 241–242 for more detailed explanation.)

WHAT TO DO WHEN CALLED UP FOR HAGBAH AND GLILAH

After the Torah reading is completed, two persons are honored with the task of lifting up the Torah, and rolling and dressing it. The one who lifts up the Torah scroll performs the task of *hagbah* (shortened from the more correct term *hagbahah*); the one who rolls up the Torah scroll and dresses it performs the task of *glilah*.

Since there are no blessings to recite, many people mistakenly have come to regard these tasks as having less religious significance than an aliyah, and so assign them to people who either cannot recite the Torah blessings or to children under the age of Bar-Mitzvah, to whom these honors may also be assigned. Although these groups should continue to be so honored, hagbah and glilah should not be denied to those who are quite able to fill more demanding roles. The Talmud views the honor we call hagbah as embodying the spiritual reward of all the aliyot combined (Megillah 32a). And tradition has, in fact, reserved it for the most distinguished members of the congregation (OH 147:1, MB;5–7).

Procedure for Hagbah

Even for hagbah, there is a correct technique to follow. Roll open the Torah scroll so that three columns of script are visible. A seam attaching two sections of parchment should also be visible, preferably centered, so that it may absorb any undue stress on the parchment that may occur when the scroll is lifted.

With one hand on each of the eitz ḥayim handles, slide the Torah scroll toward you until it is halfway off the table. Then, bending the knees, apply leverage downward. Bring the scroll to an upright position and lift it upward as you straighten yourself up. Holding the Torah aloft, turn your body in all directions, or at least somewhat to the right and left, so that the Torah script can be seen by everyone in the congregation. The whole purpose of this ritual is to enable the congregation to see the Torah script. When they do, they say:

וְזֹאת הַתּוֹרָה אֲשֶׁר שָׂם מֹשֶׁה לִפְנֵי בְּנֵי יִשְׂרָאֵל, עַל פִּי יהוה
בְּיַד מֹשֶׁה.

This is the Torah that Moses set before the Children of Israel (Deut. 4:44); by the hand of Moses according to the command of God (Num. 9:23).

55

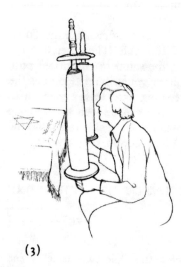

(1)

(2)

(3)

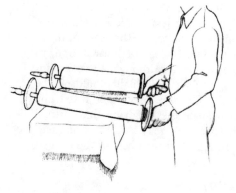

(4)

Sit down in a seat prepared for you on the bimah and let the one who is to do glilah take over with the dressing of the Torah. After he is through dressing the Torah, remain seated, holding the Torah, until the Prayer Leader is ready to take it. In some congregations, a young boy may be sent up to take the Torah from you and to hold it until it is time to return it to the Ark.

Procedure for Glilah

To do glilah, simply take hold of the eitz ḥayim handles at the top of the open scroll and roll them together. Try to keep a seam centered between the two rolls of parchment without rolling the scroll too far from where the reading ended. The right eitz ḥayim handle (to the left of the one doing glilah), which has the beginning of the scroll, should rest above the left eitz ḥayim handle. Then take the sash and bind it around the Torah; the sash should be placed about two-thirds up the scroll, just as a mezuzah is placed two-thirds of the way up a door post. There are many kinds of sash. Just make sure that the bow or the buckle is set at the front of the Torah, facing the person holding it. Now place the Torah mantle on the Torah, making sure that the front of the mantle is aligned with the front of the scroll. If there is a silver breastplate, put it on next over the mantle. There is also a pointer (*yad*) which is in the shape of a closed hand with a pointing finger. Slip that over one of the handles. If there is a crown (*keter*) to the Torah, or two finials (*rimonim*), put those on last.

When you are through dressing the Torah, do not hesitate to place a tender kiss on it before returning to your seat.

WHAT TO DO AFTER RECEIVING A SYNAGOGUE HONOR

When you return to your seat following an aliyah or after any one of the other ritual honors, you may find that some people extend their hand to you and mumble some words you do not understand. What they are saying is *yasher koaḥ*, which literally means "more power to you." (Sticklers for Hebrew grammar may use the grammatically correct form of *yishar koḥakha*.) It's the equivalent of saying "well done." The expression, found in the Talmud, is first used in an aggadic story in which Moses is complimented by God for having reacted with proper indignation in the incident of the Golden Calf when he broke the first tablets of the Ten Commandments (Shabbat 87a, Yevamot 62a).

You may respond with exactly the same words, because they have also come to mean "thank you." An alternative response is *barukh tiyeh*, which means "may you be blessed." It is particularly correct for a kohen to use this reply after the Priestly Blessing when a "yasher koaḥ" is extended to him for having recited the blessings.

WHAT TO DO IF YOU ARE A KOHEN OR A LEVITE

If you are a descendant of a priestly family—a kohen—you have some special privileges and responsibilities in the synagogue. The kohen is entitled to receive the first aliyah. So if a synagogue official should signal his intention to grant you an aliyah and your status is not known in that congregation, it is your responsibility to inform him that you are a kohen. If you miss getting the first aliyah, you may not be able to get another. Aside from Maftir, which a kohen may always receive on Sabbaths and festivals, a kohen does not have another opportunity to receive an aliyah except on Sabbath mornings when more than seven aliyot may be given. He may then be called up for aḥaron.

It is also your duty to perform the rite of the Priestly Blessing. In the diaspora, this is performed only during the Musaf Amidah on the holidays of Pesaḥ, Shavuot, Sukkot, Rosh Hashanah, and Yom Kippur. In most of Israel, this rite is performed daily during the Shaḥarit as well as Musaf Amidah.* (See pp. 132–137 for fuller explanation.)

If you are a descendant of the tribe of Levi (but not a kohen), you also have special status in the synagogue ritual. The second aliyah is reserved for the Levite. If you are to receive an aliyah, it is

---

* For detailed instructions on how to perform this rite, see *To Be a Jew*, pp. 200–206.

your responsibility to inform the person who distributes aliyot that you are a Levite.

Since kohanim must wash their hands for the ritual of the Priestly Blessing, it became customary (during the period of the Early Authorities) for Levites to pour the water over the hands of the kohanim (AH 128:15).

The Bible tells us that Moses—who was from the tribe of Levi—was instructed by God to perform that task when he consecrated his brother Aaron and Aaron's sons into the priesthood. "You shall bring Aaron and his sons forward to the entrance of the Tabernacle and wash them with water" (Exod. 40:12). It was not so much this Biblical precedent that gave rise to the custom as it was the desire to add another memorial to the Beit Hamikdash by perpetuating a role for the Levites who once had special duties to perform there, such as singing the psalms, carrying the holy vessels, and acting as gate-keepers.

So whenever the Priestly Blessing is recited, follow the kohanim when they leave their seats in the middle of the Amidah and assemble in a room outside the sanctuary to wash their hands. Your task is very simple. Take a washing cup, fill it with water, and pour it over the hands of one or more kohanim.

The water should cover the kohen's hands up to the wrists. This is so even on Yom Kippur for this washing is not meant for pleasure (OH 613:3, Rema, MB:7). If there are more Levites than kohanim present, several Levites take hold of the same cup while pouring the water over the hands of the kohen. If there are no Levites in the synagogue, the task is performed by any firstborn son. If no such person is present, the kohen washes his own hands.

WHAT TO TELL NON-JEWS VISITING THE SYNAGOGUE

There are occasions when non-Jews visit a synagogue. They may be invited to the service by Jewish friends celebrating a Bar-Mitzvah or some other special event in their lives. They may be part of a church group studying Judaism, who wish to experience a synagogue service. Or they may simply be individuals who are curious about Judaism and wish to learn more about it. Whatever the reason for the visit, a non-Jew is always welcome to attend a synagogue service. He may come only to observe the service or to join in the prayers if he so wishes. What the Jewish host should be sensitive to is that the non-Jew does not wish to offend and would appreciate knowing in advance what he may or may not do—that is, what is expected of him.

For the benefit of those who are asked for such guidance by non-Jewish friends, and for non-Jewish readers, the following simple guidelines should be borne in mind:

❧ The information contained in the first few sections of this chapter (see pp. 23–27) applies equally to everyone.

❧ The rule about a head covering in the synagogue should also be observed by non-Jews. The male visitor who does not have a head covering of his own, should take a skullcap provided by the synagogue. The skullcap itself, as I have mentioned, has no intrinsic religious sanctity, but putting it on conforms to the Jewish way of showing respect in a religious setting. (See pp. 24–25.) The female visitor, if married, should wear a hat to the synagogue. A "chapel hat," which is a piece of lace, will serve the purpose.

❧ Tallit and tefillin have ritual significance and are intended only for persons of the Jewish faith. They are not to be worn by non-Jews.

❧ It is proper that everyone in the synagogue, even those not participating in the worship service, stand when the Holy Ark is open and when the Torah is carried around the synagogue.

❧ When a prayer is said that requires the worshipers to stand, it is not necessary for those not worshiping also to stand, although they may if they wish.

Non-Jews should be given a realistic time when they are expected to arrive for services. Non-Jews who receive a printed invitation specifying the time when Sabbath morning services begin can usually be counted upon to be there punctually. Since most worshipers arrive late for the preliminary parts of the service (which they may later make up privately), non-Jewish guests could find themselves in the embarrassing position of being among the few worshipers present in the synagogue at that hour. It is therefore best to advise such guests to come to a Sabbath morning service about a half-hour after the formal start of the service. This just about coincides with the end of the preliminary sections of the service. They may be given to understand that while they are welcome to arrive at the very start of the service, the service is divided into several sections, and that they need not be there for the first part.

It would also be a courtesy to inform them in advance approximately when the service will end. Most non-Jews are accustomed to a brief half-hour or hour service. They may be totally unprepared for a complete three to three-and-a-half hour Sabbath service, typical of most traditional congregations in North America. Knowing this in advance will help them plan their day accordingly.

THE LANGUAGE OF THE SYNAGOGUE: WORDS WITH ANCIENT ECHOES

Every highly evolved human endeavor has a language of its own that the initiated know thoroughly, but that is sometimes intimidating to the newcomer. The world of the synagogue and Jewish prayer is no exception. Here, too, there are Hebrew words, names, and idioms that are used throughout most of the world by those who regularly attend the synagogue. A few of the words are not strictly Hebrew, having come down to us through Yiddish. These are used only by those with Ashkenazic background. Sephardic Jews are more likely to use the Hebrew equivalent. Familiarity with this limited vocabulary should help one to become an "insider" in this world. I have included only words that are not found or explained elsewhere in this book.

ه۶ *Davening* is the act of praying. The verb is "to daven" (in Hebrew, "l'hitpalel"). The word is from Yiddish and not Hebrew speech. It apparently stems from the Latin *divinus* and is related to the English word "divine." Davening is the act of praying to the Divine.

61

&❧ *Bentching* is the act of saying a blessing. "To bentch" is the verb. It, too, is Yiddish and when used alone is meant to be a reference to the Grace after Meals. It has a Latin root and is related to the English word "benediction," which means "blessing," and to the French *benison*. The French word in Hebrew characters בּנשׁין has practically the same pronunciation as the Yiddish word.

&❧ *Layening* is the act of reading, and in the synagogue it refers specifically to the reading of the Torah. This, too, is Yiddish, probably a form of the German word for reading "lesen." The Hebrew term is *kriat haTorah*.

&❧ *Shalosh-seudos* is often run together as "shaloshudos." It means "three meals" but refers specifically to the third Sabbath meal which is usually eaten just before the Sabbath ends. It is customary for this meal to be served in the synagogue as a simple repast. The grammatically correct term for this meal is *seudah shlishit*, which means "third meal." However, the term "shalosh-seudos" is better known—except in Israel or wherever Hebrew is commonly spoken. The deliberate use of shalosh-seudos is justified on the grounds that the religious merits inherent in all three meals are symbolized in the partaking of the last.

&❧ *Erev Shabbat* (Ashkenazic pronunciation, *erev Shabbos*) means the eve of the Sabbath. This is a reference not to Friday night, which is already Sabbath, but to all of Friday prior to sundown.

&❧ *Erev Yom Tov* likewise refers to the entire day preceding the onset of a holiday.

&❧ *Shalosh Regalim* is the overall Hebrew term for the three pilgrim festivals of Pesaḥ, Shavuot, and Sukkot, when every male Israelite was obliged to go up to Jerusalem to celebrate the festival and to worship God in the Temple (Deut. 16:16).

&❧ *Ḥol Hamoed* literally means "weekday of the festival." It refers to the intermediate days of Pesaḥ and Sukkot—that is, the days between the first two and the last two sacred days of the festival.

&❧ *Yamim Noraim* means "Days of Awe." This is a reference to both Rosh Hashanah and Yom Kippur. In a more general sense, it can also be applied to the entire ten-day period between and including the two holidays.

ً*Ner Tamid* means "Eternal Light." It refers to the lamp that is set somewhat above and to the front of the Holy Ark (Aron Kodesh). It is allowed to burn continually, and commemorates the eternal light that burned in the ancient tabernacle (Exod. 27:20–21). It is also reminiscent of the flame that was to burn continually on the altar and which was not to be extinguished (Lev. 6:6).

ً*Bimah* is the platform where the Torah is read. It is usually set apart from the Holy Ark. Part or all of the service may be conducted from there.

ً*Amud* is a small lectern between the bimah and the Holy Ark in Ashkenazic synagogues. It has traditionally stood on a lower level out of deference to the verse "From out of the depths have I called Thee, O Lord," (Psalms 130:1, Berakhot 10b). The service is conducted from the amud; the Torah reading from the bimah. In Sephardic synagogues, the entire service is conducted from the bimah.

ً*Menorah* is Hebrew for candelabrum. A menorah usually decorates the bimah or is set atop the amud. The one in the ancient Temple was of seven branches. Those used for Hannukah have nine branches.

ً*Ba'al Tefilah* is a lay person, not a professional cantor or hazzan, who is particularly good at leading the service. He has a pleasant voice, is familiar with the melodies of the liturgy, and is religiously qualified to lead the prayers.

ً*Shaliah Tzibbur* (*Shatz*, acronym) means "emissary of the congregation." He is the one actually leading the service. The Shaliah Tzibbur may be a hazzan, a ba'al tefilah, or anyone else called upon to fill the role. As indicated earlier (p. 16), I shall in this book refer to him as the Prayer Leader.

ً*Ba'al Kriah* is the person who reads the Torah; he is more commonly called Ba'al Koreh.

ً*Ba'al Tekiah* is the person who blows the shofar on Rosh Hashanah.

፟ *Berakhah* means "a blessing." The plural is *berakhot* (Ashkenazic pronunciation: *brokhos*). The special meaning of berakhah is discussed later in this chapter.

THE MAJOR LITURGICAL TRADITIONS: NUSAḤ ASHKENAZ, NUSAḤ SEPHARD, AND OTHERS

The word "nusaḥ" refers not only to the musical motif of a service (see p. 21) but also to the actual order and specific wording of the prayers, as followed by a particular community or synagogue. The two major liturgical rites are *nusaḥ Ashkenaz* (followed by Jews in Central, Eastern and Western Europe, and by their descendants), and *nusaḥ Sephard* (followed by those whose ancestors stem from Spain, the North African and Middle Eastern countries).

The differences between the two basic liturgies can be traced back to the differences that developed between the sages of Eretz Yisrael and those of Babylonia, regarding the order and content of the services. Although the Babylonian tradition prevailed everywhere, the Ashkenazic nusaḥ also reflects the influence of the tradition of Eretz Yisrael. The Sephardic nusaḥ was influenced solely by the prayer tradition of Babylonia. Among East European Ashkenazic Jews, Ḥasidic communities adopted some of the features found in the Sephardic tradition, and so a nusaḥ Sephard, slightly different from the one followed by Sephardic Jewry, is found even among Ashkenazic Jews. One variation of the Sephardic nusaḥ, followed by Lubavitcher Ḥasidim, among others, is called *nusaḥ ha'Ari*, a liturgical rite based on the rulings of Rabbi Isaac Luria, the sixteenth century Safed kabbalist.

There also developed a liturgical tradition based on the halakhic rulings of the great Ashkenazic scholar, Elijah, Gaon of Vilna. This is called *nusaḥ haGra*, which is an acronym for the Hebrew letters of his name. A great many Ashkenazic synagogues in Israel follow this nusaḥ. There are also other, less well-known rites, such as *nusaḥ Teiman*, followed by the ancient Yemenite community.

In modern times, the nusaḥ of prayer has little relationship with the two major Hebrew modes of pronunciation (*havara*): Sephardic and Ashkenazic. It is quite common for one who follows the nusaḥ Sephard in prayer to use the Ashkenazic *havara* (e.g., Ḥasidic groups in the diaspora), and for one who follows the nusaḥ Ashkenaz in prayer to recite the prayers in the Sephardic *havara* (e.g., Israelis of Ashkenazic background).

THE HEBREW BLESSING: ITS DISTINCTIVE FEATURES

The opening words of a blessing("berakhah")are always the same: *Barukh atah Adonai, eloheinu melekh ha-olam* ("Blessed art Thou, Lord our God, King of the universe"). Any prayer that either begins or ends with this fixed formula is called a blessing.

Although in everyday speech, a blessing is usually thought of as a prayer said for the good of a person—for example, God blesses us with good fortune or one person blesses another—the formal Hebrew blessing is a declaration concerning the blessedness of God.

A blessing may be a prayer giving thanks to God or one that praises Him, or it may be a prayer that petitions God. We also say a blessing for the privilege of deriving enjoyment from that which God created (e.g., blessings for food) and for the privilege of observing God's commandments (e.g., blessings said before performing a ritual mitzvah) (Maim. Hil. Berakhot 1:4). Since the blessing is central to all Jewish prayer, I will close this chapter with an explanation of its distinctive features.

The Meaning of Barukh ("Blessed")

The first words of the berakhah requires some explanation. The word *barukh* is invariably translated as "blessed" or "praised". Both translations convey the thought that it is we human beings who extend our blessing or heap our praise upon God for His having done what is described in the rest of the blessing.

Sefer haḤinukh, the classic thirteenth-century work on the six-

65

hundred and thirteen commandments, analyzes the meaning of the word barukh (No. 430). Since all honor and all wisdom and all blessing reside solely in God, nothing that man says or does can add to Him any such qualities. It is presumptuous to think that God's blessing is increased on account of our prayers. "Barukh" should therefore be regarded as descriptive of God. Just as He is an *El rahum v'hanun* ("a merciful and compassionate God"), He is also an *El barukh* ("a blessed God"). As mercy and compassion flow from Him, so does all blessing. *Barukh atah Adonai* basically means therefore that "Thou O Lord are the source, the fountainhead of all blessing."

The midrash even draws a connection between the word "berakhah", ("blessing") and "bereikhah", a "spring" or a natural "pool" (Bereshit Rabbah 39).

The Use of the Second and Third Person Forms

We now dare to use the familiar second person "atah", which means "You" or "Thou". The propriety of this wasn't at first acceptable to all the sages. Though it was the opinion of Rav, a third-century Talmudic sage, that a blessing should begin with the words *Barukh atah Adonai eloheinu* ("Blessed are Thou, Lord our God"), Samuel, a contemporary of Rav, was of the opinion that "atah", ("Thou"), should not be said. It is too intimate. The sages ruled in favor of Rav, but the approved formula for the Hebrew blessing actually takes both opinions into consideration. We begin in the second person, addressing God as "atah," Thou, or You, when we relate to Him as our Father, as the source of mercy and compassion, as the One who cares for mankind. The sense of nearness to God, in fact, is essential to Jewish prayer. It reflects the verse from Psalm 16:8: "I have set the Lord always before me." But the moment we refer to God as *melekh ha-olam*, ("King of the universe"), we become more formal and conclude the blessing in the third person, "who sanctified us . . ." or "who created the fruit of the earth." When we relate to God as a Sovereign Ruler, we assume a more respectful role. The sense of awe and of distance is reflected in the verse from Ezekiel: "Blessed is the glory of God from His abode."

While the grammatical form of the Hebrew blessing may disturb the sensitivity of grammarians, it clearly expresses the vital balance so central to Jewish thought between a sense of intimacy and closeness to God, and one of respectful distance.

Abudarham, the noted fourteenth-century scholar, in his treatise on prayer, explains the use of both the second and third person forms as an allusion to the hidden and revealed aspects of the Divine. God reveals Himself to man by what He has wrought, by the wonders He continues to perform, and by the Divine Providence or care that we discern in the affairs of men and nations. To God revealed, we use the more familiar second person. The nature of God, His mystery and His essence, however, remains hidden. To God hidden, whose ways are unfathomable, we use the more formal third person.

Having now covered the general background of Jewish prayer, let us move on to the specific content of the prayer book itself, beginning with the one prayer that is central to every worship service.

THE ORDER OF THE PRAYERS
WITHIN EACH SERVICE

SHAHARIT: *The Morning Service*
The Morning Blessings
The Verses of Song
THE SHEMA AND ITS BLESSINGS

THE AMIDAH

Supplications (on weekdays)
Hallel   (on festivals)
THE READING OF THE TORAH
(only on Sabbaths, Mondays & Thursdays)

MUSAF: ADDITIONAL AMIDAH

(only on Sabbath, festivals & Rosh Ḥodesh)

Concluding Psalms, Hymns, & Aleinu

* * *

MINḤA: *The Afternoon Service*
Ashrei (Psalm 145)

THE AMIDAH

Aleinu

* * *

MAARIV: *The Evening Service*
THE SHEMA AND ITS BLESSINGS

THE AMIDAH

Aleinu

3

The Shemoneh Esrei:
The Amidah of
"Eighteen" Blessings

THE Shemoneh Esrei is the heart of every service. It contains the basic components of prayer: praising God, petitioning Him, and thanking Him. Whenever the Talmud refers to *tefilah* ("prayer"), it means the Shemoneh Esrei, and not any other blessing, supplication, or psalm. It is The Prayer. In the various codes of Jewish law, the section dealing with the "Laws of Prayer" contains only the rules relating to the Shemoneh Esrei. The obligation to pray three times a day is fulfilled only by reciting the Shemoneh Esrei three times a day.

Shemoneh Esrei means simply "eighteen." The prayer is so called because the original version consisted of eighteen blessings. The basic formula is ancient—composed by the 120 Men of the Great Assembly in the fifth century B.C.E. Shortly after the destruction of the Second Temple in the first century C.E., the form and order of these blessings were crystallized by Simon Ha-Pakuli in Yavneh at the request of Rabbi Gamliel (Megillah 17b; Berakhot 28b). Although a nineteenth blessing was then added to this prayer (see pp. 92–93), it continued to be called "Shemoneh Esrei." The name was not changed to *Tesha*

Esrei, which means "nineteen." So ingrained is the name that people tend to call even the Sabbath and festival version of the Shemoneh Esrei by the same name, even though these prayers contain only seven blessings and are correctly designated by halakhic sources as *Tefilat Sheva,* ("the Prayer of Seven [Blessings]"). Yet people continue to call it Sabbath "Shemoneh Esrei" and Festival "Shemoneh Esrei."

This prayer is called by still another name—the "Amidah," which means "standing." The prayer is called this because it reflects our having stopped to stand in the presence of God. "Amidah," as the name of this prayer, is in widespread use among Sephardic Jews, and some contemporary prayer books have adopted it; for example, weekday Amidah, Sabbath Amidah, Festival Amidah, High Holy Day Amidah.

Because this chapter is devoted mainly to the weekday version of this prayer, I will continue to use the name "Shemoneh Esrei." But throughout the rest of this book, I will use "Amidah," if only because it is the more accurate term when referring collectively to the weekday, Sabbath, and holiday versions.

The Shemoneh Esrei is a beautifully simple prayer. Almost every phrase has its source in the Bible. Each blessing is a very ingenious collection of Biblical words and phrases pieced together to form a new composition that reflects a broad spectrum of personal needs, communal needs, and Jewish convictions. For those who faithfully say it, it has remained eternally fresh and meaningful, withstanding the test of time.

When we say the Shemoneh Esrei, we address ourselves directly to Almighty God. The outward forms that need to be observed are simple enough. What is admittedly more difficult, is to attain a level of concentration intense enough to allow us to move into another dimension. Only in that spiritual dimension is it possible to experience the uplifted feeling that comes with talking to our Father in Heaven.

LAWS AND CUSTOMS RELATING TO ITS RECITATION

The Shemoneh Esrei is said while facing in the direction of Eretz Yisrael (the Land of Israel). Worshipers in Eretz Yisrael face towards Jerusalem. Worshipers in Jerusalem face towards the Temple Mount, where the Temple (*Beit Hamikdash*) once stood. The Holy Ark in every synagogue is generally located so that when one faces the Ark, one is also standing in the proper direction vis-à-vis Israel, Jerusalem, or the Temple Mount. If one does not know in which direction to face, then, says the Talmud: "let him direct his heart to his Father in heaven" (Berakhot 30a; Maim. Hil. Tefilah 5:3).

The Shemoneh Esrei is said with feet together while standing (See p. 39). The requirement to stand at attention when praying is a matter of respect, but a Scriptural basis for it is found in Ezekiel 1:7: "And their feet were as a straight foot." This is interpreted to mean that the feet of the angels in the vision appeared as one foot (Berakhot 10b). When one stands to speak to God, one should assume the position of the ministering angels.

The Shemoneh Esrei should be said quietly to oneself, based on the example set by Hannah whose praying is described in these words: "Hannah spoke in her heart; only her lips moved, but her voice could not be heard" (Sam. I, 1:13). The sages adopted this as the proper form for prayer. That is why the Shemoneh Esrei is sometimes referred to as the "Silent Prayer," although articulation is required and the words must be audible to oneself. Those who raise their voices during this prayer are criticized as being people of little faith, as though they were insinuating that God cannot hear the soft voice that barely escapes the lips (Sotah 32b; Berakhot 31a). The soft tone of the Shemoneh Esrei is also dictated by the need to avoid disturbing the concentration of other worshipers. When alone, it is permissible to raise the voice somewhat if it aids in concentration.

Inasmuch as we also relate to God as the King of Kings, the Sovereign of the universe, no less courtesy should be shown to Him than to mortal kings. The convention that prevailed in royal courts when approaching a king thus became the basis for several customs during worship: for example, three small forward steps are taken before beginning the Shemoneh Esrei. Where space is at a premium, the practice is to move back several tiny steps before taking the three symbolic steps forward. The idea that one "approaches" God to pray is found several times in the Bible: "And Abraham approached" (Gen. 18:23), "And Elijah approached" (Kings I, 18:36). Similarly one takes three steps backward at the very end of the Shemoneh Esrei before reciting the sentence, "*Oseh shalom bimromav.*" While saying it, it is customary to slightly bow three times from the waist: first towards the left, then towards the right, then forward (OH 123:1). So did a subject take leave of his king and so do we exit from the presence of the Sovereign of the universe.

One must not permit oneself to be interrupted at any time during the recitation of the Shemoneh Esrei. Should an important personage pass by and greet you while you are saying the Shemoneh Esrei, you must not interrupt the prayer to return his greeting or even to acknowledge the greeting with a nod. Only the gravest emergency justifies the interruption of one's conversation with God (Berakhot 5:1).

The Shemoneh Esrei is said twice at every service except at the Maariv service. First it is said quietly by the congregation. It is then repeated aloud by the Prayer Leader. (The repetition is called *ḥazarat ha-Shaṭz* in Hebrew.) The Shemoneh Esrei is the only prayer that is thus repeated in its entirety. The public repetition of The Prayer was instituted for the benefit of those who were not able to recite it properly. By listening attentively and answering "Amen" at the end of each blessing, such worshipers are considered to have fulfilled their prayer obligation (Maim. Hil. Tefilah 8:9). How understanding were our sages of the religious yearnings and sensitivities of those who did not yet know how to pray.

The Shemoneh Esrei is not repeated at the Maariv service because of the Talmudic ruling which treats Maariv as having originally been optional (*reshut*), and not having the same degree of obligation (*ḥovah*). Its public recitation was therefore unnecessary (Berakhot 27b; Maim. Hil. Tefilah 1:6, 9:9).

Although it has become customary among Jews everywhere to treat Maariv with the same sense of duty and obligation as Shaḥarit and Minḥa, the nonrepetition of the Shemoneh Esrei remains witness to the Talmudic ruling about Maariv's once optional character.

THE STRUCTURE OF THE SHEMONEH ESREI

The blessings that make up the Shemoneh Esrei cover every type of prayer and respond to every human need. I once asked a class of students who did not pray regularly in the traditional manner if they were ever moved to utter a quiet prayer, a hope, a wish in the privacy of their hearts, and if so, to volunteer to tell the class what it was. After a little thought and some initial embarrassment, they began to raise their hands one by one. Everyone had, at one time or another, uttered some prayer, some wish. The content of the personal prayers varied from student to student—some were intensely personal, others reflected more general hopes dealing with the world at large. We then fit each personal prayer into a broader category and discovered that they all fell within the framework of one of the blessings of the Shemoneh Esrei.

The blessings of the Shemoneh Esrei were not haphazardly thrown together. One Talmudic midrash provides scriptural foundations for both the order and the content of the blessings (Megillah 17b–18a). Another suggests that each blessing is associated with some historic or miraculous event. Still another relates the order and content of the blessings to the prayer of Hannah (Netiv Binah I, p. 264–5).

Whatever the historic origin and the midrashic explanations, the Shemoneh Esrei also has a logical order to its arrangement. The Shemoneh Esrei is made up of three sections: an introductory section of three blessings wherein we praise God, a middle section of thirteen blessings wherein we petition Him to satisfy various needs, and a closing section of three blessings wherein we thank God and take leave of Him.

It corresponds to the ruling of Rabbi Judah who said: "A person should never petition for his requirements in the first three blessings or in the last three. For Rabbi Ḥanina taught: 'In the first blessings, one resembles a servant who praises his master, in the middle ones, one resembles a servant requesting some gift from his master, and in the last ones, one resembles a servant who has received his gift and takes his leave' " (Berakhot 34a).

It is common courtesy, when coming to someone for help, not to immediately launch into one's request. Depending on the relationship, the introductory remarks may range from a simple self-introduction, to the exchange of greetings, to a statement of sincere praise about your benefactor's virtues. Prayers uttered by Moses, David, and Solomon had followed the same pattern and set the example that the sages followed in the opening blessings of the Shemoneh Esrei (Sifre, Deut. 33:2). It was not just a matter of form. There was sincere concern about showing proper reverence to God. "And so did Rabbi Simlai expound: 'A man should always first recount the praise of the Holy One, blessed be He, and then pray [for what he needs]' " (Berakhot 32a).

The middle section of the Shemoneh Esrei covers a wide spectrum of needs. The blessings in this section contain requests that relate both to the needs of the individual and the nation. Six blessings relate to our personal well-being; six blessings to our national well-being. The personal needs are further subdivided into those of a spiritual character and those of a physical or material character.

The following chart will more vividly outline the basic structure of the Shemoneh Esrei. The name of each blessing is given in English and Hebrew. Note that the name of the blessing reflects its general theme.

INTRODUCTORY SECTION: PRAISE OF GOD

Order and Name of Blessing:	Begins with the words:
1 Fathers ("Avot")	Barukh atah
2 Powers of God ("Gevurot")	Atah gibor
3 Holiness of God ("Kedushat HaShem")	Atah kadosh

MIDDLE SECTION: REQUEST OF NEEDS

A. *Personal Needs*

Spiritual

4 Knowledge ("Binah")	Atah honen
5 Repentance ("Teshuvah")	Hashiveinu
6 Forgiveness ("Selihah")	Selah lanu

Physical, Material, and Emotional

7 Redemption-Security ("Geulah")	R'eh v'onyeinu
8 Health ("Refuah")	Refaeinu
9 Economic Prosperity ("Birkat Hashanim")	Barekh aleinu

74

The Shemoneh Esrei: The Amidah of "Eighteen" Blessings

B. Needs Of The Jewish People and Society

10	Ingathering of the Dispersed ("Kibbutz Galuyot")	Teka bashofar
11	Restoration of Justice ("Birkat Hamishpat")	Hashiva shofteinu
12	Destruction of Israel's Enemies ("Birkat Haminim")	V'lamalshinim
13	Prayer for the Righteous ("Birkat HaTzadikim")	Al hatzadikim
14	Restoration of Jerusalem ("Birkat Yerushalayim")	V'liYerushalayim
15	Coming of the Messiah ("Birkat David")	Et tzemaḥ David

C. Summary Blessing

16	Hear Our Prayer ("Tefilah")	Shema koleinu

CLOSING SECTION: THANKING GOD

17	Worship ("Avodah")	Retzei
18	Thanksgiving ("Birkat Hodaah")	Modim
19	Peace ("Birkat Shalom")	Sim shalom (or Shalom rav)

The Talmud suggests an internal logic to explain the order in which the middle blessings are arranged:

*Knowledge** is the key to all spiritual and material progress. It makes *Repentance* possible. This in turn leads to God's *Forgiveness*, which provides hope that God will grant us *Redemption* from our daily dose of problems and grant us *Health* and *Economic Prosperity*.

The needs of the nation also follow a pattern: The first step toward Israel's redemption is the *Ingathering of the Dispersed*. This step must be followed by the *Restoration of Justice*, which involves the elimination of crime, and by the *Destruction of Enemies*, including the elimination of sectarian heresies. This will permit the *Righteous* to make their influence felt, and pave the way for the *Rebuilding of Jerusalem* and the *Coming of the Messiah*. All the prayers then converge in one summary blessing that God *Hear our Prayer* (Megillah 17b–18a).

* Italicized words indicate the names of the blessings.

The first and last three blessings of the Shemoneh Esrei do not vary between weekday, Sabbath, and festival, except on holidays when passages appropriate to the holiday are incorporated. These introductory and closing sections remain essentially the same at every prayer service throughout the year. Only the middle section varies. The thirteen blessings that petition for the needs of the individual and the nation are said only on weekdays. They are omitted on the Sabbath and festivals, and replaced by a single blessing that relates to the sanctity of the day. (Only on Rosh Hashanah, does the middle section of the Musaf prayer consist of three blessings.) (See p. 121.) The primary reason for eliminating these blessings from the Sabbath and festival service is because "it is forbidden to ask for one's personal needs on the Sabbath" (Yer. Shabbat 15:3). For one to do so is to be reminded of what one is lacking, which can only sadden a worshiper, disturb his Sabbath tranquility, and strike a discordant note in the spiritual wholeness and physical contentment that the Sabbath day is intended to provide.

Let us now proceed to look into the meaning of each of the blessings of the Shemoneh Esrei.

THE INTRODUCTORY (THREE) BLESSINGS: PRAISE OF GOD

The First Blessing: Fathers ("Avot")

In the first blessing, we introduce ourselves to the Almighty and present to Him our credentials.

בָּרוּךְ אַתָּה יהוה, אֱלֹהֵינוּ וֵאלֹהֵי אֲבוֹתֵינוּ,
אֱלֹהֵי אַבְרָהָם, אֱלֹהֵי יִצְחָק, וֵאלֹהֵי יַעֲקֹב, הָאֵל
הַגָּדוֹל הַגִּבּוֹר וְהַנּוֹרָא, אֵל עֶלְיוֹן, גּוֹמֵל חֲסָדִים
טוֹבִים, וְקוֹנֵה הַכֹּל, וְזוֹכֵר חַסְדֵי אָבוֹת וּמֵבִיא

גּוֹאֵל לִבְנֵי בְנֵיהֶם לְמַעַן שְׁמוֹ בְּאַהֲבָה.
מֶלֶךְ עוֹזֵר וּמוֹשִׁיעַ וּמָגֵן. בָּרוּךְ אַתָּה יהוה, מָגֵן
אַבְרָהָם.

Blessed art Thou, Lord our God and God of our fathers,
God of Abraham, God of Isaac, and God of Jacob,
The great, mighty, and awesome God,
God Supreme, who extends loving kindness and is Master of all,
Who remembers the gracious deeds of our forefathers,
And who will bring a Redeemer with love to their children's children
   for His name's sake.
King, Helper, Savior and Protector. Blessed art Thou, Lord, Protector
   of Abraham.

By calling Him "our God" we identify ourselves as His faithful
followers. We then mention our *yichus* ("family lineage"), our relationship with Abraham, Isaac, and Jacob, with whom He had established a special covenant and to whom He made certain promises that
involve their descendants. And so we, the descendants, now humbly
claim His protection, not because of our own virtues, but because of
the merit of our forefathers (Yoma 87a). We resort to the same defense that Moses had recourse to when the Israelites sinned by worshiping the Golden Calf. The Torah tells us that God expressed a
wish then to destroy the entire nation, but Moses pleaded with Him
on the Israelites' behalf. At first, God was adamant in His refusal.
Only when Moses said: "Remember Thy servants Abraham, Isaac,
and Israel," (Exod. 32:13) did God finally accept his prayer (Shabbat
30a; Berakhot 32a). We depend on this special relationship when
expressing our conviction that God can be relied upon to bring redemption to the Jewish people.

One bends the knees and bows both at the beginning and at the
end of this first blessing when saying "*Barukh atah.*" The name of
God, "*Adonai*" should already be said while standing erect. One does
not bow again during the Shemoneh Esrei until the blessing of
Modim. The sages were wary of excessive humility and, in fact, cautioned us not to bow during the other blessings (Berakhot 34a).

The Second Blessing: Powers ("Gevurot")

In the second blessing, we extol God's greatness in giving life, in restoring life, in providing the necessities of life. We mention His awesome powers over all creation, in conformance with the verse from Psalms 29:1: "Ascribe unto the Lord glory and strength" (Megillah 17b). In doing so, we also imply the dependence of nature and all living things on God.

אַתָּה גִּבּוֹר לְעוֹלָם אֲדֹנָי, מְחַיֵּה מֵתִים אַתָּה,
רַב לְהוֹשִׁיעַ.

מַשִּׁיב הָרוּחַ וּמוֹרִיד הַגֶּשֶׁם.

מְכַלְכֵּל חַיִּים בְּחֶסֶד, מְחַיֵּה מֵתִים בְּרַחֲמִים
רַבִּים, סוֹמֵךְ נוֹפְלִים, וְרוֹפֵא חוֹלִים, וּמַתִּיר
אֲסוּרִים, וּמְקַיֵּם אֱמוּנָתוֹ לִישֵׁנֵי עָפָר. מִי כָמוֹךָ
בַּעַל גְּבוּרוֹת וּמִי דּוֹמֶה לָּךְ, מֶלֶךְ מֵמִית וּמְחַיֵּה
וּמַצְמִיחַ יְשׁוּעָה.

וְנֶאֱמָן אַתָּה לְהַחֲיוֹת מֵתִים. בָּרוּךְ אַתָּה יהוה,
מְחַיֵּה הַמֵּתִים.

Thy might is eternal, O Lord,
Who revives the dead,
Powerful in saving,
Who makes the wind to blow and the rain to fall, [*Said only in
winter*]
Who sustains the living with loving kindness,
Who revives the dead with great mercy,
Who supports the falling, heals the sick, frees the captive,
And keeps faith with the dead;
Who is like Thee, Almighty, and who resembles Thee,
O King who can bring death and give life,

And can make salvation blossom forth.
And faithful art Thou to revive the dead.
Blessed art Thou, Lord, who makes the dead live.

Power among human beings is generally defined in terms of one's ability to destroy. The most powerful persons or nations are those who can cause the greatest damage or lay waste the greatest numbers, who can subdue, imprison, or take away the freedom of people. We do not so define God's power. While God certainly has unlimited power, we emphasize that the real might of God lies in His ability to give life to man and to earth, to sustain life, to heal the sick, to free the captive, to raise the fallen.

This blessing does not even wax eloquent about the creative powers of God and the magnificent expanse over which He reigns, as does the Psalmist (see Psalms 29, 104, among others). God's powers are here defined exclusively in terms of His acts of "loving kindness" (ḥesed), by helping man when he is helpless.

In the Jewish value system, the act of loving kindness ("ḥesed") that one performs for the dead by providing them with proper burial and treating their bodies in a dignified way is called a *ḥesed shel emet* ("a true act of loving kindness"). It is so called because there can be no reciprocity attached to this selfless act. Even the High Priest, who was forbidden any contact with the dead, unable even to take part in the burial of his own parents, was required to defile himself to perform this ḥesed shel emet if he came upon an unburied corpse. The greatest expression of God's loving kindness is therefore what He can do for the dead.

The thrice-repeated emphasis in this blessing on "making the dead to live" or "reviving the dead" reflects an ancient controversy with the Samaritans, which was later taken up by the Sadducees and others, who denied this belief (Sanhedrin 10:1; Rosh Hashanah 17a). The Talmud, however, declares that God will make the dead to live again (*teḥiat hameitim*) a doctrine so central to Jewish life that its denial is deemed a heresy for which one forfeits a share in the world-to-come. Maimonides (1135–1204) includes it among his thirteen principles of faith because, aside from creation, it is the ultimate expression of Divine power (though not necessarily the ultimate spiritual reward). If God was able to create [from nothing] that which had never existed, He can certainly recreate that which had already existed.

Still, the precise meaning of this principle of faith remained open to legitimate controversy. Some, like Nachmanides (1195–1270), interpreted it literally as the eternal resurrection of the body in this world; others, like Maimonides, regarded it as a sort of "second chance" normal life that would only be temporary. Still others blurred the distinction between *tehiat hameitim* and *olam haba*, between the concept of resurrection and the belief in a spiritual hereafter that coexists parallel to the physical world, where the souls of the righteous dwell eternally in spiritual bliss (Kiddushin 39b; Rashi).*

Though a prayer for rain properly belongs in a blessing for economic sustenance and, in fact, does appear there, rain is also mentioned in this blessing as yet another example of God's power to "make the dead to live"—which is the central theme of this blessing. For through rain, God brings the barren and "dead" earth back to life and to fruitfulness (Berakhot 33a; Bereshit Rabbah 13:4).

Rain is mentioned in the passage only during the winter months (from Shemini Atzeret until the first day of Pesah) since this is the time that it is needed in Eretz Yisrael. Mention of rain is omitted during the summer months when it could ruin the crops (Sam. I, 12:17–18, Rashi). During the summer season, mention of "dew" (*morid ha-tal*) may be substituted for that of rain. Most diaspora Ashkenazim have not adopted the summer substitute. Sephardic and Hasidic liturgy does, however, follow the practice of saying "morid ha-tal", as do all Ashkenazic congregations in Eretz Yisrael. Mention of dew was never made obligatory because dew is a year-round phenomenon and is not as subject to drought. Though it is an indication of God's "greatness" (*gedulah*), dew is not an example of the theme of this blessing which is God's "power" (*gevurah*) acting seasonally upon nature or upon the human condition.

The Third Blessing: Holiness of God ("Kedushat HaShem")

In this third blessing, we continue to extol God, but concentrate on His attribute of holiness.

---

* In the early morning blessings (see pp. 187–188), the term "revival of the dead" is not meant to refer to this principle of faith, but is used to describe persons awakening from sleep who are likened unto those returning to life (Abudarham Ha Shalem, pp. 39–40).

אַתָּה קָדוֹשׁ וְשִׁמְךָ קָדוֹשׁ, וּקְדוֹשִׁים בְּכָל יוֹם
יְהַלְלוּךָ סֶּלָה. בָּרוּךְ אַתָּה יהוה, הָאֵל הַקָּדוֹשׁ.

Thou art holy, and Thy name is holy,
And those who are holy shall praise Thee every day.
Blessed art Thou, Lord, the holy God.

When the Shemoneh Esrei is repeated by the Prayer Leader,
the congregation rises immediately after the second blessing to say a
special prayer called *Kedushah*, which serves as a sort of congregational
introduction to, and elaboration of, this third blessing. The Kedushah
is not said when praying alone or during the quiet recitation of the
Shemoneh Esrei.

The Kedushah and the significance of holiness will be discussed
separately in chapter 5.

THE MIDDLE (THIRTEEN) BLESSINGS: PETITIONING GOD

The Spiritual Needs of the Individual

The Fourth Blessing: Knowledge ("Binah") *

אַתָּה חוֹנֵן לְאָדָם דַּעַת וּמְלַמֵּד לֶאֱנוֹשׁ בִּינָה.
חָנֵּנוּ מֵאִתְּךָ דֵּעָה בִּינָה וְהַשְׂכֵּל. בָּרוּךְ אַתָּה יהוה,
חוֹנֵן הַדָּעַת.

Thou grantest knowledge to man,
And teachest understanding to humans;

* This blessing is called in Hebrew by various names: "Binah" (Megillah 17b),
"Deah" (Yer. Berakhot 2:4), "Ḥokhmah" and "Ḥonein Ha-da'at" (Berakhot 33a).

81

From Thine own Self, favor us with knowledge, understanding, and
sense.
Blessed art Thou, Lord, giver of knowledge.

The middle section of the Shemoneh Esrei properly begins with
a prayer for knowledge and understanding. These are essential pre-
requisites for the genuine spiritual experience, as for all human activities. The sages said it candidly, "If there is no understanding, how
can there be prayer?" (Yer. Berakhot 4:3). They also felt that "an
ignorant person cannot be truly pious" (Avot 2:5), for true piety—
the kind that is not based on mere superstition—presupposes an
understanding of the nature of the world and a knowledge of what God
requires of us.

One notes the unusual use of the word *honein*, for "grant"
instead of the more usual *notein*. Honein literally means "to be
gracious." The implication here is that the giving of knowledge and
wisdom to man is an act of Divine grace, for by doing so God
graciously shares with man one of His own Divine qualities. It is precisely in this quality that man fundamentally differs from the rest of
the animal kingdom.

When in a dream, God asked King Solomon to make a wish, he
asked for wisdom and knowledge (Chron. II, 1:10). This then has
priority in our list of petitions.

Rabbi Abraham Isaac Hakohen Kook (1865–1935), the first
Ashkenazi Chief Rabbi of Eretz Yisrael, suggests still another reason
why the blessing for knowledge was placed before all others. When
one moves on from sanctifying God (in the third blessing) to petitioning for worldly needs, there should be no sharp distinction between
them. Knowledge and understanding is the bridge between the worlds
of the sacred and the secular. It is what enables us to direct even the
everyday mundane activities toward higher spiritual purposes (Olat
Re'iyah I pp. 273–274).

The Fifth Blessing: Repentance ("Teshuvah")

הֲשִׁיבֵ֫נוּ אָבִ֫ינוּ לְתוֹרָתֶ֫ךָ, וְקָרְבֵ֫נוּ מַלְכֵּ֫נוּ
לַעֲבוֹדָתֶ֫ךָ, וְהַחֲזִירֵ֫נוּ בִּתְשׁוּבָה שְׁלֵמָה לְפָנֶ֫יךָ.

בָּרוּךְ אַתָּה יהוה, הָרוֹצֶה בִּתְשׁוּבָה.

Return us, our Father, to Thy Torah,
And draw us closer, our King, to Thy worship,
And bring us back before Thee in complete repentance.
Blessed art Thou, Lord, who desires repentance.

Understanding can lead to repentance, to a return to God and to the observance of His Torah. This blessing is a plea that God draw us ever closer to Him and help us reach greater spiritual heights.

Only in this blessing and in the next one ("Forgiveness") is God referred to as *Avinu*, ("our Father"), and not only as *Adonai* ("Master" or "Lord"). For just as it is the duty of a father to teach his children Torah and to guide them along the correct path, so do we ask our Father in heaven to bring us closer to His Torah and help us steer a proper course in life.

Likewise, when we ask for His forgiveness, we emphasize His fatherly relationship to us by praying for a father's merciful understanding. "As a father has compassion on his children" (Psalms 103: 13), we ask that God have mercy on us and forgive us.

The fifth blessing ends with the words, "Blessed art Thou, Lord, who desires repentance." This is an expression of the traditional Jewish belief that God is *not* anxious to punish and execute judgments. The Prophet Ezekiel (33:11) makes the point: "Do I then want the death of the evildoer? I want only the return of the wicked from his ways so he may live!" Judaism does not seek the punishment but the rehabilitation of those who violate God's law. The Talmud offers the consoling thought that "He who comes to purify himself is helped [by God] to do so" (Yoma 38b).

The Sixth Blessing: Forgiveness ("Seliḥah")

סְלַח לָנוּ אָבִינוּ כִּי חָטָאנוּ, מְחַל לָנוּ מַלְכֵּנוּ
כִּי פָשָׁעְנוּ, כִּי מוֹחֵל וְסוֹלֵחַ אָתָּה. בָּרוּךְ אַתָּה
יהוה, חַנּוּן הַמַּרְבֶּה לִסְלֹחַ.

Forgive us, our Father, for we have sinned,
Pardon us, our King, for we have transgressed,
For Thou art a pardoner and forgiver.
Blessed art Thou, Lord, Gracious One who forgives abundantly.

The prophets of Israel assure us that God will forgive us in the wake of sincere repentance (Is. 55:7). This blessing emphasizes that God has set no limit to His pardoning grace. One should therefore never despair about earning Divine forgiveness.

When saying the words *ḥatanu* and *pashanu* ("we have sinned," "we have transgressed"), it is customary to lightly beat once upon the chest with one's right hand. The midrash mentions this very ancient practice as a way of symbolizing that the heart is the source of the temptation to transgress (Kohelet Rabbah 7:2).

The Physical, Emotional, and Material Needs of the Individual

The Seventh Blessing: Redemption ("Geulah")

רְאֵה בְעָנְיֵנוּ, וְרִיבָה רִיבֵנוּ, וּגְאָלֵנוּ מְהֵרָה
לְמַעַן שְׁמֶךָ, כִּי גוֹאֵל חָזָק אָתָּה. בָּרוּךְ אַתָּה
יהוה, גוֹאֵל יִשְׂרָאֵל.

Look upon us in our suffering,
And fight our struggles,
Redeem us speedily, for thy Name's sake,
For Thou art a mighty Redeemer.
Blessed art Thou, Lord, Redeemer of Israel.

The Shemoneh Esrei now turns to our physical, emotional, and material needs. First there is the need to be relieved of all sorts of daily trouble and anguish that may befall us as individuals. And though the term "redemption" has spiritual associations, being most often used in connection with the messianic redemption of the Jewish people, this is not the connotation of the word in this blessing. Rashi explains it simply: "Redemption in this blessing does not refer to redemption from exile, but that we be delivered from the troubles that constantly befall us" (Megillah 17b).

The word "suffering" as used in this blessing, may apply to all the personal difficulties—whether of body or soul—that afflict our daily lives. We pray to be delivered from all such troubles.

The Eighth Blessing: Healing ("Refuah")

רְפָאֵנוּ יהוה וְנֵרָפֵא, הוֹשִׁיעֵנוּ וְנִוָּשֵׁעָה, כִּי
תְהִלָּתֵנוּ אָתָּה, וְהַעֲלֵה רְפוּאָה שְׁלֵמָה לְכָל
מַכּוֹתֵינוּ,* כִּי אֵל מֶלֶךְ רוֹפֵא נֶאֱמָן וְרַחֲמָן אָתָּה.
בָּרוּךְ אַתָּה יהוה, רוֹפֵא חוֹלֵי עַמּוֹ יִשְׂרָאֵל.

Heal us, O Lord, and we shall be healed,
Save us and we shall be saved,
For Thou art our glory.
Send complete healing for our every illness*
For Thou, Divine King, art the faithful, merciful Physician.
Blessed are Thou, Lord, who heals the sick of His people Israel.

The opening words of this blessing paraphrase Jeremiah 17:14, where the same words are first uttered in the singular. A prayer for health and healing requires little comment except for the reminder that while it is the doctor who treats the patient, it is God who cures him.

Though this blessing, as all the others, is phrased in the plural, the sages suggested personalizing the blessing should one know of a specific person who is sick and for whose recovery one wishes to pray. The personal note may be struck by inserting the following passage into the blessing, where indicated by the asterisk:

וִיהִי רָצוֹן מִלְּפָנֶיךָ. יְיָ אֱלֹהַי וַאלֹהֵי אֲבוֹתַי. שֶׁתִּשְׁלַח
מְהֵרָה רְפוּאָה שְׁלֵמָה מִן־הַשָּׁמַיִם. רְפוּאַת הַנֶּפֶשׁ וּרְפוּאַת
הַגּוּף. לַחוֹלֶה _____ בְּתוֹךְ שְׁאָר חוֹלֵי יִשְׂרָאֵל.

Let it be Thy will, Lord our God and God of our fathers, to speedily send from heaven a full recovery, a healing of the soul and a healing of the body, to the sick (insert name) among all the other sick of Israel.

The name to use is the Hebrew name of the sick person and that of his or her mother. Thus it would be Joseph ben ("son of") Sarah, or Miriam bat ("daughter of") Sarah. (See p. 53) The Book of Psalms provides the precedent for the preference in using the mother's name instead of the father's name. When David prayed, he said: "I am Thy servant, the son of Thy maidservant" (*ani avdekha ben amatekha*) (Psalms 116:16). If the mother's name is not known, the father's name may be used.

The Ninth Blessing: Economic Prosperity ("Birkat Hashanim")

בָּרֵךְ עָלֵינוּ יהוה אֱלֹהֵינוּ אֶת הַשָּׁנָה הַזֹּאת וְאֶת

כָּל מִינֵי תְבוּאָתָהּ לְטוֹבָה, וְתֵן

בְּרָכָה ‖ טַל וּמָטָר לִבְרָכָה*

עַל פְּנֵי הָאֲדָמָה וְשַׂבְּעֵנוּ מִטּוּבָהּ, וּבָרֵךְ שְׁנָתֵנוּ

כַּשָּׁנִים הַטּוֹבוֹת. בָּרוּךְ אַתָּה יהוה, מְבָרֵךְ הַשָּׁנִים.

Bless this year for us, O Lord our God, and all its varied produce that it be for good;
Provide (dew and rain as a*) blessing on the face of the earth,
Satisfy us with Thy goodness, and bless this year like the good years.
Blessed art Thou, Lord, who blesses the years.

After deliverance from personal distress and from the incapacities of illness, the most important component in a person's physical

---

* The words "dew and rain" are limited to the winter season. In Eretz Yisrael, one begins to add these words on the 7th of Ḥeshvan, two weeks after the end of the Sukkot festival (Taanit 1:3). In the diaspora, however, there is the tradition of beginning to add these words sixty days after the start of the "Tishrei season" which falls out on the night of either December 4th or December 5th. Since the "seasons" are based on solar, not lunar, calculations (Eruvin 56a), the fixed date must be expressed in terms of the general calendar.

well-being is economic security. Though couched in agricultural terms suitable to an agricultural society (i.e., a prayer for a good crop), this blessing is essentially a prayer for *parnasah* ("a decent livelihood").

Although we live in a postindustrial society, the world's economic well-being is still very much dependent on the abundance of its harvests and of products taken out of the earth.

The prayer stresses that the year and produce be blessed "for us" (*aleinu*) and "that it be good (*l'tovah*)." At first glance, these words may seem unnecessary. Can abundance be anything but good for us? Yet the sages' choice of words is significant. For if there is waste, mismanagement, and corruption, there can be scarcity despite an abundant harvest. It is quite possible that people will be unable to afford what the blessed earth produces. "The vine will offer its fruits, but the wine will be expensive," said the sages several thousand years ago (Sotah 49b). The curse of inflation was understood even then. Abundance that cannot be enjoyed can hardly be regarded as good or as benefitting us. It is not for such abundance that we pray.

We also want God's blessings to be good for us in the long run as well. If as a result of being blessed with abundance, we indulge our vices and turn our backs on the moral and spiritual values that God wishes us to pursue, can such abundance be regarded as having been "for good"? Or if the granting of our wishes creates conditions that lead to self-destruction or that cause children to go astray, can such answered prayers be regarded as having been good or beneficial to us? Trusting that God knows what is in our long-term interest, the sages deliberately chose to pray only for economic blessings that will be both *aleinu* (to our benefit) and *l'tovah* (for our good).

Considering the great stress that Judaism places on happily serving God (*ivdu et HaShem besimḥah*), and on the religious duty to rejoice and be happy on the festivals, one may wonder why the sages did not add a blessing that asks God to grant us happiness. We ask for knowledge, for health, for economic prosperity, for peace. But for happiness, not a word! It is true that on the Sabbath and holidays, we pray that God "make us happy with Thy salvation" and "make us happy with the re-establishment [of the Temple]," but as a general blessing to add to the others on a daily basis, happiness is strangely absent. The founding fathers of the United States included the "pursuit of happiness" as one of the legitimate concerns of modern man. Why did our sages overlook it or ignore it? Why not a prayer for happiness?

Perhaps the answer is because happiness cannot be granted from On High. It must flow from man himself. God can bless us with necessities and luxuries in the realm of the material and in the realm of the spirit that might lead to happiness. But ultimately, happiness depends on personal contentment with what one has. Interestingly enough, in Hebrew, the word for "happiness" (*simḥah*) is used in the term that connotes contentment.

The Needs of the Jewish People and Society

The Tenth Blessing: Ingathering of the Dispersed
("Kibbutz Galuyot")

תְּקַע בְּשׁוֹפָר גָּדוֹל לְחֵרוּתֵנוּ, וְשָׂא נֵס לְקַבֵּץ
גָּלִיּוֹתֵינוּ, וְקַבְּצֵנוּ יַחַד מֵאַרְבַּע כַּנְפוֹת הָאָרֶץ.
בָּרוּךְ אַתָּה יהוה, מְקַבֵּץ נִדְחֵי עַמּוֹ יִשְׂרָאֵל.

Sound the great shofar [to proclaim] our freedom,
Lift up a banner for the ingathering of our exiles,
And bring us together from the four corners of the earth.
Blessed art Thou, Lord, who gathers together the dispersed of His people Israel.

We now turn to a series of prayers that relate to the national aspirations of the Jewish people. They address themselves to those developments that shall bring about the complete redemption of the Jewish people, both physically and spiritually.

There have been two major schools of thought on the ways and means of redemption. There are those who believe that redemption is a process that will happen step by step, little by little, like the rising of the sun. Gradually, and by quite natural means, Jews will be gathered together from all parts of the world; Eretz Yisrael will be reconquered and resettled in stages; and Jerusalem and the Temple will be rebuilt. There will be a spiritual return of all the people to God. At what stage in this process the Messiah appears is still another question that divides the proponents of this school of thought. However, any steps taken to hasten redemption are to be regarded as praiseworthy and desirable (Yer. Berakhot 1:1; Zohar, Vayishlaḥ; Ramban on Shir HaShirim 8:13).

Others believe that redemption will occur as does a burst of lightning. Amidst awesome miracles, the third Beit Hamikdash will appear and come down from the heavens, completely built and finished, conforming to the literal meaning of the verse in Exodus 15:17: "The sanctuary, O Lord, which *Thy* hands have established" (Rashi, Sukkah 41a; and Tosaphot, based on Midrash Tanḥuma). The Messiah will suddenly appear miraculously to bring all of diaspora Jewry back to Eretz Yisrael. Until then, one should not, indeed one may not, take any action(s) to hasten this event. Some pious Jews even base their non-Zionist or anti-Zionist attitudes on this view.

The Torah, in Deuteronomy Chapter 30, does however allude to distinct stages in the process of redemption: a) the ingathering of dispersed Jewry (verses 3–4), b) inheriting and building the land (verse 5), and c) the spiritual return of all the people to God (verses 6 and 8). Ezekiel, Chapter 36, also speaks of redemption as a gradual procedure. Authoritative opinion throughout the ages has been heavily weighted toward the first school of thought.

The very order in which the blessings of the Shemoneh Esrei were arranged by the sages would seem to reflect their belief in a chronological unfolding of the events. The tenth blessing, which prays for the reunion of all Jews in Eretz Yisrael, is followed by blessings for the rebuilding of Jerusalem and the Beit Hamikdash (fourteenth blessing) and for the coming of the Messiah (fifteenth blessing). Maimonides differs only in that he says that the Messiah will precede all these events. Any ingathering of Jews before the Messiah, according to him, is only a partial ingathering. The Messiah will complete the task (Hil. Melakhim 11:1).

In the blessing about the ingathering of the dispersed, one notes that a proclamation of freedom precedes any mention of the ingathering. History has borne this out. As long as the Jewish people were not the masters of their own land and could not chart their own history, they were in no position to accommodate a mass ingathering. Only when they proclaimed their freedom and established a sovereign Jewish state could they pass legislation that gave to every Jew who wants to, the right to come to Eretz Yisrael. That right had been denied them for almost two thousand years. Only when the Jewish people are free in their own land is it possible to translate the spiritual yearning to return to Eretz Yisrael into reality for the physical and political barriers are then eliminated. All that is needed is the will to act.

When this blessing was first composed by the Men of the Great Assembly, Jews had already returned from the Babylonian exile to rebuild the Second Temple. Yet they included this blessing among their prayers, for most of the Babylonian Jewish community did not return to Eretz Yisrael. Neither did many Jews who had fled to and settled in Egypt, Greece, Italy and other Mediterranean countries. The blessing naturally took on special significance after the destruction of the Second Temple in 70 C.E., and after the failure of the Bar-Kokhba rebellion in 135 C.E. when most of the Jewish people were forcibly exiled from Judea.

A meaningful interpretation of this blessing was suggested by Rabbi Joseph B. Soloveitchik. He said that the expression *nidhei Yisrael* ("the dispersed of Israel") (Is. 56:8, 11:12), which concludes the blessing, does not only refer to the physically dispersed but also to the spiritually dispersed, to those who have lost spiritual contact with the Jewish people and its faith. This blessing could then also be a prayer for the spiritual ingathering of the lost souls of Israel. In the same vein, the prophetic verse about the return of the children "to their borders" (Jer. 31:16) could be understood to also mean a return to their own heritage.

The Eleventh Blessing: Restoration of Justice
("Birkat Hamishpat")

הָשִׁיבָה שׁוֹפְטֵינוּ כְּבָרִאשׁוֹנָה, וְיוֹעֲצֵינוּ
כְּבַתְּחִלָּה, וְהָסֵר מִמֶּנּוּ יָגוֹן וַאֲנָחָה, וּמְלֹךְ עָלֵינוּ
אַתָּה יהוה לְבַדְּךָ בְּחֶסֶד וּבְרַחֲמִים, וְצַדְּקֵנוּ
בַּמִּשְׁפָּט. בָּרוּךְ אַתָּה יהוה, מֶלֶךְ אוֹהֵב צְדָקָה
וּמִשְׁפָּט.

Restore our judges as at first,
And our counselors as in the beginning,
Removing from us sorrow and sighing;
Rule over us, Thou alone, O Lord
With kindness and mercy,
And vindicate us in the judgment.
Blessed are Thou, Lord, King, who loves righteousness and judgment.

The return to Eretz Yisrael is to be followed by the realization of yet another Biblical prophecy: "I will restore your judges as at first" (Is. 1:26). The eleventh blessing, paraphrasing this verse, is a prayer for still another step toward full redemption.

Throughout most of history, Jews had little faith in the "justice" that was dispensed by courts in the lands where they lived. The restoration of their own courts with judges who would follow the teachings inherent in God's law makes possible the implementation of what had previously been only theoretical Hebrew civil and criminal law. This blessing means that not only the people, but also Torah law is being returned from its exile.

Jewish emphasis on the institutions of justice can be seen from the fact that the establishment of courts of law is, according to Judaism, one of the seven basic commandments incumbent upon all mankind.* As Ethics of the Fathers reminds us, "Destruction comes to the world because of the corruption of the law" (Avot 5:8).

The restoration of justice would remove the sorrow that inevitably accompanies the corruption of justice. It would also restore the Divine Presence ("Shekhina"), which cannot dwell over Israel as long as there are corrupt judges (Shabbat 139a).

The Twelfth Blessing: Destruction of Israel's Enemies ("Birkat Haminim")

וְלַמַּלְשִׁינִים אַל תְּהִי תִקְוָה, וְכָל הָרִשְׁעָה כְּרֶגַע
תֹּאבֵד, וְכָל אוֹיְבֵי עַמְּךָ מְהֵרָה יִכָּרֵתוּ, וְהַזֵּדִים

---

* The other six are the prohibitions against idolatry, blasphemy, murder, incest and adultery, robbery, and the cutting off a limb of a living animal for food (Sanhedrin 56a; Maim. Hil. Melakhim 9:1).

מְהֵרָה תְעַקֵּר וּתְשַׁבֵּר וּתְמַגֵּר וְתַכְנִיעַ בִּמְהֵרָה
בְיָמֵינוּ. בָּרוּךְ אַתָּה יהוה, שׁוֹבֵר אוֹיְבִים וּמַכְנִיעַ
זֵדִים.

For slanderers let there be no hope,
And let all wickedness instantly perish.
May all Thy enemies be quickly cut off;
And as for the malicious,
Swiftly uproot, break, cast down, and subdue
Quickly in our day.
Blessed art Thou, Lord, who breaks the power of His enemies and
  subdues the malicious.*

From time to time, as we all know, the survival of the Jewish
people is threatened. Threats may arise from hostile forces without
or from traitors within. Such threats are sometimes aimed to destroy
us physically, and sometimes to undermine us spiritually.

In one place the Talmud indicates that this blessing, which was
directed against heretical groups, was fixed in Yavneh under the leadership of Rabbi Gamliel the Elder during the second century C.E.
(Berakhot 28b) and constituted the nineteenth blessing of the Shemoneh Esrei. Eliezer Levy, however, argues from sources elsewhere
in the Talmud (Yer. Berakhot 2:4) that this blessing was one of the
original eighteen prescribed by Ezra.** The opening words of the blessing were then *Al Haminim* ("For the heretics, let there be no
hope . . ."), and it was directed against the hostile Samaritan sect.§
Later, when the Samaritan threat declined, the blessing fell into
disuse. When a new threat of religious heresy arose with the Sadducees

---

* The words of this blessing are culled from Micah 5:8, Malachi 3:19, Psalms
10:15, Isaiah 13:11, 14:5, 25:5.
** Eliezer Levy, *Yesodot Hatefilah* (Tel Aviv: Bitan Hasefer Publishing, 1952),
pp. 153–155.
§ The Samaritans were colonists who stemmed ethnically from Babylon. They
were transplanted to the province of Samaria by the conquering Assyrians in 722 B.C.E.
to displace the Israelites who were deported and taken into exile. They eventually
adopted the Mosaic code, but rejected the authority and teachings of the Prophets.
Religiously they became "quasi-Jewish." The Talmud refers to them as *Cuthim*.

(*Tzedukim*),* the blessing was revived with a new opening that mentioned the Sadducees: "For the Sadducees, let there be no hope. . . ." With the growth of new heretic sects (among them Jews who adopted Christian beliefs) who informed on fellow Jews to Roman authorities, this blessing assumed new urgency and needed to be restated—this time at Yavneh, as the Talmud indeed relates. The word V'*lamalshinim* was added: ". . . and for informers let there be no hope. . . ." To carry tales to governing authorities charging fellow Jews with all sorts of alleged crimes became one of the more despicable things a Jew could do. And so the wording remained throughout the generations. And inasmuch as "in every generation there are those who rise up to annihilate us," this prayer has unfortunately remained ever pertinent. Even today, there is no dearth of hostile forces to whom the prayer could apply. All other prayers on the same theme do not petition for the destruction of the wicked nor for their punishment, but for their return to God and to the ways of righteousness (Berakhot 10a; Sanhedrin 39b; Avodah Zarah 4b; Taanit 23b).

The Thirteenth Blessing: Prayer for the Righteous
("Birkat HaTzadikim")

עַל הַצַּדִּיקִים וְעַל הַחֲסִידִים, וְעַל זִקְנֵי עַמְּךָ
בֵּית יִשְׂרָאֵל, וְעַל פְּלֵיטַת סוֹפְרֵיהֶם, וְעַל גֵּרֵי
הַצֶּדֶק וְעָלֵינוּ, יֶהֱמוּ רַחֲמֶיךָ יהוה אֱלֹהֵינוּ,
וְתֵן שָׂכָר טוֹב לְכָל הַבּוֹטְחִים בְּשִׁמְךָ בֶּאֱמֶת,
וְשִׂים חֶלְקֵנוּ עִמָּהֶם לְעוֹלָם, וְלֹא נֵבוֹשׁ כִּי בְךָ
בָטָחְנוּ. בָּרוּךְ אַתָּה יהוה, מִשְׁעָן וּמִבְטָח
לַצַּדִּיקִים.

On the righteous and the saintly,
On the elders of Thy people, the house of Israel, and on their surviving scholars,
On the true proselyte and on ourselves,

---

* The Sadducees were a Temple oriented group who differed with the Pharisees on basic theological principles. They held to a literal interpretation of the Torah and rejected the Oral Tradition.

Let Thy compassion flow, O Lord our God.
Grant a good reward to all who sincerely trust in Thy Name;
Place our lot with them forever and let us not be shamed,
For in Thee do we trust.
Bless art Thou, Lord, the support and security of the righteous.

Since God's justice is always questioned when the wicked flourish
and the righteous suffer, this blessing petitions God to reward the
righteous and the saintly and to make their presence felt.

We also include the true proselyte in this prayer for the righteous
and the saintly. The Torah directs us to show special sensitivity to the
sincere proselyte who remolds his or her way of life in order to live
by the Jewish faith and who casts his or her lot with the Jewish
people. The Talmud numbers the proselyte among those whose souls
were present at Sinai and with whom God made His covenant
(Shevuot 39a). Furthermore, a sequence of verses in the Torah (Lev.
19:32–34) connects the *zaken* (the elder—a learned and righteous
person) and the *ger* (a word that has come to mean a convert to
Judaism) (Megillah 17b).

The Fourteenth Blessing: Restoration of Jerusalem
("Birkat Yerushalayim")

וְלִירוּשָׁלַיִם עִירְךָ בְּרַחֲמִים תָּשׁוּב, וְתִשְׁכֹּן
בְּתוֹכָהּ כַּאֲשֶׁר דִּבַּרְתָּ, וּבְנֵה אוֹתָהּ בְּקָרוֹב בְּיָמֵינוּ
בִּנְיַן עוֹלָם, וְכִסֵּא דָוִד מְהֵרָה לְתוֹכָהּ תָּכִין.
בָּרוּךְ אַתָּה יהוה, בּוֹנֵה יְרוּשָׁלָיִם.

To Jerusalem Thy city, return with compassion,
And dwell within it as Thou promised;
Rebuild it soon in our days—an everlasting structure;
And speedily establish in its midst the throne of David.
Blessed art Thou, Lord, builder of Jerusalem.

The rebuilding of Jerusalem and its re-establishment as the
capital of a Jewish state and as the spiritual fountainhead of the Jewish
faith are essential components in redemption. The ancient prophecy

that "Out of Zion [another name for Jerusalem] shall go forth the Torah and the word of God from Jerusalem" (Is. 2:3) underscores the spiritual significance that the city of Jerusalem has always had for Judaism.

When Jerusalem was in its heyday during the time of the Second Temple, the closing line of this blessing was not "who builds Jerusalem," but "who dwells in Jerusalem" (Yer. Yoma 7:1). We pray that events will someday justify the restoration of the original wording.

The Fifteenth Blessing: Coming of the Messiah ("Birkat David")

אֶת צֶמַח דָּוִד עַבְדְּךָ מְהֵרָה תַצְמִיחַ, וְקַרְנוֹ
תָּרוּם בִּישׁוּעָתֶךָ, כִּי לִישׁוּעָתְךָ קִוִּינוּ כָּל הַיּוֹם.
בָּרוּךְ אַתָּה יהוה, מַצְמִיחַ קֶרֶן יְשׁוּעָה.

The offspring of Thy servant David,
Quickly cause to flourish,
And lift up his power by Thy deliverance;
For Thy deliverance do we constantly hope.
Blessed art Thou, Lord, who makes the glory of deliverance to
   flourish.

According to tradition, the Messiah will be a descendant of the royal House of David. The "offspring of David" means the Messiah, whose coming will bring to pass the physical and spiritual redemption of the Jewish people.

Rabbi Kook makes the point that the sentence "for Thy deliverance do we constantly hope" teaches us the concept of *anticipating deliverance* even when there are no signs of it in daily events. He writes: "Just as a lookout doesn't leave his post even when everything is quiet and nothing seems to be happening, but stands ready to detect enemy movement and to react to it at a moment's notice, so do we maintain a state of constant spiritual alertness and readiness, so we may respond when the time comes. These are the two components of awaiting salvation" (Olat Re'iyah, I p. 279–280).

This blessing about the Messiah's coming and the one preceding

it about Jerusalem were originally one blessing that concluded with
the words: "God of David and Builder of Jerusalem," or according to
another version, "Builder of Jerusalem and Savior of Israel." Several
reasons have been suggested why this blessing was divided into two.*
One is based on the halakhic decision by the sages not to close a
blessing with two themes (Berakhot 49a). A contributing factor may
also have been the desire to emphasize our conviction that the
Messiah is still to come.

The fifteenth blessing concludes the series of six blessings that
relate to the redemption of the Jewish people.

The Sixteenth Blessing: Hear Our Prayer ("Tefilah")

The last blessing in the middle section of the Shemoneh Esrei
is a summary, whose eloquence lies in its simplicity and universality.
A version of it was once said by the High Priest in the Beit Hamikdash.
The sages used that prayer as a basis for formulating this blessing.
All the personal and general prayers contained in the preceding twelve
blessings now converge for one final plea to a Merciful God to hear
our voices.

שְׁמַע קוֹלֵנוּ יהוה אֱלֹהֵינוּ, חוּס וְרַחֵם עָלֵינוּ,
וְקַבֵּל בְּרַחֲמִים וּבְרָצוֹן אֶת תְּפִלָּתֵנוּ, כִּי אֵל
שׁוֹמֵעַ תְּפִלּוֹת וְתַחֲנוּנִים אָתָּה, וּמִלְּפָנֶיךָ מַלְכֵּנוּ
רֵיקָם אַל תְּשִׁיבֵנוּ, * כִּי אַתָּה שׁוֹמֵעַ תְּפִלַּת עַמְּךָ
יִשְׂרָאֵל בְּרַחֲמִים. בָּרוּךְ אַתָּה יהוה, שׁוֹמֵעַ תְּפִלָּה.

Hear our voice, O Lord our God,
Show compassion and mercy to us,
Accept our prayers with mercy and favor,
For Thou art a God who hears prayers and supplications.

* Inasmuch as Birkat Haminim had for a time been out of use, resulting in only
seventeen blessings (Yer. Berakhot 4:3), the division of Birkat Yerushalayim into two
blessings by the Babylonian sages restored the Shemoneh Esrei to eighteen blessings.
And when the ancient blessing against slanderers was revived, it was regarded as the
nineteenth blessing.

And from Thy presence, O our King, turn us not away empty;
*For Thou hearest the prayer of Thy people Israel with compassion.
Blessed art Thou, Lord, who hears prayer.

It is permissible, even desirable, to introduce extemporaneous requests within any of the petitionary blessings, but particularly in this one. These additional prayers, which may be said in any language, may relate to any need, personal or general (AH 119:1).

When the sages decided to have this blessing follow the one about messianic salvation, they perhaps wished to teach us yet another truth. Prayer will remain an essential component of the spiritual life even in a post-Messianic period. Sincere prayer will, in fact, become the hallmark of that period. Isaiah 56:7 speaks of the rebuilt Beit Hamikdash becoming a prayer center for all the peoples of the earth.

THE CONCLUDING (THREE) BLESSINGS:
THANKING GOD

The last section of the Shemoneh Esrei consists of three blessings that are the same in every Amidah throughout the year. These three blessings constitute a unit in which we ask God to receive our prayer offering, we thank Him for past, present, and future kindnesses, and we pray for peace as we take our leave.

The Seventeenth Blessing: Worship ("Avodah")

רְצֵה יהוה אֱלֹהֵינוּ בְּעַמְּךָ יִשְׂרָאֵל וּבִתְפִלָּתָם,
וְהָשֵׁב אֶת הָעֲבוֹדָה לִדְבִיר בֵּיתֶךָ, וְאִשֵּׁי יִשְׂרָאֵל
וּתְפִלָּתָם בְּאַהֲבָה תְקַבֵּל בְּרָצוֹן, וּתְהִי לְרָצוֹן
תָּמִיד עֲבוֹדַת יִשְׂרָאֵל עַמֶּךָ.

---

* This is the appropriate place to add special requests.

וְתֶחֱזֶינָה עֵינֵינוּ בְּשׁוּבְךָ לְצִיּוֹן בְּרַחֲמִים. בָּרוּךְ
אַתָּה יהוה, הַמַּחֲזִיר שְׁכִינָתוֹ לְצִיּוֹן.

Favorably receive, O Lord our God, Thy people Israel and their
prayer,
Restore the worship to Thy Temple in Zion,
Receive with love and favor the offerings of Israel and their prayer,
And may the worship of Thy people Israel always be favorably re-
ceived by Thee.
May our eyes behold Thy return to Zion in mercy.
Blessed art Thou, Lord, who restores His Divine Presence to Zion.

The blessing of Retzei specifically embodies the idea that prayer
is now the sacrificial offering, the *korban* that we bring to God in lieu
of the animal sacrifice. It is through prayer that we are now drawn
closer to Him, and that was, after all, the main purpose of the
korbanot. In former days, the kohanim asked God to favorably receive the sacrifice. And so today, we ask that God favorably receive
our service of prayer as our offering to Him (Yer. Berakhot 4:4).

Although the first few words of Retzei seem to repeat what was
already said in the preceding blessing of Shema Koleinu, the difference
in language between them is very significant. Words like "retzei"
and "l'ratzon" are nearly always used in association with the way God
is asked to respond to what *we bring to Him*, not to what *we ask of
Him*. And so in Retzei, which relates to our "prayer offerings," we ask
God to "*receive* with love." In Shema Koleinu, which relates to our
petitions, we ask God to "*hear* with mercy."

The blessing of Retzei is modeled after one that the kohanim
said in the Beit Hamikdash at the conclusion of the two daily sacrifices. The concluding words of the blessing then were:

בָּרוּךְ אַתָּה יהוה שֶׁאוֹתְךָ לְבַדְּךָ בְּיִרְאָה נַעֲבֹד.

"Blessed art Thou, Lord, for only Thee will we worship in awe."
(Berakhot 11b; Yoma 68b, Rashi)

The original last line is still said on the festivals during the Musaf service whenever the rite of the Priestly Blessing takes place.

After the destruction of the Temple, the blessing of Retzei was altered to include a prayer for the re-establishment of the Temple service and for the return of the Divine Presence to Zion. In connection with this hope, deeper insight into the meaning of *v'ishai Yisrael* ("the offerings of Israel") can be gleaned from midrashic sources. Although it is generally understood as a reference to animal sacrifices in a restored Beit Hamikdash, there is another view expressed in ancient sources that *v'ishai Yisrael* refers to "the souls of the righteous of Israel" (Menaḥot 110a, Tos. s.v. *u'Michael*). Their souls and their prayers are part of our spiritual offering. This matches the opening words of the blessing which speaks only of "Thy people Israel and their prayers" as the subject of the offering that God is asked to receive favorably.

Rabbi Joseph B. Soloveitchik reflects this view when he translates "v'ishai Yisrael" as the human "self-sacrifices" that our people made throughout history.* And what greater self-sacrifice has there indeed been, than the martyred "souls of the righteous" whose blood was shed only because they were Jews and insisted on remaining Jews.

The Eighteenth Blessing: Thanksgiving ("Birkat Hoda'ah")

מוֹדִים אֲנַחְנוּ לָךְ שָׁאַתָּה הוּא יהוה אֱלֹהֵינוּ וֵאלֹהֵי
אֲבוֹתֵינוּ לְעוֹלָם וָעֶד, צוּר חַיֵּינוּ, מָגֵן יִשְׁעֵנוּ
אַתָּה הוּא לְדוֹר וָדוֹר. נוֹדֶה לְּךָ וּנְסַפֵּר תְּהִלָּתֶךָ
עַל חַיֵּינוּ הַמְּסוּרִים בְּיָדֶךָ, וְעַל נִשְׁמוֹתֵינוּ
הַפְּקוּדוֹת לָךְ, וְעַל נִסֶּיךָ שֶׁבְּכָל יוֹם עִמָּנוּ, וְעַל
נִפְלְאוֹתֶיךָ וְטוֹבוֹתֶיךָ שֶׁבְּכָל עֵת, עֶרֶב וָבֹקֶר
וְצָהֳרָיִם. הַטּוֹב כִּי לֹא כָלוּ רַחֲמֶיךָ, וְהַמְרַחֵם
כִּי לֹא תַמּוּ חֲסָדֶיךָ, מֵעוֹלָם קִוִּינוּ לָךְ.

* "Redemption, Prayer, Talmud Torah," TRADITION, Vol. 17, No. 2, p. 71.

וְעַל כֻּלָם יִתְבָּרַךְ וְיִתְרוֹמַם שִׁמְךָ מַלְכֵּנוּ תָּמִיד
לְעוֹלָם וָעֶד.

וְכֹל הַחַיִּים יוֹדוּךָ סֶּלָה, וִיהַלְלוּ אֶת שִׁמְךָ
בֶּאֱמֶת, הָאֵל יְשׁוּעָתֵנוּ וְעֶזְרָתֵנוּ סֶלָה. בָּרוּךְ
אַתָּה יהוה, הַטּוֹב שִׁמְךָ וּלְךָ נָאֶה לְהוֹדוֹת.

We give thanks unto Thee who art the Lord our God* and God of
our fathers for all eternity.
Thou art the Strength of our lives, the Shield of our deliverance.
In every generation, we shall thank Thee and declare Thy praise
For our lives that are entrusted in Thy hand,
And for our souls that are in Thy care,
And for Thy miracles that are daily with us,
And for Thy wondrous deeds and goodness that occur at all times,
evening, morning, and noon.
Thou art the Benevolent One, for Thy mercies are never ended,
The Compassionate One, for Thy deeds of kindness do not stop,
Always have we placed our hope in Thee.
For all this, O our King, may Thy Name be always blessed and exalted
forever and ever.
All the living will forever thank Thee and praise Thy Name in truth,
O God, our eternal salvation and help.
Blessed art Thou, Lord, whose Name is Goodness; it is pleasing to
give thanks to Thee.

After petitioning God to take care of our needs, we now express
gratefulness for our very lives and for the wonders that are ever with
us. The depth of our sincerity is surely a measure of our own faith in
Divine Care.

One of the basic virtues that Judaism always encouraged in
people is to be grateful, to be appreciative, to say "thank you." Ingratitude is not only a moral flaw, it is the very essence of heresy.

* The word *modim* ("giving thanks") also means "to acknowledge." The first
words of this blessing could therefore also be translated as "We acknowledge that Thou
art the Lord our God . . . we shall thank thee."

When the Prophets castigated Israel for its sins against God, they expressed it as a condemnation of Israel's ingratitude to Him. There is no more grievous sin against God and perhaps also against man. There is none so despicable as he who is incapable of thanksgiving.

The Psalmist regarded the ability to be thankful as good for man: "It is good to give thanks to the Lord and to sing praises unto Thy Name, O Most High" (Psalm 92:2). The closing words of the blessing are even based on this verse.

A blessing of thanksgiving was also once part of the ancient Temple service. The Talmud tells us that *avodah v'hoda'ah* (the Temple service and the prayers of thanksgiving) are but two sides of the same coin (Megillah 18a).

Another version of the thanksgiving prayer is found in the siddur alongside the basic text. It is the *Modim d'Rabbanan*, the "Thanksgiving Prayer of the Rabbis," so called because it is a composite of several short thanksgiving prayers said by various Talmudic sages (Sotah 40a).

מוֹדִים אֲנַחְנוּ לָךְ שָׁאַתָּה הוּא יהוה אֱלֹהֵינוּ וֵאלֹהֵי
אֲבוֹתֵינוּ, אֱלֹהֵי כָל בָּשָׂר, יוֹצְרֵנוּ יוֹצֵר בְּרֵאשִׁית.
בְּרָכוֹת וְהוֹדָאוֹת לְשִׁמְךָ הַגָּדוֹל וְהַקָּדוֹשׁ עַל
שֶׁהֶחֱיִיתָנוּ וְקִיַּמְתָּנוּ. כֵּן תְּחַיֵּנוּ וּתְקַיְּמֵנוּ וְתֶאֱסֹף
גָּלְיוֹתֵינוּ לְחַצְרוֹת קָדְשֶׁךָ לִשְׁמֹר חֻקֶּיךָ וְלַעֲשׂוֹת
רְצוֹנֶךָ וּלְעָבְדְּךָ בְּלֵבָב שָׁלֵם, עַל שֶׁאֲנַחְנוּ מוֹדִים
לָךְ. בָּרוּךְ אֵל הַהוֹדָאוֹת.

We thank Thee who art the Lord our God and God of our fathers,
    the God of all flesh, our Creator who created the universe;
Blessings and thanksgiving to Thy great and holy Name for having
    given us life and sustained us.
So mayest Thou continue to keep us in life and sustain us, and gather
    our dispersed to the courts of Thine holy Temple to keep Thy
    statutes, to do Thy will, and to worship Thee wholeheartedly.

101

For making it possible to thank Thee;
Blessed is the God to whom thanksgivings are due.

This prayer is not said during the quiet recitation of the
Shemoneh Esrei, nor is it said by the Prayer Leader. It is said only
by the congregation to accompany the Prayer Leader when he recites
the standard Thanksgiving blessing.

A reason for this practice is suggested by Abudarham in his
treatise on prayer: while it is fitting to petition God through an
emissary, it is not seemly to thank Him through one. This is something
that everyone should do for himself. So when the Prayer Leader
recites the standard text of this blessing, each worshiper quietly adds
the Modim d'Rabbanan.

One also bows during this blessing—once at the beginning when
saying *Modim anahnu lakh,* and again at the very end of the blessing
when saying *Baruch atah.*

The Nineteenth Blessing: The Peace Blessing ("Birkat Shalom")

שִׂים שָׁלוֹם טוֹבָה וּבְרָכָה, חֵן וָחֶסֶד וְרַחֲמִים
עָלֵינוּ וְעַל כָּל יִשְׂרָאֵל עַמֶּךָ. בָּרְכֵנוּ אָבִינוּ
כֻּלָּנוּ כְּאֶחָד בְּאוֹר פָּנֶיךָ, כִּי בְאוֹר פָּנֶיךָ נָתַתָּ
לָּנוּ יהוה אֱלֹהֵינוּ תּוֹרַת חַיִּים וְאַהֲבַת חֶסֶד,
וּצְדָקָה וּבְרָכָה וְרַחֲמִים וְחַיִּים וְשָׁלוֹם. וְטוֹב
בְּעֵינֶיךָ לְבָרֵךְ אֶת עַמְּךָ יִשְׂרָאֵל בְּכָל עֵת וּבְכָל
שָׁעָה בִּשְׁלוֹמֶךָ. בָּרוּךְ אַתָּה יהוה, הַמְבָרֵךְ אֶת
עַמּוֹ יִשְׂרָאֵל בַּשָּׁלוֹם.

Establish peace, well-being, blessing, grace, loving kindness, and mercy
upon us and upon all Israel, Thy people.
Bless us, our Father, all of us as one, by the light of Thy presence,
For by the light of Thy presence have you given us, O Lord our God,

A Torah of life, love of kindness, justice, blessing, compassion, life, and peace.
And it is good in Thy sight to bless Thy people Israel at all times and in every hour with Thy peace.
Blessed art Thou, Lord, who blesses His people Israel with peace.

Peace is the greatest blessing of all and the Shemoneh Esrei concludes with this prayer.

Some ancient nations envisioned their national glory in terms of war, and perhaps some nations still do. Israel, even when she was compelled to wage war, always considered peace as the ideal to strive for—peace between herself and other nations, and domestic peace among the people.

A blessing for the peace of Klal Yisrael ("the collective body of Israel") also concluded the ancient Temple service. This was separate from the three-verse Priestly Blessing, which is phrased in the singular, and which ends with a prayer for the peace of the individual. (See p. 133.) (Maim. Commentary on Mishnah; Tamid 5:1)

This Peace Blessing, phrased in the plural, covers the same series of themes as does the Priestly Blessing. Since the Priestly Blessing was not said in the afternoons or evenings, a shorter version of the Peace Blessing, whose theme is restricted to peace is now said at Minḥa and Maariv services in the Ashkenazic rite. The shorter version begins with the words *Shalom rav*.

שָׁלוֹם רָב עַל יִשְׂרָאֵל עַמְּךָ תָּשִׂים לְעוֹלָם,
כִּי אַתָּה הוּא מֶלֶךְ אָדוֹן לְכָל הַשָּׁלוֹם. וְטוֹב
בְּעֵינֶיךָ לְבָרֵךְ אֶת עַמְּךָ יִשְׂרָאֵל בְּכָל עֵת וּבְכָל
שָׁעָה בִּשְׁלוֹמֶךָ. בָּרוּךְ אַתָּה יהוה, הַמְבָרֵךְ אֶת
עַמּוֹ יִשְׂרָאֵל בַּשָּׁלוֹם.

Grant peace to Thy people Israel forever, for Thou art the sovereign Master of all peace;

103

And it is good in Thine eyes to bless Thy people Israel at all times
and in every hour with Thy peace.
Blessed art Thou, Lord, who blesses His people Israel with peace.

In the Ḥasidic rite, this shorter version is said only at Maariv
thus indicating that Maariv is of a different level of obligation than
Shaḥarit and Minḥa. In the Sephardic rite, it is not said at all.

The Shemoneh Esrei now formally concludes with the recitation of:

יִהְיוּ לְרָצוֹן אִמְרֵי־פִי וְהֶגְיוֹן לִבִּי לְפָנֶיךָ, יהוה צוּרִי וְגֹאֲלִי:

May the words of my mouth and the meditation of my heart be
acceptable to Thee, O Lord, my Strength and my Redeemer.

(Since this verse is in the meditation that follows the Shemoneh
Esrei, some say it only then.) This concluding verse, an integral part
of the Shemoneh Esrei, stands in juxtaposition to a parallel introductory verse that is said before starting the Shemoneh Esrei:

אֲדֹנָי, שְׂפָתַי תִּפְתָּח וּפִי יַגִּיד תְּהִלָּתֶךָ:

Lord, open my lips and my mouth will declare Thy praise.
(Berakhot 4b)

The Meditation of Mar, Son of Rabina
In the silent recitation of the Shemoneh Esrei, it has become
customary for the individual to add a personal supplication. The
Talmud mentions eleven sages and the supplications that each customarily added to the Shemoneh Esrei (Berakhot 16b–17a). The one by
Mar, son of Rabina, a fourth-century rabbi, became a favorite and
found its way into the prayer book.

אֱלֹהַי, נְצֹר לְשׁוֹנִי מֵרָע וּשְׂפָתַי מִדַּבֵּר מִרְמָה, וְלִמְקַלְלַי
נַפְשִׁי תִדֹּם, וְנַפְשִׁי כֶּעָפָר לַכֹּל תִּהְיֶה. פְּתַח לִבִּי בְּתוֹרָתֶךָ,

וּבְמִצְוֹתֶיךָ תִּרְדֹּף נַפְשִׁי. וְכָל הַחוֹשְׁבִים עָלַי רָעָה, מְהֵרָה
הָפֵר עֲצָתָם וְקַלְקֵל מַחֲשַׁבְתָּם.

My God, guard my tongue from evil, and my lips from speaking with
deceit.

Let my soul be silent to them that curse me; yea, let my soul be as
the dust unto all.

Open my heart to Thy Torah, and let my soul pursue Thy commandments.

And all who think evil against me, quickly annul their designs and
frustrate their intentions.

There is nothing more crucial to the true spiritual life and to the
establishment of harmony among people than controlling the tongue
—keeping it from "spreading falsehoods" (*motzi shem ra*) and from
gossiping. Even if the gossip is true, it is still called *lashon hara*
("an evil tongue"). This, the Talmud regards as a most insidious and
widespread sin (Bava Batra 165a). So we pray for God's help in acting properly toward others, and to stoically endure the impropriety of
other's actions toward us (Gitin 36b).

The Biblical source for the opening words used by Mar is
Psalms 33:14. The continuation of the prayer, where it says: "Open
my heart to Thy Torah," is in keeping with the Talmudic teaching
that it is not sufficient to only abstain from doing evil. One must also
strive to do good (Avodah Zarah 19b). "Turn away from evil and do
good" (Psalms 34:15, 37:27).

The Sephardic liturgy introduces an additional silent prayer at
this point to complement the one by Mar:

May it be Thy will, O Lord, our God, and God of our fathers, that no
person be jealous of me nor I of others, that I not become angry
and that I not anger Thee; save me from the evil inclination, and
place humility in my heart . . .

Both Sephardic and Ashkenazic rites conclude with the following prayer which was later added to the meditation:

עֲשֵׂה לְמַעַן שְׁמֶךָ, עֲשֵׂה לְמַעַן יְמִינֶךָ, עֲשֵׂה לְמַעַן קְדֻשָּׁתֶךָ

עֲשֵׂה לְמַעַן תּוֹרָתֶךָ. לְמַעַן יֵחָלְצוּן יְדִידֶיךָ הוֹשִׁיעָה יְמִינְךָ

וַעֲנֵנִי: יִהְיוּ לְרָצוֹן אִמְרֵי פִי וְהֶגְיוֹן לִבִּי לְפָנֶיךָ, יהוה צוּרִי וְגוֹאֲלִי

עֹשֶׂה שָׁלוֹם בִּמְרוֹמָיו, הוּא יַעֲשֶׂה שָׁלוֹם עָלֵינוּ וְעַל כָּל יִשְׂרָאֵל,

וְאִמְרוּ אָמֵן.

Do it for the sake of Thy Name, for the sake of Thy might, for the
sake of Thy holiness, for the sake of Thy Torah.

In order that Thy loved ones may be saved, save me through Thy
might and answer my prayer.

May the words of my mouth and the meditation of my heart be
acceptable to Thee, O God my Strength and my Redeemer.

May He who makes peace in the heavens, make peace for us and for
all Israel, and say Amen.

For rules pertaining to the repetition of the Shemoneh Esrei
(Amidah) by the Prayer Leader, see pp. 345–346.

THE CONDENSED SHEMONEH ESREI:
HAVINEINU

The sages prescribed a condensed form of the Shemoneh Esrei for
those times when one is distressed, or so pressed for time that one is
unable to concentrate, or is in a place where one can be interrupted
at any moment (Berakhot 29a: Maim. Hil. Tefilah 2:2: OH 110:1).
This version condenses the thirteen middle blessings into a single
inclusive one. The first and last sets of three blessings remain intact.
This blessing is known by its opening word *havineinu*. Each phrase
corresponds to one of the thirteen blessings.

הֲבִינֵנוּ יהוה אֱלֹהֵינוּ לָדַעַת דְּרָכֶיךָ, וּמוֹל אֶת לְבָבֵנוּ

לְיִרְאָתֶךָ, וְתִסְלַח לָנוּ לִהְיוֹת גְּאוּלִים, וְרַחֲקֵנוּ מִמַּכְאוֹב,

106

וְדַשְּׁנֵּנוּ בִּנְאוֹת אַרְצֶךָ, וּנְפוּצוֹתֵינוּ מֵאַרְבַּע תְּקַבֵּץ, וְהַתּוֹעִים
עַל דַּעְתְּךָ יִשָּׁפֵטוּ, וְעַל הָרְשָׁעִים תָּנִיף יָדֶךָ, וְיִשְׂמְחוּ צַדִּיקִים
בְּבִנְיַן עִירֶךָ וּבְתִקּוּן הֵיכָלֶךָ, וּבִצְמִיחַת קֶרֶן לְדָוִד עַבְדֶּךָ
וּבַעֲרִיכַת נֵר לְבֶן יִשַׁי מְשִׁיחֶךָ. טֶרֶם נִקְרָא אַתָּה תַעֲנֶה.
בָּרוּךְ אַתָּה יהוה, שׁוֹמֵעַ תְּפִלָּה.

O Lord our God, grant us understanding to know Thy ways,
Purify our hearts to revere Thee,
And forgive us,
So that we are redeemed.
Remove us from pain,
And satisfy us with the goodness of thine earth.
Gather our scattered people from the four [corners of the world],
Judge those who transgress Thy will,
And lift up Thy hand against the wicked,
Then shall the righteous rejoice
  with the rebuilding of Thy city and the re-establishment of Thy
  sanctuary,
  with the flourishing of the might of David, Thy servant, and the
  establishing of the glory of the son of Jesse, Thy Messiah.
Even before we call, Thou wilt answer.
Blessed art Thou, Lord, who hears prayer.

Some Talmudic sages were of the opinion that this condensed
version of the Shemoneh Esrei should be the standard text for anyone
who could not properly recite the complete Shemoneh Esrei (Berakhot 28b). Maimonides ruled according to this view and included
unfamiliarity with the Shemoneh Esrei as one of the conditions that
justifies use of the condensed Shemoneh Esrei.

The condensed form must also be said in accordance with all
the rules that apply to the full Shemoneh Esrei.

The condensed form may not, however, be said at a Maariv
service at the end of a Sabbath or festival day, because *Havdalah* is
required as part of the fourth blessing. Nor may it be said during the
winter months when the prayer for rain must be said in the ninth
blessing (Berakhot 29a).

THE SHORT PRAYER

If one finds oneself in dangerous surroundings (such as being a soldier on a front line) and one cannot recite even the condensed Shemoneh Esrei, the rabbis suggest the recitation of a short prayer that may be said in any position: sitting, walking, or lying down (OH 110:3).

צָרְכֵי עַמְּךָ יִשְׂרָאֵל מְרֻבִּים וְדַעְתָּם קְצָרָה. יְהִי רָצוֹן מִלְּפָנֶיךָ יהוה אֱלֹהֵינוּ
וֵאלֹהֵי אֲבוֹתֵינוּ שֶׁתִּתֵּן לְכָל אֶחָד וְאֶחָד כְּדֵי פַרְנָסָתוֹ וּלְכָל גְּוִיָּה וּגְוִיָּה דִּי
מַחְסוֹרָהּ.

The needs of Thy people are many and they are unable to express their wants.

May it be Thy will, O Lord our God and God of our fathers, to give each and every one his daily sustenance and to every one whatever he lacks.

Should the emergency pass, one remains obligated to say the full Shemoneh Esrei, the one prayer which, as we have seen, reflects a comprehensive Jewish relationship to God.

CHAPTER

4

The Amidah for the
Sabbath and Festivals

THE AMIDAH PRAYER for the Sabbath day and the festivals is considerably shorter than the weekday version. It consists of only seven blessings. The first three and last three blessings are the same as those said during the week, but the middle section differs. In lieu of thirteen blessings that stress our needs, there is a single blessing that emphasizes the sanctity of the day.

This is because of the ruling by the sages that: "it is forbidden to ask for the fulfillment of personal (physical) needs," on the Sabbath (Yer. Shabbat 15:3). To do so, and thus focus one's attention on things lacking or on sufferings, might sadden a person, disturb his tranquility, and strike a discordant note in the spiritual serenity that the Sabbath day is intended to provide. Because of the honor due the Sabbath, "the sages did not burden" us with the full Amidah (Berakhot 21a). The same applies to the festivals.

And so the middle blessing in the Sabbath and festival Amidah is a composite of praise and thanksgiving. It consists of a brief paragraph called *Kedushat Hayom* ("Sanctification of the Day") and it is the same in every service.

אֱלֹהֵֽינוּ וֵאלֹהֵי אֲבוֹתֵֽינוּ, רְצֵה בִמְנוּחָתֵֽנוּ.
קַדְּשֵֽׁנוּ בְּמִצְוֹתֶֽיךָ וְתֵן חֶלְקֵֽנוּ בְּתוֹרָתֶֽךָ, שַׂבְּעֵֽנוּ
מִטּוּבֶֽךָ וְשַׂמְּחֵֽנוּ בִּישׁוּעָתֶֽךָ, וְטַהֵר לִבֵּֽנוּ לְעָבְדְּךָ
בֶּאֱמֶת. וְהַנְחִילֵֽנוּ יהוה אֱלֹהֵֽינוּ בְּאַהֲבָה וּבְרָצוֹן
שַׁבַּת קָדְשֶֽׁךָ, וְיָנֽוּחוּ בָהּ יִשְׂרָאֵל מְקַדְּשֵׁי שְׁמֶֽךָ.
בָּרוּךְ אַתָּה יהוה, מְקַדֵּשׁ הַשַּׁבָּת.

Our God and God of our Father, be pleased with our rest.
Sanctify us through Thy commandments,
And set our portion in Thy Torah.
Gratify us with Thy goodness,
Gladden us through Thy salvation,
And purify our hearts to serve Thee in truth.
Give us Thy holy Sabbath, Lord our God, with love and favor as
 our heritage.
And may Israel, who sanctifies Thy Name, rest on it.
Blessed art Thou, Lord, who sanctifies the Sabbath.

To be sure, this prayer also contains petitions, but they are of a spiritual or communal nature in keeping with the Sabbath spirit.

The series of requests that begins: "Sanctify us through Thy commandments" and concludes: "to serve Thee in truth" is the same in every Sabbath, Festival, and High Holy Day Amidah. Some see in these lines an echo of the overall themes covered by the middle blessings of the weekday Amidah. "Sanctify us . . ." relates to spiritual needs; "gratify us . . ." refers to physical needs; while the phrase about "Thy salvation" pertains to national needs and aspirations.

110

VARIATIONS WITHIN THE SABBATH AMIDAH

Until about the first century B.C.E., the Amidah prayer for every Sabbath was exactly the same. Then began the expansion of the middle blessing of the Amidah with the addition of one or more introductory paragraphs to the basic blessing. This process of addition took place over a period of a thousand years and was not completed until the Geonic period. These introductory paragraphs differ in each of the Sabbath services.

At the Sabbath eve service, the middle blessing begins with *Atah kidashta*; at the Sabbath morning service, it begins with *Yismah Moshe*; and at the Sabbath afternoon service, it begins with *Atah Ehad*. The variations in theme are intended to symbolize the different stages in the development of the Sabbath.

The Sabbath had been accorded its sanctity long before there was a Jewish people and long before the Torah was given to them. The seventh day of the week had been sanctified by God as an integral part of Divine Creation and has universal significance. This is the Sabbath of Creation.

The Sabbath took on a specifically Jewish dimension as a result of the Ten Commandments that were revealed to Israel at Sinai—an event that took place on the Sabbath. This is the Sabbath of the Giving of the Torah.

In addition to the Sabbath experienced in the present world, the sages speak of the Sabbath of the future, the Sabbath that will be kept in the messianic period. This is the Sabbath of Redemption.

The variations in the middle blessing can be said to reflect several concepts that are basic to Judaism: Creation, Revelation, and Redemption.

At the Friday night service: The introductory paragraphs stress God's sanctification of the Sabbath as it relates to the creation of the world.

111

Atah Kidashta

אַתָּה קִדַּשְׁתָּ אֶת יוֹם הַשְּׁבִיעִי לִשְׁמֶךָ, תַּכְלִית
מַעֲשֵׂה שָׁמַיִם וָאָרֶץ, וּבֵרַכְתּוֹ מִכָּל הַיָּמִים,
וְקִדַּשְׁתּוֹ מִכָּל הַזְּמַנִּים, וְכֵן כָּתוּב בְּתוֹרָתֶךָ:

Thou sanctified the seventh day unto Thine own Name
As the culmination of creation of heaven and earth;
Thou blessed it above all days, and hallowed it above all seasons;
As is written in Thy Torah:

In this passage, we say that God sanctified the seventh day
lishemekha ("unto Thine own Name"). This means that the seventh
day was not set aside just for the rest and leisure of man but as a way
to bring man closer to God, to acknowledge and praise Him as Creator.
A Biblical quotation then follows:

Vayekhulu (Gen. 2: 1–3)

וַיְכֻלּוּ הַשָּׁמַיִם וְהָאָרֶץ וְכָל צְבָאָם: וַיְכַל אֱלֹהִים
בַּיּוֹם הַשְּׁבִיעִי מְלַאכְתּוֹ אֲשֶׁר עָשָׂה, וַיִּשְׁבֹּת בַּיּוֹם
הַשְּׁבִיעִי מִכָּל מְלַאכְתּוֹ אֲשֶׁר עָשָׂה: וַיְבָרֶךְ אֱלֹהִים
אֶת יוֹם הַשְּׁבִיעִי וַיְקַדֵּשׁ אֹתוֹ, כִּי בוֹ שָׁבַת מִכָּל
מְלַאכְתּוֹ אֲשֶׁר בָּרָא אֱלֹהִים לַעֲשׂוֹת:

Completed were the heaven and the earth and all their array.
On the seventh day, God finished the work that He had made;
On the seventh day, He rested from all the work that He had made;
Then God blessed the seventh day and sanctified it, because on it
   God ceased from all the work that He created to function thence-
   forth.

The last Hebrew word in the passage, *la'asot*, is there to teach us
some special truth. Otherwise, the word is superfluous. It seems to
suggest that God created a world whose task is to keep developing
beyond the original creation.

112

Yismeḥu (in Sephardic nusaḥ only)

יִשְׂמְחוּ בְמַלְכוּתְךָ שׁוֹמְרֵי שַׁבָּת וְקוֹרְאֵי עֹנֶג.
עַם מְקַדְּשֵׁי שְׁבִיעִי, כֻּלָּם יִשְׂבְּעוּ וְיִתְעַנְּגוּ מִטּוּבֶךָ,
וּבַשְּׁבִיעִי רָצִיתָ בּוֹ וְקִדַּשְׁתּוֹ, חֶמְדַּת יָמִים אוֹתוֹ
קָרָאתָ, זֵכֶר לְמַעֲשֵׂה בְרֵאשִׁית.

Those who keep the Sabbath and call it a delight shall rejoice in
   Thy kingdom;
A nation that sanctifies the seventh day will be sated and delighted
   with Thy goodness;
The seventh [day] Thou desired and sanctified;
Thou called it the precious of days,
A remembrance to creation.

At the Sabbath morning service: The introductory paragraphs
speak of God's command to Israel to keep the Sabbath as set forth
in the Ten Commandments.

Yismaḥ Moshe

יִשְׂמַח מֹשֶׁה בְּמַתְּנַת חֶלְקוֹ, כִּי עֶבֶד נֶאֱמָן
קָרָאתָ לּוֹ, כְּלִיל תִּפְאֶרֶת בְּרֹאשׁוֹ נָתַתָּ, בְּעָמְדוֹ
לְפָנֶיךָ עַל הַר סִינַי, וּשְׁנֵי לוּחוֹת אֲבָנִים הוֹרִיד
בְּיָדוֹ, וְכָתוּב בָּהֶם שְׁמִירַת שַׁבָּת, וְכֵן כָּתוּב
בְּתוֹרָתֶךָ :

Moses rejoiced in the portion assigned to him,
Thou did call him a faithful servant;
Thou placed a crown of glory upon his head, when he stood before
   Thee on Mt. Sinai,

113

And brought down in his hand two stone tablets on which was written: the [law of] keeping the Sabbath.

As is written in Thy Torah:

During the Talmudic period, the Biblical quote which followed this passage was taken from the Ten Commandments, which was indeed the most logical source. This was changed later when the rabbis sought alternatives to quoting the Ten Commandments when stressing essential doctrines of faith so as to counteract the influence of heretical sects who tried to convince the people that the only part of the Torah they need accept as true and binding was the Ten Commandments (also the Shema [see p. 344]). Since the Sabbath is emphasized in ten different passages in the Torah, there were many alternatives to choose from and they chose the following:

Veshamru (Exod. 31:16–17)

וְשָׁמְרוּ בְנֵי יִשְׂרָאֵל אֶת הַשַּׁבָּת, לַעֲשׂוֹת אֶת
הַשַּׁבָּת לְדֹרֹתָם בְּרִית עוֹלָם. בֵּינִי וּבֵין בְּנֵי יִשְׂרָאֵל
אוֹת הִיא לְעֹלָם, כִּי שֵׁשֶׁת יָמִים עָשָׂה יהוה אֶת
הַשָּׁמַיִם וְאֶת הָאָרֶץ, וּבַיּוֹם הַשְּׁבִיעִי שָׁבַת וַיִּנָּפַשׁ:

The children of Israel shall keep the Sabbath,
Observing the Sabbath throughout the generations as a covenant for all time,
It shall be a sign for all time between Myself and the children of Israel;
For in six days the Lord made heaven and earth,
And on the seventh day He ceased from work and rested.

Velo Netato

While the universality of the Sabbath is emphasized in the Maariv Amidah, the unique Jewish relationship to the Sabbath is emphasized in the Shaḥarit Amidah. This is why the theme of rejoicing in the Sabbath is prefaced in the Shaḥarit Amidah by several verses reminding us that God did not give the Sabbath to the other nations.

114

וְלֹא נְתַתּוֹ יהוה אֱלֹהֵינוּ לְגוֹיֵי הָאֲרָצוֹת, וְלֹא
הִנְחַלְתּוֹ מַלְכֵּנוּ לְעוֹבְדֵי פְסִילִים, וְגַם בִּמְנוּחָתוֹ
לֹא יִשְׁכְּנוּ עֲרֵלִים, כִּי לְיִשְׂרָאֵל עַמְּךָ נְתַתּוֹ
בְּאַהֲבָה, לְזֶרַע יַעֲקֹב אֲשֶׁר בָּם בָּחָרְתָּ. עַם
מְקַדְּשֵׁי שְׁבִיעִי, כֻּלָּם יִשְׂבְּעוּ וְיִתְעַנְּגוּ מִטּוּבֶךָ,
וּבַשְּׁבִיעִי רָצִיתָ בּוֹ וְקִדַּשְׁתּוֹ, חֶמְדַּת יָמִים אוֹתוֹ
קָרָאתָ, זֵכֶר לְמַעֲשֵׂה בְרֵאשִׁית.

Thou did not give it, O Lord our God, to the other nations of the
world;
Nor did Thou, O our King, make it the heritage of idol worshipers;
In its serenity, the heathen will not dwell,
For unto Israel, Thy people, and to the seed of Jacob whom Thou
chose,
Did Thou give it in love.

———

A nation that sanctifies the seventh day will be sated and delighted
with Thy goodness;
The seventh [day] Thou desired and sanctified;
Thou called it the precious of days,
A remembrance to creation.

At the Sabbath afternoon service: The introductory paragraph
stresses the unity of God as well as the singularity of the Jewish people.
While the passage lauds the Sabbath as a day of perfect rest, the sages
read into the passage veiled references to the tranquility of the messianic era and also of the spiritual world-to-come, which is pictured in
the religious literature as possessing a Sabbath-like atmosphere in
which the righteous souls shall eternally bask.

Atah Eḥad

אַתָּה אֶחָד וְשִׁמְךָ אֶחָד, וּמִי כְּעַמְּךָ יִשְׂרָאֵל

גּוֹי אֶחָד בָּאָרֶץ. תִּפְאֶרֶת גְּדֻלָּה, וַעֲטֶרֶת יְשׁוּעָה,
יוֹם מְנוּחָה וּקְדֻשָּׁה לְעַמְּךָ נָתָתָּ. אַבְרָהָם יָגֵל,
יִצְחָק יְרַנֵּן, יַעֲקֹב וּבָנָיו יָנוּחוּ בוֹ. מְנוּחַת אַהֲבָה
וּנְדָבָה, מְנוּחַת אֱמֶת וֶאֱמוּנָה, מְנוּחַת שָׁלוֹם וְשַׁלְוָה
וְהַשְׁקֵט וָבֶטַח, מְנוּחָה שְׁלֵמָה שָׁאַתָּה רוֹצֶה בָּהּ,
יַכִּירוּ בָנֶיךָ וְיֵדְעוּ כִּי מֵאִתְּךָ הִיא מְנוּחָתָם וְעַל
מְנוּחָתָם יַקְדִּישׁוּ אֶת שְׁמֶךָ.

Thou art One and Thy Name is One,
And who is like Thy people Israel, a nation unique on earth.
Glorious greatness and a crown of salvation,
A day of rest and holiness hast Thou given to Thy people.
A day on which Abraham was glad, Isaac rejoiced, and in which Jacob
   and his children have found rest;
A rest of love and generosity,
A rest of truth and faithfulness,
A rest of peace and tranquility, of calm and security,
A perfect rest of [the kind] that Thou desirest.
Thy children shall recognize and know that their rest comes from
   Thee,
And that by their rest, they sanctify Thy Name.

The *Atah Ehad* passage gives expression to the three singular
elements unique to Jewish faith: God, Israel, and the Sabbath. As
God is one and there is none like Him, as Israel is one, unique among
the nations, so is the Sabbath special among the days of the week.

The passage, "Yismehu," expressing Israel's rejoicing in the Sabbath, is omitted from the Minha Amidah, because of a tradition
dating back to the Geonic period that Moses died on a Sabbath afternoon. A passage emphasizing rejoicing was therefore deemed inappropriate for this service. This same tradition is the basis for saying
Tzidkatkha tzedek after the Amidah on Sabbath afternoons. This
short passage affirms Divine righteousness, a form of *tzidduk hadin*
said in the wake of a tragic event.

116

THE MUSAF AMIDAH

On the Sabbath (also on the festivals, the High Holy Days and Rosh Hodesh), an additional Amidah is added to the morning prayers. It is called *Tefilat Musaf*, which means simply "Additional Prayer." It is said following the Torah reading.

The Musaf Amidah also has only seven blessings, and the basic blessing in the middle section is the same one that is recited at the other three services. Indeed, at one time, the entire Musaf Amidah may have been identical with the others. A basic difference developed only in the later Talmudic period. Although every service was intended to correspond to its respective Temple offering, no other Amidah makes specific mention of the sacrificial offerings. The middle blessings of the others either petition for God's grace and mercy or praise Him. In the Musaf, on the other hand, the sacrificial offerings form a central theme in the middle blessing. As a result of the desire to perpetuate the memory of the Temple, the blessing of Kedushat Hayom (the "Sanctity of the Day") was expanded to recall the offerings of the day (Yer. Berakhot 4:6).

This is especially true of the Musaf said on the three festivals of Pesaḥ, Shavuot, and Sukkot. When the Temple stood, these festivals, unlike the Sabbath, were celebrated by a pilgrimage to Jerusalem and by personal attendance at the Temple worship (Deut. 16:16). Thus, the loss of the Temple and the exile were felt with particular pain on these holidays. The Musaf Amidah reflects this pain with an impassioned plea for the ingathering of the exiled nation from all corners of the earth, and for the restoration of the Temple service.

Inasmuch as there may be many worshipers for whom the mere description of the sacrifices or the thought of it at some future time conjures up distasteful associations, and whose hearts are not wholly at ease with such a prayer, let me explain this prayer for the restoration of the Temple service.

First a word about the spiritual significance of the Temple sacrifice and why it had been so important to the people.

The Hebrew word for sacrifice, *korban* (pl. *korbanot*), contains within itself the word *karov* which means "near." *L'hakriv* ("to sacrifice") can be literally translated as "to cause to draw near." By bringing korbanot, by giving up something precious to them, the people were drawn closer to God. It was the way they expressed their gratitude to God. It was the way they asked for pardon and atoned for their sins after repenting. It was the way they joined in the celebration of a pilgrimage festival. It was the way they expressed their humility before God and their obedience to His will. These were done through obligatory sacrifices and voluntary offerings, through communal and personal sacrifices.

Although use of the term "sacrifices" ("korbanot") immediately conjures up visions of animal sacrifices, several types of offerings made up the Temple service. One type was called *zevahim* (s. *zevah*) and this consisted of most of the kosher animals and of such kosher fowl as doves and pigeons. I might point out that most of these korbanot were eaten by the priests. Another type was called *menahot* (s. *minha*) and this consisted of flour offerings. It took the form of fine flour and of such baked goods as hallah bread and matzah wafers. These were generally mixed with olive oil and frankincense. A third type was called *nesakhim* (s. *nesakh*). This was liquid—wine or water—that was poured on the altar.

Meat, wine, and bread were all precious commodities, and a person was reluctant to part with them. Nachmanides (1194–1270) saw the animal sacrifices as having intrinsic worth and serving a powerful psycho-moral purpose in which the corrupt individual was subjected to a vicarious death experience, one that impelled him to confront the meaning of his own life (Ramban, Lev. 1:9).

Although Maimonides sees the sacrificial system as a necessary adjunct to a rebuilt Temple (Hil. Melakhim 11:1) it is also true that he takes a limited view of korbanot. He argues that the sacrificial system had been commanded not for its own sake, but as a pedagogical concession in order to wean the Israelites away from idolatry and "to establish the truly great principle of our faith, the existence and unity of God." The custom of sacrifice as a way of worship was then so ingrained among people in general, the Israelites included, that to have forbidden them to engage in the only form of worship they understood, would have gone against their nature and they would have been incapable of obeying. The symbolic action provided by the sacrifices was therefore permitted to continue, though in severely restricted fashion, by confining it to just one site—the Temple in Jerusalem; by limiting its practice to just one group—the kohanim, who acted on behalf of the people; and by outlawing the intolerable practices then associated with idolatry—child sacrifice, temple prostitution, and self-mutilation. "All these restrictions," writes Maimonides, "served to limit this kind of worship, and keep it within those bounds within which God did not think it necessary to abolish the sacrificial system altogether. But prayer and supplication can be offered everywhere and by every person" (*Guide to the Perplexed* III:32).

Indeed, as we have seen, even when the Temple was in existence, prayer had already become widespread in synagogues. It was even an essential component of the sacrificial ritual. Still, there was doubt as to whether prayer could ever fully replace sacrifice as the way to worship God. Only after the destruction of the Temple was the doubt resolved. Prayer became the accepted means through which the Jew could give expression to the basic concept underlying korbanot. The same spiritual benefits that had resulted from the sacrifices, "the worship of the doing" (*avodah she'b'maaseh*), were now seen as emanating from prayer, "the worship of the heart" (*avodah she'b'lev*).

For support, the sages quoted the Prophets: "We will render [the offering of] our lips in place of the bulls" (Hosea 14:3). The Talmud pictures a discussion between God and Abraham on how Israel might be forgiven its sins. Abraham says: "Well and good, while the Temple is in existence. When the Temple will no longer be, what will be then?" Answers the Almighty: "I have already provided for them in the Torah the order of the sacrifices. Whenever they read it, I will credit them with having brought the offerings before Me and grant them pardon for all their transgressions" (Megillah 31b; Taanit 27b).

Some sages did not hesitate to regard the substitute (prayer) as spiritually superior to the original (sacrifice), and as a goal to which Judaism had, in fact, aspired even while the Temple sacrifices were in effect. The Talmud records the opinion of one sage, Rabbi Elazer, who deduced from a scriptural text that "prayer is greater than sacrifices" (Berakhot 32b).

Thus while we have long since come to rely on prayer and on just reading about sacrifice, prayers for the restoration of the Temple and its worship service (the Avodah) continue to be said because they are the symbols of the messianic era and of Divine redemption.

Whether the rebuilding of the Third Beit Hamikdash will be accompanied by the restoration of animal sacrifices is an altogether different question. To argue that question today is quite futile. When it does become possible, even those now opposed may feel quite differently about it, even as those now in favor may then find halakhic reasons to object. The issues then may be entirely different. First, it is widely accepted that sacrifices cannot be restored until after the Messiah arrives and the Third Beit Hamikdash is rebuilt. Furthermore, those who pray most ardently for a restoration of the sacrificial system for they see it as a renewal of the Temple's pristine glory are the very first to admit that *under present-day circumstances,* even if the Temple Mount were physically restored to our possession, the halakhic problems inherent in a restoration of the Temple service are insurmountable.

How is it possible to verify the genealogical purity of present-day kohanim and *prove* their ancestry. The Torah warned that anyone not a kohen dare not approach the altar. How is it possible to precisely locate the site of the altar? It is forbidden to sacrifice at any other location. How is it possible to make the priestly vestments, without which kohanim cannot officiate, if the fabrics and dyes from which they have to be made are no longer available? How is it possible to obtain the jewels for the breastplate if the prescribed method by which they are to be made is no longer at our disposal? These and other questions pose serious halakhic problems that contemporary religious authorities simply cannot resolve.

The answers to all questions relating to the restoration of the sacrificial system therefore lie in the future, awaiting the advent of the Messiah and his rebuilding of the Temple.

We do not meanwhile take it upon ourselves arbitrarily to abrogate commandments and rituals of the Torah even in theory, no matter why they were given to us in the first place, or even if they no longer seem to be relevant. Such authority is not ours to exercise. Maimonides, at the very end of his Mishneh Torah Book of Avodah, classifies all korbanot in that category of religious law known as ḥukim, whose reasons are not known to us and whose sense escapes us. Of all such laws, he says, "Let them not be regarded with contempt." Paraphrasing Exodus 19:21, 22, he says, "Let one not break through to ascend to the Lord, lest He break out against him. One's thinking about [ḥukim] must not be like one's thinking concerning secular matters" (Hil. Me'ilah 8:8).

If we accept Judaism's basic creed that the Torah represents the infinite wisdom of God, then we should have sufficient faith to believe that the halakha—through which the will and wisdom of God have continued to reveal themselves throughout history—and perhaps restored prophecy will, when the time comes, guide the way to answers and correct actions.

THE MUSAF AMIDAH OF ROSH HASHANAH

The Musaf of Rosh Hashanah is noticeably different in form, content, and emphasis from every other Musaf Amidah of the year, although it, too, includes the passages describing the offering of the day and the loss of the Temple. First, the middle section consists not of one relatively short blessing but of three long blessings. It is in fact the longest Amidah of the year. Second, the emphasis in these blessings is on God's role as Sovereign of the universe, as a Judge who is compassionate and merciful and who holds the key to our redemption.

The first of the middle blessings is known as *Malkhuyot*, ("Kingship"). It emphasizes God's sovereignty over the world. The second is known as *Zikhronot*, ("Remembrances"). It dwells on God's remembering the deeds of all men and the covenant He made with Abraham, Isaac, and Jacob. The third blessing, *Shofarot*, the ("Sounding of the Shofar"), speaks of God's revelation to Israel and of ultimate redemption. It is in the context of this blessing that we also pray, as on the festivals, for the return of Israel to its own land and for the restoration of the Temple service. Furthermore, this Musaf is dramatized above all others said during the year because each of the three middle blessings concludes with the sounding of the shofar. In the Ashkenazic rite, the shofar is blown only during the Prayer Leader's repetition of the Amidah. In the Sephardic and Hasidic rites, the shofar is blown also during the silent Amidah.

CHAPTER

5

Kedushah and Other
Additions to the Amidah

KEDUSHAH

A MOMENT of particular significance occurs during the Prayer
Leader's repetition of the Amidah. Immediately following the second
blessing, the congregation rises to join the Prayer Leader in publicly
proclaiming the holiness of God. A prayer called "Kedushah," which
means "holiness," is introduced as a preface to the third blessing. The
heart of the prayer is a three-verse response by the congregation.

The first verse, taken from the Prophet Isaiah's vision of the
seraphim angels surrounding the Divine Throne, proclaims the holiness of God with the words:

קָדוֹשׁ, קָדוֹשׁ, קָדוֹשׁ יהוה צְבָאוֹת, מְלֹא כָל הָאָרֶץ כְּבוֹדוֹ:

Kadosh, Kadosh, Kadosh, Adonai tzevaot. Melo khol ha-aretz kevodo.

Holy, Holy, Holy is the Lord of hosts! The whole earth is filled with
His glory.

(Isaiah 6:3)

The second verse is taken from Ezekiel's vision of Heaven. The words are those he heard carried by the rushing winds and spoken by the heavenly hosts:

בָּרוּךְ כְּבוֹד יהוה מִמְּקוֹמוֹ:

Barukh kevod Adonai mimekomo.

Blessed is the glory of the Lord from His abode.

(Ezekiel 3:12)

The third verse, from Psalms, has less of a mystical background. It is a proclamation not originally ascribed to angels, but to people who declare:

יִמְלֹךְ יהוה לְעוֹלָם, אֱלֹהַיִךְ צִיּוֹן לְדֹר וָדֹר, הַלְלוּיָה:

Yimlokh Adonai l'olam,
Elohaiyikh tziyon ledor va-dor; hallelu-yah.

The Lord shall reign forever,
Thy God, O Zion, for all generations; praise the Lord.

(Psalm 146:10)

In the Musaf Amidah on Sabbaths and festivals, the Kedushah has the extra congregational responses of:

שְׁמַע יִשְׂרָאֵל, יהוה אֱלֹהֵינוּ, יהוה אֶחָד:

Shema Yisrael Adonai Eloheinu Adonai Eḥad
Hear O Israel, the Lord our God, the Lord is One

אֲנִי יהוה אֱלֹהֵיכֶם:

Ani Adonai Eloheikhem.

I am the Lord your God.

123

These last two responses, which are the first verse and last few words of the Shema, were added almost a thousand years after Ezra first prescribed the saying of Kedushah. In the fifth century c.e., religious persecution in Persia prohibiting Jews from publicly reciting the Shema led the sages in that country to slip these responses regularly into the Kedushah. Government inspectors sent to enforce the prohibition would leave the synagogue before the repetition of the Amidah, satisfied that the Shema had not been recited. The Shema was so beautifully woven into the fabric of the original text that even after these persecutions ceased, it was retained in the Musaf Kedushah to commemorate these events and became established usage everywhere.

Significance of the Kedushah

The pious, apart from any obligation to pray, go out of their way to say Kedushah. Even one who has already said his prayers will eagerly join a group that is saying Kedushah. What is so special about it? Why does the thrice-holy declaration of *Kadosh, Kadosh, Kadosh* carry such extraordinary significance? It may be that the saying of Kedushah came to be seen as an opportunity to observe a special teaching of the Torah: "I will be sanctified in the midst of the children of Israel" (Lev. 22:32). Kedushah is an opportunity to sanctify God, to publicly proclaim His holiness.

Side by side with a deep faith in the existence of God and in His Providence, there is an awareness of God's mystery. After we exhaust all philosophical speculation, rational analyses, or mystical insights, God still remains beyond our understanding. His secret remains impenetrable.

The Torah tells us that Moses sought to learn that secret and to discover the essence of God. He pleaded with God: "Show me Thy glory." But even Moses, the greatest of all prophets, the only one who is described as having spoken to God "face to face" was refused. "You cannot see My face, for man cannot see Me and live" (Exod. 33:20).

We ascribe many qualities to God. We know Him by many names: Creator, Omnipresent, Almighty, Omnipotent, Omniscient, Infinite, Eternal, All-Merciful. There is, however, one name that does not describe an attribute but relates instead to His essence, His mystery. We say that God is the Holy One, *HaKadosh.* (When we call God by this name, we tend to add the phrase *barukh hu* ["blessed is He"].) We ascribe holiness to God so often, and accept it as so self-evident, that holy has become synonymous with God and everything related to Him. But we give little thought to what "holy" really means.

What does it mean to declare that God is holy? Is it the same as saying that the Sabbath is a holy day, that Israel is a holy people, or that some human being is a holy person?

Jewish tradition interprets "holy" as meaning "separated from," but in a way that also implies a higher spiritual level. When applied to people, places, or time, the concept is more easily explained and more readily understood.

Life consists of a spiritual ladder with rungs leading upward to the greatest spiritual heights or downward into the depths of moral depravity and spiritual chaos. Holiness in people depends on their being able to develop a religious-moral sensitivity that enables them to distinguish the right from the wrong, the true from the false, the good from the bad, the pure from the impure. A holy person is one whose personal behavior reflects that sensitivity.

To be holy, then, means to be separated, but only from that which is vulgar and profane in life, from that which the Torah forbids, and not from the full range of human and community life. Holiness, in Judaism, is not defined as a separation from life; it is not an ascetic withdrawal from life or a denial to oneself of the legitimate pleasures sanctioned by Torah.

According to Rabbi Abraham Isaac HaKohen Kook, the very highest level of human holiness is, in fact, reached when one strives for the spiritual perfection of society as a whole. However proper it is to strive for one's own spiritual perfection with its attendant inner happiness and sense of tranquility, it remains, in a sense, a narrowly self-seeking goal. Holiness requires the individual to be part of the community—to help improve it and perfect it—and to do so because such is the will of God and is an act of homage to Him (Olat Re'iyah I, pp. 271–272).

But holiness in man or society is still a matter of degree. There are varying levels of holiness, just as there are varying levels of defilement. Sometimes these levels of holiness reflect the degree of intensity of one's faith in God, as one's behavior might reflect varying degrees of sensitivity to religious moral questions. Sometimes these different levels—this hierarchy in holiness, as it were—are the result of spiritual functions assigned by God to different individuals or groups. The difference in holiness between the Kohen Gadol ("High Priest") and other kohanim, between a kohen and other Jews, between Israel and other nations, between the Sabbath and the other days of the week, even between the Sabbath and a festival—results from the different roles each was assigned.

God's holiness is not, however, in the same class as that of man's. God may have said to Israel: "You shall be holy, for I am holy," but no real equation can be made. Man can aspire toward holiness on his own level, but his can never become like that of God. Man's holiness, however great, remains imperfect, because man is imperfect. God's holiness is absolute and perfect. Furthermore, unlike man's holiness, Divine holiness is not a function of behavior, for it is inherent in the very nature of His being. It tells us not what God does, but what God is!

The rabbinic scholar, David Tzvi Hoffman, finds this difference alluded to in the way the Masoretic text spells the word *kadosh* throughout the book of Leviticus. Whenever the reference is to man, it is spelled קדֹש , with the vowel letter *vav* missing. Whenever the reference is to God, it is spelled in full: קדֹוֹש . God's holiness is complete.

Onkelos, in the Aramaic translation of Isaiah 6:3, interprets the thrice-holy proclamation "Holy, Holy, Holy!" to mean that God is holy in the heavens, on earth, and in time. The commentary on the Bible by Rabbi Meir Leib ben Yeḥiel Mikhael (1809–1879), who is known as the Malbim, explains how:

> God is separated from earth in that He is not made of matter;
> He is separated from time in that He is everlasting, eternal. He has
>   no beginning and no end;
> But He is also separated from the heavens in that He has no form.

Not only is God above and beyond man and his world, but the angels proclaim God to be above and beyond their world as well. If the angels so proclaim, can mortal man say less? Thus the same words of homage that the celestial beings paid to God—as recounted by Isaiah in a prophetic vision—are repeated by His faithful followers on earth. This proclamation acknowledges the mystery inherent in God's holiness, namely that He is in and part of, yet totally separate from, everything on earth or in heaven. He reveals Himself to us in time, yet is totally apart from it. In a way that no mortal or even any celestial being can ever be, He is Holy, Holy, Holy!

The Invitation to Say Kedushah

One of the most noticeable differences between the Ashkenazic and Sephardic rites is found in the Kedushah, though not in the verses that the congregation must say. The difference is in the introductory words to the Kedushah, which at one time were said only by the Prayer Leader and not by the congregation. They constitute an invitation to the congregation to say the Kedushah. Only during the last few centuries has it become customary for the congregation also to say these introductory words: "as though we are inviting ourselves to say Kedushah" (AH 125:2).

Among Ashkenazim, the introductory sentence to the Kedushah is:

נְקַדֵּשׁ אֶת שִׁמְךָ בָּעוֹלָם, כְּשֵׁם שֶׁמַּקְדִּישִׁים אוֹתוֹ בִּשְׁמֵי מָרוֹם. כַּכָּתוּב עַל יַד נְבִיאֶךָ: וְקָרָא זֶה אֶל זֶה וְאָמַר:

We will sanctify Thy name in the world,
Just as they [the angels] sanctify it in the heavenly heights.
As is written by Thy prophet: And one [angel] would call to the other and say:

Among Sephardim and Ḥasidim, the introductory sentence is:

נַקְדִּישָׁךְ וְנַעֲרִיצָךְ כְּנֹעַם שִׂיחַ סוֹד שַׂרְפֵי קֹדֶשׁ, הַמְשַׁלְּשִׁים לְךָ קְדֻשָּׁה, כַּכָּתוּב עַל יַד נְבִיאֶךָ: וְקָרָא זֶה אֶל זֶה וְאָמַר:

We will sanctify and acclaim Thee in the pleasant words of the
assembly of holy seraphim, who thrice proclaim Thy holiness.
As is written by Thy prophet: And one would call to the other and
say:

In the Musaf Amidah for Sabbaths and festivals, the introductory
sentence for the Kedushah among Ashkenazim is:

נַעֲרִיצְךָ וְנַקְדִּישְׁךָ כְּסוֹד שִׂיחַ שַׂרְפֵי קֹדֶשׁ,
הַמַּקְדִּישִׁים שִׁמְךָ בַּקֹּדֶשׁ, כַּכָּתוּב עַל יַד נְבִיאֶךָ:
וְקָרָא זֶה אֶל זֶה וְאָמַר:

We will acclaim and sanctify Thee according to the words of the
assembly of holy seraphim, who sanctify Thy name in the
Sanctuary [on High].
As is written by Thy prophet: And one would call to the other
and say:

This was the version used by Jews in Eretz Yisrael. The Babylonian version, adopted by Sephardic Jews and also by Ashkenazic
Ḥasidim, is as follows:

כֶּתֶר יִתְּנוּ לְךָ, יהוה אֱלֹהֵינוּ, מַלְאָכִים הֲמוֹנֵי
מַעְלָה, עִם עַמְּךָ יִשְׂרָאֵל קְבוּצֵי מַטָּה,
יַחַד כֻּלָּם קְדֻשָּׁה לְךָ יְשַׁלֵּשׁוּ, כַּדָּבָר הָאָמוּר
עַל יַד נְבִיאֶךָ: וְקָרָא זֶה אֶל זֶה וְאָמַר:

A crown [of praise] will be given Thee, Lord our God, by the multi-
tude of angels on high,
Together with Thy people Israel assembled below.
In unison, all of them will thrice acclaim Thy holiness.
As was said by Thy prophet: And one would call to the other and say:

Ashkenazic usage is based on the siddur of Saadia Gaon. Although a Babylonian, he was influenced by the text used among the

Jews of Eretz Yisrael. The Sephardic usage is based on the siddur of Amram Gaon, which was the text that prevailed among the Jews of Babylonia.

The Connecting Verses in Kedushah

In addition to the invitation to say Kedushah, the Prayer Leader also says several additional verses that lead into the responses said by the congregation. These phrases are very short during the weekday, but are somewhat longer on Sabbaths and festivals. Unlike the introductory verse, these connecting verses hardly differ between Ashkenazim and Sephardim.

It is not necessary for the congregation to say these connecting verses, and at one time they were said only by the Prayer Leader. In many communities this is still so. It has, however, become common in most congregations, especially on Sabbaths and festivals, for everyone in the congregation to say them.

Rules Relating to Kedushah

৪৯ Kedushah is said only in the presence of a minyan.

৪৯ It is said while standing at attention, feet together.

৪৯ One may not interrupt the Kedushah to engage in conversation.

৪৯ Even if one only happens to be present and is not participating in the prayer service, one should stop whatever one is doing and join in saying Kedushah.

৪৯ It is customary to raise oneself slightly on one's toes when saying *Kadosh, Kadosh, Kadosh.* This symbolizes the movement of the angels described in Isaiah as: "And with two wings, they fluttered about." The raising of the body also symbolizes an uplifting of the spirit.

৪৯ If one is in the midst of saying the Amidah when the congregation begins to say Kedushah, one does not interrupt the Amidah in order to join in saying Kedushah. One should stop to listen to the

Kedushah, but not respond. In this case, listening is regarded as the equivalent of responding. (OH 104:7).

YA'ALEH V'YAVO

On all the holidays and on Rosh Hodesh, a prayer known as *Ya'aleh V'yavo* is added to every Amidah except Musaf. It is incorporated into the blessing of Retzei, which asks God to accept the offerings of His people. The Talmud refers to the prayer as *m'ein ham'ora*, which means "a synopsis of the event" (Shabbat 24a). This same term, "m'ein ham'ora," is also used as a reference to the passages added to the Amidah on Hanukkah and Purim, both of which describe the historical events being celebrated. Yet Ya'aleh V'yavo does not appear to describe any particular event. Apart from mentioning the name of the holiday, which could easily have been introduced into Retzei without resorting to an additional passage, Ya'aleh V'yavo raises the question of whether there is anything else in this prayer that justifies its being called a "synopsis of the event."

Rabbi Levi Yitzhak Rabinowitz suggests that Ya'aleh V'yavo actually depicts the bringing of a festival offering to the altar, which also explains why the prayer is said only on holidays on which a musaf offering was to be brought. The opening words following "God and God of our fathers" are not an exaggerated use of synonyms by a liturgist who got carried away. Rather, they capture the scene of festival days in the time of the Temple, when Jews came on pilgrimage to Jerusalem, laden with voluntary offerings to the Temple. There was a procedure and a system to the bringing of the voluntary offerings. We can imagine the elaborate ritual that took place as each pilgrim reached the foot of the steps leading up to the altar. The instructions of a supervising kohen might well have been as follows:

And let this act be remembered [by God]
("*yizakher*");
Let the gift be recorded ("*yipaked*");
Let him be heard [to make his declaration]
("*yishama*");
Let the gift be accepted ("*yeiratzeh*");
Appear [before the officiating kohen]
("*yei'ra-eh*");
Draw near [to the altar] ("*yageea*");
Come forward ("*yavo*");
Ascend the steps ("*ya'aleh*");

This then is the "synopsis of the event." But the prayer does not limit itself only to the past. If it did, it would have been inserted in the Blessing of Thanksgiving, as were the passages concerning Ḥanukkah and Purim. Ya'aleh V'yavo is also a prayer for the present and the future. Although the Temple is no more, and we can no longer bring our material gifts there, we can and do bring to God the *gift of our remembrances*. We remember our Fathers, the Messiah, Jerusalem the Holy City, and all the House of Israel that are united in brotherhood as a people. These remembrances, which reaffirm the basic teachings of Judaism, are our festive-day offerings to God. We pray that they be accepted. The same words that describe an ancient scene are now used to enumerate the eight stages by which our verbal remembrances come before God.

אֱלֹהֵינוּ וֵאלֹהֵי אֲבוֹתֵינוּ, יַעֲלֶה וְיָבוֹא וְיַגִּיעַ, וְיֵרָאֶה
וְיֵרָצֶה וְיִשָּׁמַע, וְיִפָּקֵד וְיִזָּכֵר זִכְרוֹנֵנוּ וּפִקְדוֹנֵנוּ וְזִכְרוֹן
אֲבוֹתֵינוּ, וְזִכְרוֹן מָשִׁיחַ בֶּן דָּוִד עַבְדֶּךָ, וְזִכְרוֹן יְרוּשָׁלַיִם
עִיר קָדְשֶׁךָ, וְזִכְרוֹן כָּל עַמְּךָ בֵּית יִשְׂרָאֵל, לְפָנֶיךָ, לִפְלֵיטָה
לְטוֹבָה, לְחֵן וּלְחֶסֶד וּלְרַחֲמִים, לְחַיִּים וּלְשָׁלוֹם בְּיוֹם
בראש חדש רֹאשׁ הַחֹדֶשׁ / בפסח חַג הַמַּצּוֹת / בסוכות חַג הַסֻּכּוֹת
הַזֶּה. זָכְרֵנוּ יהוה אֱלֹהֵינוּ בּוֹ לְטוֹבָה, וּפָקְדֵנוּ בוֹ לִבְרָכָה,
וְהוֹשִׁיעֵנוּ בוֹ לְחַיִּים. וּבִדְבַר יְשׁוּעָה וְרַחֲמִים חוּס וְחָנֵּנוּ

131

וְרַחֵם עָלֵינוּ וְהוֹשִׁיעֵנוּ, כִּי אֵלֶיךָ עֵינֵינוּ, כִּי אֵל מֶלֶךְ חַנּוּן
וְרַחוּם אָתָּה.

Our God and God of our Fathers,
May there ascend, come forward, draw near, appear, be accepted, be
    heard, counted and remembered before Thee
Our remembrances and our recollections:
The remembrance of our fathers,
The remembrance of the Messiah, son of Thy servant David,
The remembrance of Jerusalem, Thy Holy City,
And the remembrance of all Thy people, the House of Israel,
[So that we may in turn receive from Thee]
Deliverance, goodness, grace, loving kindness, mercy, life, and peace
    on this day of

.   .   .   .

Remember us, Lord our God on this day for good;*
Think of us [on this day] for blessing;*
Save us [on this day] for a good life.*
By the promise of salvation and mercy, spare us and be gracious to us,
    have mercy upon us and save us,
For our eyes are turned to Thee,
For Thou art a gracious and merciful God King.

Ya'aleh V'yavo is never said in the Musaf Amidah because in the
middle blessing of the Musaf Amidah, mention is already made of the
festival sacrifice and the Temple ritual. On days that Ya'aleh V'yavo
is said in the Amidah, it is also said in the Grace after Meals.

THE PRIESTLY BLESSING: BIRKAT KOHANIM

The Torah instructs the kohen to bless the people, and prescribes the words of the blessing. In Hebrew, it consists of fifteen
words, divided into three short verses of three, five, and seven words
respectively:

* It is customary for the congregation to answer "Amen" at these points.

יְבָרֶכְךָ יהוה וְיִשְׁמְרֶךָ: יָאֵר יהוה פָּנָיו אֵלֶיךָ וִיחֻנֶּךָּ:
יִשָּׂא יהוה פָּנָיו אֵלֶיךָ וְיָשֵׂם לְךָ שָׁלוֹם:

May the Lord bless you and watch over you.
May the Lord cause His countenance to shine upon you and be
gracious to you.
May the Lord bestow His favor upon you and grant you peace.

(Num. 6:24–26)

The Targum, the ancient Aramaic translation of the Torah,
provides an authoritative insight into the meaning of these three
verses. The first is intended to be a blessing for success in one's work
and for protection in dangerous situations. The second verse is a request for enlightenment through study of Torah. The third verse is a
plea that God, in His grace, listen to us when we turn to Him in
prayer; it concludes with a prayer for peace in every area of life.

Lest there be the impression that the blessing is derived from the
status, power, or merit of the kohen, or that he is the source of blessing,
the Torah follows immediately with: "Thus shall they put My name
upon the children of Israel, and *I* will bless them." God alone is the
source of blessing. The kohanim are merely instruments through
whom the blessing is conveyed to the people. The kohanim say the
words of the blessing; only God bestows it.

The ritual of the Priestly Blessing ("Birkat Kohanim̈"), was an
integral part of the ancient Temple service. It took place every day,
immediately following the daily morning offering (Tamid 7:2; Maim.
Hil. Tefilah 14:14).

But the blessing did not stay confined to the Temple. It became
part of communal prayer assemblies even before there was a synagogue,
and then was incorporated into the ritual of the synagogue. During
the period of the First Temple, the rite of the Priestly Blessing was
performed throughout the country wherever the Anshei Ma'amad
met for prayer (Sotah 7:6; Taanit 4:1). (See pp. 12–14.)

The rite is also called in Hebrew *nesiat kapayim* ("lifting up of
the hands"), for this is the position assumed by the kohanim when

they administer the blessing. The basis for their doing so is in the Torah: "And Aaron lifted up his hands to the people and blessed them" (Lev. 9:22). However, the more popular term for the rite is *dukhen*, which comes from the Hebrew word *dukhan* ("platform") and refers to the platform in the Temple upon which the kohanim stood when they said the blessing. The Talmud refers to the rite as "going up to the *dukhan*" (Shabbat 118a).

The Ritual Procedure

In the synagogue, the rite takes place just before the last blessing of the Amidah, the Blessing of Peace. When the Prayer Leader begins the blessing of Retzei, the kohanim ascend to the area before the Holy Ark (Sotah 38b). In ascending, they face the Ark and wait to be called.

When the Prayer Leader concludes the Thanksgiving Blessing, he [or someone else designated for that purpose] calls out "kohanim." If only one kohen is on the bimah, the call is omitted. The kohanim then begin to recite in unison the blessing said before performing this religious duty.

> Blessed art Thou, Lord our God, King of the universe, who sanctified us with the sanctity of Aaron, and commanded us to bless His people Israel with love.

Halfway through this blessing, the kohanim turn toward the congregation, their faces and hands covered by a tallit.

The Prayer Leader then chants each word of the Priestly Blessing for the kohanim to repeat. He should do so in a subdued voice, for his role is only that of prompter. The kohanim in turn should say each word of the blessing loudly and distinctly. The special chant used for this blessing is reserved specifically for this rite.

The role of the congregation during all this is only to stand as one stands in prayer, head bowed and eyes cast down as a sign of respect and humility, carefully listening to the words being uttered by the kohanim. As they conclude each verse of the blessing—following the words *veyishmarekha, vihuneka, shalom*—the congregation responds with "Amen."

The congregation should stand facing the kohanim. Those to the side of the kohanim need not move, but worshipers sitting behind the kohanim should leave their places to stand in front of the kohanim. Otherwise they are not considered to be within the scope of the blessing (OH 128:23–24; MB:95).

It is the practice to lower one's eyes and not look at the kohanim while they recite the Birkat Kohanim. This is to prevent distraction and to permit better concentration on the words of the blessing (Maim. Hil. Tefilah 14:7). It is also a matter of respect. A rather bizarre practice, however, has evolved in some places. Some people have taken to turning their backs to the kohanim during the rite to prevent unintentional glances from occurring.

There is a reason for this odd behavior. The Talmud says that those who would look at the kohanim in the Temple while they are saying the Priestly Blessing, "their eyes became dimmed" (Ḥagigah 16a). The reason, explains Rashi, is that the radiance of the Divine Presence in the Beit Hamikdash emanated from the fingers of the kohanim. This reason hinges upon the use of the Tetragrammaton (*Shem Hameforash*) by the kohanim in the Temple. (See p. 146 fn.) While the Talmudic statement did not apply when Birkat Kohanim was said outside the Temple, when the Shem Hameforash was not used, one may readily understand how it might mistakenly have been applied also to the synagogue, imbuing some people with a fear of being struck blind.

The feelings and intentions of the people who turn their backs may be understandable, but their behavior is nevertheless wrong. By turning their backs to the kohanim, they appear to be protesting, as though they were saying, "Do not include me in the blessing." Though dissociation from the blessing and an affront to the kohanim are certainly the furthest things from their minds, that is exactly the implication of their behavior. Furthermore, it is totally contrary to the halakhah, which requires us to face the kohanim.

Most prayer books list a series of short verses of praise and thanksgiving for the congregation to recite while the kohanim say each word of the blessing. The Talmud records a debate among the sages as to whether the people are required to respond to the Priestly Blessing with verses of thanksgiving and praise to God or to remain silent. One view held that a person should respond. "Can you imagine a servant who, when he is being blessed, does not graciously acknowledge and thank the one blessing him?" But the opposing view of

Rabbi Ḥanina bar Papa prevailed: "Can you imagine a servant who, while he is being blessed, is not attentive to what is being said to him?" Though the folk custom is to say these verses and they are included in most prayer books, the halakha is that these verses should not be said. (Sotah 40a; AH 128:39).

In most prayer books, two other prayers to be recited after each verse of the Birkat Kohanim, are also found. These are personal meditations and are not really part of the rite. The first of these, beginning with the words *Ribbono Shel Olam* ("Lord of the Universe") is based on the statement by a Talmudic sage that, "If one has had a bad dream . . . let him stand before the kohanim at the time when they spread out their hands [to say the Priestly Blessing] and say. . . ." He then suggests the first personal prayer. The second prayer, *Yehi Ratzon* ("May it be Thy will") is a beautiful personal meditation composed in the seventeenth century as a conclusion to Birkat Kohanim. The recitation of neither of these prayers is required. If said, care should be taken not to say them during the time that the kohanim are chanting the words of the Priestly Blessing.

In most of Israel and among Sephardic Jews everywhere, kohanim go up to dukhen every day of the year in accordance with the ancient Temple practice. They do this during the Shaḥarit Amidah and whenever the Musaf is said during the Musaf Amidah. On Yom Kippur, they also say it during the Neilah service (Taanit 26b).

Ashkenazic practice in the diaspora, however, is to perform the rite only during the Musaf Amidah on the Biblical festivals (exclusive of ḥol hamoed). The justification for limiting the Priestly Blessing to these days is based on a scriptural lesson that only in an atmosphere of cheerfulness should a kohen bless the people. In the hard-pressed Jewish communities of the diaspora, this mood was felt to be lacking throughout most of the year (OH 128:44 Rema). On Yom Tov, however, when the "simḥah" ("joy") of the festival is paramount—and even on Yom Kippur when the simḥah of forgiveness is dominant—the criterion of "cheerfulness" was considered to have been met.*

Birkat Kohanim is the only mitzvah whose accompanying blessing stipulates that it must be performed *b'ahavah* ("with love"). If

---

* In some communities it is customary to omit this rite if the festival falls on a Sabbath. There is no halakhic basis for this custom.

a person is to bestow God's blessing upon others, he must have a feeling of love for his fellow Jews. It is for this reason that a kohen who is quarreling with people in the congregation, should not go up to dukhen, but should step out of the synagogue.

The ceremony is short, simple, and dramatic. Properly performed, Birkat Kohanim can be awe inspiring.

AL HANISIM: FOR THE MIRACLES

On the holidays of Ḥanukkah and Purim, "Modim" (the Blessing of Thanksgiving) is expanded to include a "synopsis of the event" being celebrated. The additional prayer begins with the words *Al hanisim* ("For the miracles"). It was incorporated into this particular blessing because it is a prayer of thanksgiving and not a prayer of petition (Shabbat 24a, Tos., s.v. *mazkir*).

עַל הַנִּסִּים וְעַל הַפֻּרְקָן וְעַל הַגְּבוּרוֹת וְעַל הַתְּשׁוּעוֹת וְעַל הַמִּלְחָמוֹת שֶׁעָשִׂיתָ לַאֲבוֹתֵינוּ בַּיָּמִים הָהֶם בַּזְּמַן הַזֶּה.

[We thank Thee] for the miracles, for the redemption, for the mighty deeds and victories, and for the battles that Thou didst perform for our fathers in those days, during this season.

Following this introductory sentence are two sections: one briefly describing the basic events of Ḥanukkah, the other of Purim. The worshiper says the passage appropriate to the holiday. Common to both paragraphs is the theme that although men fought the wars and were involved in the victories described, it was God who made these victories possible. In the case of Ḥanukkah, He made it possible for the strong to be defeated by the weak, the many by the few, the impure by the pure, the wicked by the righteous, and the arrogant by those who studied Torah. In the case of Purim, He caused the evil counsel of Haman to be overturned, his plans to be upset, and his subsequent punishment. The victories of Israel are not ascribed to the people's superior power or greater fighting ability, but to Divine Providence. God reveals His saving powers in the great events of Jewish history. Thanksgiving is therefore in place.

ATAH ḤONANTANU: THE DECLARATION OF HAVDALAH

It is a mitzvah to declare the sanctity of the Sabbath day, both when it begins and when it ends. At the start of the Sabbath, we do this in the middle blessing of the Maariv Amidah and again over a cup of wine before eating at the dinner table. This declaration we called *Kiddush* (the "Sanctification"). At the end of the Sabbath, we do this in the fourth blessing of the first weekday Amidah, which is re- cited at the Maariv service on Saturday night, and once again over a cup of wine. This declaration we call *Havdalah* (the "Separation"), for in it we proclaim the separation of the sacred Sabbath from the other days of the week. The home ritual of Havdalah is explained more fully in chapter 17. Here we will deal only with the havdalah passage recited during the Amidah.

אַתָּה חוֹנַנְתָּנוּ לְמַדַּע תּוֹרָתֶךָ, וַתְּלַמְּדֵנוּ לַעֲשׂוֹת
חֻקֵּי רְצוֹנֶךָ וַתַּבְדֵּל יהוה אֱלֹהֵינוּ בֵּין קֹדֶשׁ לְחֹל,
בֵּין אוֹר לְחֹשֶׁךְ, בֵּין יִשְׂרָאֵל לָעַמִּים, בֵּין יוֹם
הַשְּׁבִיעִי לְשֵׁשֶׁת יְמֵי הַמַּעֲשֶׂה. אָבִינוּ מַלְכֵּנוּ הָחֵל
עָלֵינוּ הַיָּמִים הַבָּאִים לִקְרָאתֵנוּ לְשָׁלוֹם חֲשׂוֹכִים
מִכָּל חֵטְא וּמְנֻקִּים מִכָּל עָוֹן וּמְדֻבָּקִים בְּיִרְאָתֶךָ.

Thou hast favored us with knowledge of Thy Torah,
And taught us to perform the laws of Thy will.

Thou hast made a separation, Lord our God, between the sacred and
the everyday, between light and darkness, between Israel and the
nations, between the seventh day and the six days of work.
Our Father, Our King, bring upon us these coming days in peace,
withheld from all sin, cleansed of all iniquity, and devoted to
revering Thee.

This Havdalah passage is most often referred to by its first
Hebrew words, *Atah Honantanu*. The separations mentioned in the
havdalah prayer are not physical, but spiritual and moral. Its recitation marks the formal conclusion of the Sabbath for the individual.
Atah Honantanu is not an independent blessing but is said as part
of the fourth blessing of the weekday Amidah, the Blessing of
Knowledge.

The Talmud offers two reasons for reciting it as part of the fourth
blessing. One reason is that the concept of havdalah makes distinc-
tions between the sacred and the everyday a matter of knowledge and
wisdom. "If there is no knowledge [of what God requires of us], how
can there be havdalah?" In other words, how can there be an awareness of the differences between the sacred and the everyday, the
Sabbath and the weekday? Therefore it is only right that it be part
of the blessing that asks God for "knowledge, understanding, and
discernment." The other reason is that since the recitation of Havdalah
concludes the Sabbath, it is only proper that it be part of the very first
of the weekday blessings and that it precede all other petitions. On
the Sabbath, it will be recalled, one may not ask for the satisfaction
of personal needs. (Yer. Berakhot 5:2, 33a).

Atah Honantanu also contains a short heartfelt plea that begins
with the words *Avinu Malkeinu* ("Our Father, Our King"). The
deepest concern of those who composed the prayer, said as the Sabbath ends and Jews once again return to the world of secular activities,
was not just for material well-being but for the purity of the soul.

When the Sabbath is not followed by a weekday, but by a festival
day, a slightly different version of havdalah is said in the Maariv
Amidah of the festival. It begins with the word *Vatodi'einu*. In this
passage, we add to the list of separations enumerated in the other
version of Havdalah, the distinction between the greater "holiness of
the Sabbath" and the lesser "holiness of the festival." Because of its

stylistic beauty, the sages called this passage a precious "pearl" (*marganita*) (Berakhot 33b).

Havdalah, as a prayer in the Amidah and as a ritual, is simply an extension of the prayer and ritual of Kiddush. Similarly, the concept of havdalah is an extension of the concept of kedushah (see pp. 124–127), a motif that runs through the entire fabric of our faith. Both words, havdalah and kiddush, are translated—one directly, the other indirectly—as "set apart." If there is no sense of separation, there can be no sense of holiness.

The debate among the sages regarding the proper words to use to conclude the havdalah ritual illustrates the interrelationship between these two concepts. Samuel proposed the words: "Blessed art Thou, Lord our God, who separates the holy from the everyday." Rav, however, proposed the words: "Blessed art Thou, Lord our God, who sanctifies Israel" (Pesaḥim 104a). Though we follow the ruling of Samuel, the view of Rav points to the purpose of having Israel set the holy apart from the everyday and the Sabbath apart from the weekday. The purpose is to sanctify Israel.

ANEINU: ANSWER US, O LORD

On fast days, a prayer that reflects the mood of these days is added to the Shemoneh Esrei. The congregation says this prayer as part of the Shema Koleinu blessing, the last of the intermediate blessings. The Prayer Leader says it as a separate blessing between the Blessings of Redemption ("Geulah") and that of Healing ("Refuah"). The prayer then concludes with the words: "Blessed art Thou, Lord, who answers in time of trouble."

The opening words of the passage, *Aneinu, Adonai, aneinu,* "Answer us, O Lord, answer us . . ." were derived from a prayer uttered by the Prophet Elijah (Kings I, 18:37).

NAḤEM: COMFORT US, O LORD

On Tisha b'Av, the fast day which commemorates the destruction of the First and Second Temples and the fall of the city of Jerusalem (in 586 B.C.E. and 70 C.E. respectively), a special prayer is added to the blessing on Jerusalem at the Minḥa service. This prayer asks God to comfort those who mourn the destruction of Zion and Jerusalem. The prayer begins with the word *Naḥem*, "Comfort, Lord our God, the mourners of Zion and the mourners of Jerusalem. . . ." It concludes with "Blessed art Thou, Lord, who brings comfort to Zion and rebuilds Jerusalem."

Naḥem is said only at the Minḥa service in the Ashkenazic tradition. One reason it is not said at either the Maariv service at the inception of the fast or at the Shaḥarit service the following morning is that for the greater part of the day the Jew is compared to a bereaved person before the funeral. According to Jewish tradition, comfort is not extended to bereaved while the deceased "is still before him." Only during the late afternoon, by which time we are compared to a mourner after the funeral, is the prayer of comfort recited.

Since the Six Day War, when the eastern half of Jerusalem was liberated and restored to Jewish sovereignty, this particular prayer has been the subject of much religious controversy. The reason: one sentence in the prayer, in the present tense, describes Jerusalem as "laid waste in her dwellings, despised in the downfall of her glory, desolate without inhabitants, sitting with her head covered [in shame] . . . ." These words are patently no longer a description of Jerusalem's condition. Rabbi Ovadia Yosef, Sephardic Chief Rabbi of Israel, represents those who resist any change in the prayer, insisting that the words, if no longer relevant to Jerusalem's present-day physical condition, are still in some sense applicable to the spiritual condition of Jerusalem, the cosmopolitan capital of Israel. He forbids any change in the text. Rabbi Hayim David Halevy, Chief Rabbi of Tel Aviv, vehemently disputes this position and regards the saying of the passage as "speaking a falsehood before God." He quotes from *Sefer haḤinukh*:606, "We must learn to be very precise in our words and careful in the language of our prayers and supplications before God to say only that which is accurate." He himself therefore adopted the practice of changing the tense of the word "sitting" to "sat," and adding the word *she-haitah* ("used to be") at the beginning of the passage, in order to put it all in the past tense. This now describes Jerusalem from its destruction up until recent times (Asei L'kha Rav I:14, II:36–39).

The celebration of Jerusalem's new political status and physical development, and the corresponding adjustment of prayer terminology, does not affect the fact that Jews remain in mourning over the destruction of the Temple. As long as the third Beit Hamikdash is not rebuilt and the Temple Mount remains in the hands of non-Jews who have put their own house of worship on Judaism's most sacred site, we need to pray for God's comfort.

FOR THE TEN DAYS OF REPENTANCE

Beginning with Rosh Hashanah and concluding with Yom Kippur, a series of short additions, reflecting the theme of the period are inserted in the first two and last two blessings of the Amidah. A slight change is made in the conclusion of the third and eleventh blessings to stress the role of God as King and Judge.

In the middle of the first blessing, we add:

זָכְרֵנוּ לְחַיִּים, מֶלֶךְ חָפֵץ בַּחַיִּים, וְכָתְבֵנוּ בְּסֵפֶר הַחַיִּים, לְמַעַנְךָ אֱלֹהִים חַיִּים.

Remember us unto life, O King who delights in life.
Inscribe us in the Book of Life, for Thine own sake, O living God.

In the middle of the second blessing, we add:

מִי כָמוֹךָ אַב הָרַחֲמִים, זוֹכֵר יְצוּרָיו לְחַיִּים בְּרַחֲמִים.

142

Who is like Thee, Merciful Father, who in mercy remembers His creatures for life.

In the ending of the third blessing, *hamelekh hakadosh* ("the holy King"), is substituted for *ha-el hakadosh* ("the holy God"). In the ending of the eleventh blessing (Judgment), *hamelekh hamishpat* ("the King of Judgment") is substituted for *melekh oheiv tzedakah u'mishpat* ("the King who loves righteousness and judgment").

In the next to last blessing (Thanksgiving), we add:

$$\text{וּכְתֹב לְחַיִּים טוֹבִים כָּל בְּנֵי בְרִיתֶךָ.}$$

Inscribe all the children of Thy covenant for a good life.

In the very last blessing (Peace), we add:

$$\text{בְּסֵפֶר חַיִּים בְּרָכָה וְשָׁלוֹם, וּפַרְנָסָה טוֹבָה,}$$
$$\text{נִזָּכֵר וְנִכָּתֵב לְפָנֶיךָ, אֲנַחְנוּ וְכָל עַמְּךָ בֵּית}$$
$$\text{יִשְׂרָאֵל, לְחַיִּים טוֹבִים וּלְשָׁלוֹם}$$

In the book of life, blessing, peace, and good sustenance,
May we be remembered and inscribed before Thee;
We and all Thy people, the House of Israel, for a good life and for
peace.

It is necessary to stop and repeat the entire Amidah only if one forgets to say the alternate version in the third blessing. If one forgets to say any of the other passages, it is not necessary to repeat the Amidah.

CHAPTER

6

The Shema and

Its Blessings

שְׁמַע יִשְׂרָאֵל, יהוה אֱלֹהֵינוּ, יהוה אֶחָד:

Shema Yisrael, Adonai eloheinu, Adonai eḥad
Hear O Israel, the Lord is our God, the Lord is One.

(Deut. 6:4)

THE SHEMA is not a prayer in the ordinary sense of the word, but for thousands of years it has been an integral part of the prayer service. The Shema is a declaration of faith, a pledge of allegiance to One God, an affirmation of Judaism. It is the first "prayer" that children are taught to say. It is the last utterance of martyrs. It is said on arising in the morning and on going to sleep at night. It is said when one is praising God and when one is beseeching Him. The faithful Jew says it even when questioning Him. The Shema is said when our lives are full of hope; it is said when all hope is gone and the end is near. Whether in moments of joy or despair, in thankfulness or in resignation, it is the expression of Jewish conviction, the historic proclamation of Judaism's central creed.

The obligation to recite the Shema is independent of the obligation to pray. It is spelled out in the ensuing verse: "And these words that I command you this day . . . talk of them . . . when you lie down and when you rise up." This was interpreted to mean at night and in the morning (Berakhot 1:3).

In addition to its prescribed recitation as part of the morning and evening service, the importance of the Shema is emphasized by the reappearance of the verse throughout other parts of the service. We find the Shema in the early morning blessings. On Sabbaths and festivals, it is said in the Kedushah of the Musaf Amidah and when the Torah is taken out of the Ark. On Rosh Hashanah, it is part of the Musaf Amidah, and on Yom Kippur, it marks the conclusion of the day. It climaxes the seventh and last circling of the bimah during the Hoshanot prayers on Hoshana Rabbah. It is said as part of a bedtime prayer and as part of the deathbed confessional.

It was the view of Rabbi Judah Ha-Nasi, compiler of the Mishnah, that the Torah enjoins us to recite only this one verse (Berakhot 13b). Others, however, were of the opinion that the Torah obligation encompasses much more than that, yet they differ on how much more. Whatever the case, three passages are now said mornings and evenings to fulfill the mitzvah of saying Shema.

The first passage is a continuation of the Shema verse. It is from Deuteronomy, Chapter 6, verses 5–9, and begins with the word V'ahavta ("You shall love"). The second passage is from Deuteronomy, Chapter 11, verses 13–21, and begins with the word V'hayah ("It shall be"). The third passage is from Numbers, Chapter 15, verses 37–41, and begins with the words Vayomer Adonai ("The Lord spoke").

The reading of all three passages in this order is called Kriat Shema ("Reading of the Shema"). In the Ashkenazic pronunciation, it is called Krias Shema. In colloquial Yiddish, these two Hebrew words are frequently run together and its pronunciation somewhat corrupted to sound like krishma.

The Shema was also once read as part of the ancient Temple service. All three paragraphs were then recited aloud by the kohanim following the daily morning offering (Tamid 5:1). The people assembled in the Temple courtyard did not join in this reading, but on hearing the first sentence of the Shema, they responded with:

בָּרוּךְ שֵׁם כְּבוֹד מַלְכוּתוֹ לְעוֹלָם וָעֶד.

Barukh shem kvod malkhuto l'olam va-ed.
Blessed is the name of His Glorious Majesty forever and ever.

This response is not a quotation of any biblical verse though it bears some similarities to a verse in Psalms (72:19). This response was first used by the people upon hearing the Tetragrammaton* uttered by the High Priest (*Kohen Gadol*) in the Temple on Yom Kippur. They would then prostrate themselves and say: "Blessed is the name of His Glorious Majesty forever and ever." The Hebrew response is simple, beautiful, and moving. This became the response to all blessings recited by the kohanim in the Temple, including the Priestly Blessing. It was used in lieu of "Amen." It was also the response to the declaration: "Hear O Israel, the Lord is our God, the Lord is One!" (Taanit 16b; Yoma 6:2; 3:8).

This response was later transferred to the synagogue as a standard part of the Shema. To indicate that this sentence is not part of the Biblical passage of the Shema, it is customary to say it in a more subdued voice than the rest of the Shema (Pesaḥim 56a). The only exception to this is on Yom Kippur when it is deliberately said aloud.

A beautiful aggadah explains the origin of the response and the tradition of saying it quietly. The aggadah ascribes it to the Patriarch Jacob, also known as Israel, who gasped this response on his deathbed, when he was assured by his twelve sons, who were then gathered about him, that they too believed in the One God and would carry on the faith (Pesaḥim 56a; Bereshit Rabbah 98:4; Devarim Rabbah 2:25). It is said quietly to symbolize Jacob's having said it quietly out of weakness.

One should also take note of three small words that always appear in the siddur just before the Shema:

---

* Tetragrammaton is the name of God spelled out by four Hebrew letters: the *yud*, the *hay*, the *vav*, the *hay*. It was never pronounced as written except by the kohanim in the Temple. In prayer, we read it as "Adonai," meaning "Master" or "Lord." When not in prayer, we read it as HaShem ("the Name").

אֵל מֶלֶךְ נֶאֱמָן

El melekh ne'eman

God, Faithful King.

(Shabbat 119b)

These words are not said when one is praying with a congregation. They are said only when praying alone. (The first letters of these three words, (א) aleph, (מ) mem, (ן) nun, spell out the Hebrew word "Amen.") The reason for adding these three words to the Shema is to bring the number of words in the Shema up to 248, to symbolize the proverbial 248 parts of the human body, thus indicating that the worshiper dedicates his entire body to the service of God. When praying with a congregation, it is the Prayer Leader who brings the number of words in the Shema up to 248. He does this by saying aloud the last two words of the Shema: "*Adonai eloheikhem* " with the first word in the next blessing, *emet* ("true"). In this way, the conclusion of the Shema is made to parallel the verse in Jeremiah 10:10: "The Lord God is true." (Berakhot 2:2).

The Shema may be said somewhat more audibly than the Amidah. In prayer, which is said very quietly, we address ourselves to God, and for Him we do not need to raise our voices. It is in fact a shortcoming (Berakhot 24b, 31a). But the Shema is instructional; by saying it we reaffirm and teach ourselves principles of Jewish faith. "For this, one should clearly hear what one is saying" (Berakhot 15a; OH 62:3).

Jewish law requires a greater measure of kavanah when saying the first verse of the Shema. The need for this higher degree of kavanah has led to the custom of closing one's eyes or covering them with one's hand when reciting it. This is to eliminate every distraction and to help one concentrate on the meaning of what is being said. Rabbi Judah Ha-Nasi first set the example for the practice. The Talmud says that "when [he] covered his face with his hands, he would affirm the yoke of Divine rule" (Berakhot 13b).

Unlike the Amidah, which must be said while standing, the Shema may be said while standing or sitting (Berakhot 1:3). For a long time the Jews of Eretz Yisrael stood up for the Shema (a) because of its importance and (b) because it was an act of witnessing

147

God (and testimony in a Jewish court is always given while standing). But in ninth-century Babylonia, during the days of Amram Gaon, the Karaites exploited the widespread practice of standing for the Shema to demonstrate that only the Shema passages of the Torah (and, as we have seen, the Ten Commandments) were important and of Divine origin. To disavow such views, the religious leaders ruled that the Shema be said while seated. And so it has remained. If one has been standing throughout the prayer service, one may continue to stand for the Shema. But if already seated, one should not deliberately rise for it.

It is customary for worshipers wearing a tallit to gather the fringes from the four corners of the tallit before beginning the morning Shema, and to hold them in the left hand—the hand on which the tefillin is bound—during the recitation. In the third paragraph of the Shema, when the word "tzitzit" is said (three times) and also when the Shema is concluded with the word "emet," the fringes are put to the lips and kissed as a sign of affection for the commandments.

THE MEANING OF THE SHEMA

Let us now study the text of the Shema beyond the first two verses already discussed.

In the very first paragraph of the Shema, we declare our "acceptance of the yoke of Divine rule" (*kabalat ol malkhut shamayim*). This consists of three elements: an affirmation of belief in His unity and in His sovereignty over the world; a deep, abiding, and unconditional love of God; and the study of His teachings (Maim. Hil. Kriat Shema 1:2).

The second paragraph of the Shema moves from principles of faith to the application of faith, from the theoretical to the practical. We declare our "acceptance of the yoke of the commandments" (*kabalat ol mitzvot*), which is the undertaking to carry out the specific regulations, the mitzvot, as evidence of our loyalty to God.

The third paragraph deals mainly with one specific commandment: the putting of fringes ("tzitzit") on the corners of four-cornered garments as a reminder to us of all the commandments. It also mentions the exodus from Egypt. Since we are obliged to read daily a Torah passage that refers to the Exodus, this third passage of the Shema serves to fulfill that duty too (Berakhot 12b; Menaḥot 43b).

V'ahavta—The First Paragraph of the Shema

וְאָהַבְתָּ אֵת יהוה אֱלֹהֶיךָ, בְּכָל לְבָבְךָ וּבְכָל
נַפְשְׁךָ וּבְכָל מְאֹדֶךָ: וְהָיוּ הַדְּבָרִים הָאֵלֶּה, אֲשֶׁר
אָנֹכִי מְצַוְּךָ הַיּוֹם, עַל לְבָבֶךָ: וְשִׁנַּנְתָּם לְבָנֶיךָ
וְדִבַּרְתָּ בָּם, בְּשִׁבְתְּךָ בְּבֵיתֶךָ, וּבְלֶכְתְּךָ בַדֶּרֶךְ,
וּבְשָׁכְבְּךָ וּבְקוּמֶךָ: וּקְשַׁרְתָּם לְאוֹת עַל יָדֶךָ, וְהָיוּ
לְטֹטָפֹת בֵּין עֵינֶיךָ: וּכְתַבְתָּם עַל מְזוֹת בֵּיתֶךָ
וּבִשְׁעָרֶיךָ:

Love the Lord your God with all your heart, with all your soul, with
all your means.
And these words which I command you this day shall be taken to
your heart.
Teach them diligently to your children, and talk of them when you
sit in your house, when you walk on the road, when you lie down
and when you rise up.
Bind them for a sign upon your hand and for frontlets between your
eyes.
Write them on the doorposts of your house and on your gates.

|Deut. 6:5–9)

This first paragraph of the Shema emphasizes several basic religious duties: 1) to love God intensely; 2) to teach the Torah to our children; 3) to talk of Torah on every possible occasion; 4) to put tefillin on our arms and heads; and 5) to place mezuzot on the doorposts of our homes.

149

The Mishnah says that to love God "with all your heart" means with both impulses [of the heart], the evil impulse* as well as the good impulse; "with all your soul" means even though He takes your soul [life]; "with all your means" means with all your wealth or with whatever God has allotted you (Berakhot 54a). Love of God must be unconditional, in times of blessing and in times of suffering.

Love of God expresses itself best—as in all love—by a willingness to sacrifice and to do things on behalf of the loved one. It implies the readiness to sanctify His name (see pp. 216–217), which means to behave in ways that make God beloved to others, Jew and non-Jew alike. (See Berakhot 17a). Pure love, not the fear of punishment nor the inducement of reward, is the *highest* level in man's relationship to God.

Maimonides suggests that this level may be reached by studying all that God created; in other words, everything that would today be classified as the natural sciences. We would thus learn to appreciate the infinite wisdom that brought all of nature and all living creatures into being and that makes them function as they do. One could then not help but be inspired to love, praise, and glorify God and seek to understand Him better (Hil. Yesodei Hatorah 2:2; Hil Teshuvah 10:6).

While there is no inherent conflict between the natural sciences and Jewish faith, and there are many great men of science who are also men of deep religious faith, the discipline of science as it is taught below the graduate levels tends to stress scientific dogma rather than scientific thinking. This encourages religious skepticism. The way to God today can be found more directly, and is being found by very many, through intensive study of His Torah. With Torah as a basis, the natural sciences are more apt to lead to additional awe of God— and love for Him. The sequence of petitions in the fifth blessing of the weekday Amidah may well provide a clue to the most workable formula: first "Return us to Thy Torah," then "Draw us near to worship Thee," and only then "Lead us back in full repentance."

Also embedded in this all-important paragraph is the obligation

---

* What the sages meant by the "evil impulse" was the urge to satisfy certain physical or psychological drives. The sexual drive, the drive to build for personal comfort, and the drive to achieve can all be disciplined to conform and serve Divine purposes. When properly directed, the evil impulse is a necessary and indispensable component in life and in creative progress (Bereshit Rabbah 9:7).

to transmit the Jewish heritage by teaching Torah to our children. V'*shinantam*, the word we translate as "teach diligently" does not literally mean "teach." It really means "review it again and again" until becoming extremely well-versed in Torah.

The next sentence is the basis for reciting this paragraph twice a day: "And you shall talk of them . . . when you lie down and when you rise up."

The commandments regarding tefillin and mezuzah, the physical symbols of the covenant, complete the first paragraph of the Shema.

V'haya—The Second Paragraph of the Shema

Whereas the first paragraph of the Shema emphasizes the study of Torah, the second paragraph emphasizes the observance of Torah. Whereas the first paragraph is in the second person *singular*, the second paragraph is couched in the second person *plural*. (The English translation, of course, does not clearly reflect this difference.) In the first paragraph, Moses addresses the individual Jew. In the second paragraph, he addresses the collective body of Israel.

וְהָיָה, אִם שָׁמֹעַ תִּשְׁמְעוּ אֶל מִצְוֹתַי, אֲשֶׁר אָנֹכִי
מְצַוֶּה אֶתְכֶם הַיּוֹם, לְאַהֲבָה אֶת יהוה אֱלֹהֵיכֶם
וּלְעָבְדוֹ, בְּכָל לְבַבְכֶם וּבְכָל נַפְשְׁכֶם: וְנָתַתִּי
מְטַר אַרְצְכֶם בְּעִתּוֹ, יוֹרֶה וּמַלְקוֹשׁ, וְאָסַפְתָּ
דְגָנֶךָ וְתִירֹשְׁךָ וְיִצְהָרֶךָ: וְנָתַתִּי עֵשֶׂב בְּשָׂדְךָ
לִבְהֶמְתֶּךָ, וְאָכַלְתָּ וְשָׂבָעְתָּ: הִשָּׁמְרוּ לָכֶם פֶּן
יִפְתֶּה לְבַבְכֶם, וְסַרְתֶּם וַעֲבַדְתֶּם אֱלֹהִים אֲחֵרִים
וְהִשְׁתַּחֲוִיתֶם לָהֶם: וְחָרָה אַף יהוה בָּכֶם, וְעָצַר
אֶת הַשָּׁמַיִם וְלֹא יִהְיֶה מָטָר, וְהָאֲדָמָה לֹא תִתֵּן
אֶת יְבוּלָהּ, וַאֲבַדְתֶּם מְהֵרָה מֵעַל הָאָרֶץ הַטֹּבָה,
אֲשֶׁר יהוה נֹתֵן לָכֶם: וְשַׂמְתֶּם אֶת דְּבָרַי אֵלֶּה עַל

151

לְבַבְכֶם וְעַל נַפְשְׁכֶם, וּקְשַׁרְתֶּם אֹתָם לְאוֹת עַל
יֶדְכֶם, וְהָיוּ לְטוֹטָפֹת בֵּין עֵינֵיכֶם: וְלִמַּדְתֶּם אֹתָם
אֶת בְּנֵיכֶם לְדַבֵּר בָּם, בְּשִׁבְתְּךָ בְּבֵיתֶךָ, וּבְלֶכְתְּךָ
בַדֶּרֶךְ, וּבְשָׁכְבְּךָ וּבְקוּמֶךָ: וּכְתַבְתָּם עַל מְזוּזוֹת
בֵּיתֶךָ וּבִשְׁעָרֶיךָ: לְמַעַן יִרְבּוּ יְמֵיכֶם וִימֵי בְנֵיכֶם
עַל הָאֲדָמָה אֲשֶׁר נִשְׁבַּע יהוה לַאֲבֹתֵיכֶם לָתֵת
לָהֶם, כִּימֵי הַשָּׁמַיִם עַל הָאָרֶץ:

It shall be, that if you obey My commandments that I command you
this day to love the Lord your God and serve Him with all your heart
and with all your soul, then will I send the rain for your land in its
season, the early [autumn] rain and the late [spring] rain, and you
will gather in your grain, your wine, and your oil. And I will provide
grass in your field for your cattle, and you shall eat and be sated.
Be careful that your heart be not tempted and you turn away to serve
other gods and bow to them. For then God will be furious with you
and will block the heavens and there will be no rain and the land
will not yield its produce, and you will perish quickly from the good
land that God gives you. Take these My words to your hearts and
to your souls, and bind them for a sign on your hands and for frontlets
between your eyes. Teach them to your children: to speak them when
you sit in your house and when you walk on the road, when you lie
down and when you rise up. Write them on the doorposts of your
house and on your gates. So that your days and the days of your
children may be prolonged upon the land, which God swore to give
to your forefathers, as the days of the heavens [are prolonged] upon
the earth.   (Deut. 11:13–31)

Although the commandments concerning tefillin, mezuzah, and
the study of Torah are repeated toward the end of the second paragraph, most of the paragraph is devoted to what constitutes an essen-

tial element in Jewish belief: the principle of reward and punishment. God promises to send blessings if His commandments are kept, and to withhold His blessing, even to cause us to be cast out of the land, if they are ignored. The promise of reward and the threat of punishment, reflected in the second paragraph of the Shema, are of a communal nature, directed to the collective body of Israel.

The promise to prolong our days and those of our children upon the land is also to be understood in the communal sense. It is not a promise of added years of life to the individual, but the extension of life for the Jewish people in their own land. The Jewish people's continued residence in Eretz Yisrael very much depends upon remaining true to their historical religious mission on earth.

The notion of reward and punishment emanates from the Jewish concept of God as an ethical and just Being. It is also based on the premise that man has free will and that each person is responsible for his own actions. When Israel was told to "choose life so that you and your children may live" (Deut. 30:19), it was not a royal decree to be obeyed under threat of punishment; it was good advice, a sound piece of guidance such as a doctor might give his patients, warning them of the possible consequences should they not heed his instructions. Basically, Israel was presented with a choice of two different paths: "Behold, I have given you this day life and good, death and evil . . ." (Deut. 30:15). The final choice is not predetermined. It is up to each person to choose his way, while fully aware of the implications in store for himself and for the nation as a whole.

Judaism's belief in reward and punishment is also tied in with still another basic Jewish concept: Divine Care or Providence (*Hashgahah Pratit*). God didn't just create the world and the people in it and then turn His back on them, unconcerned with what happens. He is very much concerned with the world and cares for mankind. He wants people to meet His highest expectations; He is sorely grieved when they do not. But He didn't create human robots nor did He wish to do so. The greatest tribute to God is when man chooses, of his own free will, to walk in His ways. If God had created human robots, then no person would be responsible for his own actions. If a person were programmed to do God's every bidding, he would deserve no reward for living a good and saintly life, nor would it be just to punish him for wrongdoing. Reward and punishment can ethically follow only if one is held accountable for one's own actions; this in turn depends on possessing free will.

A perplexing theological dilemma has arisen over the fact that in human experience the system does not always seem to work as perfectly as it should. We see "righteous people suffering and wicked people prospering." The problem is an ancient one. The Talmud speaks of Moses himself confronting the Almighty with the same question (Berakhot 7a). Many answers are suggested, none totally satisfying. The predominant answer running through Jewish thought is that material criteria are not the only way to measure God's pleasure or displeasure. God rewards by granting eternal life in *olam haba* ("world-to-come"). He punishes by cutting off that spiritual afterlife.

If reward and punishment are to be meted out in the spiritual hereafter, why then does the Torah consistently dwell on them in the here and now? Maimonides provides an explanation that views worldly blessings as a factor in the spiritual life. He says that God's promise of blessing in this world is to free us from the need to devote all our time and energy to physical survival and the fulfillment of our material needs. In the presence of such obstacles as sickness, poverty, fear, despair, and anxiety, a person is too troubled and too concerned with his daily existence to be able to devote himself to spiritual concerns. The material benefits are intended to free us to study Torah, and to provide us with the means to do good works—so as to deserve the ultimate reward in the world-to-come. (Maim. Hil. Teshuvah 9:1).

Vayomer—The Third Paragraph of the Shema

The third paragraph of the Shema has to do with the commandment of tzitzit. The reason for the observance is clearly stated in the passage: it is to remind us of God's commandments and to keep us from acting out the heretical thoughts of our hearts or the immoral yearnings of our eyes. One may be unable to prevent fantasies or control thoughts, but behavior can be regulated. We are reminded here that holiness of Israel is the main purpose for keeping the commandments. (See pp. 125–127 for an explanation of holiness.)

154

וַיֹּאמֶר יהוה אֶל מֹשֶׁה לֵּאמֹר: דַּבֵּר אֶל בְּנֵי
יִשְׂרָאֵל וְאָמַרְתָּ אֲלֵהֶם, וְעָשׂוּ לָהֶם צִיצִת עַל
כַּנְפֵי בִגְדֵיהֶם לְדֹרֹתָם, וְנָתְנוּ עַל צִיצִת הַכָּנָף
פְּתִיל תְּכֵלֶת: וְהָיָה לָכֶם לְצִיצִת, וּרְאִיתֶם
אֹתוֹ, וּזְכַרְתֶּם אֶת כָּל מִצְוֹת יהוה וַעֲשִׂיתֶם אֹתָם,
וְלֹא תָתוּרוּ אַחֲרֵי לְבַבְכֶם וְאַחֲרֵי עֵינֵיכֶם, אֲשֶׁר
אַתֶּם זֹנִים אַחֲרֵיהֶם: לְמַעַן תִּזְכְּרוּ וַעֲשִׂיתֶם אֶת
כָּל מִצְוֹתָי, וִהְיִיתֶם קְדֹשִׁים לֵאלֹהֵיכֶם: אֲנִי יהוה
אֱלֹהֵיכֶם, אֲשֶׁר הוֹצֵאתִי אֶתְכֶם מֵאֶרֶץ מִצְרַיִם,
לִהְיוֹת לָכֶם לֵאלֹהִים, אֲנִי יהוה אֱלֹהֵיכֶם:

The Lord spoke to Moses, saying, "Speak to the children of Israel and tell them to make for themselves tzitzit ("fringes") on the corners of their garments throughout their generations, putting a thread of blue upon the corner tzitzit. They will be for you tzitzit, you will see them and be reminded of all the Lord's commandments, and do them, and not turn aside toward your hearts and your eyes and stray after them. So that you remember and do all My commandments and be holy to your God. I am the Lord your God who brought you out of the land of Egypt to be your God; I am the Lord your God. Truth.

(Num. 15:37–41)

(The last word of the Shema, "Truth," is actually the first word of the next prayer and is not part of the Biblical passage.)

How does the mere act of looking upon tzitzit serve to remind one of God's commandments? I suggest that it's like a uniform worn by soldiers in an army. When wearing a uniform, one is especially mindful to whom one owes one's allegiance.

Inasmuch as the Torah says that the tzitzit shall be "for you to look upon" and this is not possible in the darkness of the night without artificial light, this commandment is in force only during the day. There is no obligation to wear tzitzit at night. Consequently, the

Talmud questions the appropriateness of saying this paragraph as part of the evening Shema. It then explains that this third paragraph is said at night because it also makes reference to the exodus from Egypt, an event that is a mitzvah to recall twice daily, by night as well as by day.

This third paragraph of the Shema completes the mitzvot that Israel was instructed to keep as aids to resist transgression and as symbols of the Jewish faith. Says the Talmud: "Beloved is Israel [to God], for the Holy One, blessed be He, surrounded them with the commandments of tefillin for their heads, tefillin for their arms, tzitzit for their clothing, and mezuzot for their doors" (Menaḥot 43b).

THE BLESSINGS ACCOMPANYING
THE SHEMA

Since it is a mitzvah to recite the Shema, it would only seem proper for the sages to have required us to preface the performance of this mitzvah by first saying a blessing, just as is said before performing any mitzvah. The blessing might have been: "Blessed art Thou, Lord our God, King of the universe, who sanctified us with His commandments and commanded us to read the Shema" (likro et Shema, or al keriat Shema). This blessing formula is used for all mitzvot, with each mitzvah having its own appropriate ending: to listen to the sound of the Shofar, to put on the tefillin, to light the Sabbath candles, concerning the eating of matzah, and so forth. But the sages did not require us to say a special blessing before reciting the Shema, and this deserves an explanation.

Technically, the blessing recited in the preliminary section of the morning service "to engage in words of the Torah" (la'asok b'divrei Torah), covers the Shema, which after all consists of passages from the Torah. But another explanation has to do with the reason for saying a blessing before other religious duties. The reason that a blessing is said before them is twofold: (a) to witness that the purpose of the act is not just to light candles, eat a piece of matzah or blow a shofar, but to obey a Divine commandment, and (b) to acknowledge the yoke of Divine rule (*kabalat ol malkhut shamayim*)—for mentioning God's name and His sovereign title (*shem umalkhut*) is essential to every blessing. Since the Shema, by its very nature, already serves these two purposes, the standard blessing is rendered superfluous.

The sages did, however, formulate blessings reflecting central religious ideas of Judaism to accompany the twice-daily recitation of the Shema. The Mishnah rules: "In the morning, one recites two blessings before the Shema and one after it. In the evenings, two blessings before and two after" (Berakhot 1:4). The blessings surrounding the Shema emphasize: God as the creator of the universe; God's revelation and eternal love for the people of Israel; and God's redemption of Israel. The two blessings before the Shema serve as theological stepping stones to the Shema's proclamation of faith, while the blessing following the Shema refers to the anticipated result of such faith. Though worded somewhat differently, the same basic themes run through both the morning and evening services.

These blessings each have a name. Before the morning Shema, the first blessing is called the blessing of *Yotzer* ("Creator"); the second is called the blessing of *Ahavah* ("Love"); and the one after the Shema is called the blessing of *Geulah* ("Redemption").

Before the evening Shema, the first blessing is called *Maariv*, the same as that of the service. The names of the next two blessings are the same as those said in the morning. After the evening Shema, the second blessing is called *Hashkiveinu*. Its theme is retiring for the night and the need for Divine protection.

The First Blessing Before the Shema

The first blessing before the Shema emphasizes a basic tenet of the Jewish faith: God is the Creator of the universe and everything within it, and creation, instead of being just a one-time event, is an ongoing process in which God's creative role is maintained. By acknowledging "the daily renewal of creation," we affirm God's continued role in the creation. Unlike a craftsman who fashions an object and then has nothing more to do with it, God, in His goodness and compassion, maintains control of His creation and takes an abiding interest in its development.

Birkat Yotzer ("Blessing the Creator")

> Blessed art Thou, Lord our God, King of the universe, who forms light and creates darkness, who makes peace and creates all things.
> Who mercifully sheds light upon the earth and upon all who dwell on it.
> And who in His goodness, renews the works of creation every day continually.
> "How many are Thy works O Lord, in wisdom hast Thou made them all, the earth is filled with Thy creations!"
>
> . . . .
>
> He is the Lord of wonders, who in His goodness renews the works of creation every day continually.
> As it is said, "[Give thanks] to Him who makes great lights,
> For His loving kindness endures forever."
> Cause a new light to shine upon Zion,
> And may we all be worthy to soon enjoy its brightness.
> Blessed art Thou, Lord, Creator of the luminaries.

Birkat Maariv ("Evening Blessing")

> Blessed art Thou, Lord our God, King of the universe, who with His word brings on the evenings,
> With wisdom opens the gates,
> With understanding alters the phases, varies the seasons,
> And arranges the stars in their heavenly orbit according to His will.
> He creates day and night.
> He rolls away the light from before the darkness and the darkness from before the light,
> He makes the day to pass and the night to come, and divides between day and night;
> Lord of hosts in His name.
> A living and everlasting God, who shall constantly reign over us forever and ever.
> Blessed art Thou, Lord, who brings on the evenings.

Day and night are mentioned in both versions of the blessing in keeping with the Talmudic dictum that "The theme of day should be mentioned by night and the theme of night should be mentioned by day" (Berakhot 11b). The purpose is to emphasize that one God rules over all and to disavow a once-prevailing dualistic doctrine that day and night, and good and evil were ruled by different deities.

The Shema and Its Blessings

The opening words of this blessing (in the morning) have their source in Isaiah 45:7: "Who fashions light and creates darkness, who makes peace and who creates evil, I am the Lord who does all this!" In the composition of the blessing, the biblical words "who creates evil" (*u'vorei ra*) were changed to "who creates all things" (*u'vorei et hakol*). When some Talmudic sages questioned the change, others responded that the authors of the blessing preferred to use a more elegant and felicitous phrase (*lishna ma'alya*), and to avoid the use of the word "evil." Besides, they answered, "all things" includes evil.

To ascribe to a God who is all-good, the creation of evil, is at first a most disturbing concept. For what purpose would God wish to permit evil? The answer is: to give a person the freedom to choose between good and evil! (See p. 153.) So He pleads with us to do right. He cajoles us. He cautions us. He threatens us. But He stops short of forcing us. The Torah says it well: "See, I have placed before you this day life and goodness, death and evil . . . you shall choose life . . ." (Deut. 30:15, 19). It is by *choosing* to worship God, to *willingly* follow in His ways, that man brings to God the most precious of offerings—his own self.

The Kedushah in the First Blessing

The unusual length of the first blessing before the morning Shema is due to the addition of the Kedushah (the prayer of Sanctification). (See pp. 122–130.) The Kedushah is based on passages in Isaiah and Ezekiel describing these Prophets' visions, in which ministering angels extol, praise, and laud the Almighty. It was added to this blessing to emphasize that even the heavenly angels pay homage to God and affirm His sovereignty over the universe.

Unlike the Kedushah during the repetition of the Amidah, which is said standing, this Kedushah is said while seated and is therefore called Kedushah d'Yeshivah ("Sitting Kedushah"). It is also called Kedushah d'Yotzer because it is part of the Yotzer blessing. We may sit while saying it because we are not now declaring God's holiness (in which case it would be mandatory to stand); we are only reading a passage that tells what the angels are doing. It is for this reason that one may say this Kedushah even when praying alone. If it were *our* prayer of sanctification and not just a description of heavenly doings, it would require a minyan just like the Kedushah of the

159

Amidah. To dispell all doubt about this point, the Sitting Kedushah omits the third major sentence of the standard Kedushah: *Yimlokh Adonai l'olam* . . ., for this verse was not part of what the angels said in the vision of the Prophets.

The Second Blessing Before the Shema

The second blessing before the Shema in both the morning and evening service moves on to the next theological stepping stone. In this blessing, we relate not to the exalted Creator whose relationship is with all mankind, but to a Father and Teacher who, by giving us His Torah, established a special relationship with us. God's choice of Israel for this role was an act of pure and everlasting love; it was not the result of any superior quality on Israel's part. The theme of pure love runs through the entire blessing: God's love for His world, and His special love for Israel, reciprocated by Israel's love for Him and His Torah.

Ahavah Rabbah ("Blessing of Great Love"—in the morning)

With great love did Thou love us, O Lord our God,
With great and abundant compassion did Thou have mercy on us,
Our Father, our King, for the sake of our forefathers who trusted in
    Thee
And to whom Thou did teach the laws of life;
Be gracious to us and teach us too.

.   .   .   .

Our Father, Merciful Father, ever-Compassionate One,
Be merciful to us, and enable our hearts to understand and gain sense,
To hear, to learn, and to teach,
To keep, to do and to fulfill—with love—
All the words of instruction of Thy Torah.

.   .   .   .

Enlighten our eyes to Thy Torah, and cause our hearts to cling to
    Thy commandments;
Unite our hearts to love and revere Thy name, so that we shall never
    be brought to shame.
Because we trust in Thy holy, great and revered name, we shall rejoice
    and be glad in Thy salvation.

160

Bring us together in peace from the four corners of the earth....
Blessed art Thou, Lord, who chooses His people Israel with love.

Ahavat Olam ("Blessing of Eternal Love"—in the evening)

With everlasting love did Thou love Thy people, the House of Israel;
Torah and commandments, statutes and judgments did Thou teach
us;
Therefore, O Lord our God, when we lie down and when we rise up,
we will speak of Thy statutes;
And we will forever rejoice in the words of Thy Torah and in Thy
commandments, for they are our life and the length of our days,
and on them will we meditate day and night.
May Thou never remove Thy love from us.
Blessed art Thou, Lord, who loves His people Israel.

The slight variation in wording of the blessings for the morning
and evening services stems from the two versions that existed among
the sages of the Talmud. Samuel preferred the version that begins
with the words *Ahavah Rabbah* ("great love"), but the majority of
the rabbis were in favor of the version that begins with the words
Ahavat Olam ("eternal love") (Berakhot 11b). This therefore became the version used in the Sephardic rite, both morning and
evening. In the post-Talmudic period, the Geonim decided that both
should be said: Ahavah Rabbah at the morning service and Ahavat
Olam at the evening service. Such is the practice in the Ashkenazic
rite.

The difference in the wording may seem trivial, yet enormous
meaning lies embedded in it. Picture two young people declaring
their great love for one another, when they first marry in the morning
of their lives. The test of their relationship is whether that great love
becomes an enduring, abiding love that will also bind them in the
evening of their lives. Early love, no matter how great or passionate,
can be short-lived. God's great love for Israel, we proclaim, is not short-
lived. It is everlasting!

The Blessing After the Shema
Birkat Geulah ("The Blessing of Redemption")

The blessing immediately after the Shema, both at the morning
and evening service, touches upon still another basic tenet of Jewish

faith. In it we acknowledge God's deliverance of the children of Israel from Egypt and the wonders He wrought when they crossed the Sea of Reeds (*Yam Suf.*) It is the "Blessing of Redemption." In both services, this blessing quotes from the Song of Moses:

מִי כָמֹכָה בָּאֵלִם, יהוה, מִי כָּמֹכָה נֶאְדָּר
בַּקֹּדֶשׁ, נוֹרָא תְהִלֹּת, עֹשֵׂה פֶלֶא:

Who is like Thee, O Lord, among the gods!
Who is like Thee, magnificent in holiness, awesome in praises, doer of wonders!

(Exod. 15:11)

We also repeat the proclamation that the children of Israel said at that time:

יהוה יִמְלֹךְ לְעֹלָם וָעֶד:

Adonai yimlokh l'olam va-ed

The Lord shall reign for ever and ever.

(Exod. 15:18)

The expression "Rock of Israel" (*Tzur Yisrael*), a reference to God in the last paragraph of this blessing said in the morning, is taken from Isaiah 30:29. The same phrase was incorporated into The State of Israel's Declaration of Independence, signed on May 14, 1948:

"With trust in the Rock of Israel, we affix our signatures in testimony to this declaration."

The Blessing of Redemption should be said immediately before the Amidah, since the Talmud rules that "Tefilah (meaning the Amidah) should be joined to geulah ('redemption')" (Berakhot 4b, 9b). At the Shaharit service this is indeed the case. At the Maariv service, the Blessing of Hashkiveinu is regarded as an extension of the redemption theme and not in conflict with this requirement.

162

One reason for this ruling is to connect the theme of Israel's redemption in the past, as reflected both in the Shema and in the Blessing of Geulah which follows it, with the theme of Israel's redemption in the future, as reflected in the very first blessing of the Amidah: "Who will bring a Redeemer with love to their children's children for His name's sake."

The Second Blessing After the Evening Shema
Hashkiveinu ("The Blessing for Retiring")

Unlike the morning Shema, the evening Shema is followed by two blessings. The second is particularly relevant for the night. It is called the Blessing of Hashkiveinu ("Cause us to lie down").

> Cause us to lie down in peace, O Lord our God, and to rise up again unto life, O our King.
> Spread over us the canopy of Thy peace,
> Improve us with the good advice from Thy presence and save us for Thy name's sake.
> Shield us, and remove from us: enemy, pestilence, sword, famine and sorrow.
> Remove the adversary from before us and from behind us.
> Shelter us in the shadow of Thy wings.
> For Thou art our protecting and saving God, and a gracious and merciful God King;
> Guard our going forth and our coming in, for life and peace, now and forevermore.
> Blessed art Thou, Lord, who protects His people Israel forever.

On the Sabbath, the conclusion of the blessing is changed to read:

> Spread over us Thy canopy of peace.
> Blessed art Thou, Lord, who spreads the canopy of peace over us and over all His people Israel and over Jerusalem.

In Babylonia, the center of Jewish life during the Talmudic period, the nights were especially frightening. Sparsely populated areas and rural roads were dangerous. Criminals roamed and violence was prevalent. "Remove the adversary from before us and from behind us." . . . "Guard our going forth and our coming in" needs no elaboration. It meant simply just that. (I would surmise that many urban-dwelling people today, who know nothing about the blessing of Hashkiveinu give expression to similarly worded prayers.) The concluding words of the blessing are changed on the Sabbath and on the festivals to suggest that on these holy days we require less protection against harmful elements. On these days, the people did not work in the unprotected fields, but spent the day in the relative safety of their own homes and neighborhoods. "The canopy of peace" was characteristic of the Sabbath in the physical as well as spiritual sense.

One verse in the blessing, "Remove the adversary from before us and from behind us," may, however, have a meaning that goes beyond the sense of imminent physical danger. The word we translate as "adversary" is rendered in the Hebrew text by the word *satan*. In the Hebraic idiom, this word does not mean a "Satan" who fights against God. Judaism recognizes no independent spiritual power other than God. "Satan" refers to the evil impulses within man that prevent him from following his good inclinations and thus lead him astray. The verse might therefore also be translated as "Remove every evil impulse from before us and from behind us."

The Third Blessing After the Evening Shema: To Say It or Not to Say It

In the Ashkenazic liturgy, there is still one more prayer in the evening weekday service—a collection of eighteen verses, which separate the Shema and its Blessings from the Shemoneh Esrei. It begins with the words: *Barukh Adonai l'olam* ("Blessed be the Lord forever and ever").

This prayer has an interesting history. During the Talmudic period in Babylonia, the governing authorities did not permit synagogues within the residential areas, only in the open fields. As the nights were dangerous, the men who gathered in the synagogues at the end of a day's work to say the Shema did not wish to linger too long. Inasmuch as the Babylonian sages ruled that the evening Amidah was optional, they prescribed eighteen short verses to correspond to, and take the place of the Eighteen Blessings. A short concluding blessing

(*Yiru Eineinu*) and Kaddish ended the brief service (Abudarham Ha Shalem p. 141).

This prayer of eighteen verses was never said on Friday nights, for the eighteen-blessing Amidah is not said on the Sabbath. And because the men were not out in the fields on Saturdays and holidays, it was also not said on those nights. This historical precedent is the reason why this prayer is still not said on Saturday nights by many communities that say it during the rest of the week.

The sages of Eretz Yisrael who had ruled that the evening Amidah was also obligatory and therefore was not to be separated from the Shema and its Blessings, never sanctioned the introduction of this intervening prayer into the evening service. It is for this reason that this prayer is not found in the Sephardic rite nor in the Ashkenazic rite followed in Eretz Yisrael.

BORKHU: THE CALL TO PRAYER

At one time, the morning service in the synagogue consisted only of the Shema and its Blessings, followed by the Amidah. The preliminary sections were said privately, either at home or in the synagogue while waiting for the congregational service to begin. In other words, Shaḥarit, the morning service, began with the Shema and its Blessings, just as Maariv, the evening service, still does.

It was therefore appropriate for the Prayer Leader to announce the start of the worship service by summoning the congregation to prayer. This he did by calling out:

בָּרְכוּ אֶת יהוה הַמְבֹרָךְ.

Borkhu et Adonai hamevorakh!

Bless the Lord who is blessed!

The congregation responded by saying:

בָּרוּךְ יהוה הַמְבֹרָךְ לְעוֹלָם וָעֶד.

Barukh Adonai hamevorakh l'olam va-ed

Blessed is the Lord who is eternally blessed.

(Sifri Devarim 32:3)

Borkhu remained the introduction to the Shema and its Blessings and to the Amidah which follows, in both the morning and evening service.

The formulation of this call was at first questioned. The Talmud teaches that "one may not exclude oneself from the group (Berakhot 49b)." In calling upon the congregation in the second person plural to "Bless the Lord . . ." there is the slightest implication that the Prayer Leader is excluding himself from what he is telling the group to do. The problem was resolved by having the Prayer Leader repeat the response, thereby identifying with the congregational reply. Others were not bothered by the problem at all. By adding the word *hamevorakh*, ("who is blessed") to his call, the Prayer Leader indicates his own inclusion.

When the Prayer Leader says "Borkhu," he bows slightly from the waist. The congregation does likewise when responding.

The same call to the congregation is said before the blessings on the Torah.

7

The Verses of Song— Pesukei d'Zimra (The Introductory Prayers)

T HE Shema and the Amidah constitute the heart of the morning prayer service. But for people of deep faith, prayers are not merely a religious duty they must attend to and be done with. Such people seek to pour their hearts out to God. They want to sing His praises. A short prayer service is no favor to people who are conscious of God's presence at all times, and who are grateful to Him for life's every simple—and often taken for granted—activity. Throughout history, the truly religious were guided by the Talmudic dictum that "One should always first recount the praises of the Holy One, blessed be He, and then pray" (Berakhot 32a). They were also ever mindful of the need to get into the proper frame of mind for their obligatory prayer. And so they added prayers and more prayers to the basic prayer service: some preceded the obligatory prayers, others followed. These prayers, at first informal and optional, were a genuine spiritual expression of people who would not be confined to fixed prayer and standard formulas. These additional prayers gradually found acceptance among kindred spirits in the Jewish community. Eventually, the private custom of the pious few was adopted as the norm for the community.

In this manner, introductory and supplementary prayers grew around the basic prayer service. This was especially true of the morning service, which now has two distinct preliminary sections. Most of the additional prayers are excerpts from the Bible; some were the personal prayers of individual sages. The development that made them part of the synagogue service occurred over many centuries.

At the very beginning of the daily siddur are two preliminary sections. The first is called "Morning Blessings" (*Birkhot HaShaḥar*). The second is called "Verses of Song" (*Pesukei d'Zimra*). I will explain the second section first because that is how the synagogue service developed both historically and halakhically. It is also easier this way to visualize how the various parts of the service fit into the total structure. (The first preliminary section will be the subject of the next chapter.) I should point out that the order in which the prayers are explained in this chapter do not correspond to the order they follow in the siddur.

THE SIX PSALMS AND THEIR BLESSINGS

Pesukei d'Zimra is an introduction to prayer. At first, it consisted only of the last six chapters from the Book of Psalms (Psalms 145–150), which are devoted entirely to praise of God. Rabbi Jose, a second-century Talmudic sage, attests to the popularity of saying these psalms. In expressing his view regarding a whole series of religious practices that were then entirely optional, he said, "Let my lot [meaning in this life and in the afterlife] be with those who complete hallel every day" (Shabbat 118b). The Talmud then proceeds to explain that Rabbi Jose was not referring to the group of psalms that we designate today as Hallel and recite only on holidays (see p. 264), but to the groups of psalms that we say every day, and call *Pesukei d'Zimra*. This is known as "the daily hallel."

This remained an entirely optional part of the service for a long time, as a sort of voluntary offering. Saadia Gaon explained it this way: "Our nation willingly offered to read songs and praises to the Holy One, blessed be He. . . ." Maimonides put it this way: "The sages regarded as praiseworthy those who every day read the psalms from Tehilah l'David (Psalm 145) until the end of the book . . ." (Hil. Tefilah 7:12). It was said mainly by pious individuals who were meticulous about putting themselves into the proper spirit for the obligatory prayers (Berakhot 5:1).

Expositors of the prayer book have generally viewed this section of psalms as a way to uplift the soul, purify thoughts, and make us worthy to approach God in prayer. Pesukei d'Zimra is said in preparation for the Shema and the Amidah.

The halakhic rationale for reciting this introductory section is based on the Talmudic ruling that "One should not rise to pray from a mood of sadness . . . or lightheadedness or vain talk . . . but from joy that comes with doing a mitzvah." This state of mind should result from a conscientious and thoughtful recitation of these "Verses of Song" (Berakhot 31a; Rashi).

The Shulḥan Arukh stresses that the Pesukei d'Zimra must not be said hurriedly, but slowly and deliberately (OH 51:8). To rush through these psalms, as is often done by those who pray regularly, is to distort their very purpose. One who is so pressed for time that he finds it necessary to rush through the Pesukei d'Zimra should weigh the following advice from the Talmud: "A man's words before the Holy One, blessed be He, should always be few" (Berakhot 61a). It is better to say less and to say it wholeheartedly.

Since the saying of Pesukei d'Zimra was looked upon with favor and was seen to possess religious merit, the rabbis prescribed a blessing to precede it and to follow it (just as the regular Hallel opens and closes with a blessing). The opening blessing is *Barukh She'amar*, and the closing blessing is *Yishtabah*.

Barukh She'amar; the opening blessing:

בָּרוּךְ שֶׁאָמַר וְהָיָה הָעוֹלָם, בָּרוּךְ הוּא, בָּרוּךְ

עוֹשֶׂה בְרֵאשִׁית, בָּרוּךְ אוֹמֵר וְעוֹשֶׂה, בָּרוּךְ גּוֹזֵר
וּמְקַיֵּם, בָּרוּךְ מְרַחֵם עַל הָאָרֶץ, בָּרוּךְ מְרַחֵם
עַל הַבְּרִיּוֹת, בָּרוּךְ מְשַׁלֵּם שָׂכָר טוֹב לִירֵאָיו,
בָּרוּךְ חַי לָעַד וְקַיָּם לָנֶצַח, בָּרוּךְ פּוֹדֶה וּמַצִּיל,
בָּרוּךְ שְׁמוֹ.

בָּרוּךְ אַתָּה יהוה אֱלֹהֵינוּ מֶלֶךְ הָעוֹלָם, הָאֵל,
הָאָב הָרַחֲמָן, הַמְהֻלָּל בְּפִי עַמּוֹ, מְשֻׁבָּח וּמְפֹאָר
בִּלְשׁוֹן חֲסִידָיו וַעֲבָדָיו, וּבְשִׁירֵי דָוִד עַבְדֶּךָ
נְהַלֶּלְךָ יהוה אֱלֹהֵינוּ בִּשְׁבָחוֹת וּבִזְמִירוֹת.
נְגַדֶּלְךָ וּנְשַׁבֵּחֲךָ וּנְפָאֶרְךָ וְנַזְכִּיר שִׁמְךָ וְנַמְלִיכְךָ
מַלְכֵּנוּ אֱלֹהֵינוּ, יָחִיד, חֵי הָעוֹלָמִים מֶלֶךְ מְשֻׁבָּח
וּמְפֹאָר עֲדֵי עַד שְׁמוֹ הַגָּדוֹל. בָּרוּךְ אַתָּה יהוה,
מֶלֶךְ מְהֻלָּל בַּתִּשְׁבָּחוֹת.

Blessed is the One who willed it, and the world came into being,
   blessed be He;
Blessed is the One who creates the universe,
Blessed is the One who wills and does,
Blessed is the One who decrees and fulfills,
Blessed is the One who is compassionate toward the world,
Blessed is the One who is compassionate to all creatures,
Blessed is the One who rewards those who serve Him,
Blessed is the One who lives forever, existing eternally,
Blessed is the One who redeems and saves, blessed is His name.

Blessed art Thou, Lord our God, King of the universe, God merciful
   Father, who is praised by the mouth of His people, lauded and
   glorified on the tongues of those who follow and serve Him.
We will praise Thee, Lord our God, with the psalms of Thy servant

David; with praises and songs will we magnify, praise and glorify Thee, and recall Thy name.

We shall proclaim Thee our King, O our God, the Only One, life of all worlds.

O King, whose great name is forever praised and glorified.

Blessed art Thou, Lord, King extolled with psalms of praise.

Yishtabaḥ; the closing blessing:

יִשְׁתַּבַּח שִׁמְךָ לָעַד, מַלְכֵּנוּ, הָאֵל הַמֶּלֶךְ הַגָּדוֹל
וְהַקָּדוֹשׁ בַּשָּׁמַיִם וּבָאָרֶץ. כִּי לְךָ נָאֶה, יהוה
אֱלֹהֵינוּ וֵאלֹהֵי אֲבוֹתֵינוּ, שִׁיר וּשְׁבָחָה, הַלֵּל
וְזִמְרָה, עֹז וּמֶמְשָׁלָה, נֶצַח, גְּדֻלָּה וּגְבוּרָה, תְּהִלָּה
וְתִפְאֶרֶת, קְדֻשָּׁה וּמַלְכוּת, בְּרָכוֹת וְהוֹדָאוֹת
מֵעַתָּה וְעַד עוֹלָם. בָּרוּךְ אַתָּה יהוה, אֵל מֶלֶךְ
גָּדוֹל בַּתִּשְׁבָּחוֹת, אֵל הַהוֹדָאוֹת, אֲדוֹן הַנִּפְלָאוֹת,
הַבּוֹחֵר בְּשִׁירֵי זִמְרָה, מֶלֶךְ, אֵל, חֵי הָעוֹלָמִים.

Praised be Thy Name forever, O our King, God, the great and holy King of heaven and earth.

For befitting Thee, O God and God of our fathers is: song and praise, hymn and psalm, strength and dominion, eternity, greatness and power, praise and glory, holiness and sovereignty, blessings and thanksgiving, now and forevermore.

Blessed art Thou, Lord, Sovereign God, great in praise;

God of praises, Lord of wonders, who selects songs of praise;

Sovereign, God, the life of all worlds.

Since Yishtabaḥ is a concluding blessing, it is not said unless the opening blessing, Barukh She'amar, and at least one of the six psalms of the Pesukei d'Zimra are said first. It is customary to stand when saying the blessings of Barukh She'amar and Yishtabaḥ.

The most noteworthy of the six psalms in the Pesukei d'Zimra is the first one, Psalm 145, which begins with the words *Tehilah l'David* ("a Psalm of David") and is better known as *Ashrei*. "Ashrei" is the first word in each of the two verses (Psalms 84:5 and 144:15) that preface Tehilah l'David.

The spiritual significance of this psalm was stressed by Rabbi Elazar who said: "All who say 'Tehilah l'David' three times every day are assured of their place in the world-to-come." It is therefore said again toward the end of the Shaḥarit service and once again at the Minḥa service. Its prominence among the psalms is also reflected in the halakhic ruling that if one arrives late at services and there is only time to say one psalm before continuing to pray together with the congregation, Ashrei should be that psalm, sandwiched between the blessings of Barukh She'amar and Yishtabaḥ. (See pp. 343–344.)

This psalm owes its special significance to its sixteenth verse, *Potei-aḥ et yadekha umasbia l'khol ḥai ratzon* ("Thou openest Thy hand and satisfiest [the need of] every living thing") (Berakhot 4b). God is recognized here as the ultimate source in the maintenance of all life. The psalm may also owe some of its popularity to the fact that its verses are arranged alphabetically,* which has made it easier to remember and recite by heart.

Prayer book commentaries point out that Psalm 34, *L'David b'Shanoto*, is also arranged alphabetically and that it, too, contains a verse similar in thought to the salient verse in Ashrei. This verse is: *V'dorshei Adonai lo yaḥ'seru khol tov* ("Those that seek God do not lack of all that is good"). Why then did the sages not give equal stress to this psalm? The same question is asked about Psalm 111, *Halleluyah, Odeh Adonai*, which is also arranged alphabetically and contains a verse that says: "He has given food to those who revere Him." They considered Psalm 145 superior, according to the Gaon of Vilna, because it emphasizes that God provides sustenance for *all living creatures*, whereas Psalms 34 and 111 mention only "those who seek God" or "who revere Him" as the beneficiaries of His goodness.

The final sentence in Psalm 150 (the last one of the Pesukei d'Zimra psalms) is repeated. The repetition signals the end of a book

---

* A verse beginning with the letter *nun* is missing. The reason given by the Talmud is that "nun" may suggest the Hebrew word *naflah*, meaning "fallen," and might imply a reference to Amos 5:2, which speaks of the fall of Israel. This the Psalmist wished to avoid. The "nun" is made good, however, in the middle of the next verse, where it appears in a more positive context, depicting God as supporting the fallen.

or of a section. For this same reason, the verse *Adonai yimlokh l'olam va-ed* is repeated at the end of the Song at the Sea (see pp. 173–174).

Other prayers were gradually grafted on to the basic unit of six psalms with their opening and closing blessings. I shall now explain them briefly.

THE PREFACE TO ASHREI: YEHI KH'VOD

Immediately preceding Ashrei is a collection of eighteen scattered verses from Psalms. It begins with the words *Yehi Kh'vod* ("Let the glory of the Lord last forever"). The two passages complement one another. Whereas Ashrei emphasizes God's loving kindness, His readiness to help, console, and sustain His creatures, Yehi Kh'vod emphasizes God's might, His control of nature, and His design of the history of nations. Also God's name is therein alluded to twenty-one times, corresponding to the twenty-one verses in Ashrei.

THE SONG AT THE SEA: SHIRAT HAYAM

The Song at the Sea (*Shirat HaYam*) refers to the song of victory that Moses and the Israelites sang after crossing the Sea of Reeds ("Yam Suf") to escape the pursuing Egyptians (Exod. 15: 1–18). It is also called by its first two Hebrew words, *Az Yashir* ("Then Sang [Moses]").

During Temple days, this song, in conjunction with the Minḥa offering, was chanted every Sabbath afternoon by the Levites. (Rosh Hashanah 31a). After the destruction of the Temple, communities in Eretz Yisrael, wishing to perpetuate as much of Temple worship as was possible, introduced the recitation of this song into the daily Pesukei d'Zimra. The practice caught on and spread to Jewish communities elsewhere. At first, it was said only on the Sabbath and after Pesukei d'Zimra's concluding blessing (Maim. Hil. Tefilah 7:13), but eventually it became an integral part of the daily Pesukei d'Zimra. It is now said just before the concluding blessing Yishtabaḥ, immediately following the six basic psalms.

Shirat HaYam is more than just a song of victory. By extolling God's saving power, it becomes an affirmation of our belief in God's role in history, and an acceptance of His sovereignty over all the earth. If the psalms of the Pesukei d'Zimra depict God's might in the works of nature, Shirat HaYam describes how He revealed His might in history and in the affairs of nations. Shirat HaYam expresses Israel's faith in God, the result of the people's encounter with His wondrous miracles. "This is my God and I will glorify Him," sang our ancestors, as we do today.

As a fitting introduction to Shirat HaYam, there are several verses from Chronicles I (29:10–13): *Vayevarekh David* ("And David blessed . . ."), followed by several verses from the book of Nehemiah (9:6–11). These verses conclude by recalling the miracles wrought by God at Yam Suf. It is customary to stand when reciting this entire section, beginning with *Vayevarekh David* (OH 51).

THE THANKSGIVING SONGS: HODU AND MIZMOR L'TODAH

I have referred several times to the Temple practice in which the Levites accompanied the daily sacrificial offerings with songs of prayer. These songs consisted of both praise and thanksgiving to God (Chron. I, 23:30). The Pesukei d'Zimra are the psalms of praise. *Hodu* and *Mizmor l'Todah* are the songs of thanksgiving. These too eventually became part of the daily prayers.

Mizmor l'Todah (Psalm 100) is a psalm of thanksgiving. In the days of the Temple, it was recited in conjunction with the thanksgiving offering, which included loaves of leavened and of unleavened bread (Lev. 7:12–13). The brevity of this psalm belies its religious import. Tradition ascribes its origin to Moses (Yer. Shevuot 1:8). The Midrash furthermore declares that "in the distant future all sacrificial offerings will be abolished, except for the thanksgiving offering; all prayers will be abolished, except for the thanksgiving prayer" (Vayikra Rabbah 27:12, 9:7). Even in a spiritually perfect society, where universally virtuous conduct would render superfluous the prayers and offerings that relate to atonement from sin, thanksgiving to God for His everpresent mercies will forever remain.

Psalm 100

> A psalm of thanksgiving; acclaim the Lord, all the world!
> Serve the Lord in joy, come before Him with jubilation.
> Know that the Lord, He is God,
> He made us, and we are His, His people and the sheep of His pasture.
> Come into His gates with thanksgiving, and into His courts with praise;
> Give thanks unto Him and bless His Name.
> For the Lord is good; His loving kindness is everlasting,
> And His faithfulness endureth from generation to generation.

This psalm expresses our gratitude to God for miracles that daily happen to us but to which we may be totally oblivious. As the Talmud says: "What is the meaning of the verse in Psalm 72 that says that God does wonders alone? That even the one who benefits from the miracle is unaware of it." (Niddah 31a). Indeed, how often is one saved from imminent danger without even knowing it?

Because this psalm also symbolizes the thanksgiving offering with which it was initially associated, it is not said on those days when the *korban todah* ("thanksgiving offering") was not brought. The days on which Mizmor l'Todah is not said are the following:

· Sabbaths and festivals—because the thanksgiving offering, being voluntary, was not brought on those days because it was subject to the Sabbath restrictions.
· the intermediate days of Pesah—because the thanksgiving offering included leavened bread (*hametz*).
· the day before Pesah—because one might not have been able to complete the eating of the offering by the time hametz became forbidden in the morning hours. Besides it was forbidden to restrict the eating of a sacrifice to a period less than what the Torah prescribed.
· the day before Yom Kippur—because the offering (which could ordinarily be eaten all day and all night) might not be totally consumed before the fast set in.

175

The longer thanksgiving prayer is Hodu. The first part of this prayer was first sung by David after he recovered the Holy Ark from the Philistines and brought it, amidst much rejoicing, to the City of David [Jerusalem] (Chron. I, 16:8–36). It too became a standard chant that the Levites sang each day in the Temple.

The association of Hodu with the Temple sacrificial service is the reason why, in the Sephardic rite, Hodu is said immediately after the reading of the daily sacrifices in the Morning Blessings, before the Pesukei d'Zimra. But in the Ashkenazic rite, Hodu is said after the blessing of Barukh She'amar, because it is regarded as belonging to the Verses of Song wherein we declare our thanks to and praise of God.

PSALM 30: THE BRIDGE

The title of this psalm, *Mizmor Shir Ḥanukat Habayit*, tells us that it was composed by David as "a song for the dedication of the house." The reference cannot be to the Temple in Jerusalem, which was not yet built, though some commentaries see it in the light of a prophetic expression (Radak). Other commentaries consider it likely that the "house" referred to is the one built for David by Hiram, King of Sidon (Sam. II, 5:11). Still, the title of the psalm made it an appropriate choice for recitation at the dedication of both the first and second Temples and during the rededication of the Temple following the Maccabean victories which Ḥanukkah celebrates.

The title of the psalm actually bears no relationship to the verses that follow. The psalm is a tribute to God, an expression of gratitude for having been saved from a deathly illness and restored to health:

> I will extol Thee, O Lord, for Thou hast drawn me up, and have not allowed my foes to rejoice over me.
> O Lord my God, I cried out to Thee, and Thou didst heal me.
> O Lord, Thou raised my soul from the grave,
> Thou kept me alive that I should not descend to the pit.

The psalm goes well beyond the illness and the healing of one individual. It touches upon the universal human condition. It takes

note of the arrogant self-assurance so typical of the successful individual, who foolishly believes that he will always be able to rely on
his own resources:

> I said in my prosperity, I shall never be moved,
> And when it was Thy will, O Lord, Thou made my mountain [myself]
> stand strong;
> But then Thou hid Thy face, and I was confounded.

In recalling the plea he made to God during his illness, David
expresses a thought that is central to the Book of Psalms and to all
of Judaism: the affirmation of the supreme value of life. There is no
merit in death, for "the dead do not praise the Lord" (Ps. 115:17).
Only the living can do so. In Hallel, David says: "I will not die but
live and recount the works of the Lord" (Ps. 118:17). Here David
also says:

> What profit is there [to Thee O Lord] in my blood if I die?
> Can the dust give thanks to Thee? Can it declare Thy truth?

The psalm concludes upon a note of thanksgiving for God's
having turned his despair into joy:

> Thou hast turned for me my mourning into dancing;
> Thou hast opened my sackcloth, and girded me with gladness.
> So that my soul may sing praise to Thee, and not be silent;
> O Lord my God, I will give thanks unto Thee forever.

It is this last part of the psalm that has made it appropriate for
occasions of victory and celebration. David's experience in having
been delivered from total defeat became symbolic of the history of the
Jewish people.

The Malbim commentary suggests that the "house" mentioned
in the opening verse does not refer to a building at all, but symbolizes
the human body which houses the spirit of man. The essence of man
is his soul, his spirit. The physical body is but a structure in which the
spirit dwells. David's recuperation from his near-fatal illness was
therefore an apt occasion for dedicating his "house" to the service of
God.

The assurance of the psalm that God's anger is momentary, but
that His goodness is lifelong, that "weeping may tarry for the night,

but joy comes in the morning," reflects an optimism that may have been the reason for its popular acceptance into the daily prayers. Hearts burdened by troubles found it reassuring.

Some regard this psalm as the conclusion to the section of the early Morning Blessings; others look upon it as an introduction to the Verses of Song. Whatever the case, it stands alone, bridging the two preliminary sections of the morning service.

ADDITIONAL PSALMS FOR SABBATHS AND FESTIVALS

Rabbi Moses Isserles notes that it is customary on the Sabbath to introduce additional songs of praise in the Pesukei d'Zimra (OH 281, Rema). The leisure provided by the Sabbath and festival day made it possible to lengthen the service by the recitation of additional psalms. No one had to rush off to work. Abudarham writes that the reason for reciting additional psalms on the Sabbath and the festival is simply to distinguish these days from the weekday.

In the Ashkenazic tradition, nine additional psalms are introduced in the early part of the Pesukei d'Zimra: they follow the opening blessing of Barukh She'amar. The additional psalms relate either to the theme of creation, which culminated with the Sabbath, or to the Revelation and the giving of the Torah, which took place on the Sabbath (Shabbat 88a). In the Sephardic tradition, there are a total of fourteen additional psalms plus a poem of mystical significance called Ha-Aderet ve-Ha-emunah ("The Power and the Faith"). These are all said before the blessing of Barukh She'amar.

One of the additional psalms recited on the Sabbath and festivals is Psalm 136, which the Talmud calls Hallel HaGadol, "the Great Hallel" (Pesaḥim 118a). It may have been called by this name to differentiate it from the Hallel said on the festivals (Psalms 113–118). Rabbi Yoḥanan, however, said that it was called "great" because it refers to God as the One who "gives food to *all* creatures" and provides for the daily sustenance of all mankind. This is the same idea that is projected in Ashrei, and accounts for the significance of the latter. A grammatical analysis of Psalm 136 would indeed show that all the verses in the psalm lead up to the penultimate sentence of this one climaxing verse. It is the only verse which begins with a direct statement about what God does, and provides the reason for giving thanks. All the preceding verses are subordinate to the very first sentence, elaborating on the greatness of Him to whom we give thanks.

The sages possessed a rare appreciation of what it takes to feed a world. They were overwhelmed by the magnitude of the responsibility. They expressed the thought that "providing food for man is as difficult a feat as [and no less a miracle than] the splitting of Yam Suf" (Pesaḥim 118a). Indeed, the history of nations and the lives of individuals may well be portrayed in terms of economic conditions and motivations.

The Great Hallel would in ancient times be said on special occasions. Parts of it were recited at the dedication of Solomon's Temple (Chron. II, 7:6, 5:13, 7:3); it was said when the rains came in the wake of a fast day that had been called to pray for rain (Taanit 3:9); and it was recited on Passover eve when the Paschal lamb was eaten, which is why we now say it at the Passover seder (Pesaḥim 118a).

There are twenty-six lines of verse in Hallel HaGadol, each ending with the refrain: Ki l'olam ḥasdo ("For His loving kindness is everlasting"). This refrain was the people's response to each phrase said by the Levites.

Rabbi Joshua ben Levi explains that these twenty-six verses correspond to the twenty-six generations who lived from Creation until the giving of the Torah at Sinai. Inasmuch as these generations did not yet possess the Torah, their nourishment in a Torah-less world was made possible only because of God's loving kindness. After the Torah was given, even though it was given only to Israel, the entire world came to be sustained and nourished by virtue of the Torah's spiritual merit.

The mere fact that the Torah exists and is adhered to by at least one community of people on earth provides a spiritual umbrella which protects all of mankind from the Divine retribution mankind might otherwise deserve. It is not unlike the situation in which Abraham pleaded with God not to destroy the cities of Sodom and Gomorrah for the sake of the fifty, the forty-five, the forty, the thirty, the twenty, or even the ten righteous people who might be found there. God agreed. The Divine Judgment on these cities was carried out only because there could not even be found a minimum of ten righteous persons who could be counted "as one righteous community" to balance the wicked community of Sodom. Less than ten does not count as a community, only as a scattering of individuals.

The notion that the entire world is sustained by the spiritual merit of Torah might at first be regarded as a bit of spiritual arrogance; but if anything, it is indicative not of Judaism's parochialism but of the universality of its concerns. The only alternative to such "arrogance" would be to claim that the spiritual merit of Torah saves only the faithful and those who abide by it, while all the rest of the world is beyond its spiritual protection and therefore damned.

There are, of course, religions that claim to be universal, but are in reality parochial. Their "universality" is not expressed by extending their theological umbrella and spiritual protection over the rest of the world, as does Judaism, but, on the contrary, they espouse creeds that insist upon spiritual hegemony.

THE BLESSING OF SONG: NISHMAT

One of the most beautiful poetic adorations in all of liturgical literature is called *Nishmat* ("the soul of"), which is also the first word of the prayer: "The soul of every living thing shall bless Thy Name." Of unknown authorship, it is partially cited in the Talmud as a prayer of thanksgiving for the rainfall that follows a drought (Berakhot 59b; Taanit 6b).

The Talmud calls this prayer *Birkat Ha-Shir* (the "Blessing of Song"), even though it is not technically a blessing since it does not contain the standard blessing formula. It is now said regularly only on

Sabbaths and festivals, immediately following Shirat Ha-Yam ("Song at the Sea"). It is also said at the Passover seder.

The "Song" referred to in the Talmudic name for this prayer may be all the songs of praise in Pesukei d'Zimra. This view is supported by the fact that Nishmat is said at the very end of the entire section and leads right into the closing blessing for Pesukei d'Zimra. As such, it may be regarded as a preamble to Yishtabah, the closing blessing. Or it may have been called this because it itself is a beautiful song.

Others believe that Nishmat was originally an embellishment to Hallel said at the Passover seder. This view is based on the Talmudic discussion that calls for reciting Nishmat after Hallel over the fourth cup of wine (Pesahim 117b–118a).

Regardless of what the Talmudic name of Nishmat was originally intended to denote, the words have a powerful spiritual impact. Not without some misgiving, I offer several excerpts in translation, knowing no translation can possibly capture the breathtaking imagery and vivid portraiture that comes across in the Hebrew.

> The soul of every living being shall bless Thy name, O Lord our God;
> The spirit of every mortal will forever extol and exalt Thy mention,
>   O our King.
> From eternity to eternity, Thou art God;
> Besides Thee we have no King, who in all times of trouble and distress,
>   redeems and saves,
>   sets free and rescues,
>   sustains and is compassionate,
> We have no King but Thee . . .

> The Lord neither slumbers nor sleeps;
> He awakens those who sleep and arouses those who slumber,
> He makes the mute talk,
> He frees the captives, supports the falling, and straightens those who
>   are bent down,
> To Thee alone we give thanks.

> Were our mouths filled with song as is the sea [with water],
> And our tongues with exaltation as of the tumultuous waves,
> Were our lips full of adoration as the spacious skies,
> And our eyes shining like the sun and the moon,

Were our hands outstretched as the eagle's [wings] in the sky,
And our feet as swift as wild deer—
We would still be incapable of thanking Thee sufficiently,
And of blessing Thy name,
Lord our God and God of our fathers,
For even one thousandth of the countless millions of goodnesses that
    Thou bestowed upon our fathers and upon us.

CHAPTER

8

The Morning Blessings—
Birkhot HaShahar
(The Preliminary Prayers)

PEOPLE imbued with an awareness of God's presence do not confine their prayers to designated places of worship, nor restrict their prayers to formal worship services. People of great faith tend to be conscious of God's role in everything they do, from the moment they arise in the morning to the moment they retire at night. Our religious teachers were such people. And to instill within us that same consciousness, they taught us to bless, praise, and thank God for many things that most people simply tend to take for granted. These blessings relate to the pleasures and benefits, both spiritual and material, that we daily derive just from being alive, from the satisfaction of basic needs, and from our contact with nature and society. Many of these blessings will be discussed separately in chapter 15. But those related to rising in the morning became the core of yet another unit of preliminary prayers in the morning service.

We now turn to the very beginning of the daily prayer book, the first part of the morning service. Here we have a section of prayers and blessings that were not intended at first to be part of a prayer service. They were to be said privately at home prior to the synagogue service. The order of the blessings followed the order in which things are generally done upon arising. These personal blessings were gradually transferred to the synagogue, and most, though not all of them, came to be said publicly before the start of the formal service. The reason for this development was that there were people, not versed in the blessings, who were not able to say them privately. In the synagogue, these blessings would be recited aloud by a Prayer Leader, and the people could at least answer "Amen" to them. To this day, there are congregations where the worshipers say the morning blessings at home before coming to the synagogue, or do so privately upon arriving in the synagogue, so that the public service in these congregations begins with Pesukei d'Zimra. But most congregations follow the practice of beginning the daily morning service with the series of blessings said upon arising. (See pp. 191–193.) Collectively known as the Morning Blessings ("Birkhot HaShaḥar"), its name has been given to this entire section.

Although this preliminary section is relatively short, it is made up of a greater assortment of blessings, prayers, and Torah study units than any other part of the siddur. It is so rich and varied in content, and touches upon so many different themes in Jewish thought, philosophy, ethics, and halakha, that it would be simple to expand this one section into an entire book or to base a whole year's course of study on it. Courses designed to teach tefilah (Jewish prayer) starting at the beginning of the siddur often fail to go beyond this preliminary section. This is unfortunate because, after all it is really only an introduction to the prayer service.

Although the prayers in this unit consisted mostly of passages from the Torah and Talmud, their arrangement was never halakhically fixed, as were the other parts of the service. The order of the prayers in this section differs not only between Ashkenazic and Sephardic prayer books, but sometimes between different prayer books of the same liturgical rite. The order in which these prayers are discussed in this book may therefore vary from that found in some prayer books. In several instances, I deliberately do not follow the order of any prayer book, in order to explain the origin of the prayer more clearly and to place it in its proper perspective.

The Talmud says that "A person is required to recite one hundred *berakhot* ("blessings") every day" (Menaḥot 43b). The guidance sought from the Geonim by distant Jewish communities on how to fulfill this requirement, may well have been the final stimulus that led to the appearance of the first siddur. Credited toward the daily goal of one hundred blessings are all the blessings said during the three prayer services and those said before and after meals. The Morning Blessings provide a great boost for reaching the daily mark.

THE BLESSING FOR WASHING HANDS: AL NETILAT YADAYIM

The very first blessing in this section is for washing hands:

Blessed art Thou, Lord our God, King of the universe, who sanctified us with His commandments and commanded us concerning the washing of hands.

To wash one's hands in the morning (and also before meals) is one of the mitzvot legislated by the sages (Ḥulin 106a; Sotah 4b; OH 4:1, 158:1). The reasons are both hygienic and spiritual. In addition to insuring physical cleanliness, the washing of hands symbolizes the removal of defilement and impurity, and the restoration of spiritual cleanliness. It also serves as a reminder of the ancient Temple service in which the kohen was required to wash his hands before beginning the daily ritual (Exodus 30:20). His was an act of consecration. We emulate that act.

Although blessings are usually recited before performing a mitzvah, the proper time for saying this blessing, both in the morning and before meals, is after washing, but before drying the hands (OH 4:1; MB:2). The blessing is always delayed until after the washing because hands are sometimes so dirty that it is not proper to say a blessing then. The blessing for the morning washing is properly said after dressing; many people say it, however, at the start of the morning prayers. This blessing is not recited aloud by the Prayer Leader in the synagogue.

One should note the unusual word used for "washing hands." The conventional Hebrew word for washing is *rohetz*, and one would expect to say *al rehitzat yadayim*. Instead, we say *al netilat yadayim*, which literally means "the lifting up of the hands." The use of this expression for washing of the hands implies that it is a ceremony symbolizing that the hands are "lifted" to a higher level and are being consecrated for nobler deeds in fulfillment of God's commandments. We wash them out of respect to our Maker (Shabbat 50b).

THE BLESSING FOR CREATING MAN: ASHER YATZAR

A blessing that praises God for creating the wondrous mechanism of the body, and for its ability to preserve our health and our lives, is one of the first things said every morning.

Blessed art Thou, Lord our God, King of the universe, who has formed man in wisdom and created in him many ducts and organs. It is well known that if but one of these be opened [that should be closed], or if one of these be closed [that should be open], it would be impossible to survive and to stand before Thee. Blessed art Thou, Lord, who heals all flesh and works wondrous things.

Judaism appreciates the wonderfully intricate and delicately balanced mechanism that is the human body and the house of the human soul. The better one understands the complexity of the human body, the more meaningful this blessing becomes. Unless the body is alive and functioning, a person cannot fulfill his spiritual purpose "to stand before Thee." "The dead do not praise the Lord," says the Psalmist. This blessing thus reflects the importance that Judaism generally attaches to proper health care.

This is another blessing not recited aloud by the Prayer Leader in the synagogue, but is said privately by each worshiper before the start of the service.

THE BLESSING FOR RESTORING MAN'S SOUL: ELOHAI NESHAMAH

After the blessing for the creation of the human body comes a blessing in which we thank God for having created within us a pure soul that He, in His loving kindness, daily restores to us. The prayer also confidently suggests that our daily reawakening forecasts the restoration of our souls in the hereafter.

> O my God, the soul that Thou placed within me is pure;
> Thou created it, Thou fashioned it, Thou breathed it into me, Thou preserves it within me;
> And Thou wilt one day take it from me, and henceforth restore it to me.
> As long as my soul is within me,
> I give thanks to Thee, Lord my God, and God of my fathers, Master of all creation, Lord of all souls.
> Blessed art Thou, Lord, who restores the souls to [those who sleep like] the dead.

The Hebrew idiom at the conclusion of the blessing, *pegarim meitim*, from Isaiah 37:36, means literally "dead bodies," and many prayer books translate it this way. Yet according to Abudarham and others, "dead" in this prayer is used to denote a state of sleep rather than actual death. It should properly be translated as "tired and weary as the dead"—or, as we might say, "dead-tired." The sages had drawn a parallel between death and sleep when they expressed the notion that "sleep constitutes one-sixtieth of death" (Berakhot 57b). When asleep, man's soul is not functional. Only upon awakening, does it become reactivated. Rabbi Avraham Landau, the Rebbe of Czechanova, argues that even the part of the prayer which speaks of God "one day" taking our souls, refers not to death and the hereafter but to the days ahead and their morrows (Tzelota d'Avraham I, pp. 18–19).

This blessing also emphasizes a basic theological concept in Judaism that is at odds with the Christian notion that man is born in original sin. Said the sages, "Just as God is pure, so is man's soul pure" (Berakhot 10a).

Since the theme of this blessing is logically associated with the theme of the Asher Yatzar blessing, both of which relate to what God created, they should be said in succession, as is done in the Sephardic rite as well as in some Ashkenazic congregations. In most Ashkenazic prayer books however, Elohai Neshamah is found a little further on, just before the series of blessings said upon arising. This is probably due to the fact that Elohai Neshamah is listed in the Talmud together with the other morning blessings; indeed it is the first in the series (Berakhot 6ob).

THE TORAH STUDY BLESSINGS:
BIRKHOT HATORAH

One of God's commandments to the Jewish people is to study Torah daily. The essence of Judaism is expressed through the study and the keeping of Torah. Since the daily prayers contain many passages from the Torah, their recitation is regarded as a form of Torah study and satisfies the *minimum* daily requirement. Blessings related to the observance of this mitzvah are therefore said at the very beginning of the prayer service before any of these Biblical passages are read. Two blessings are recited:

First Blessing:

> Blessed art Thou, Lord our God, King of the universe, who sanctified us by His commandments, and commanded us to occupy ourselves with the words of Torah. Make the words of Thy Torah pleasant in our mouth, Lord our God, and in the mouth of Thy people, the House of Israel, so that we and our offspring and the offspring of Thy people, the House of Israel, may all know Thy Name and study Thy Torah. Blessed art Thou, Lord, who teaches the Torah to His people Israel.

Second Blessing:

> Blessed art Thou, Lord our God, King of the universe, who has chosen us from among all peoples and given us His Torah. Blessed art Thou, Lord, who gives the Torah.

The first blessing addresses itself to the performance of the mitzvah. The second blessing, also said when one is called up for an aliyah, is a blessing of thanksgiving for having been selected to receive the Torah at Sinai.

One reason for saying two blessings (rather than the customary single blessing) before observing this particular mitzvah (to study Torah) is to symbolize the dual nature of Torah: the Written (Scripture) and the Oral (Talmud, which consists of Mishnah and Gemara).

Maimonides is of the opinion that the first blessing should be counted as two separate blessings. He maintains that the sentence beginning with V'*ha-arev na* ("Make the words of Thy Torah pleasant in our mouth") is a separate blessing and not a continuation of the first one. Thus there are three Torah blessings symbolizing the three divisions of Torah that should be studied daily: Scripture, Mishnah, and Gemara (AH 47:13).

TORAH STUDY PASSAGES

So as not to delay the observance of the mitzvah for which the Torah study blessings were said, it became customary immediately to follow the Torah blessings with several passages from the Torah and the Talmud. Though several of the Early Authorities did not regard this as halakhically essential (Berakhot 11b; Tos. s.v. *she-kvar*), the practice took hold and was widely adopted. Since the sages took the position that daily Torah study should consist of selections from Scripture, Mishnah, and Gemara, passages were chosen from each area (Kedushin 30a).

Two different sections of Torah study were developed, one in Eretz Yisrael, the other in Babylonia. Custom varied as to which one of these, or if both were said (Maim. Hil. Tefilah 7:11). The first is short and immediately follows the Torah blessings. The second is longer and is found toward the end of the preliminary section.

In the first section, the Torah passage consists of the verses of the Priestly Blessing, (Num. 6:24–26) (see p. 133).

The Mishnah selection is from Peah 1:1:

These are the obligations that have no limits: the corner of the field to be garnered by the poor, the gift of the first fruit, the pilgrimage offering, deeds of kindness, and study of the Torah.

The Gemara selection is culled from Shabbat 127a:

These are the things, the fruits of which a man enjoys in this world while the principal remains for him [to enjoy] in the world-to-come: They are: honoring father and mother, deeds of kindness, early attendance, morning and evening, at the house of study, hospitality, visiting the sick, dowering the bride, accompanying the dead to the grave, devotion in prayer, and making peace between people—but the study of Torah is equal to all of them.*

Both selections stress the importance of Torah study, and seek to emphasize that, while one had discharged his duty, one should not feel that one has done justice to the study of Torah merely by reading these passages.

Torah study is said to be equal to all the other mitzvot combined only because the study of Torah is supposed to lead to the observance of all other mitzvot.

In the second Torah study unit, the Torah and Mishnah selections consist of lengthy excerpts that deal with the laws of the Temple sacrifices. For the Gemara passage there is a midrash (whose analysis is equivalent to Gemara) that begins with: "Rabbi Ishmael says." The latter passage summarizes the thirteen rules of exegesis used by the Oral Tradition to expound the Torah. (Further on in this chapter, I will explain why these were selected for the second study unit.)

---

* In six other instances the sages conferred a special status to certain mitzvot by calling them equal to all the other mitzvot combined. The others are: Shabbat (Yer. Berakhot 1:8), Tzedakah (Bava Batra 9a), Living in Eretz Yisrael (Sifri, R'eh), Circumcision (Nedarim 32a), Tzitzit (Menaḥot 43b), and Rejection of idolatry (Horayot 8:1).

THE BLESSINGS UPON ARISING

The Talmud (Berakhot 6ob) lists a series of blessings that a person should say upon arising. The synagogue service usually begins with these blessings. They all open with the standard formula for a blessing, "Blessed art Thou, Lord our God, King of the universe," and conclude as follows:

... who has given the rooster intelligence to distinguish between day and night.

... who opens the eyes of the blind.

... who clothes the naked.

... who releases the bound.

... who raises up those who are bowed down.

... who sets forth the earth upon the waters.

... who directs the steps of man.

... who provided for my every need.

... who girds Israel with might.

... who crowns Israel with glory.

... who gives strength to the weary.

... who removes sleep from my eyes and slumber from my eyelids ...
Blessed art Thou, Lord, who bestows great kindnesses on His people Israel.

All these blessings relate in some way to the act of waking, arising, dressing, and going about our daily affairs. Some have double meanings. They recognize God's role in everything a person does and in the satisfaction of every human need.

In the very first blessing, we thank God for giving the rooster the intelligence to distinguish between day and night. The crowing of the rooster awakens the person from his sleep and gets him started on a new day. The wording of the blessing is taken from Job 38:36. Since being able to *hear* the rooster crow is essential to taking advantage of its "wake-up service," the blessing is an indirect expression of gratitude to God for the daily "restoration" of our hearing.

Since our eyes were closed and did not see while asleep, we are compared to the blind, to whom sight is now restored. "Opening the eyes," may also connote gaining understanding and wisdom.

When asleep, our motionless limbs, while unbound, are certainly restrained; awake, we are free to stretch them and move about. To be able to rise and stand erect on our feet testifies to the way God created us, as the solid earth on which we set down our feet attests to how He formed the world. For all this we are grateful.

"Who clothes the naked" is an allusion to God having clothed Adam and Eve (Genesis 3:7). But it is also a reminder that providing clothing for the needy is one of the great mitzvot among the Jewish people (Sotah 14a). The same blessing is said when putting on a new garment.

God's providence is attested to in two blessings: "who directs the steps of man," and "who provided for my every need." The latter was intended as a blessing to be said in conjunction with putting on one's shoes, shoes symbolizing the last of the necessities, the culmination of one's needs. Furthermore going barefoot is an impediment to earning a livelihood, while the wearing of shoes makes it possible to get about and provide for one's daily needs. Some authorities have ruled that this blessing should be omitted on Yom Kippur and Tisha b'Av, when it is forbidden to wear regular leather-made shoes. Others have ruled that it should nevertheless be said since these blessings were meant to reflect the collective experience of all mankind and not of only the individual on any given day (AH 46:13).

"Who girds Israel with strength" was associated with putting on a waist belt, the traditional symbol of strength, for in it men kept their weapons. The blessing was also endowed with moral meaning, for the belt was also seen as symbolically dividing the upper and lower parts of the body, the one signifying man's spirit, the others man's lust, thus contributing to the moral discipline and strength of the nation. "Who crowns Israel with glory" was associated with putting on one's headwear as a sign of respect to God. The blessing may also be an allusion to the tefillin. Both these blessings, in addition to evoking several spiritual associations, also contributed to the morale of Jews who daily struggled against those who would destroy them.

The series of blessings then reverts to the general theme of what takes place when one awakens: strength is restored to the weary and sleep is removed from the eyes. These are all possible because of God's loving kindness. They are all reasons to be thankful.

The last blessing in the series is longer than all the rest. It thanks God "for removing sleep from my eyes," thereby associating it with the act of washing one's face in the morning. But it goes on to make several heartfelt requests:

> May it be Thy will, O Lord our God and God of our fathers, that we become accustomed to walk in the way of Thy Torah, and to cling to Thy precepts. Lead us not into sin or transgression and iniquity, or into temptation or disgrace; let not the impulse toward evil rule over us; keep us far from evil men and worthless companions; and help us cling to the impulse toward good and to good deeds. Bend our will to Thine. Give us this day and every day grace, favor, and mercy—in Thy sight and in the sight of all men, and bestow upon us Thy loving kindness. Blessed art Thou, Lord, who bestows loving kindness upon his people Israel.
>
> (Berakhot 60b)

These are all requests of a spiritual and social nature. There is an awareness here of the challenges and temptations that await people in their daily struggle for advancement and fulfillment. So we begin each day with a plea to God that He help us stay on the right path, and regard His doing so as an act of loving kindness.

THE THREE BLESSINGS OF "WHO HAS NOT MADE ME"

The attitude of the Talmudic sages to women is best reflected in such statements as: "The Holy One, blessed be He, gave a greater measure of understanding to woman than to man" (Niddah 45b); "A man, to know peace in his home, should honor his wife even more than his own self" (Yevamot 62b); "God's love is not like that of the human being; for Him the son and the daughter are equal." The status of the Jewish woman, though more circumscribed than that of the Jewish male, was historically always higher and more privileged than that of her non-Jewish counterpart.

How then does one explain the inclusion into the daily prayer book of a blessing that has been the source of much controversy and misunderstanding, and that offends many Jewish women? The blessing in question has its origin in the teaching of a Talmudic sage, Rabbi Judah: "a person should recite the following three blessings each day." The conclusions of these blessings are:

who has not made me a non-Jew (*shelo asani goy*)

who has not made me an ignorant person (*shelo asani boor*)

who has not made me a woman (*shelo asani ishah*)
(Tosefta Berakhot, Vilna Shas 6:23)

Rabbi Judah's statement clearly states that the reason for this third blessing is "Because women are not required to observe [all] the mitzvot."

The blessing which thanks God "for not having made me a *boor*" (an ignorant person) was rejected by the sages and it never became part of the liturgy. The reason given for suggesting this blessing is that "an ignorant person cannot be a sin-fearing person." Since an ignorant person does not know Torah and does not know what is permitted and what is forbidden, he obviously does not keep all the mitzvot. Rashi explains the rejection: The blessings make sense when speaking of a non-Jew or of a woman, inasmuch as they are not halakhically obligated to keep all or some of the commandments. But an ignorant man is still *obligated* to keep all the commandments; he is *not exempt* from their observance (Rashi, Menaḥot 43b). A blessing which thanks God "for not having made me a slave" (*shelo asani aved*) was substituted instead.

The common denominator of all three conditions: being a non-Jew, a slave, and a woman—is their halakhic exemption from observing all or some of the mitzvot. A Jewish woman is exempt from most religious duties that have to be carried out at fixed times.* It is not so much that one gives thanks for not being a woman, but rather that one is grateful for the obligation to observe *all* religious rites.

---

* The exceptions include the following biblical and rabbinic mitzvot: reciting or hearing Kiddush and Havdalah; eating matzah on the first night of Passover; listening to the reading of the Megillah on Purim; lighting candles on Ḥanukkah and on the Sabbath; drinking four cups of wine at the Passover seder; and rejoicing in the festivals.

It is important to understand the context of faith and the spiritual motivation that inspired the composition of this series of blessings. The devout Jew did not look upon the religious observances as an oppressive burden from which he sought relief, or as so heavy a load that it needed to be lightened. The duties and responsibilities that were attached to serving God were performed with alacrity, love, and devotion. They subscribed to the dictum: "Be strong as a leopard, light as an eagle, fleet as a hart, strong as a lion, to do the will of Thy Father in Heaven" (Avot 5:23). To be a Jew was a privilege. It meant being chosen by God for a special mission on earth. It meant the promise of eternal life in the world-to-come. Such people would not trade places with anyone who was not required to observe the full range of mitzvot. The obligation to observe the mitzvot was a privilege that made their lives meaningful.

The fact that people in the exempted categories could choose to abide by the commandments, even if not obliged to do so, did not detract from the significance of the blessings. Rabbi Ḥanina stated: "Greater [is the reward of] the one who is commanded [to do a mitzvah] and does it, than [of] the one who does it though not commanded to do it" (Kiddushin 31a). And though one might logically argue the opposite point of view, Rabbi Ḥanina's dictum was apparently accepted among the sages as a guiding principle in many matters.

Perhaps there were other considerations in sanctioning the blessing of "Who Has Not Made Me A Woman." But whatever attitudes later generations read into these blessings, we cannot remain oblivious to the stated intent of those who composed the blessings and made them part of our liturgical heritage. By their own testimony, it was not to offend or imply inferiority, but to show gratitude for the full load of mitzvot that the Torah placed upon the free male Jew.

I am aware that any explanation of the motives for the traditional blessings said by the man may not satisfy devout Jewish feminists, who do not want to be exempt from religious duties. The resolution of this problem, however, will have to be left to other forums. Further discussion of this issue is obviously not within the scope of this book.

The three "Who Has Not Made Me" blessings follow the first of The Blessings Upon Arising in the Ashkenazic rite. By reciting them immediately after *Asher Yatzar, Elohai Neshamah,* and *Notan la-sekhvi vinah,* we establish a unit acknowledging the way we were created.

In the Sephardic rite, however, this point was not found sufficiently compelling. And since these three blessings are not part of the series of morning blessings prescribed in the Talmud for saying upon arising, they were inserted toward the end of the series.

THE WOMAN'S BLESSING

Sometime after the Geonic period, it became customary for women to substitute *she-asani kirtzono* ("who has made me according to His will"), for the "male" blessing.*

Some may interpret this blessing as a grudging resignation to a lesser state, or as the acceptance of one's fate. But Rabbi Aaron Soloveitchik, a leading contemporary Talmudic scholar, views it as a blessing that affirms woman's innate superiority over man. It is God's wish, he says, that human beings achieve the Divine qualities of compassion and mercy. Woman is naturally closer to that level of perfection than is man. She was given the gift of mercy and compassion. Is not God Himself addressed as *Raḥum,* the Compassionate One? And is not *reḥem,* the Hebrew word for womb (the part of the body that more than any other distinguishes woman from man and symbolizes her essence) a form of the same word that means compassion? A woman can therefore proudly claim to have been fashioned "according to His will."

Man, on the other hand, cannot make the same claim. Although given the gift of power and strength to conquer the earth and subdue it, man lacks the natural qualities by which he may achieve the spiritual ideal. He starts with a baser nature than does woman, and is therefore in need of greater refinement. Since mitzvot are seen as a means

---

* Converts to Judaism, male or female, do not say *shelo asani goy* ("who has not made me a non-Jew"). Instead, they say (m.) *she'asani ger* or (f.) *she'asani giyoret* ("who has made me a proselyte").

of purifying a person's soul and perfecting his character, man needs to keep more mitzvot because he has further to go toward the ideal.

Man, at the moment of his creation, was not yet "according to His will." Astute readers of the Bible also point out that each thing created was of a higher form than that which preceded it. The female followed the male, and only then was Man's creation complete.

This interpretation of the woman's blessing has support from the Zohar, the kabbalistic commentary on the Torah, which declares that the ideal man is the one who possesses the strength of a man and the compassion of a woman.

THE PERSONAL PRAYER OF RABBI JUDAH:
YEHI RATZON

The Talmudic sages were in the habit of adding personal prayers before and after the Amidah. Some of these found their way into the prayer book. One composed by Rabbi Judah Ha-Nasi, who compiled the Mishnah toward the end of the second century, was added to the preliminary prayers. It begins with the words *Yehi Ratzon* ("May it be Thy will").

> May it be Thy will, O Lord my God and God of my fathers, to deliver me this day and every day from insolent men and impudence, from evil men and bad friends, from a bad neighbor and from any mishaps and destructive influences, from difficult litigation and from a stubborn litigant, be he a member of the covenant [a Jew] or be he not a member of the covenant [a non-Jew].
>
> (Berakhot 16b)

Halakhic commentaries note that one may augment this prayer with one's own personal pleas.

THE BINDING OF ISAAC: THE AKEDAH

The willingness of Abraham to sacrifice his beloved son Isaac and Isaac's readiness to be that offering, because both father and son believed that such was God's wish is an event that has captured the imagination of religious and secular thinkers, Jew and non-Jew alike, throughout the centuries. The Torah portion (Gen. 22:1–19) that describes this event is called the *Akedah* ("the Binding"). It became the selected Torah reading for the second day of Rosh Hashanah. But it is also recited in the preliminary section of the morning service to highlight the praiseworthiness of our ancestors who were prepared to unquestioningly place their trust in God.

The Biblical excerpt is preceded and followed by paragraphs that elaborate on the theme of the Akedah. The introductory and concluding paragraphs are a portion of the Zikhronot blessing said in the Amidah of Rosh Hashanah.

INSPIRATIONAL AND PENITENTIAL: L'OLAM YEHEI ADAM

L'olam Yehei Adam—"At all times let a man revere God in private as in public; acknowledge the truth, and speak the truth in his heart; let him rise early and say. . . ."

This introduction and the part that leads up to a description of the sacrificial offerings is a beautiful and moving unit of prayer. It is the "agonizing cry of a generation passing through the fires of persecution, in a time when Jewish *public* worship was forbidden" (J.H. Hertz). Although made up of excerpts from Bible and Talmud, it was compiled into a separate prayer unit in about 456 C.E., when the Persian ruler, Yezdejard II, prohibited Babylonian Jewry from keeping the Sabbath, and outlawed the public reading of the Shema. This prayer was intended as a private substitute for the public morning service, and it avows some of the basic doctrines of Judaism. The first line of the Shema (and in some versions, the entire first paragraph) was worked into this prayer, so that the worshipers were able to recite the Shema without drawing attention to it. When this particular persecution passed, these prayers were retained in the liturgical tradition of the Jewish people. Obviously it has touched responsive chords in subsequent generations.

THE SACRIFICIAL READINGS: A SECOND TORAH STUDY SECTION

One concise section of Torah study was discussed earlier in the chapter. (See p. 189.) A second and longer Torah study unit, completes this first part of the service. It consists of passages from the Bible (Numbers 28:1–8) and Mishnah (Zevaḥim 5) that deal with the sacrificial offerings which were the core of the daily Temple service.

Considering how little interest these passages have held for many generations—indeed, they are omitted in many synagogues—the question arises why they were selected when so many other excerpts dealing with more meaningful and pertinent subjects could have been chosen?

The answer lies in the spiritual significance that was assigned to the reading *about* sacrifices, which was considered an acceptable substitute for bringing sacrifices. Biblical verses were interpreted to mean that "one who studies the portion of the burnt-offering is as though he actually brings a burnt-offering; one who studies the portion of the minḥa offering is as though he actually brings a minḥa offering. . . ." (Menaḥot 110a). (See p. 119.)

It was precisely this perspective that brought about the selection of these particular Bible and Mishnah passages for this second Torah study section. Maimonides himself defended the study of such passages in general: "It is proper to involve oneself in the study of korbanot, and not to say as do most people today that there is no need to know these things in our times" (*Commentary on the Mishnah, Menaḥot*, chap. 13).

The concluding part of this Torah study unit begins with: "Rabbi Ishmael says." It is a midrash that lists the thirteen exegetical principles used by the sages to interpret Scripture. It is the foundation of the Oral Torah, which is reason enough for it to have been selected to complete this study unit. The fact that this midrash (Sifra) appears as an introduction to the book of Leviticus where most of the sacrificial laws are found is another reason for adding it on to the sacrificial readings.

This midrash concludes the first preliminary part of the morning service.

OTHER PRAYERS

Other prayers found at the very beginning of the siddur are: a) The blessings and prayers for putting on the tallit and the tefillin; b) Two verses to say when entering a synagogue: *Mah Tovu*, "How goodly are thy tents O Jacob, thy dwelling places O Israel" (Numbers 24:5) and V'*ani*, "As for me, in the abundance of Thy loving kindness will I come into Thy house" (the latter verse contains exactly ten Hebrew words and was used to determine if there were ten people present for the minyan. Jewish tradition does not count people by numbers; using the words of a verse instead of numbers is an acceptable alternative); and c) the hymns of *Adon Olam* and *Yigdal*. Most people are familiar with them because they are popular hymns that also conclude the Sabbath and festival services.

Adon Olam

Adon Olam ("Eternal Lord") is a poetic hymn to God whose author is thought to be Solomon ibn Gabirol (1021–1058), the poet-philosopher who lived in Spain. It consists of ten lines: the first six express the Jewish concept of God, and the last four tell how the man of faith relates to God, the trust he feels in Him. The last words of the hymn, "God is with me, I shall not fear," are taken from Psalm 118:6, one of the passages of Hallel.

Yigdal

Yigdal is a poetic hymn attributed to Daniel ben Judah, the Dayan (judge in a Jewish court of law) of Rome who lived during the late fourteenth century. It consists of thirteen lines and is a poetic formulation of the Thirteen Principles of Faith that Maimonides elaborated on in his *Commentary on the Mishnah* (these principles are in the introduction to Chapter Ten of Sanhedrin). Maimonides' summary of Jewish creed had also been reduced to a concise statement in prose by an unknown author. This composition is known as *Ani Ma'amin* ("I Believe"). Although not a part of the service, Ani Ma'amin is found in most prayer books at the very end of the daily morning service.

Since the kabbalists objected to the idea of reducing all of Jewish faith to just 13 principles, and insisted that all 613 mitzvot be regarded as principles, the Hasidic rite omits the Yigdal hymn from its prayer books. (It is also not found in Sephardic prayer books.) Nevertheless, Jewish philosophers persisted in their attempts to pinpoint the primary principles in the creed of Judaism. Joseph Albo, who lived in Spain (circa 1380–1444), condensed the basic Jewish creed into three essential principles—belief in God, in revelation, and in reward and punishment. It should be noted, however, that each one of his principles incorporates several of those listed by Maimonides.

The Yigdal hymn succeeded in gaining popularity among the masses and was set alongside Adon Olam as a favorite for congregational singing. It is usually sung at the close of the evening festival services.

Supplications and Other Supplementary Prayers

TAḤANUN

FOLLOWING the weekday Shemoneh Esrei, at Shaḥarit and Minḥa, is a prayer unit called *Taḥanun* (pl. *taḥanunim*), which means "supplication." Taḥanun is relatively short, but on Monday and Thursday mornings, it is augmented by a lengthy section of supplications that begins with the words *v'hu raḥum* and consists of seven paragraphs and a penitential hymn.

The word "taḥanun" is derived from Daniel 9:3: "And I will turn my face· to the Lord God to request by prayer and supplications . . ." (see also verses 17–20). The supplication was a form of personal entreaty that was distinct from fixed or regular prayer. The same is implied by Kings I 8:54, where it says that "Solomon finished praying to God this entire prayer and supplication."

Since these Biblical verses seem to indicate that prayer was always followed by supplication, the Talmudic sages developed the habit of adding a personal appeal to God after saying the obligatory prayers (Berakhot 16b–17a). They pleaded with God that He show extra mercy and kindness in matters about which they were especially sensitive or that exceedingly troubled them.

The personal entreaties of eleven sages are recorded in the Talmud. One such plea, by Mar, son of Rabina, eventually became the closing prayer of the silent Amidah. (See p. 104.) Another, by Rabbi Judah Ha-Nasi, was incorporated into the early Morning Blessings. (See p. 197.) Taḥanun developed in keeping with that tradition.

It gradually became customary for most worshipers to add their own words of personal supplication after the prayer services ended (Berakhot 31a). For many centuries, these extemporaneous supplications or entreaties were wholly spontaneous, unstructured, and optional. Everyone expressed what was uppermost in his mind and what lay heaviest upon his heart. It was not until after the fourteenth century that a standardized text for taḥanun began to crystallize and became part of the structured congregational service. The text consisted of verses culled from the Bible. The short daily Taḥanun now consists of Psalm 6 with a brief introduction, a hymn to the Guardian of Israel, and a closing paragraph.

Psalm 6 with its introduction is especially meaningful to any person who, as King David was, is in distress, trouble, or ill health.

And David said to Gad [the prophet], I am deeply troubled; let me fall into the hand of the Lord for His mercies are many, but let me not fall into the hand of man.   (Samuel II 24:14)

O Merciful and Gracious One, I have sinned before Thee.
O Lord full of mercy, have pity on me and receive my entreaties.

Psalm 6

O Lord rebuke me not in Thine anger, nor chastise me in Thine indignation.
Be gracious to me, O Lord, for I am wretched,
Heal me, O Lord, for my bones are trembling.
My soul also is terrified; and Thou, O Lord, how long?
Return, O Lord, extricate me from my plight, save me for the sake of Thy loving kindness.
For in death there is no remembrance of Thee; in the grave, who shall give Thee thanks?

I am weary with my groaning; every night I make my bed to swim
  [with tears];
With my tears, I melt away my couch.
My eye is dimmed from vexation; it grows old because of all my
  adversaries.
Let me be, all of you who do wrong,
For the Lord heard the voice of my weeping.
The Lord heard my supplication; the Lord will receive my prayer.
Let all my enemies be ashamed and frightened;
They shall turn back, they shall be suddenly ashamed.

The posture assumed while saying this part of the daily Taḥanun
is to be seated, bent over, with the face lowered on the left forearm.
For one to be able then to read the prayer from the siddur, it must be
held below the eyes. During the morning service when tefillin are
worn on the left arm, the head is lowered on the right forearm.

This posture is symbolic of Temple practice, in which the people
knelt and fell prostrate until their faces touched the ground—a gesture
of absolute humility and total self-effacement indicating total sub-
mission to God. Because of the original posture assumed for this
prayer, Taḥanun is still known as *nefilat apayim* ("falling on the
face"). The modified way in which we now "fall on the face" has
Talmudic precedent: "Said R. Hiyya bar Abin: I saw Abaya and Rava
supplicating," which Rashi interprets as "leaning over on their sides

and not actually falling on their faces" (Rashi, Megillah 23a, Berakhot 34b). In the post-Talmudic period, a further modification (the posture we assume today) evolved.

When saying Taḥanun in a place where there is no Ark, we do not assume this posture. This is in keeping with the spirit of the verse in Joshua (7:6), where it says that he "fell on his face on the ground *before the Ark of the Lord.*"

The very last paragraph of Taḥanun, that begins with V*a'anaḥnu lo neida mah na'aseh,* emphasizes that we have exhausted every solution "and do not know what is left for us to do" (Chron. II, 20:12). What this means to say is that we have exhausted every form of prayer in seeking Divine aid. We *sat* in prayer (during the Shema and its Blessings). We *stood* in prayer (during the Shemoneh Esrei). We *"fell"* on our faces (during these supplications).* What else is now left for us to do but to conclude the supplication with: "Help us, God of our salvation, for the sake of *Thy* Name's glory; save us and pardon our sins for *Thy* Name's sake."

In the Sephardic liturgy, Psalm 25 is said instead of Psalm 6. Sephardic and even some Ashkenazic congregations preface the Taḥanun with the short form of V*idui,* the confessional prayer (*Ashamnu*), and a Biblical passage from Exod. 34:6 that describes the thirteen attributes of God.

THE LONG V'HU RAḤUM

A series of supplications, known as the long V'hu Raḥum, is added to Taḥanun on Monday and Thursday mornings. It is surely the saddest and most touching part of the prayer book. The words vividly reflect a people's indescribable suffering and daily agony. Like a magnet, the long V'hu Raḥum draws us into sharing the fear and anguish that was the lot of many generations of Jews, particularly during the Middle Ages when these supplications were written. Its

* The Bible describes Moses in three postures of prayer: "And I sat on the mountain" (Deut. 9:9); "And I stood on the mountain" (Deut. 10:10); "And I fell before the Lord" (Deut. 9:18).

pleas are filled with pathos. Although repetitive, it does not bore or tire. The repetition only deepens the stirring portrayal of despair and helplessness. Its basic theme is that God Himself is our last hope, indeed our only hope. Only He can save us from all the suffering, only He can come to our rescue and bring us salvation.

This prayer does not seek scapegoats for our troubles. We do not blame God; we do not try to find solace in blaming the oppressor. We accuse only ourselves of being at fault. Our weaknesses, our sins, and our failings have put us into such a dire situation. We plead guilty and throw ourselves entirely upon God's mercy. Only at the very end of the long V'hu Raḥum do we offer up a character reference on our own behalf: We are the people "who twice every day declare the unity of Thy name with love, Shema Yisrael, . . . Hear O Israel, the Lord our God, the Lord is One."

The reasons why Taḥanun is augmented by additional supplications on Mondays and Thursdays is because tradition regards these as especially favorable days for God to respond to our pleas. It was on the fifth day of the week that Moses ascended Mt. Sinai to receive the second set of the Ten Commandments. (The first set he had smashed when he returned to find the Israelites worshiping the Golden Calf.) And forty days later, on the second day of the week, he descended carrying not only the Tablets of the Law but also bringing with him God's forgiveness for the sin of the Golden Calf. And since court sessions in ancient Israel were also held on Mondays and Thursdays, the traditional market days, these days were seen as days of judgment on High when it would be appropriate to intensify our pleas to the Court On High (Bava Kama 82a; Tos. s.v. *kedei* and *v'donin*).

It may seem inappropriate to prosperous Jews living in the Western world under conditions of security and freedom and who are accustomed to asserting their rights to say the long V'hu Raḥum. And it may even seem a sign of weakness to Israelis, capable of defending themselves or punishing assailants, to say a prayer that emphasizes our sense of utter helplessness. It is true that V'hu Raḥum does not reflect our actual condition, and thank God for that. Although we still have enemies who seek to destroy us (and fair-weather friends who would not come to the rescue), we do not feel ourselves to be an object "of scorn and derision among nations, counted as sheep, led to the slaughter, to be slain and destroyed, to be smitten and shamed." And we are determined that such things shall never again come to pass.

God has graciously seen fit to restore national sovereignty to the Jewish people in this generation. Jews in every country share the prestige that comes with such independence. Why then do we continue to say Taḥanun, especially the V'hu Raḥum portion? Because there are Jews still living in lands where they are oppressed and where their rights are curtailed. And because we are a people for whom the past represents a lesson that, if heeded, will help ensure our future. That is why we mourn on Tisha b'Av and celebrate on Passover. If the long V'hu Raḥum only brings to mind the Jewish condition during the horrors of the Holocaust, still so near in time and fresh in our minds, it merits repetition each Monday and Thursday.

WHEN TAḤANUN IS NOT SAID, AND WHY

Since Tahanun concerns tragedy and sorrow, it is not said on a day that has even the slightest festive character, either of a personal or national kind. Taḥanun is therefore omitted on:

- Sabbaths and festivals (Pesaḥ, Shavuot, Sukkot, Rosh Hashanah, and Yom Kippur)
- Rosh Ḥodesh
- Ḥanukkah
- Tu b'Shevat, the New Year for Trees (15th day of Shevat)
- Purim and Shushan Purim (14th and 15th days of Adar)
- Purim Katan (14th and 15th days of Adar I, during a leap year)
- The entire month of Nisan
- Yom ha-Atzmaut (5th day of Iyar)
- Pesaḥ Sheni (14th day of Iyar)
- Lag b'Omer (18th day of Iyar)
- Yom Yerushalayim (28th day of Iyar)
- From the 1st day of Sivan through the day after Shavuot (8th day of Sivan); and according to some, through the 12th day of Sivan
- Tisha b'Av (9th day of Av)
- Fifteenth day of Av, the day of an ancient festival

· From Yom Kippur through the day after Sukkot; and according to some, until the end of Tishrei

Taḥanun is also omitted from the Minḥa service on the day before any of the above. On the days before Rosh Hashanah and Yom Kippur, it is omitted even in Shaḥarit.

Taḥanun is not said in the synagogue if a bridegroom, whose wedding is to take place that day or evening, is present at morning or afternoon services. Nor is it said in the synagogue during the seven day period following the wedding if the bridegroom is in attendance. If it is a remarriage for *both* parties, the celebration period is three days.

Taḥanun is not said if the father of a child to be circumcised, or the sandek, the one who holds the infant during circumcision, or the mohel who is to perform the circumcision is present at services that day. If a circumcision is scheduled to take place in the synagogue itself, a practice widespread in many places, Taḥanun is not said on that day by the congregation, even if none of the three principal participants is present. The event itself calls for the elimination of Taḥanun. The mitzvah of circumcision was received with joy, and its fulfillment should therefore be accompanied by joy (Shabbat 130a).

In Ḥasidic congregations, Taḥanun is omitted on the day when the yahrzeit of one's Rebbe (head of a Ḥasidic sect) is observed. Among Ḥasidim, the yahrzeit of a Rebbe is not a day for sorrow, but for spiritual renewal and religious celebration (Yevamot 122a; Rashi, s.v. *t'lata riglei*).

Taḥanun is also omitted at services that are conducted in a house of mourning. This requires a word of explanation. One can readily understand why Taḥanun is not said on days that bear a festive character. We do not want the sorrow expressed by Taḥanun to dampen the spirit of religious joy that we feel on these significant occasions. But in a house of mourning, Taḥanun would seem to be quite fitting. Yet it is omitted precisely because the mourner has been subjected to Divine judgment and we are sensitive about saying prayers that highlight the judgmental rather than the compassionate and merciful aspects of God's relationship to us. The mourner has grief enough. Let us not say anything that would add to it.

Nowhere else in religious worship do we find such a striking example of how the entire congregation is made to share the joy or sorrow of the individual. The rules that govern the omission of Taḥanun from the services are an expression of the Jewish community's concern with and responsibility for the individual. No Jew is ever alone. He is always part of an extended family that shares his sorrow and his joy.

The reason for omitting Taḥanun in a house of mourning does not apply to Tisha b'Av, which is a day of national mourning. Yet there exists an ancient tradition that extends back to the Talmudic period of not saying Taḥanun on that day, because "Tisha b'Av is called *moed* ("festival") (OH 559:4).

The reason is difficult to understand because Tisha b'Av can by no stretch of the imagination be called a festival, and because the verse in Lamentations upon which the reason is ostensibly based does not really say that at all. The verse reads: *Kara alai moed lishbor baḥurai* ("He [God] had set a time in which to crush my young men") (Lamentations 1:15). There moed is used in its most literal sense, "an appointed season," a "set time." A festival is a *moed l'simḥah* ("a season appointed for joy"); but Tisha b'Av is certainly not such a season. Even the Talmudic interpretation of this verse, which translates moed specifically as "festival," applies it to Rosh Ḥodesh, not Tisha b'Av (Taanit 29a; Shevuot 10a).

So the reason given for not saying Taḥanun on account of Tisha b'Av being "called a festival" requires an explanation that goes beyond the baffling reason offered in all the sources.

The explanation is based on midrashic sources which fix Tisha b'Av as the day when the Messiah was born. They did not mean this in a literal, historic sense, but meant to say that on the very day of the Temple's destruction, there was also sown the seeds for Jewish redemption (Eikhah Rabbah 1:57). The famous story of the four sages who came to Jerusalem and came upon the destroyed Temple Mount reflects this view. It is told that when Rabbi Gamliel, Rabbi Eliezer ben Azariah, Rabbi Joshua, and Rabbi Akiva reached the Temple Mount and caught sight of a fox slinking out of the Holy of Holies, the first three rabbis began to weep. But Rabbi Akiva appeared joyful. When the others wondered at his strange behavior and questioned it, he replied to them: "If the prophecy concerning the destruction of the Temple came to pass, I am confident that the prophecy concerning redemption will also come to pass. Upon hearing this, they said to him: 'Akiva, you have comforted us, Akiva, you have comforted us'" (Makkot 24b).

This rabbinic view finds expression in Targum Yonatan, the Aramaic translation of the Bible, of yet another verse in Lamentations (2:22), where the word "moed" is also found. The Targum there clearly sheds light on what the tradition might have meant by nebulously associating the word "moed" (with its connotation of festival) with Tisha b'Av. According to the Targum, the prophet did not mean to use moed as a reference to Tisha b'Av as it is observed today (a day of mourning), but as a reference to Tisha b'Av, *as it is destined to become in the Messianic era*, when it will indeed be turned into a festival like Passover, and transformed from a day of sorrow to rejoicing, from mourning to celebration, from a day of darkness and gloom to one of light and joy.

This is the symbolism and the message that the sages, by their demonstrative act of omitting Taḥanun, wished to communicate on this day of national grief; and this is also what the tradition meant to convey when it cryptically transmitted the fact that Tisha b'Av is called "moed" as the reason for not saying Taḥanun (Mekor Ḥayim HaShalem IV, 205:9).

PRAYERS CONCLUDING THE SERVICE

The concluding portion of the daily morning service consists of the following prayers: Ashrei (Psalm 145), Lamnatzei-aḥ (Psalm 20), U'va L'tziyon, Aleinu, and The Psalm of the Day.

On the Sabbath and festivals, the concluding portion consists of Ein Keloheinu, Aleinu, the Psalm of the Day, and the hymn of An'im Zmirot. Most congregations then conclude the Sabbath and festival service with the hymn of either Adon Olam or Yigdal.

Ein Keloheinu is also said at the weekday service in all Sephardic and Ḥasidic congregations. In Eretz Yisrael, it is also said in all Ashkenazic congregations.

Ashrei (Psalm 145)

The psalm which is the core of the Pesukei d'Zimra is repeated in the concluding part of the service.

On those days when Musaf is said (Sabbaths, festivals, Rosh Ḥodesh), Ashrei is said before the Musaf Amidah and not at the very end of the service.

Lamnatzei-aḥ (Psalm 20)

The opening verse of Psalm 20 is: "The Lord will answer you in the day of trouble." Since this psalm is in the mode of a supplication and begins with a verse that refers to a day of trouble, it is not said on such major festive days as the intermediate days of Passover and Sukkot, Ḥanukkah, Purim, Rosh Ḥodesh, the day before Yom Kippur, and the day before Passover, Yom Atzmaut and Yom Yerushalayim. According to the rite followed by Sephardim and many Ḥasidim, Lamnatzei-aḥ is considered to be an extension of Taḥanun and is therefore omitted whenever Taḥanun is omitted. But Ashkenazim regard Psalm 20 as a preface to the prayer, U'va L'tziyon. Since one theory accounting for the introduction of U'va L'tziyon into the service relates it to times of persecution, Psalm 20 was chosen to precede it because it takes note of troublesome times. But it also brings a message of hope, "The Lord will answer you . . . ." According to this view, Lamnatzei-aḥ should be said even on those days when Taḥanun is omitted, except on the days indicated.

U'va L'tziyon

The opening words of the prayer are *U'va l'tziyon goel* ("And a redeemer shall come to Zion."). Its first two verses are from Isaiah (59:20–21). The formal, but lesser known name of the prayer is *Kedushah d'Sidra*, so called because the heart of the prayer is the three verses that comprise Kedushah (the prayer of sanctification), which is said during the repetition of the Amidah. (See p. 122.) It was called *d'Sidra* because this Kedushah at one time followed the reading of a sidra or portion of the Prophets, which would customarily be read at the end of the daily services. That the opening verses are from the Prophets, reflects a trace of this practice.

The motivation for introducing this Kedushah toward the end of the synagogue service may have been to accommodate latecomers who missed Kedushah during the repetition of the Amidah. Since latecomers were generally the uneducated who did not understand Hebrew, the three Biblical verses that make up Kedushah were said first in the original Hebrew and then repeated in the Aramaic translation, the vernacular of Babylonian Jewry during the Talmudic period. And so has it come down to us in the prayer. Kedushah in U'va L'tziyon appears in both languages.

Inasmuch as Sabbath and festival services would start at a later hour, making it possible for even habitual latecomers to take part in the standard Kedushah, it never became customary to recite U'va L'tziyon on Sabbath and festival mornings. It is, however, said at the beginning of the Minḥa service on Sabbaths and festivals. It is said at this time on these days not because of possible latecomers, but it is said for the same reason that the Rabbinical Kaddish was recited. It was the practice to conduct Torah study sessions for the public on Sabbath afternoons before the Minḥa service. These sessions were concluded with prayers that stressed the ideas of redemption and the sanctification of God's name. One of these was Kaddish; Kedushah d'Sidra was another.

According to Tzemaḥ Gaon, this Kedushah, like the Kedushah of the Amidah, requires the presence of a minyan. Prevailing opinion is that the Kedushah d'Sidra may be said privately as is the Kedushah d'Yeshiva. (See p. 159.)

After U'va L'tziyon, the full Kaddish is recited, indicating the conclusion of the prescribed service. (See pp. 221–222.) It is now permissible to remove one's tefillin.

Aleinu

One of the noblest expressions of the universal character of Jewish monotheism is a prayer, consisting of two paragraphs, called "Aleinu," which is its opening word. The author of the prayer is reputed to be the Babylonian sage, Rav, who lived in the third century c.e. It was originally said only in the Musaf Amidah of Rosh Hashanah, as the introduction to the Malkhuyot blessing. It is still said at that time. Sometime during the early thirteenth century, Aleinu also became the closing prayer of each daily service throughout the year.

The choice of Aleinu to close every service may have been inspired by the fact that during the twelfth-century persecutions in France and elsewhere, Aleinu had become—in addition to the Shema —the dying song chanted by many Jewish martyrs.

The first paragraph of Aleinu deals with the present; the second paragraph speaks of the distant future, the messianic era.

In the first paragraph, we acknowledge Israel's distinct character among the nations of the earth. This distinctiveness, however, is not premised on narrow parochial qualifications, but on Israel's acceptance of the One Universal God who created heaven and earth.

The second paragraph anticipates sharing this distinction with all the nations of the earth. We look forward to the day when all men will worship the One Universal God, not necessarily by converting to Judaism but by acknowledging His sovereignty. Only then (with the acceptance of the ethical duties that flow from that acknowledgment) will mankind be perfected.

Since Aleinu is both a sublime declaration of faith and an act of witnessing God, it became customary to stand while saying it. When coming to the words Va'anaḥnu korim u'mishtaḥavim ("for we bend the knee and bow in worship") we slightly bend the knee and bow at the waist.

When these same words are said during the repetition of the Musaf Amidah on Rosh Hashanah and Yom Kippur, the ancient custom is to kneel down to the ground and fall prostrate before the open Ark. (See p. 40.)

Psalm of the Day

During the Temple period, it was the practice of the Levites to chant a special psalm for each day of the week at the end of the service (Tamid 7:4). As late the the twelfth century, Maimonides writes that "some of the people customarily read after each day's supplications the psalm that the Levites had said that day in the Temple" (Seder Tefilot). The custom took root and the Psalm of the Day eventually became standard practice in every synagogue.

On special occasions, an additional psalm or two are added to the daily psalm. Psalm 27 is added to the morning and evening service beginning with the first of Elul, the month before the High Holy Days; it is said until Shemini Atzeret. In a house of mourning, Psalm 49 (*Lamnatzei-aḥ livnei Koraḥ*) or Psalm 16 (*Mikhtam l'David*) is added. During the week of Ḥanukkah, Psalm 30 (*Mizmor Shir Ḥanukat Habayit*) is said. On Rosh Ḥodesh, Psalm 104 (*Borkhi Nafshi*) is added.

In the Sephardic tradition, the Psalm of the Day is said before Aleinu, so that the service concludes with Aleinu. (On days when a Musaf Amidah is said, the Psalm of the Day is said following the Shaḥarit Amidah, just before the Torah reading service.) In the Ashkenazic tradition, the daily psalm and all other special psalms are always said following the Aleinu at the very end of the service.

Ein Keloheinu

A very popular hymn of praise to God known as Ein Keloheinu is one of the concluding prayers said daily in the Sephardic and Ḥasidic rites. In the Ashkenazic rite of the diaspora, however, it is said only on Sabbaths and festivals. Its opening line seems to have been inspired by a sentence in the prayer of Hannah: "There is no holy one like the Lord, there is none beside Thee; There is no rock like our God" (Sam. I 2:2). A Talmudic discussion about God's uniqueness (Berakhot 10a) calls attention to this verse and its meaning. The hymn may once have been arranged so that the question "Who is like our God?" (the second line of verse) came first, followed by the answer "There is none like our God!" (the first line of verse). The current version in use reverses the order, and the line beginning with "Who" becomes an exclamatory declaration, rather than a question. The preference for this arrangement may have been due to the fact that in this way, the first letter from each of the first three lines form an acrostic of "Amen."

In this hymn, God is designated by four different names arranged according to the order in which they appear in the Torah:

Elohim: an appellation for God, found in the very first verse of Genesis (*Eloheinu* means "our God").

Adon: means "Master." It was first used by Abraham (Gen. 15:2). The Talmud says that Abraham was the first to address God as Adonai, my Master (Berakhot 7b). (*Adoneinu* means "our Master.")

Melekh: means "King." This usage is implied in Exodus 15:18, where it says that "the Lord will *reign* for ever and

	ever." Direct use of the name Melekh is found in Numbers 23:21. (*Malkeinu* means "our King.")
Moshi-a:	means the "Deliverer." It is implied in Deuteronomy 33:29, where it says that Israel is "a people delivered by the Lord" (*Moshi'einu* means "our Deliverer").

This hymn is followed by a Talmudic passage (Keritot 6a) that is a recipe for the incense (*ketoret*) that was twice daily burned in the Beit Hamikdash on a special altar called the Altar of Incense.

The Ein Keloheinu unit is concluded with the recitation of a Mishnah containing the names of the psalms said daily in the Temple by the Levites and with two very short aggadic excerpts from the Talmud. One is from Megillah 28b ("At the school of Elijah, they taught"). The other is, "Said Rabbi Elazar," a passage which concludes a number of Talmudic tractates: Berakhot, Yevamot, Nazir, Tamid, and Keritot.

These aggadic passages are added to the Mishnah passage to allow for the recitation of a Rabbinical Kaddish at this point. Since the Rabbinical Kaddish has been prescribed by the sages as a conclusion to the teaching of aggadah, the Rabbinical Kaddish is not recited after the study or reading of Mishnah or of other halakhic passages (OH 54:3; MB:9; MA:3).

To permit this Kaddish to be said, it has become customary to conclude readings from the Mishnah or other halakha with aggadic passages.

CHAPTER

10

~~~~~~

The Kaddish

No PRAYER in all of Jewish liturgy arouses greater emotion than *Kaddish*. No prayer instills greater reverence. No prayer projects more mystery. It is usually thought of as a prayer for the dead, but it is not that at all. There are prayers for the dead, but Kaddish meaning "sanctification" is not one of them. Yet it is Kaddish that is recited by grief-stricken families at funerals and by mourners at memorial assemblies. It is Kaddish that sons are required to recite for eleven months following the death of a parent. Wherein lies the secret of this prayer's power and significance? What does it mean— for the dead and for the living?

Its opening words, *yitgadal v'yitkadash* (Ashkenazic pronunciation: *yisgadal v'yiskadash*) were inspired by Ezekiel 38:23, where the prophet envisions a time when God will become great and hallowed in the eyes of all nations; they shall learn "that I am the Lord." Its mood emanates from an awareness of God's infinite power and majesty. Kaddish is a hymn that praises God and yearns for the speedy establishment of God's kingdom on earth.

To sanctify God's name publicly has been the historic duty of the Jew. To testify boldly to our faith in His existence and in His sovereignty has been the Jewish mission on earth.

There were times when to sanctify the Name of God, *Kiddush*

HaShem, meant only one thing: to be led to the Roman crucifixion, or to the Christian auto-da-fé, or to the Nazi gas chamber with the Shema on our lips. It meant being killed only because we were Jews, or because we refused to yield our faith. It meant offering our lives on behalf of the Holy One, blessed be He. It meant to die a martyr.

But it was not always so. In less oppressive times the Jewish duty to sanctify God's Name publicly was (and is) expressed not by the way we die but by the way we live. When we act in such a way as to bring honor to our faith, to the Torah, and to our people, we are in essence sanctifying God's Name. When what we do produces added reverence for Him—if it inspires the verbal or mental response "praised be God"—that, too, is a sanctification of His Name.

The simplest manifestation of Kiddush HaShem is a public declaration of our belief that God is great and holy, which elicits from others the response *Yehei Shmei rabba mevorakh l'olam ul'almei almaya* ("May His great Name be blessed forever and ever"). That is what we do when we say Kaddish, for the whole purpose of saying Kaddish is not merely to praise God—many other prayers also do that—but to elicit the aforementioned response from listeners. The response is the heart of the Kaddish and should be said aloud.

Kaddish is therefore not said when one is praying alone. Its very essence is as a public prayer. If the minimum number of people that constitute a congregation ("a public assembly") is not met, the public nature of the sanctification of God's Name is missing. And if there cannot be a public response, the reason for saying Kaddish disappears.

The response is the crux of the Kaddish. This is indicated by the fact that the entire prayer may once have been solely identified by it. For although the name "Kaddish" and the text (even the earliest version) are not found either in Scripture or in the Talmud, explicit references to the response *Yehei Shmei rabba . . .* are made throughout Talmudic literature. The significance of this response is emphasized everywhere: "Rabbi Joshua ben Levi said, 'He who responds *Amen, Yehei Shmei rabba . . .* with absolute devotion, merits that any evil decrees against him be abolished.' Rabbi Ḥiyya bar Abba said in the name of Rabbi Jonathan, 'Even if one has a taint of idolatry, one is forgiven' " (Shabbat 119b). According to Raba, the world itself is sustained by the religious merit accrued by the recitation of *Yehei Shmei rabba* (Sotah 49a). "The one who answers *Yehei Shmei rabba*

is assured that he is worthy of the world-to-come" (Berakhot 57a).
"When Israel enters its synagogues and study houses and responds
Yehei Shmei rabba . . . , the Holy One, blessed be He, says, 'How
fortunate is the King who is thus praised in His own House' " (Berakhot 3a).*

One indication that Kaddish was not a prayer deliberately composed for the synagogue but an outgrowth of the informal prayers
recited in the *Beit Midrash* ("the study hall") is the fact that
"Adonai" or "Elohim," the name of God as it appears in all other
prayers and blessings, does not appear in Kaddish. Instead we find the
less formal appellations that were widely used in the daily language
of the people and that may be said even outside the context of a
formal blessing: *Kudsha Brikh Hu*, ("the Holy One, blessed be He")
and *Avuhon di bi'shmaya* ("their Father in heaven"). Even *HaShem*
("The Name"), an informal reference to God, popular in our times,
is found in Kaddish, as: *Shemei* ("His Name").

The Kaddish

יִתְגַּדַּל וְיִתְקַדַּשׁ שְׁמֵהּ רַבָּא, בְּעָלְמָא דִּי בְרָא כִרְעוּתֵהּ,
וְיַמְלִיךְ מַלְכוּתֵהּ בְּחַיֵּיכוֹן וּבְיוֹמֵיכוֹן וּבְחַיֵּי דְכָל בֵּית יִשְׂרָאֵל
בַּעֲגָלָא וּבִזְמַן קָרִיב, וְאִמְרוּ אָמֵן.

יְהֵא שְׁמֵהּ רַבָּא מְבָרַךְ לְעָלַם וּלְעָלְמֵי עָלְמַיָּא.

יִתְבָּרַךְ וְיִשְׁתַּבַּח וְיִתְפָּאַר וְיִתְרוֹמַם וְיִתְנַשֵּׂא וְיִתְהַדָּר
וְיִתְעַלֶּה וְיִתְהַלָּל שְׁמֵהּ דְּקֻדְשָׁא בְּרִיךְ הוּא, לְעֵלָּא מִן כָּל
בִּרְכָתָא וְשִׁירָתָא, תֻּשְׁבְּחָתָא וְנֶחֱמָתָא דַּאֲמִירָן בְּעָלְמָא,
וְאִמְרוּ אָמֵן.

---

* This response bears a resemblance to a verse in Psalms (113:2) and to the
Hebrew response to Borkhu.

The Kaddish

Magnified and sanctified be His great name in the world which He created according to His will.
And may He establish His kingdom
During your life and during your days, and during the life of all the house of Israel, speedily and in the near future, and say Amen.

(Response: May His great Name be blessed forever and ever.)

Blessed, praised and glorified, exalted, extolled and honored, adored and lauded be the Name of the Holy One, blessed be He, beyond all blessings and hymns, praises and songs that are uttered in the world, and say Amen.

This earliest version of Kaddish goes back to the period of the Second Temple. Although this Kaddish is complete (AH 56:8), we refer to it as the "Half Kaddish," because the full Kaddish now includes two more sentences that began to be recited around the eighth century C.E. These sentences reflect the traditional yearning for peace and begin with *Yehei shlomo rabba* and *Oseh shalom*.

יְהֵא שְׁלָמָא רַבָּא מִן שְׁמַיָּא וְחַיִּים עָלֵינוּ וְעַל כָּל יִשְׂרָאֵל,
וְאִמְרוּ אָמֵן.
עֹשֶׂה שָׁלוֹם בִּמְרוֹמָיו, הוּא יַעֲשֶׂה בְרַחֲמָיו שָׁלוֹם עָלֵינוּ
וְעַל כָּל יִשְׂרָאֵל, וְאִמְרוּ אָמֵן.

May there be abundant peace from heaven and life for us and for all Israel, and say Amen.
May He who makes peace in the heavens, make peace for us and for all Israel, and say Amen.

The very last sentence is the same one that concludes the Amidah and the Grace after Meals. This fuller Kaddish is the one that we today refer to as the "Mourner's Kaddish."
The Sephardic version of the Half Kaddish contains a relatively minor variation. Four words are added to the second sentence, after the word *malkhutei* ("His kingdom"). They are:

וְיַצְמַח פֻּרְקָנֵהּ וִיקָרֵב מְשִׁיחֵהּ,

V'yatzmaḥ purkanei vikarev meshiḥei.
And make His salvation spring forth, and bring nigh the Messiah.

The otherwise amazing uniformity of Kaddish throughout the Jewish world attests to its antiquity.

THE RABBINICAL KADDISH

Kaddish was not said at first by mourners. It was a prayer said by the rabbis when they finished their lecture-sermons on Sabbath afternoons. The Talmud calls it "the Yehei Shmei Rabbah of the Aggadah" (Sotah 49a) because it was said only after the study of aggadah or midrash, not after the study of halakha. And since this practice developed in Babylonia, where most of the people spoke and understood only Aramaic, Kaddish was said in the vernacular to enable the people to understand what was being said (Berakhot 3a, Tos. s.v. v'onin). That is why Kaddish has come down to us primarily in Aramaic and not in Hebrew.

Kaddish is still said after a study session that includes midrashic or aggadic portions, or after reading them as part of the service—only here we call it Kaddish d'Rabbanan ("Kaddish of the Rabbis" or "Rabbinical Kaddish").* It differs from the regular Kaddish by the inclusion of a prayer for rabbis, scholars, and their disciples.

עַל יִשְׂרָאֵל וְעַל רַבָּנָן וְעַל תַּלְמִידֵיהוֹן וְעַל כָּל תַּלְמִידֵי
תַלְמִידֵיהוֹן, וְעַל כָּל מַאן דְּעָסְקִין בְּאוֹרַיְתָא, דִּי בְּאַתְרָא
הָדֵין, וְדִי בְכָל אֲתַר וַאֲתַר, יְהֵא לְהוֹן וּלְכוֹן שְׁלָמָא רַבָּא,

---

* Anyone may say this Kaddish, but it is now customary for mourner's to say the Rabbinical Kaddish in addition to the Mourner's Kaddish.

חִנָּא וְחִסְדָּא וְרַחֲמֵי, וְחַיֵּי אֲרִיכֵי וּמְזוֹנֵי רְוִיחֵי וּפֻרְקָנָא
מִן קֳדָם אֲבוּהוֹן דִּי בִשְׁמַיָּא, וְאִמְרוּ אָמֵן.

Unto Israel, and unto the rabbis, and unto their disciples, and unto all the disciples of their disciples, and unto all who engage in the study of Torah, in this or in any other place, unto them, and unto you, let there be abundant peace, grace, loving kindness, mercy, long life, ample sustenance, and salvation from their Father in heaven, and say Amen.

THE WHOLE KADDISH

Already in Talmudic times, it had become customary also to conclude prayer services with Kaddish. Thus Kaddish, which started out as a prayer said by the rabbis in the Beit Midrash moved into the synagogue, where it was said by the Prayer Leader to mark the end of the service. The Kaddish that concludes the service came to be known as *Kaddish Titkabal*, because it contains a special verse that begins with the word *titkabal* ("let be accepted").* It asks God to accept all the prayers that were recited. This verse replaces the passage on behalf of the rabbis and their disciples.

תִּתְקַבֵּל צְלוֹתְהוֹן וּבָעוּתְהוֹן דְּכָל יִשְׂרָאֵל קֳדָם אֲבוּהוֹן
דִּי בִשְׁמַיָּא, וְאִמְרוּ אָמֵן.

Let the prayers and supplications of all Israel be accepted by their Father in heaven, and say Amen.

This Kaddish is now called *Kaddish Shalem* ("Whole Kaddish" or "Full Kaddish"). The Prayer Leader says it to indicate the comple-

* In some prayer books, the word is *titkabeil*, which is the Hebrew form of the same word.

tion of the prescribed service, though some supplementary prayers may still follow.

It gradually became customary for the Prayer Leader also to say Kaddish to introduce the Amidah and to indicate the end of subdivisions within the service. However, in this case he said only the original Kaddish, or what is now called the "Half Kaddish." Neither the verse of titkabal nor the last two sentences about peace were included. The Prayer Leader now says this Half Kaddish following the Pesukei d'Zimra in the morning service. He says it after the Amidah or the Taḥanun, as the case may be; and he says it after the Torah reading. He also says it before the Amidah at Minḥa, Maariv, and Musaf services.

In this way did Kaddish become one of the prayers most frequently said by the Prayer Leader.

WHY MOURNERS SAY KADDISH

The first mention of the custom that mourners say Kaddish at the end of the service is found in Or Zarua, a thirteenth century halakhic work by one of the Early Authorities. In the sixteenth century, Rabbi Moses Isserles still speaks of the "custom" of reciting Kaddish for a period of eleven months after the death of a father or mother (YD 376:4, Rema). The Kaddish after Aleinu, the last prayer in the service, was specifically designated as the Kaddish for mourners. This Kaddish became known as Kaddish Yatom ("Mourner's Kaddish", literally, "Orphan's Kaddish").

Since Kaddish makes no direct reference to the dead or to a hereafter, why did it become the prayer that mourners say?

One explanation is that it is an expression by a bereaved person of his acceptance of the Divine judgment (tzidduk hadin). In a time of tragedy and loss, one might become bitter toward the Lord and reject Him. At precisely such a time, we rise to praise Him and publicly to affirm our belief in His righteousness. Kaddish reflects the mood of Job's declaration: "The Lord gave and the Lord took away, let the name of the Lord be blessed" (Job 1:21). It also reflects the verse from Psalms: "I found trouble and sorrow. But I called upon the name of the Lord ..." (116:3–4).

A second explanation is that the Kaddish is a prayer for the dead in an indirect sense. Its recitation by the living is a factor in redeeming the soul of the deceased. If the children of recently deceased parents rise to sanctify God's name in public, that redounds to the merit of the deceased. God's judgment of the dead person takes this act of the children into account. So does "a child acquit the parent" (Sanhedrin 104a). Kaddish is therefore a way in which children can continue to show respect and concern for their parents even after they have died. This is in keeping with the commandment to "Honor thy father and mother," a law that is in force when they are dead as much as when they are alive.

The inspiration for mourners to adopt Kaddish as their special prayer, and the curious mystical hold it has had over mourners over the centuries, even though it was never codified, may have been based on a legend told about Rabbi Akiva who lived in the second century C.E. It is said that he once saw a man struggling under a heavy load of wood. Rabbi Akiva stopped the man and said, "Why must you do this difficult work? If you are a slave and this labor is forced upon you, I will redeem you from your master and set you free. And if it is because you are poor and you must earn your livelihood this way, I will enrich you." But the man responded with obvious fright, "Please let me go and do not detain me, lest I anger those in charge of me." The man's reply puzzled Akiva. "Who are you and what is this all about?' he asked. The man replied, "I am one of those unfortunate souls condemned to the agonies of hell-fire, and every day I am sent to bring my own wood for my own torment." "Is there then no way for you to be relieved of this suffering?" asked Akiva. "Yes," the man answered. "I heard it said that if my little son, whom I left behind, were to say in public *Yitgadal v'yitkadash* and the others would answer *Yehei Shmei rabba mevorakh*, or if he were to say *Borkhu et Adonai hamevorakh* and the congregation would answer *Barukh Adonai hamevorakh l'olam va-ed*, I would be set free from this judgment." Akiva then asked the man for the pertinent details and promised to locate his child and teach him Torah so that he could stand before the congregation and say Yitgadal in praise of God. The legend goes on to describe how Akiva searched for the child, found him, taught him Torah, the Shema, the Amidah, the Grace after Meals, and prepared him to stand before the congregation to recite Yitgadal. When the boy did this, the father's soul was delivered from its judgment and permitted its eternal rest. The man then appeared to Akiva in a dream and thanked him: "May it be God's will that you rest in peace for you made it possible for me to be at peace" (Netiv Binah I, pp. 367–368).

Although Judaism does not claim to know what takes place after death and does not dwell on descriptions of the hereafter, it does teach that there is a spiritual world-to-come where God rewards the righteous and punishes the wicked. How He does this, however, remains a mystery. The legend of Rabbi Akiva and of the child who saves his father from eternal punishment emphasizes an important truth—the everlasting bond that remains between parents and children. The connection is not severed even after death. As the actions of parents influence the lives of children, so the faith and the good deeds of children help determine the spiritual destiny met by the souls of parents.

THE GREAT KADDISH

Tractate Soferim mentions still another passage, a later addition to the Kaddish, which Maimonides includes in his standard text of the Rabbinical Kaddish. The passage, beginning with b'alma d'hu atid l'ithadta, contains a prayer for the rebuilding of Jerusalem and the Temple and refers to a world-to-come where the dead will be revived and raised to eternal life. The passage replaces the first paragraph of the regular Kaddish.

יִתְגַּדַּל וְיִתְקַדַּשׁ שְׁמֵהּ רַבָּא, בְּעָלְמָא דְהוּא עָתִיד לְאִתְחַדְתָּא, וּלְאַחֲיָא מֵתַיָּא, וּלְאַסָּקָא לְחַיֵּי עָלְמָא, וּלְמִבְנֵי קַרְתָּא דִירוּשְׁלֵם, וּלְשַׁכְלֵל הֵיכָלֵהּ בְּגַוַּהּ, וּלְמֶעֱקַר פּוּלְחָנָא

The Kaddish

נוּכְרָאָה מֵאַרְעָא, וּלְאָתָבָא פּוּלְחָנָא דִשְׁמַיָּה לְאַתְרָה,
וְיַמְלִיךְ קוּדְשָׁא בְּרִיךְ הוּא בְּמַלְכוּתֵה וִיקָרֵהּ, בְּחַיֵּיכוֹן
וּבְיוֹמֵיכוֹן, וּבְחַיֵּי דְכָל בֵּית יִשְׂרָאֵל, בַּעֲגָלָא וּבִזְמַן קָרִיב,
וְאִמְרוּ אָמֵן.

Magnified and sanctified be His great name in the world that is to be created anew, where He will revive the dead and raise them up into life eternal;

He will rebuild the city of Jerusalem and establish His Temple in its midst;

He will uproot all alien worship from the earth and restore the worship of [God in] heaven;

And the Holy One, blessed be He, will reign in His kingdom and in glory.

During your life and during your days, and during the life of all the house of Israel, speedily and in the near future, and say Amen.

As a form of Rabbinical Kaddish said at the conclusion of Torah study, this Kaddish was said to emphasize the Talmudic teaching that "all who engage in the study of Torah will be granted life in the world-to-come" (Avodah Zarah 3b). This Kaddish is the one that is still said at a *siyum*, when a tractate of the Talmud is completed. It is known as "the great Kaddish" or "the long Kaddish."

Direct reference to the revival of the dead, to life eternal, to a world-to-come, was apparently not sufficiently compelling for it to be adopted as the Mourner's Kaddish. But it did become the Kaddish that mourners say at the graveside at the time of burial. It is for this reason that this Kaddish is also referred to in English as the "Burial Kaddish." Inasmuch as its recitation at a burial is associated with the Justification of Judgment prayer, it is not said on those occasions when the latter prayer is not said. This corresponds to the days when Taḥanun is omitted (YD 376).

RULES RELATING TO SAYING KADDISH

&· Kaddish is said only in the presence of a minyan.

&· Kaddish is never recited independently. It is said only following a psalm or a prayer that has also been said in the presence of a minyan (OH 54:3, Rema).

&· The one who says Kaddish always stands. What the other worshipers do varies with the congregation.

&· In the past, only one person at a time said Kaddish. If there was more than one mourner present, they took turns. It is now customary for all the mourners in the congregation to say Kaddish in unison.

&· The Mourner's Kaddish may be said by a young child under the age of thirteen if he has lost one of his parents.

&· While a daughter is under no religious obligation to recite Kaddish daily, she is not forbidden to do so. Some religious authorities who do not share this view feel that a daughter can show honor to a deceased parent in an alternative manner. If she had been instructed by her parents to keep an added specific religious duty, and she does so, this accrues even more merit for the deceased than does the Kaddish. Even if parents leave behind only daughters, in which case no one is required to say Kaddish, this is a way to achieve the same spiritual benefits.

&· The Mourner's Kaddish is recited for eleven months, according to the Hebrew calendar. This period is reckoned from the day of death. This also holds true for a leap year when there are thirteen months in the Hebrew calendar year. It is also said on the yahrzeit.

&· One may say Kaddish for relatives other than parents. A father may say it for a child who has died, brothers may say it for one another, a son-in-law may say it for his in-laws. It is proper for an adopted son to say Kaddish for adoptive parents if they raised him.

&· The Rabbinical Kaddish, the Half Kaddish, and the Whole Kaddish may be said by a Prayer Leader who is not a mourner and has both parents living.

11

~~~~~~

Responses in Prayer

AMEN

THE Hebrew word *amen* has entered almost every language in the world and is today one of the most universally known words. It is also one of the most ancient, originating in the Torah as a response of affirmation. In Deuteronomy 27:16–26, we find a series of pronouncements by the Levites to which the people responded "Amen." The Book of Chronicles I (16:35) clearly indicates that in the time of King David, the second king of Israel (c.1000 B.C.E.), the people responded with "Amen" upon hearing the blessing: "Blessed be the Lord God of Israel from now and unto all eternity."* In Sephardic Hebrew, the "a" in "Amen" is pronounced as *ah*. The Ashkenazic pronunciation is *aw*. The accent in both cases is on the second syllable.

When a person says the word "Amen," he indicates his endorsement of the words that he has just heard, and affirms his belief in the truth of what has been said. He acknowledges his identification with the prayer or the blessing, as though he himself had said it. Where "Amen" follows a petitionary blessing or a prayer of supplication, it also carries the meaning of "so may it be."

The Talmudic sages saw great significance in this word. Rabbi

---

* The diligent reader who wishes to find "Amen" elsewhere in the Bible, should see Numbers 5:22; Kings I 1:36; Psalms 41:14; Jeremiah 11:5, 28:6; and Nehemiah 5:13.

Hanina stressed that the three Hebrew letters that make up the word "Amen" stand for the three Hebrew words *El Melekh Ne'eman,* ("God, Faithful King"). As such "Amen" is an acknowledgment of the yoke of the Divine Kingdom (Shabbat 119b).

The sages regarded the response of "Amen" as a fulfillment of the verse: "When I proclaim the name of the Lord, give glory to our God!" (Deut. 32:3). What this means, they said, is that Moses said to the Israelites, "When I bless the name of God, you declare God's greatness by answering 'Amen' " (OH 215; MB: 8).

The halakha has ruled that anyone who hears another recite a blessing is required to respond with "Amen" upon its conclusion (OH 215:2 and 124:6).

This ruling was particularly significant before printed prayer books came into widespread use. Since most people were not able to pray by heart, they could fulfill their prayer obligation by listening to the prayers said by the Prayer Leader and answering "Amen." The response was equated with the recitation itself. Even after printed prayer books became commonplace and most people were able to recite the prayers for themselves, the Prayer Leader's repetition of the Amidah and the congregation's response of "Amen" remained integral and meaningful parts of Jewish worship.

OTHER RESPONSES

"Amen" is not the only congregational response that is part of Jewish prayer. Another is *barukh hu, u'varukh shemo* ("Blessed is He, and blessed is His Name!"). This is the correct response when hearing the name of God ("Adonai") in the opening part of a blessing, *Barukh atah Adonai* (OH 124:5).

One does not respond with *barukh hu u'varukh shemo* to any blessing that is being said with the intent to fulfill the obligation of the listener. This is usually the case with blessings for the shofar and for the reading of the Megillah, and occasionally with the Kiddush and Havdalah. This response is not said at such times because it is tantamount to interrupting oneself in the middle of a berakhah. If, however, one has already fulfilled his personal obligation regarding a mitzvah and then hears someone else recite a blessing for it, the response is in order.

The response to the words *Borkhu et Adonai hamevorakh,* said by one who is called up to the Torah for an aliyah, is *Barukh Adonai hamevorakh l'olam va-ed.*

When the Prayer Leader says the three sentences of the Priestly Blessing in the repetition of the Amidah, the congregational response is: *kein yehi ratzon!* (*"So may His will be!"*). We do not respond "Amen" in this instance, because the Prayer Leader is not actually blessing the people. He is only reading a passage that quotes the blessing. When the kohanim say these same sentences during the ritual of the Priestly Blessing, the congregation then responds with "Amen."

In the preliminary part of the morning service (Pesukei d'Zimra), there are many chapters from the Book of Psalms. The last word in many of these passages is *Halleluyah* (*"Praise the Lord"*). In the days of the Temple, this word was the congregational response to every sentence of Hallel.

The short response is actually a time-honored form of prayer; it provided a way for those people who could not recite or concentrate on lengthy prayers to participate in and be fully part of the worship service. It had its origin in the Temple service and was carried over into the synagogue.

In our own day, the short response is often treated as insignificant. This neglect does it an injustice. It should be restored to its rightful status.

RULES FOR SAYING "AMEN"

Even with so simple a response as "Amen," there are a number of rules to keep in mind:

ֶ֎ One does not respond "Amen" to a blessing that one recites oneself. The exception to this rule is the third blessing in the Grace after Meals (*Birkat Hamazon*), where "Amen" is said to mark the end of the original Grace and thus becomes an integral part of the blessing's conclusion (see p. 294). In such other prayers as Kaddish, Mi Shebeirakh, El Malei Raḥamim, and the Blessing of the Month, "Amen" is often said by the one reciting it, not as a response but as an instruction to the listeners, v'imru Amen ("and say Amen").

᠈᠍᠍᠍᠍᠍᠍᠍᠍᠍᠍ If one is in the midst of saying prayers that may not be interrupted, one may not stop even to say "Amen."

᠈᠍᠍᠍᠍᠍᠍᠍᠍᠍ "Amen" may be said even when hearing a blessing recited by a non-Jew (OH 215:2, Rema).

᠈᠍᠍᠍᠍᠍᠍᠍᠍᠍ It is forbidden to respond "Amen" to a blessing that is said needlessly and so takes the name of the Lord in vain (OH 215:4).

᠈᠍᠍᠍᠍᠍᠍᠍᠍᠍ For educational purposes, one should respond "Amen" to a blessing recited by a child, and thereby set an example for the child (OH 215:3, 124:7).

᠈᠍᠍᠍᠍᠍᠍᠍᠍᠍ One should not say "Amen" in a louder tone than the blessing itself (OH 124:12; Berakhot 45a).

᠈᠍᠍᠍᠍᠍᠍᠍᠍᠍ "Amen" should be pronounced unhurriedly and distinctly. The first vowel must not be said so quickly as to lose the vowel sound altogether. The last letter must not be slurred so that the n sound is dropped (OH 124:8; Berakhot 47a).

᠈᠍᠍᠍᠍᠍᠍᠍᠍᠍ "Amen" is said only after the blessing is entirely completed. The last syllables of the blessing must not be cut off by the response (OH 124:8; Berakhot 47a).

᠈᠍᠍᠍᠍᠍᠍᠍᠍᠍ One should not say "Amen" for a blessing that one does not actually hear and one has no idea to what blessing he is responding. Such a response is called an "orphaned Amen," because it has no "parent." But if a person hears the congregation reciting "Amen" and knows to which blessing they are responding, he may join in the response (OH 124:8, 11).

᠈᠍᠍᠍᠍᠍᠍᠍᠍᠍ Contemporary authorities have ruled that "Amen" is not said when a blessing is heard over television, radio, or on a recording.

CHAPTER

12

The Torah Reading Service

THE SACRED BOOKS of the Jewish people were always considered to be the inheritance of the entire community of Israel. They were never the exclusive possession of a privileged elite, as was often the case with sacred texts among other religious communities. The priests, the prophets, the elders, and the rabbis may all have been charged with safeguarding the sacred books and entrusted with the authority to interpret them for the people, but these groups were to enjoy no monopoly on the study of Torah and the knowledge thereof. They were, in fact, given the responsibility for spreading a knowledge of Torah among all the people. The key to the survival of Judaism depended on universal religious education; ignorance of Torah was not to be condoned. The Torah makes this point over and over again. Moses himself showed the way by teaching the Torah before a large public. "And Moses took the Book of the Covenant and read it to the people" (Exod. 24:7). One Torah commandment specifically calls for reading the entire book of Deuteronomy to an assembly of all the people: "Assemble the people, men and women and little children, and the stranger within your gates that they may hear and that they may learn and [thus] revere the Lord your God and observe to do all the words of this Torah" (Deut. 31:12). This particular assembly had to be called only once in seven years (at the end of each Sabbatical

231

year) during the festival of Sukkot. But the principle of continuing adult education was clearly established—and this at the very outset of our existence as a faith community. The sacred books were not secret documents.

Tradition attributes to Moses the practice of publicly reading portions of the Torah on Sabbaths, festivals, and Rosh Ḥodesh—the last having been much more of a semi-festival in ancient times than it is today (Yer. Megillah 4:1). This practice may help explain the meaning of the Biblical expression *mikra-ei kodesh* as a reference to these sacred days. This term is generally translated as "sacred assemblies," because "mikra-ei" implies "being called together or assembled," and "kodesh" means "holy" or "sacred." But "mikra" also means "reading" and is a term that was later applied to Scripture. The sages read both meanings into the term "mikra-ei kodesh"; for them it meant the sacred days on which the people assembled to listen to the reading of Scripture.

There was at first no established order to the public reading of Scripture. But there is no denying the impact that this extraordinary tradition has had on the religious life of the Jewish people throughout history. The systematic reading of Torah on Sabbaths and the festivals was a significant educational influence among adult Jews. This was especially so because the Torah was not just read but also explained. Torah had to be understood. In the biblical Book of Nehemiah we read that ". . . the Levites . . . read from the book in the Torah of God distinctly, and they explained the meaning and caused them to understand the reading" (8:8). And when Hebrew ceased to be the spoken tongue of the masses—after the return of the Jews from their Babylonian exile, where the vernacular was Aramaic—a translator, known as a *meturgeman*, was brought in to translate each sentence aloud as it was read. And later, during the Talmudic period, it became the practice of the rabbis to expound at length on the meaning of the text. The Talmud tells of Rabbi Ashi, Mar Zutra, and Meremar regularly doing so at the Shaḥarit service (Berakhot 30a); of Rabbi Joseph doing so before the Musaf service (Berakhot 28b, Rashi); and of other rabbis doing so before the Minḥa service. The rabbis used parables to vividly bring home the lesson of the Scriptural text in its application to the daily life of the people. This was the origin of the sermon or *drashah*—a long-established tradition among Jews—whose purpose was to explain Torah and teach Judaism to the assembled public. This is still the prime purpose of the sermon.

The Talmud relates that it was Ezra the Scribe who introduced the practice of reading the Torah also on Monday and Thursday mornings and Sabbath afternoons (Bava Kama 82a; Yer. Megillah 4:1). Monday and Thursday were the market days when the farmers came to the nearest towns to do their shopping and trading (Bava Batra 22a). These days provided an excellent opportunity to assemble the people for short periods in order to teach them some Torah. As the town merchants, being otherwise occupied, were not free to attend these Monday and Thursday assemblies, the extra Sabbath afternoon reading was instituted for their benefit.

The Talmud also gives a spiritual reason for the two mid-week readings and, in so doing, suggests that the practice predated Ezra, who may have formalized the Monday and Thursday Torah reading but did not originate it. The sages always regarded water as the symbol of Torah. What water is to the body—a source of life, a fount of refreshment—Torah is to the soul. When Isaiah said, "All ye who thirst, go to the water," (55:1), he was speaking not literally, but figuratively. He was addressing himself to all who thirst for the spirit, and telling them to quench that thirst by turning to Torah.

So when the Israelites in the wilderness are described as having become weary because they "walked for three days . . . and did not find water" (Exod. 15:22), the sages saw this as an object lesson. The weariness, they said, resulted from having gone three days without the spiritual sustenance of Torah. That, the sages tell us, is why long before Ezra the prophets ruled that the Torah should be read on Monday and Thursday in addition to the Sabbath. This ruling ensures that no three-day period would go by without the spiritual sustenance provided by a public Torah reading.

Although there have been periods when the tradition of the public Torah reading was neglected, it has been continuously observed in Jewish communities everywhere ever since the Maccabean period, during the second century B.C.E. Furthermore, the sages decided to prohibit the earlier practice of choosing Biblical passages at random for the Sabbath reading and to substitute consecutive reading. On Sabbath afternoon, on Monday and Thursday mornings, and on the following Sabbath morning, the Torah reading has to begin where it left off on the previous Sabbath morning (Megillah 31b).

While adhering to the rule of consecutive reading, two traditions emerged: one in Eretz Yisrael, the other in Babylonia. In Eretz Yisrael, the Torah was divided into 155 portions. It took three years to read through the entire Five Books of Moses (Megillah 29b). In some of the communities, the division resulted in 175 portions, so that it took three and one-half years to complete the cycle (Soferim 16:10).

Among Babylonian Jewry, the Torah was divided into fifty-four portions (each called a *parshah*) according to the number of weeks in a leap year—a division that became the accepted halakhic norm for Jewry everywhere. In normal years, when there are only fifty weeks, double portions are read on some Sabbaths, so as to complete the reading of all Five Books of Moses within a one-year period. The annual celebration of Simḥat Torah on the second day of Shemini Atzeret is an outgrowth of this tradition.

The only time when a break in the weekly continuity of the Torah reading is sanctioned is when a festival falls on the Sabbath. The festival reading then takes precedence over the weekly portion, in keeping with the Biblical verse: "And Moses spoke of the festivals of God to the children of Israel" (Lev. 23:44). From this verse, the sages derived the obligation to read about each festival on the festival day (Megillah 3:6).

Although the public reading of Torah (an educational undertaking) is a much more ancient tradition among Jews than is congregational prayer, and developed independently of prayer, it was only natural that with the evolution of congregational worship, Torah reading would be joined to the service and become an integral part of it. It completed the circle—creating a dialogue. In prayer, man talks to God; through the Torah reading, God talks to man.

THE TORAH SCROLL—FROM AND TO THE HOLY ARK

The importance of the Torah reading is highlighted by the fact that the most ceremonial part of any synagogue service, especially on Sabbaths and festivals, is related to removing the Torah from the Holy Ark and returning it again. The congregation rises. The Ark is opened. There is a procession in which the Torah is carried around the synagogue. People reach out to kiss it. Prayers are sung in melodious unison.

The ritual is introduced on Sabbaths and festivals with several verses that begin as follows:

אֵין כָּמוֹךָ בָאֱלֹהִים, אֲדֹנָי, וְאֵין כְּמַעֲשֶׂיךָ:

There is none like unto Thee among the gods, O Lord, and there are no works like Thine.　　　　　　　　　　　(Tractate Soferim)

In the Sephardic and Ḥasidic rites, a verse from Deuteronomy is said before the preceding:

אַתָּה הָרְאֵתָ לָדַעַת, כִּי יהוה הוּא הָאֱלֹהִים,
אֵין עוֹד מִלְּבַדּוֹ:

You have been made to recognize that the Lord is God; there is none besides Him.　　　　　　　　　　　(Deut. 4:35)

The Ark is then opened, and the congregation says a one-sentence passage from Numbers (10:35) that relates to the past, when the Ark of the Covenant was carried forward in the wilderness of Sinai. Now follows a one-sentence quote from Isaiah (2:3) that relates to the future, the messianic period.

וַיְהִי בִּנְסֹעַ הָאָרֹן וַיֹּאמֶר מֹשֶׁה : קוּמָה יהוה
וְיָפֻצוּ אֹיְבֶיךָ וְיָנֻסוּ מְשַׂנְאֶיךָ מִפָּנֶיךָ: כִּי מִצִּיּוֹן
תֵּצֵא תוֹרָה, וּדְבַר יהוה מִירוּשָׁלָיִם: בָּרוּךְ שֶׁנָּתַן
תּוֹרָה לְעַמּוֹ יִשְׂרָאֵל בִּקְדֻשָּׁתוֹ.

And it came to pass, when the Ark was carried forward, that Moses
said:
Rise up O Lord, and Thine enemies be scattered, and them that hate
Thee flee before Thee.
For out of Zion shall go forth Torah, and the word of the Lord from
Jerusalem.

Since the middle of the sixteenth century, it has been customary
to add a personal meditation at this point—a prayer known as "Brikh
Shemei" ("Blessed is the Name"). It is a beautiful prayer, written in
Aramaic and found in the Zohar (Shemot 26), the classic kabbalistic
commentary upon the Torah. It is said before the open Ark.

Blessed is the Name of the Lord of the universe. Blessed is Thy crown
and Thy abode. May Thy good will always abide with Thy people
Israel. Reveal the saving might of Thy right hand to Thy people in
Thy sanctuary. Affect us by the goodness of Thy light and accept our
prayers in compassion.
May it be Thy will to prolong our lives in well-being and let us be
counted among the righteous, so that Thou mayest have compassion
on me and protect me and mine and all that belong to Thy people
Israel.
Thou art He who sustains and provides for all; Thou art He who rules
over all; Thou art He who rules over kings, and dominion is Thine.
I am the servant of the Holy One, blessed be He, before whom and
before whose glorious Torah I bow at all times.
Not in man do I place my trust, nor on any angel* do I rely, only
in the God of Heaven, who is the true God, whose Torah is true,
whose prophets are true, and who performs many deeds of goodness
and truth.

* The Aramaic *bar-elohim* is found in Daniel 3:25, where it means "an angel";
the literal translation is, however, "son of God." This sentence in the prayer may well
have been meant as a disclaimer of Christianity, which rests its faith on a "son of
God." Judaism affirms only "the God of Heaven . . . ."

In Him do I place my trust and unto His holy and glorious name will I say praises.

May it be Thy will to open my heart to Thy Torah and to fulfill the good wishes of my heart and of the hearts of all Thy people Israel for good, for life, and for peace.

On the festivals, a Biblical verse that lists the Thirteen Attributes of God, and a prayer for our personal welfare, are said before Brikh Shemei. On Rosh Hashanah and Yom Kippur, the personal prayer pleads for forgiveness and pardon. Both versions begin with the words "Ribbono shel olam" ("Master of the universe"). Written by Nathan of Hanover in the latter part of the seventeenth century, the simple and moving words evoke a deep response.

When the Prayer Leader takes the Torah scroll in his arms, he lifts it up and, on weekdays, says the following:

גַּדְּלוּ לַיהוה אִתִּי וּנְרוֹמְמָה שְׁמוֹ יַחְדָּו:

Gadlu la'Adonai iti, uneromemah shemo yaḥdav

Exalt the Lord together with me and let us together extol His name.

(Psalms 34:4)

On Sabbaths, festivals, and the High Holy Days, the Prayer Leader prefaces this with two other verses that are repeated by the congregation. One is the verse of Shema Yisrael: "Hear O Israel, the Lord our God, the Lord is one." The other is:

אֶחָד אֱלֹהֵינוּ, גָּדוֹל אֲדוֹנֵינוּ, קָדוֹשׁ שְׁמוֹ.

Eḥad eloheinu, gadol adoneinu, kadosh shemo

One is our God, great is our Lord, holy is His Name.

(Soferim 14:8)

The congregational response to Gadlu on Sabbaths and weekdays is:

לְךָ יהוה הַגְּדֻלָּה וְהַגְּבוּרָה וְהַתִּפְאֶרֶת וְהַנֵּצַח וְהַהוֹד,
כִּי כֹל בַּשָּׁמַיִם וּבָאָרֶץ. לְךָ יהוה הַמַּמְלָכָה וְהַמִּתְנַשֵּׂא
לְכֹל לְרֹאשׁ:

רוֹמְמוּ יהוה אֱלֹהֵינוּ וְהִשְׁתַּחֲווּ לַהֲדֹם רַגְלָיו קָדוֹשׁ הוּא:
רוֹמְמוּ יהוה אֱלֹהֵינוּ וְהִשְׁתַּחֲווּ לְהַר קָדְשׁוֹ כִּי קָדוֹשׁ יהוה
אֱלֹהֵינוּ:

Thine O Lord is the greatness and the power, the glory and the victory
and the majesty; for all that is in heaven and on earth [is thine];
Thine O Lord is the kingdom, and Thou art exalted above all.

(Chron. I, 29:11)

Exalt the Lord our God and bow down at His Temple, holy is He;
Exalt the Lord our God and bow down at His holy mountain, for the
Lord our God is holy.

(Psalms 99:5, 9)

While the congregation chants this response, the Torah is carried from the Ark to the bimah or table from where it is read. Particularly on Sabbaths and festivals do the synagogue's dignitaries join
in a procession behind the Torah.

Later, when the Torah is returned to the Ark, the Prayer Leader
takes it into his arms and says:

יְהַלְלוּ אֶת שֵׁם יהוה, כִּי נִשְׂגָּב שְׁמוֹ לְבַדּוֹ

Y'hallelu et shem Adonai, ki nisgav shemo levado . . . .

Let them praise the name of the Lord for only His Name is
exalted . . . .

This is the first part of a verse from Psalms (148:13). The
congregation finishes the verse and continues with the very next one:

הוֹדוֹ עַל אֶרֶץ וְשָׁמָיִם: וַיָּרֶם קֶרֶן לְעַמּוֹ, תְּהִלָּה

לְכָל חֲסִידָיוֹ, לִבְנֵי יִשְׂרָאֵל עַם קְרֹבוֹ, הַלְלוּיָהּ:

. . . His glory is beyond earth and heaven.
He has raised the honor of His people.
[He is] a glory for all His faithful,
For the children of Israel, a people close to Him,
Praise the Lord.

The Torah is then carried back to the Ark, again in procession. During the procession, the congregation says Psalm 24 (on week-days) or Psalm 29 (on Sabbaths and festivals). While the Torah is being put back into the Ark, the congregation says a passage, the first verse of which is a continuation of the Biblical passage that was said when the Torah was first taken out of the Ark:

And when [the Ark] rested, he [Moses] said: "Return, O Lord, unto the tens of thousands of Israel".

(Num. 10:36)

The last verse in the passage is from the end of the Book of Lamentations: "Return us unto Thee, O Lord, and we shall return, renew our days as of old."

THE TORAH BLESSINGS

These blessings began to be said when different worshipers were called up to read a portion of the Torah from the Torah scroll. Origi-nally the first Torah blessing was said solely by the first person before he began to read; the second blessing was said only by the last person after he had completed his reading. Those in between read their portion without reciting any blessings at all. This explains why Borkhu, a call to prayer and an invitation to bless God, precedes the first blessing. The first person said it because it was the begin-ning of the Torah reading service, just as the Borkhu said before the Shema marked the beginning of the public worship service. Only during the later Talmudic period, did the sages rule that every one who came up to read from the Torah also had to recite both blessings. This innovation was introduced so as not to deprive any member of the congregation—those arriving after the start of the Torah reading or those leaving before its end—of the chance to hear both blessings (Megillah 21b).

When the number of people capable of reading from the Torah scroll drastically declined in the post-Talmudic period, another innovation was introduced. So as not to embarrass those who could not themselves read, it became customary for one person to read on behalf of all who were called up. Those called to the Torah now had only the blessings to recite, a relatively easy task that was, and is, within the scope of anyone with even the most elementary training. Those capable of reading from the Torah still read along with the Torah Reader in a quiet voice.

The first Torah blessing emphasizes that God chose Israel to receive His Torah. The blessing is a reference to that spiritual event at Sinai.

In the second blessing, the use of the phrase *"planted* within us eternal life" is a reference to the Oral Torah. It parallels Ecclesiastes 12:11: "The words of the sages are *planted* . . ." The Oral Torah, as the key to the continuity, growth, and development of Jewish law, assures the spiritual eternity of the Jewish people.

(The Torah Blessings, the names and the number of aliyot, and detailed instructions on what to do when receiving an aliyah are given in chapter 2, pp. 49–54.)

HAGBAH: RAISING THE TORAH SCROLL

Following a custom that goes back at least to the seventh century C.E., we raise an open Torah scroll in order to hold the Torah script up to the view of the entire congregation (Soferim 14:7:6–8). The custom enjoys a Biblical precedent. "And Ezra opened the Book in the sight of all the people . . ." (Neh. 8:5). The essence of this ritual lies in the opportunity for everyone to see the Torah script and for them to proclaim, "This is the Torah that Moses placed before the children of Israel . . ." (OH 134:2). It was and remains a dramatic moment in the service.

The Torah Reading Service

There is a striking difference between Ashkenazim and Sephardim about the timing of this ritual. In Ashkenazic congregations, the Torah scroll is raised *after* the Torah reading is completed. In Sephardic congregations, the Torah scroll is raised *before* beginning the Torah reading.

The response of the congregation consists of excerpts from two different Biblical verses. The first excerpt is:

וְזֹאת הַתּוֹרָה אֲשֶׁר שָׂם מֹשֶׁה לִפְנֵי בְּנֵי יִשְׂרָאֵל,

V'zot ha-Torah asher sam Moshe lifnei b'nei Yisrael . . .

This is the Torah that Moses placed before the children of Israel . . .

(Deut. 4:44)

The second excerpt (not found in Sephardic prayer books) is:

עַל פִּי יהוה בְּיַד מֹשֶׁה.

al pi Adonai b'yad Mosheh

according to the command of the Lord, by the hand of Moses

(Numbers 9:23)

Although these two excerpts are now run together in Ashkenazic congregations, it is possible that the first excerpt was once said only by the one who raised the Torah, while the second excerpt was the response of the congregation.

(Detailed instructions on how to perform Hagbah are given in chapter 2, pp. 55–56.)

HAFTARAH: READING FROM THE PROPHETS

The Torah reading on Sabbaths and festivals is followed by a short selection from one of the books of the Prophets. Hence, the reading from the Prophets became known as "Haftarah," which means "Concluding Portion." The one called up to read the Haftarah is called the "Maftir" (literally, "one who concludes"). This practice is a very ancient one and precedes the Talmudic period. When and how it started is not known.

The Haftarah is read only at the morning service on Sabbaths and the major festivals. It is not read during a weekday, even if it is Rosh Ḥodesh or ḥol hamoed; nor is it read on Ḥanukkah or Purim. While these are days of celebration, work is not forbidden; and since people would go off to work, the sages did not want to burden them with a longer morning service on these days (Megillah 21a). At Minḥa, a Haftarah is read only on Yom Kippur, Tisha b'Av, and the minor fast days (Megillah 31a).

Unlike the Torah reading, the Haftarah reading need not be consecutive. The criteria used to select the portion of the Prophets was that there be some thematic relationship to the weekly Torah reading or to the special significance of that day or period.

MAFTIR: THE TORAH READING PRECEDING THE HAFTARAH

The Talmudic sages also fixed the rule that the reading of the Haftarah could not be done independently of the Torah reading. The Maftir, the person called up to read from the Prophets, first had to read a portion from the Torah (Megillah 23a; Sotah 39b). This Torah portion is now also designated as Maftir, to distinguish it from the Haftarah, the reading from the Prophets. On an ordinary Sabbath, the Maftir consists of rereading the last few verses (at least three) of the weekly Torah portion. On the festivals, the Sabbath of Rosh Ḥodesh, the Sabbath of Ḥanukkah, and on the Four Special Sabbaths that precede Pesaḥ, the Maftir consists of a special reading from another Torah scroll. The reason given for this ruling was "the honor of the Torah." If the Haftarah reading were independent of the Torah reading, and equal honor extended to both, there might be conveyed the erroneous impression that the Torah and the Prophets are of equal sanctity and authority. And this is not so. The books of the Prophets, though a part of the Bible, are not equal to Torah. By making the reading of the Haftarah dependent on first reading a Torah portion, the sages wished to stress the notion that the books of the Prophets are rooted in Torah, that their teachings are based on Torah, and that their Divine messages were meant to strengthen the loyalty of the people to the teachings of the Torah; in short, they could not be treated independently of Torah.

It is for this reason also that the Maftir aliyah is not counted among the official seven or five aliyot to the Torah on the Sabbaths or the festivals. Maftir is an addition to the required number. And while only an adult male, one over thirteen years of age, may be called to the reading of the Torah, a child under thirteen may be called upon to read the Maftir and Haftarah. (The only exception to this is Parshat Zakhor, when the special Maftir reading is regarded as a Biblical requirement.) Despite the deliberate strategy of downgrading the halakhic status of the Haftarah in relation to the Torah, it has remained a signal honor to receive this aliyah. Persons who merit a special distinction in the synagogue, or who celebrate a special event in their lives, are still accorded the honor of reciting the Haftarah and its accompanying blessings.

THE HAFTARAH BLESSINGS

In addition to the two Torah blessings for the brief Torah reading over which he presides, the Maftir also recites five blessings for the Haftarah reading: one before the Haftarah and four after it. The five blessings collectively symbolize the five books of Moses, whose teachings the Prophets came to implement.

The Blessing Before the Haftarah

The single blessing before the Haftarah expresses praise for the prophets of Israel and affirms the truth of their message. Since there were false prophets who arose from time to time to draw the people away from Torah, the blessing stresses that the true prophets chosen by God were "good," and through them He continues to guide Israel.

בָּרוּךְ אַתָּה יהוה אֱלֹהֵינוּ מֶלֶךְ הָעוֹלָם, אֲשֶׁר
בָּחַר בִּנְבִיאִים טוֹבִים וְרָצָה בְדִבְרֵיהֶם הַנֶּאֱמָרִים
בֶּאֱמֶת. בָּרוּךְ אַתָּה יהוה, הַבּוֹחֵר בַּתּוֹרָה וּבְמֹשֶׁה
עַבְדּוֹ וּבְיִשְׂרָאֵל עַמּוֹ וּבִנְבִיאֵי הָאֱמֶת וָצֶדֶק.

Blessed art Thou, Lord our God, King of the universe, who has chosen good prophets and who was pleased with their words, spoken in truth. Blessed art Thou, Lord, who chooses the Torah and His servant Moses and His people Israel and prophets of truth and righteousness.

The Four Blessings After the Haftarah

The first blessing that follows the Haftarah emphasizes God's truthfulness and His faithfulness in fulfilling His prophecies.

The second blessing is a prayer for the return of the Jewish people to Zion (another name for Jerusalem). Jerusalem can only rejoice if her children return to dwell in her. All the later Hebrew prophets conveyed this same message.

The third blessing is also a prayer for the fulfillment of a prophecy: that Elijah the prophet should gladden us with the news of the coming of the Messiah. The restoration of the House of David is an aspect of the Messianic redemption. This blessing is similar to the theme of the fifteenth blessing in the daily Amidah. (See p. 95.)

The fourth and final blessing is an overall blessing of thanksgiving for the Torah, for the privilege of worshiping God, for the prophets, for the Sabbath that was given to Israel, and for all that God has bestowed on us. It includes the hope that all mankind will someday bless His name.

בָּרוּךְ אַתָּה יהוה אֱלֹהֵינוּ מֶלֶךְ הָעוֹלָם, צוּר
כָּל הָעוֹלָמִים, צַדִּיק בְּכָל הַדּוֹרוֹת, הָאֵל הַנֶּאֱמָן,
הָאוֹמֵר וְעוֹשֶׂה, הַמְדַבֵּר וּמְקַיֵּם, שֶׁכָּל דְּבָרָיו
אֱמֶת וָצֶדֶק. נֶאֱמָן אַתָּה הוּא יהוה אֱלֹהֵינוּ
וְנֶאֱמָנִים דְּבָרֶיךָ, וְדָבָר אֶחָד מִדְּבָרֶיךָ אָחוֹר

לֹא יָשׁוּב רֵיקָם, כִּי אֵל מֶלֶךְ נֶאֱמָן וְרַחֲמָן אָֽתָּה.
בָּרוּךְ אַתָּה יהוה, הָאֵל הַנֶּאֱמָן בְּכָל דְּבָרָיו.

רַחֵם עַל צִיּוֹן, כִּי הִיא בֵּית חַיֵּֽינוּ, וְלַעֲלֽוּבַת
נֶֽפֶשׁ תּוֹשִֽׁיעַ בִּמְהֵרָה בְיָמֵֽינוּ. בָּרוּךְ אַתָּה יהוה,
מְשַׂמֵּֽחַ צִיּוֹן בְּבָנֶֽיהָ.

שַׂמְּחֵֽנוּ יהוה אֱלֹהֵֽינוּ בְּאֵלִיָּֽהוּ הַנָּבִיא עַבְדֶּֽךָ,
וּבְמַלְכוּת בֵּית דָּוִד מְשִׁיחֶֽךָ, בִּמְהֵרָה יָבוֹא וְיָגֵל
לִבֵּֽנוּ. עַל כִּסְאוֹ לֹא יֵֽשֶׁב־זָר, וְלֹא יִנְחֲלוּ עוֹד
אֲחֵרִים אֶת כְּבוֹדוֹ, כִּי בְשֵׁם קָדְשְׁךָ נִשְׁבַּֽעְתָּ לּוֹ,
שֶׁלֹּא יִכְבֶּה נֵרוֹ לְעוֹלָם וָעֶד. בָּרוּךְ אַתָּה יהוה,
מָגֵן דָּוִד.

עַל הַתּוֹרָה וְעַל הָעֲבוֹדָה וְעַל הַנְּבִיאִים וְעַל
יוֹם הַשַּׁבָּת הַזֶּה, שֶׁנָּתַֽתָּ לָּֽנוּ, יהוה אֱלֹהֵֽינוּ, לִקְדֻשָּׁה
וְלִמְנוּחָה, לְכָבוֹד וּלְתִפְאָֽרֶת. עַל הַכֹּל, יהוה
אֱלֹהֵֽינוּ, אֲנַֽחְנוּ מוֹדִים לָךְ וּמְבָרְכִים אוֹתָךְ.
יִתְבָּרַךְ שִׁמְךָ בְּפִי כָּל חַי תָּמִיד לְעוֹלָם וָעֶד.
בָּרוּךְ אַתָּה יהוה, מְקַדֵּשׁ הַשַּׁבָּת.

Blessed art Thou, Lord our God, King of the universe, Rock of all
worlds, righteous through all generations, the faithful God who
says and does, who speaks and fulfills, for all His words are true
and just.
Faithful art Thou, Lord our God, and faithful are Thy words,
Not one of Thy promises will remain unfulfilled,
For Thou art a faithful and merciful God King.
Blessed art Thou, Lord, the God who is faithful in all His words.

Have mercy on Zion, for it is the focus of our lives;

245

Save her wretched of soul speedily in our own day.
Blessed art Thou, Lord, who makes Zion rejoice in her children.

Gladden us, O Lord our God, with [the coming of] Elijah, the
prophet, Thy servant,
And with the kingdom of the House of David, Thy annointed;
May he soon come and make our hearts rejoice.
Let no stranger sit on his throne, nor let others any longer inherit
his glory.
For Thou did swear to him by Thy Holy name, that his light would
never be extinguished.
Blessed art Thou, Lord, Shield of David.

For the Torah, for the worship, for the prophets,
And for this Sabbath day that Thou, O Lord our God did give us,
For holiness and rest, for honor and glory;—for everything, O Lord
our God,
We thank Thee and bless Thee;
Blessed be Thy name in the mouth of every living being continually
and forever;
Blessed art Thou, Lord, who sanctifies the Sabbath.

There are slight variations in the last blessing on the festivals,
as well as on Rosh Hashanah and Yom Kippur. The name of the
holiday is substituted for "the Sabbath" (or added to it, as the case
may be). The ending of the last Haftarah blessing always parallels
the conclusion of the middle blessing in the Musaf Amidah of that
day (except on the Sabbath that occurs during hol hamoed Pesah).
In his commentary on the prayer book, Rabbi Issachar Jacobson
raises the question why the sages saw fit to embellish the Haftarah
with so many more blessings than accompany the Torah reading. This
is particularly perplexing in view of the sages' consistency in main-
taining a lesser halakhic status for the Haftarah. Furthermore, why
did they include seemingly unrelated blessings about Zion and the
kingdom of David? The answer he suggests is based on the assumption that the reading from the prophets was first instituted in reaction
to the Samaritans, a sect that accepted the Books of Moses as sacred
scripture but rejected the sanctity of the prophetic writings. The
blessings for the Haftarah were formulated, then, to emphasize all the

ideological points of difference from the Samaritans (Netiv Binah II, p. 230).

And so in the blessing before the Haftarah, we affirm—contrary to Samaritan belief—that just as God chose the Written Torah, Moses, and Israel, so did He choose the prophets and their teachings.

In the blessings after the Haftarah, we affirm our faith in the centrality of Jerusalem—in contrast to the Samaritans, who considered Shekhem (Nablus) as the religious center of their faith and who chose Mt. Gerizim instead of Mt. Zion for their holy temple. We also emphasize the view that the Messiah will come from the House of David, of the tribe of Judah; and we pray that "no stranger sit on his throne." This is in contrast to the Samaritans, who placed their Messianic aspirations on one who will come forth from the tribe of Ephraim.

The whole purpose of reading the Haftarah was thus to strengthen Jewish faith in the sanctity of the prophetic writings, in the holiness of Jerusalem, and in the messianic destiny of the Davidic dynasty. The Haftarah blessings clearly reflect this purpose.

We may no longer be struggling against Samaritans or Zoroastrians, or Sadducees, or Karaites, but these blessings, as do all the others in the prayer book, continue to bring the essential doctrines of Judaism and the basic beliefs of the Jewish people to the attention of all who come to pray as Jews.

THE GABBAIM AND THEIR DUTIES

From the very beginning, it was customary for someone to stand alongside the person who read from the Torah and to provide whatever assistance was necessary. He would stand prepared quietly to correct the pronunciation or trop. That one does not stand alone on the bimah when reading from the Torah is based on a Talmudic teaching which emphasizes the point that God gave the Torah to Israel through an intermediary (Moses). In that same spirit, we arrange to always have at least three persons standing on the bimah.

The Torah Reader is then, so to speak, the intermediary between the synagogue official who summons people to the Torah (as God summoned Israel) and the one called to the Torah who represents the people receiving the Torah (OH 141:4; MB:16). Inasmuch as a meturgeman, who translated each Torah sentence as it was read, later also took his place on the bimah, two people always flanked the one reading from the Torah.

This arrangement has come down to us in the practice of two synagogue officials who stand on either side of the Reading Table while the Torah is read. The men who do so are called *gabbaim* (sing. *gabbai*).

It would be correct to identify the two gabbaim as an *honor guard* to the Torah. But they also have definite responsibilities. The most important is the very same responsibility that first gave rise to this practice. The Torah Reader reads from a scroll that is not punctuated and has no vowel signs. It is easy for him to make a mistake. It is the duty of the gabbaim carefully to follow the reading from a printed text and quietly to correct the Torah Reader should he err.

One of the two gabbaim is usually assigned the responsibility of calling the people up to the Torah and reciting the special Mi She'beirakh prayers after each aliyah. In some congregations, these duties are left to the sexton.

The gabbai should be the one to cover the Torah scroll with its mantle after each man called to the Torah completes the second blessing. He does this so the Torah scroll will not lie ignored while the Mi She'beirakh is recited. When the next person called up is ready to begin the first blessing, he removes the mantle.

THE FATHER'S BLESSING AT A SON'S BAR-MITZVAH

It is customary for the father of a Bar-Mitzvah boy to recite a special blessing on the day that the boy is first called to the Torah. The father says it after his son concludes the second Torah blessing. The father's blessing is:

The Torah Reading Service

Barukh sheptarani mei'ansho shelazeh.

Blessed is [He] who has acquitted me from this one's [the boy's]
punishment.   (Bereshit Rabbah 63:14)

The rationale for saying this blessing is that until the age of
thirteen, it is the father's responsibility to see that his son studies
Torah; from that age onward, the responsibility for keeping this
mitzvah devolves entirely upon the son. If the son neglects to do so,
the father is exempt from whatever spiritual punishment is due for
this transgression of omission.

Despite the father's blessing, with its disclaimer of formal responsibility, he would be remiss in his duties if he were to regard himself as absolved of all responsibility for continuing to provide his
children, daughters as well as sons, with much-needed spiritual and
moral guidance, and with the opportunities for them to pursue Torah
study. The halakhic duty to advise and counsel remains in force (OH
225:2, Rema; MB 6–8). The steps taken by parents to guide children
during their formative adolescent years may be their greatest invest-
ment in their own ultimate peace of mind; it is, in fact, its own reward.
In the words of Proverbs: "Correct your child and he will give you
rest; yea, he will give delight unto your soul" (29:17).

THE BLESSING OF "GOMEL"

Judaism teaches us that it is a great virtue to say "thank you."
And so in many of the daily prayers, we render thanksgiving to God
for the benefits that He regularly bestows upon us. But occasionally a
person has special reason to be grateful. The Talmud says that anyone who survives a serious illness, or is freed from imprisonment,
or returns from a perilous journey through a wilderness, or from a sea
voyage, that person is required to give thanks to God (Berakhot 54b).

The inspiration for this Talmudic ruling comes from Psalm 107,
which describes deliverance from four kinds of dangers common in
those times. After each danger, the Psalmist says: "Let them give
thanks to the Lord for His mercy, and for His wonders to human
beings" (Ps. 107:8, 15, 21, 31).

The blessing, known as *Birkat haGomel* is said in the presence of a minyan. To publicly acknowledge God's saving deed, while implying that we are undeserving of His concern, is a greater tribute to God's loving kindness than if we were to say it privately. This way, one also lets others know about the personal miracle that God has performed. If a minyan cannot be convened, however, the blessing may be said without one (OH 219:3; MB:8).

The Gomel blessing is as follows:

בָּרוּךְ אַתָּה יהוה אֱלֹהֵינוּ מֶלֶךְ הָעוֹלָם, הַגּוֹמֵל לְחַיָּבִים טוֹבוֹת, שֶׁגְּמָלַנִי כָּל טוֹב.

Barukh atah Adonai eloheinu melekh ha-olam ha-gomel l'hayavim tovot, she'gemalani kol tov.

Blessed art Thou, Lord our God, King of the universe who bestows favors on the undeserving, for having shown me every goodness.

Those who hear this blessing respond, in addition to "Amen," as follows:

מִי שֶׁגְּמָלְךָ טוֹב, הוּא יִגְמָלְךָ כָּל טוֹב, סֶלָה.

Mi she-gemalkha kol tov, hu yigmalkha kol tov selah.

May He who bestowed every goodness upon you, continue to bestow every goodness upon you forever.

It is now customary for men to say this blessing when called to the Torah for an aliyah. It is said aloud immediately after the second Torah blessing. If for any reason, one does not receive an aliyah that day, one may still come up to the bimah, usually at the conclusion of the Torah reading, to publicly recite the blessing.

Although it is not customary for women to recite this blessing, it is proper for them to do so. Some say it at home in the presence of male and female family and friends—even in the absence of a formal minyan of ten men. It is especially appropriate to do so after childbirth.

Religious authorities are divided on the question of whether the Gomel blessing is said only in the four specific instances cited in the Talmud or after safely passing through any dangerous situation. Ashkenazic practice follows the latter view (OH 219:9; MA:10).

The blessing is surely required today in the aftermath of an accident, or any serious illness where one's life is in peril.

Some religious authorities require the recitation of the blessing after every plane flight, even if routine and uneventful. They compare a plane flight to a ship going out to sea. The issue here is not whether the plane crosses an ocean, but the fact that there has been a severance from terra firma. An airplane, like a ship, loses contact with land, and the danger inherent in that separation is even greater for a plane than for a ship. The safe return to terra firma is the wondrous act for which thanksgiving is given (Igrot Moshe OH II:59). Other authorities feel that the Gomel blessing ought to be reserved for those moments when one truly feels a sense of relief from danger and special gratefulness to God. They object to the everyday use of this blessing and question whether routine travel in modern aircraft whose safety record surpasses the automobile qualifies as a perilous journey, for which the blessing was originally prescribed.

MI SHE'BEIRAKH: A PRAYER FOR ALL OCCASIONS

The opening words of Mi She'beirakh are: *"He who blessed* our fathers, Abraham, Isaac and Jacob, may He bless . . . ."* There is no standard text beyond this. What follows depends on the occasion and the purpose.

It is now customary for the gabbai or the sexton to invoke this prayer when the one who is called up to the Torah finishes reciting the Torah blessings. In this case the words that follow are:

> May He bless . . . son of . . . who has come up to honor God and the Torah. May the Holy One, blessed be He, protect and deliver him from all distress and illness and send blessing and success upon every-

thing he does, together with all of Israel his brethren, and let us say Amen.

This prayer is also said by the gabbai or the sexton on behalf of a sick person. Any worshiper is entitled to request that it be said. In this case, the words that follow the opening formula are:

. . . may He heal . . . son/daughter of . . . who is ill. May the Holy One, blessed be He, be filled with mercy for him/her, to heal and cure him/her, to strengthen him/her to perfect health, and to speedily send him/her a complete recovery, both in spirit and in body, and let us say Amen.

Should the person called to the Torah request this prayer, the gabbai will say it at the same time that he says the usual Mi She'beirakh.

There is a Mi She'beirakh on behalf of a couple about to be married. When a groom is called to the Torah before the wedding (aufruf), the prayer invokes God's blessing upon the bride and bridegroom with a wish for their happiness and for their success in building a faithful Jewish home.

When a child is born, a Mi She'beirakh is recited for the health of the mother and the newborn child. If the newborn is a girl, the Mi She'beirakh also includes a formula for naming the child. (A male child is named at the Circumcision.)

The Mi She'beirakh recited after a Bar-Mitzvah boy is called to the Torah makes reference to this event and expresses the hope that he will continue to serve God all his life and be a source of pride and joy to his parents and to the Jewish people.

Still other Mi-She'beirakh prayers are said after the Torah reading on Sabbaths and festivals, before the scrolls are returned to the Ark. The best-known is one for the entire congregation and cites those who devote themselves to good works, and who extend themselves on behalf of the community.

The Mi She'beirakh formula may have also been used at one time for reciting a prayer for the king. Today it is called "A Prayer for the Government" and is said after the reading of the Torah in every country where Jews live. Its opening words are now *Hanotein teshuah lamelakhim* ("He who grants victory to rulers . . ."). (See Netiv Binah II, p. 234.)

Though the custom of praying for the welfare of the government did not become part of synagogue liturgy until about the fourteenth century, it is based on an ancient tradition. The prophet Jeremiah wrote to the Jews who were exiled from Judea to Babylonia: "Seek the welfare of the city to which the Lord exiled you, and pray to God for her, for in her peace will you also find peace" (Jer. 29:7). In the book of Ezra (6:10), we read that the Jews "prayed for the life of the king and his sons."

The Mishnah records the view of Rabbi Ḥaninah "to pray for the welfare of the government for were it not for the fear of the government, men would swallow each other up alive" (Avot 3:2). This is a frightening description of anarchy, but the Talmud's explanation of this assessment highlights its essential truth, not only for primitive society, but for many places in the world today. Commenting upon a verse in Ḥabakuk (1:14) that compares men to the fish in the sea, the Talmud says: "Just as with the fish in the sea, the big fish swallow up the small fish, so among people, were it not for the fear of the rulers, people would swallow each other up alive" (Avodah Zarah 3:2). Apart from those instances where the government itself is the greatest menace to the people, were it not for the laws, the courts, and the police, the law of the jungle would prevail. And so a prayer for the welfare of those institutions which contribute to a stable and orderly society became an integral part of synagogue custom.

In addition to the Mi She'beirakh prayers said during and after the reading of the Torah, there are two more prayers that do not begin with the Mi She'beirakh prescript, but that nevertheless are an extension of its spirit and form. These two prayers are said only on Sabbaths. They were originally said in Aramaic and have come down to us in that language. They begin with the words *Yekum purkan* ("May salvation arise"). The first Yekum Purkan, composed in Babylonia, is a prayer for the scholars, the rabbis, and the heads of the yeshivot and their disciples. The second Yekum Purkan, composed in Europe at a much later date, is in the same style, and is a prayer for the whole congregation, like the Hebrew Mi She'beirakh mentioned earlier. But while the latter cites those who perform public service, the second Yekum Purkan cites those who study Torah.

In our own times, a prayer composed by the Chief Rabbinate of Israel for the welfare of the State of Israel has also been incorporated into this series of prayers recited after the Torah reading. In Israel, the prayer for the state is accompanied by yet another Mi She'beirakh that invokes God's blessing upon the soldiers who serve in Israel's Defense Forces.

Attention should be called to a custom that once considerably lengthened the service and invited restlessness, but which is now practiced in only a few places. The person receiving an aliyah requests to have a Mi She'beirakh blessing invoked upon family or friends. Where this is practiced, the people blessed are mentioned by name. When requesting this blessing the custom involves the person's adding a pledge of charity to a specific cause, usually the synagogue itself. The abuse of this custom in some synagogues made the Hebrew word used to announce the amount "that he pledged" (she'nader) synonymous in Yiddish slang with mendicity.

UPON COMPLETING ONE OF THE FIVE BOOKS OF MOSES: ḤAZAK, ḤAZAK!

When the last sentence of each of the Five Books of Moses is about to be read, everyone rises in anticipation of proclaiming at the end of the reading:

Ḥazak, ḥazak v'nitḥazek

Be strong! be strong! and let us be strengthened [in our efforts].

This is a cry of encouragement to continue with the reading of the next Book, and to return to this one again in due course. The triple use of *ḥazak* may symbolize the past, present, and future.

The inspiration for saying these words in connection with finishing a section of the Torah may have come from the Talmudic dictum that "Four [elements] need to be strengthened [in Man]: Torah, good deeds, prayer, and occupation (*derekh eretz*)" (Berakhot 32b). The scriptural basis for this saying lies in the following verses:

To be strengthened in Torah:

Only be strong and very brave so that you may observe all the Torah that Moses My servant commanded you. (Josh. 1:7)

To be strengthened in prayer:

Be strong and let your heart be brave, and hope in the Lord.
(Psalms 27:14)

To be strengthened in good deeds and derekh eretz:

Be strong and let us strengthen ourselves for our people and for the cities of God. (Sam. II 10:12)

13

Welcoming the Sabbath:
Kabbalat Shabbat

THE FRIDAY evening prayer service has a character all its own. It is marked by congregational singing and by a mood of joyous anticipation. The most striking difference in the contents of this service from that of all other nights of the week is the addition of a preliminary service called *Kabbalat Shabbat* ("Welcoming the Sabbath"). This addition is of relatively recent origin. It was introduced by the kabbalistic scholars of Safed during the middle of the sixteenth century. From there it spread to Jewish communities all over the world, gradually gaining acceptance as an integral part of the Friday evening service.

However popular it became, it is not considered obligatory. The nonobligatory status is still reflected in a practice, followed in many congregations, of conducting this part of the service from the bimah where the Torah is read and not from the podium ("amud") where the prayers are conducted. There are even communities where local tradition dictates that the Prayer Leader does not put on a tallit for Kabbalat Shabbat. This, in effect, stresses the same point.

Welcoming the Sabbath: Kabbalat Shabbat

The idiom "kabbalat Shabbat" has two distinct connotations. One implies "welcoming"; the other implies "acceptance." In halakhic literature, it is the latter connotation that is dominant. Just as on a fast day, one could "accept" the fast earlier than the time set for its obligatory commencement, by declaring it to be in effect for oneself from that moment on—so a person could declare even before sundown that for him the Sabbath has begun. Any statement that takes note of the start of the Sabbath constitutes its acceptance. This is the moment of kabbalat Shabbat.

That is what the sages meant by kabbalat Shabbat when they used these words in ruling that the saying of Borkhu (at the start of the Maariv service) constituted the precise moment when one accepted the Sabbath. From that moment on, all work was forbidden even if the sun had not yet set. When it became customary to preface Maariv with Psalm 92 (A Psalm: A Song for the Sabbath Day), this became the moment of kabbalat Shabbat. For the woman who lights the Sabbath candles, it is customarily that act which marks the acceptance of the Sabbath (see OH 263:10, Rema).

Ever since Kabbalat Shabbat became the title to a section of prayers that consists of songs and hymns welcoming the Sabbath, it is the connotation of welcome that has become the more established.

The Kabbalat Shabbat service consists of three distinct components:

1. A series of six psalms (Psalms 95–99 and 29) followed by a short mystical poem.
2. The hymn *Lekhah Dodi* ("Come, My Friend").
3. Psalm 92 (A Psalm: A Song for the Sabbath Day) and Psalm 93.

THE SIX PSALMS

The custom of reciting six psalms before the hymn of Lekhah Dodi, which is the heart of this service, is ascribed to Rabbi Moshe Cordovero (1522–1570). The first of these psalms begins with the words *Lekhu n'ranenah l'Adonai* ("Come, let us sing before the

Lord"). The six psalms all express the theme of God's sovereignty, and symbolize the six working days of the week. For each day, we say a psalm that acknowledges God as King and Ruler of the universe. A psalm for the seventh day is said right after Lekhah Dodi.

There is a view that the recitation of six psalms before the start of the Sabbath can be traced back to the ninth century c.e. According to this view, the recitation of six psalms, not necessarily the same ones we say today, was instituted in Babylonia to commemorate the long, discontinued practice of blowing six shofar blasts to signal the approaching Sabbath. This would be done at regular intervals every Friday afternoon during the days of the Temple (Shabbat 35b).

The last of the six psalms, Psalm 29, Mizmor l'David, has special symbolic significance. The Talmud suggests a connection between this psalm and the Amidah. The reason that the weekday Amidah was first organized around eighteen blessings and the Sabbath Amidah around seven blessings was to relate it to the psalm where God's name is mentioned eighteen times, while the phrase "voice of God" (kol Adonai) is used seven times (Berakhot 28b, 29a). The Talmud also suggests that this psalm contains an allusion to the order and theme of the first three blessings in the Amidah (Megillah 17b). This psalm's symbolic association with the weekday and Sabbath Amidah may explain why it was chosen to mark the transition from the weekday to the Sabbath and why it became customary to stand while saying it.

A short prayer of the mystics, Ana, bekhoaḥ, was appended to Psalm 29 by the kabbalists. The prayer is ascribed to a second century Talmudic sage, Neḥunya ben ha-Kanah. It mentions seven designations for the "names of God": Nora ("Awesome One"), Gibor ("Mighty One"), Ḥasin ("Almighty"), Kadosh ("Holy One"), Yaḥid ("One and Only"), Ga-eh ("Exalted One"), Yodeia Ta-alumot ("Knower of Inmost Thoughts"). These designations are said to correspond to the seven "voices of God" mentioned in Psalm 29. Furthermore, this prayer contains forty-two words that correspond to a composite name of God, a phrase consisting of forty-two letters that was once used as a substitute for the Tetragrammaton (Kiddushin 71a). That name and its meaning are unknown to us today. (See Maim. Guide to the Perplexed, I:62).

THE HYMN OF LEKHAH DODI

The hymn of Lekhah Dodi was composed by Rabbi Shlomo Halevy Alkabetz (1505–1584), one of the kabbalists of Safed. He arranged the poetical composition so that the first letter of each stanza spells out the name of the author, a practice quite common among liturgical poets. Although several versions of a hymn by this name had been circulating at that time, this is the one that was adopted by Rabbi Isaac Luria, the foremost authority among the kabbalistic masters.

After the Minḥa service, as the sun cast its setting rays over the distant hilltops, this saintly mystic and his disciples would go out into the fields to stand on one of Safed's magnificent slopes. Gazing out upon plunging ravines and soaring heights, they would open their hearts in song as the sunset swelled into a cadence of changing colors:

לְכָה דוֹדִי לִקְרַאת כַּלָּה, פְּנֵי שַׁבָּת נְקַבְּלָה.

Lekhah dodi, likrat kallah;
P'nai Shabbat, nekablah.

Come, my dear friend, to meet the bride;
The Sabbath presence, let us welcome.

This refrain concludes each of the nine stanzas of the hymn, in which Biblical phrases are pieced together to create a liturgical mosaic. Only the first two and the last stanzas relate to the Sabbath theme. The rest reflect the Jewish longing for redemption, which includes the restoration of Jerusalem and the coming of the Messiah. Each of these other six stanzas describes another stage in the process of redemption.

The words of the refrain and the last two words of the hymn were taken from the Talmud. The Talmud relates that every Sabbath eve, Rabbi Ḥanina would don his finest garments and declare: "Come, let us go out to meet the Sabbath Queen." Rabbi Yannai likewise put on his festive clothes and declared: "Come, O Bride, Come, O Bride" (Shabbat 119a; Bava Kama 32b).

We no longer go outdoors to welcome the Sabbath Bride. But we do turn around to face westward in the direction of the setting sun, which signals the arrival of the Sabbath. This we do while reciting the last stanza of the Lekha Dodi hymn. A slight bow is effected when saying *Bo'i Kallah, Bo'i Kallah,* "Come, O Bride, Come, O Bride."

The personification of the Sabbath as a Bride and as a Queen, both of which convey the imagery of beauty and radiance, testifies to the tremendous affection that the Sabbath enjoyed among the people. The Midrash is the basis for the idea that God mated the Jewish people with the Sabbath (Bereshit Rabbah 11:9). Hence, the notion of a beloved bride whose arrival is eagerly awaited and joyously welcomed.

PSALM 92: A SONG FOR THE SABBATH DAY

Psalm 92 is a psalm of thanksgiving. It sings the praises of God, who in the fullness of time will destroy the wicked and cause the righteous to blossom forth. It also raises the ancient problem about the prosperity of the wicked and the misfortune of the righteous and answers by saying, appearances to the contrary notwithstanding, the wicked are doomed to destruction, the righteous are destined to endure. The wise understand this; fools do not.

Apart from its title, "Mizmor Shir l'Yom Ha-Shabbat," ("A Psalm, a Song for the Sabbath Day"), there is no other mention of the Sabbath in this psalm. It may have been designated for the Sabbath simply because this was the psalm that the Levites sang in the Temple on the Sabbath day. But inasmuch as its theme of reward and punishment involves the belief in a world-to-come (see the discussion on pp. 153–154), the title could be a veiled reference to Olam Haba ("world-to-come"), which is described in the Mishnah as a *yom she'kulo Shabbat* ("a day which is all-Sabbath").

Whatever the case, the saying of this psalm marks the formal start of the Sabbath. We stand when saying it, out of deference to the incoming Sabbath, much as we might rise to greet a distinguished visitor upon his entrance.

This psalm is also said twice on Sabbath mornings, once during the Pesukei d'Zimra, and again at the end of the service as the psalm of the day. It has become customary to add the five short verses of Psalm 93 to Psalm 92.

BAMEH MADLIKIN: WITH WHAT MAY WE LIGHT?

Bameh Madlikin ("With What May We Light [the Sabbath lamps]?"), are the opening words of a Mishnah (Shabbat, Chapter Two). The reading of this entire chapter of Mishnah was first introduced into the service by the Babylonian Geonim in the ninth century, and since then it has been part of the Friday evening prayer service, said either after Maariv or after Minḥa. It is now most commonly said, in the Ashkenazic and Sephardic rites, following the psalm for the Sabbath day, just before Maariv (OH 270:1; MB:2).

The saying of this Talmudic chapter as part of the Friday evening service has nothing to do with Kabbalat Shabbat. Its introduction to the service may have a prosaic explanation, that accounts for the fact that at one time in the Ashkenazic rite, Bameh Madlikin was said at the very end of Maariv. This was done simply to prolong the service so as to allow latecomers to finish their prayers before the congregation dispersed. Walking back alone from the synagogue after dark was a dangerous thing to do in Babylonia in those days. Out of consideration for everyone's safety, the congregation was kept a while longer in the synagogue so that all could leave together. In numbers, there was greater safety.

This particular chapter was picked for this purpose since it deals with rules that relate to preparing for the Sabbath. It discusses the selection of proper wicks and oils for the Sabbath lights, and contains a statement of the three things a man must remind his household on Sabbath eve toward dusk: "Did you tithe? Did you prepare the *eruv*?* Light the Sabbath lights!"

* The eruv is an arrangement that halakhically combines adjoining courtyards or domains, forming a legal unit for the purpose of carrying or removing items on the Sabbath from one domain to another.

There is reason to suspect that there was still another motivation for choosing this particular chapter over so many others. Since almost all of it deals with the lighting of the Sabbath lights, it may have been chosen deliberately to emphasize the obligation of kindling lights for the Sabbath. This was in sharp contrast with the practice of the Karaite sect, who did not recognize the validity of the Oral Torah (Talmud). It was their view that not only did the Torah forbid the kindling of a fire on the Sabbath, it also forbade keeping a fire burning on the Sabbath. In keeping with this strict interpretation of Scripture, they sat in darkness throughout the Sabbath. In Bameh Madlikin, the halakha as it was handed down through the rabbis is emphasized.

In the older Sephardic rite, Bameh Madlikin used to be said immediately after Minḥa, because it contains reminders of what still needs to be done to prepare for the Sabbath. If someone truly forgot something, there would still be time to take care of it at the last minute. If it were delayed till after Maariv, the value of the reminder would be lost.

A short aggadic passage from the end of Tractate Berakhot (64a) concludes Bameh Madlikin. Since the Rabbinical Kaddish is recited only after aggadah and not after the study of halakha, this makes it possible to conclude this part of the service with Kaddish. Since halakhic discourses are ordinarily concluded with another aggadic passage from the end of Tractate Makkot (attributed to Rabbi Ḥanania ben Akashya), two reasons are given for the choice of this passage. One reason is that this aggadah concludes with a prayer for peace, and therefore parallels the conclusion of other prayers, such as the Amidah and the Kaddish, that also conclude with such a prayer. But it may also have been chosen because it was said in the name of Rabbi Ḥanina. Since the entire Kabbalat Shabbat service can be said to have been inspired by Rabbi Ḥanina, who said, "Come, let us go out to greet the Sabbath Queen," it is only fitting to conclude Kabbalat Shabbat with an aggadic lesson attributed to him.

WHEN THE SABBATH COINCIDES WITH A FESTIVAL

At first, most of the Kabbalat Shabbat service was omitted only when Friday coincided with a festival. This rule was later extended to include those Fridays that coincided with the intermediate days of a festival (ḥol hamoed), and that preceded the festival days that fell on the Sabbath.

In the Ashkenazic rite, only the Psalm for the Sabbath Day is said before Maariv. In the Sephardic and Ḥasidic rites, Psalm 29 (Mizmor l'David), and the first two and last two stanzas of Lekhah Dodi are also said preceding the Psalm for the Sabbath Day.

The traditional reason for shortening the Welcome to the Sabbath is not to offend the festival. If two guests were invited to a home, one a more important personage than the other, the wise and sensitive host would take care not to treat one guest with more deference or fanfare than the other.

Bameh Madlikin is omitted on these occasions for an entirely different reason. When Friday coincided with a festival, there was no need to prolong the service to accommodate latecomers, since it was not a work day. Furthermore tithing is not permitted on such a day; consequently the reminder to do so, contained in Bameh Madlikin, would be misleading.

CHAPTER

14

Prayers for Special Occasions

ANNIVERSARIES of major events in Jewish history inspire special remembrance. These are all reflected in the prayer book, through the addition of prayers or blessings intended for special occasions of this kind. This chapter will be devoted to explaining some of these prayers.

HALLEL: HYMNS OF PRAISE

Six psalms (113–118), collectively known as *Hallel* (Hymns of Praise), are said immediately following the Shaḥarit Amidah on the major festivals of Pesaḥ, Shavuot, and Sukkot, on the minor holiday of Ḥanukkah, and on Rosh Ḥodesh. These hymns, composed by King David, were the spontaneous outpourings of his heart in response to God's wondrous miracles and saving powers. The beauty of David's compositions remains unsurpassed, and as the sages did not want to leave the singing of God's praises to chance, they made the recitation of these psalms a religious obligation for the Biblical festivals of Pesaḥ, Shavuot, and Sukkot. Some are of the opinion that the recitation of Hallel on these festivals should be regarded as a mitzvah of the Torah, satisfying a Biblical obligation.

The Talmud also tells us that the prophets prescribed that hymns of praise to God are to be said whenever we celebrate historic events that commemorate the deliverance of our people from dire peril (Pesaḥim 117a). Saying Hallel on Ḥanukkah, aside from "publicizing the miracle," is in keeping with this requirement. This is also the halakhic basis for the ruling of the Israeli Chief Rabbinate in our own day for saying Hallel on *Yom Atzmaut* (the "Day of [Israeli] Independence"), and on *Yom Yerushalayim* ("Jerusalem Day").

The mood and tempo of Hallel make it most appropriate for festivals and for days of national rejoicing. It expresses jubilation and celebration. The music to which it is sung reflects high spirits and exuberance. The verse from Psalm 118 sums up the spirit of the entire Hallel: "This is the day which the Lord God made, we will be glad and rejoice therein."

Hallel is conspicuous by its omission on Rosh Hashanah and Yom Kippur, days that are otherwise counted among the Biblical festivals (*moadim*), and by its omission on Purim, a holiday which also celebrates a deliverance from danger. Hallel is not said on Rosh Hashanah and Yom Kippur because these festivals were not intended for excessive rejoicing. "They are days of repentance, reverence and awe," explains Maimonides. The Talmud elaborates on why Hallel is especially inappropriate for these Days of Judgment: "Is it seemly for the King to be sitting on His throne of judgment with the Books of Life and of Death open before Him and for the people to sing joyful praises to Him?" (Arakhin 10b).

The sages give different reasons for not saying Hallel on Purim. First, Hallel is not said for miracles that happen outside the borders of Eretz Yisrael. Purim of course celebrates an event that occurred in Persia. Second, the special reading of Megillat Esther on Purim is a form of praise equivalent to Hallel. (Maim. Hil. Hanukkah 3:6.) Third, and perhaps the most convincing reason of all, is that while the Jews of Persia were saved and there was real cause for celebration, they did not gain complete freedom. They remained under foreign rule, subjects of King Artaxerxes (Aḥasuerus)—and Hallel is not said for such a partial deliverance (Arakhin 10b).

A peculiarity in the saying of Hallel is the omission of the first eleven verses of Psalm 115 and of Psalm 116 on the last six days of Passover and on Rosh Ḥodesh. When Hallel is said with these omissions, it is called "Half Hallel," although I prefer the term abridged Hallel because the omission of two short passages hardly cuts it in half. Why is a shorter or abridged Hallel said on these days?

The Midrash offers an ethical, humanitarian explanation for the practice on the last day(s) of Passover. The last day(s) of Passover commemorates the crossing of Yam Suf by the Israelites, an event that climaxed their successful escape from the pursuing Egyptians. While this final chapter in the exodus from Egypt merits joyous praise of God, countless Egyptian soldiers did drown in the sea at the time. Jewish ethics is guided by the verse in Proverbs (24:17) "Rejoice not over the fall of your enemy . . ." One midrash pictures God as rebuking the ministering angels who wished to offer to Him a paean of praise: "Creations of My hands are drowning in the sea, and you would sing to Me!" Because Egyptians suffered in the process of our deliverance, the sages decreed that Hallel be shortened to symbolize the lessening of the festival joy (Yalkut Shimoni 247).

And since an abridged Hallel is said on the sacred last day(s) of Pesaḥ, when we abstain from all work, it is not regarded as seemly to say a complete Hallel on the less sacred, intermediate days of the holiday when some work is permitted. And so, out of deference to the last days, the abridged Hallel is said also during ḥol hamoed.

The Talmud, however, offers an halakhic explanation for not saying the complete Hallel on the last six days of Pesaḥ though it is said throughout the week of Sukkot. Each day of Sukkot has its own distinct sacrificial offerings unlike Pesaḥ when each day's offering remains the same. Each day of Sukkot is therefore endowed with the status of an independent holiday requiring its own full expression of joy. Greater significance is thus conferred on the intermediate days of Sukkot than upon those of Pesaḥ (Arakhin 10a, b).

The saying of an abridged Hallel on Rosh Ḥodesh is based on entirely different considerations. Although Scripture associates it with the festivals, Rosh Ḥodesh was not one of the days for which the Mishnah prescribes the saying of Hallel. This is because it is not a day sanctified by abstention from work (Arakhin 10b). Hallel was introduced into the liturgy of Rosh Ḥodesh as a result of a custom that originated in Babylonia during the later Talmudic period. The

Babylonian custom, however, was to say only the abridged form in order to call attention to its then nonobligatory character. And so it has remained (Taanit 28b).

Like all religious duties, even those of rabbinic origin, the recitation of Hallel is preceded by the recitation of a blessing. Maimonides ruled that the Hallel on Rosh Ḥodesh should not be accompanied by a blessing since the saying of Hallel on Rosh Ḥodesh is only a custom, and one does not recite a blessing over a custom (Hil. Ḥanukkah 3:7). Maimonides' ruling on this point is adhered to by Sephardic congregations, but among Ashkenazim it did not prevail, and the blessing is said even on Rosh Ḥodesh.* The blessing for Hallel is:

> Blessed art Thou, Lord our God, King of the universe, who sanctified us with His commandments and commanded us to read the Hallel.

In time, it became customary also to conclude Hallel with a blessing ending with, ". . . Blessed art Thou, Lord, a King extolled in psalms of praise."

We stand when saying Hallel because it is a testimony to God's wondrous deeds and powers, and because testimony in Jewish courts is always given while standing. Also, it is in keeping with the verses: "*Give praise*, ye servants of the Lord; you who *stand* in the house of the Lord" (Psalms 135:1–2).

Hallel was not meant to be said on the nights of the festivals because the first paragraph of Hallel (Psalm 113) speaks of praising God's name "from the rising of the sun until its setting" (Megillah 20b). The first night(s) of Passover is an exception. Hallel is said on Passover night because the climax of the Passover miracle took place at night, and Hallel (in Psalm 114) makes specific reference to the exodus from Egypt. From Isaiah 30:29, we can surmise that this exception has ancient roots.

In the synagogue, Hallel is said at the Maariv service in Sephardic congregations and in all Israeli congregations. At the seder table, Hallel is said as part of the *Haggadah*, but without its blessings. Hallel is said in part just before the seder meal; in part, after the meal. One reason for splitting up Hallel is because the first part makes direct

---

* In the nusaḥ Ari—the rite followed by Lubavitch Ḥasidim—only the Prayer Leader says the opening and closing blessings of Hallel on Rosh Ḥodesh.

reference to the exodus and so belongs in the first part of the Hagaddah, which retells the story of the exodus. The rest of Hallel speaks of the present and the future, so it is placed with the prayers in the second part of the Hagaddah. Another reason for dividing the Hallel at the seder has to do with the significance of saying some prayers, especially hymns of praise, in conjunction with a cup of wine. (Arakhin 11a.) By splitting the Hallel, we provide a peg for all four cups of wine. Kiddush is said over the first of the four prescribed cups of wine; the Grace after Meals is said over the third cup; the two parts of Hallel are said over the second and fourth cups.

At the seder, we do not stand, but remain seated for Hallel. The reason for this exception to the rule is that seder custom requires us to recline throughout the seder as a symbol of our freedom.

The reference in Hallel to the Exodus has bestowed upon this series of six psalms the designation "Egyptian Hallel" (*Hallel ha-Mitzri*), thus distinguishing it from "the great Hallel" and "the daily Hallel." (Berakhot 56a.)

The recitation of Hallel on Yom Atzmaut and Yom Yerushalayim is far from being a settled practice; it remains in the realm of contemporary religious controversy and may for a long time to come. The situation described by Maimonides regarding the way Hallel was recited in his day by the Prayer Leader and the congregation could well describe the situation with respect to this controversy in our own times. He said: "In our times, I have seen different customs prevailing in different places. And no one is like the other" (Hil. Ḥanukkah 3:14).

There are those today who say the complete Hallel with the prescribed blessings on both Yom Atzmaut and Yom Yerushalayim; there are those who say Hallel but omit the blessings; there are those who do not say Hallel at all. And there are those who distinguish between Yom Atzmaut and Yom Yerushalayim, saying Hallel (with and without the blessings) on the latter day but not on the former.

Religious authorities and pious Jews are aligned on all sides of the question. The controversy basically divides Torah-observant Jews into Zionists and non-Zionists. And while fine points of Jewish law are debated, the conclusions are greatly influenced by how one relates to Israel's re-establishment after a two-thousand-year hiatus, to the ingathering of Jews from all corners of the globe, and to the wondrous military victories that accompanied her rebirth and have on several occasions delivered her from mortal danger. Are all these events to be seen as the beginning of the process of redemption of which the prophets had spoken? If so, there is definitely a spiritual dimension and theological significance inherent in what has happened. These days deserve to be sanctified by the Jewish people and added to their religious calendar; and praise to God for what has been wrought is not only in order, it is mandatory.

Or are these events only to be seen as important political and military achievements which, while allowing the Jewish people through Divine Providence to make impressive gains toward independence and self-rule on their ancestral soil, say nothing about the imminence of their redemption? Those who take this view do not express their satisfaction with the existence of a Jewish state by saying Hallel. On the contrary, by their decision not to say Hallel, they pointedly demonstrate their unhappiness over the many religious and spiritual imperfections found in Israeli society.

I should note that those who do not abide by the ruling of the Chief Rabbinate of Israel on the question of Hallel do not generally accept its authority on all halakhic questions, precisely because such authority functions within the framework of a secular state. They rely on their own Torah authorities for guidance on all matters.

Pertinent to this question is another dispute that has been debated over the centuries: Is *teshuvah* (the return to God by the entire Jewish people) a necessary prerequisite to Divine redemption, or can the process of redemption begin even before we are spiritually worthy of it?

Those who insist that universal teshuvah is a prerequisite of redemption minimize the theological significance of Israel's re-establishment. Those who say that teshuvah is not a prerequisite but rather the result of redemption are more likely to discern the signs of Divine redemption in contemporary history. Thus, they look more kindly upon the instruments of that Divine redemption, even if such agents take the form of secularist political leaders or a less than spiritually perfect people. (See related discussion, pp. 88–89.)

Between these two divergent ideological positions affecting the saying or not saying of Hallel is a third group who, though identified with the proponents of Hallel, are not certain whether all the halakhic criteria for the saying of Hallel have indeed been met by these events. They therefore say the stanzas of Hallel but omit the opening and closing blessings. They follow the general rule governing blessings: If there is any doubt about whether or not to say a blessing, one does not say it.

In singing God's praises, Hallel alludes to five different themes: the exodus from Egypt, the crossing of the Yam Suf, the giving of the Torah, eternal life, and the coming of the Messiah (Pesaḥim 118a). These themes carry us from events of the past, to those of the present, and on to those of the distant future. Because of this chronological continuity in Hallel, it may only be said in the prescribed order. (OH 422:6, MB:26).

Hallel was once sung in the Beit Hamikdash. The Temple is gone but the sentiments and the spirit generated by such prayers as Hallel continue to live on in the contemporary synagogue.

YIZKOR AND OTHER MEMORIAL PRAYERS

Four times a year a memorial service for the dead takes place in the synagogue following the Torah and Haftarah reading: on Yom Kippur, on the last day of Passover, on the second day of Shavuot, and on the eighth day of Sukkot (Shemini Atzeret). The prayer said at that time is called *Yizkor*, from the opening words *Yizkor Elohim* ("May God remember . . ."). It is said by every person who has ever suffered the loss of a parent or of other loved ones.* The deceased is mentioned by name in the prayer. Yizkor also contains a pledge to charity, for we believe that an act of charity, in addition to its intrinsic merit, will contribute to redeeming the soul of the departed.

Yizkor is said on Yom Kippur because it is a Day of Judgment, when the dead as well as the living need atonement. The pledge to charity is also in keeping with the special theme of the day, namely that "Prayer, repentance, and charity avert the severe decree."

* Some authorities favor its omission during the first year after death since its recitation during this period when the tragedy is still so fresh in mind, may cause an undue sense of grief to dampen the joy of the festival.

Yizkor is said on the other three festivals because the Torah reading for those days includes the verse: "They shall not appear before the Lord empty-handed, but each with his own gift, according to the blessing that the Lord your God bestowed upon you" (Deut. 16:17). Yizkor with its pledge to charity serves this purpose too.

Another memorial prayer begins with the words *El malei raḥamim* ("God, full of compassion"). This prayer, whose name is often abbreviated to simply *Malei*, is recited at the Yizkor service by the Prayer Leader on behalf of all the deceased for whom the Yizkor prayer was said. The Malei prayer is also said at funeral services; and it is said on the *yahrzeit* in the synagogue on behalf of the deceased by the sexton or the gabbai.* Naturally, a member of the family must be present at services to request the prayer.

Still another memorial begins with the words "Av haraḥamim" ("Merciful Father"). The recitation of this prayer, however, is not confined to those who have suffered a personal loss. It is said by the entire congregation for the departed souls of all the martyred dead of the Jewish people, and thus it is a fitting conclusion to the Yizkor memorial service.

Av Haraḥamim, as a memorial prayer, is not restricted to the Yizkor memorial service. At first, it was also said on the Sabbaths before Shavuot and Tisha b'Av, since both of these weeks commemorate events during the period of the Crusades when many Jewish communities were destroyed and many Jews suffered martyrdom. Now it is said regularly in most congregations after the Torah reading as part of the weekly Sabbath service, except on festive Sabbaths and on Sabbaths preceding Rosh Ḥodesh exclusive of the Sefira period when it is nevertheless said (OH 284: 7, Rema).

---

* The Malei prayer is not said on days when Taḥanum is omitted. Should a yahrzeit fall on such a day, the recitation of the Malei prayer is advanced to a day when it may be said.

ANNOUNCING THE NEW MONTH:
BIRKAT HAHODESH

On the Sabbath before the start of every new Hebrew month, a Prayer for the [New] Month (*Birkat HaHodesh*) is said immediately following the reading of the Haftarah. It is said only eleven times a year (twelve times in a leap year) because it is not said on the Sabbath before the month of Tishrei—the first of Tishrei is celebrated as Rosh Hashanah ("the New Year") and not as Rosh Hodesh ("New Month") (Eruvin 40a).

The heart of the prayer is actually an announcement mentioning the name of the incoming month and the day or days on which Rosh Hodesh will be celebrated. The original name for this prayer, still found in Sephardic prayer books, is in fact "the Announcement of the New Month" rather than "the Blessing for the Month."

The *announcement* is still highlighted in contemporary synagogues by the manner in which the ritual is conducted. When the Prayer Leader makes the announcement and proclaims the day(s) on which Rosh Hodesh will be observed, he holds a Torah scroll in his arms.

Until a fixed calendar was introduced, the Sanhedrin, the supreme religious court sitting in Jerusalem, would receive witnesses who came to testify that they sighted the new moon, and on the basis of this testimony the court declared that day to be Rosh Hodesh. Since the month in the Hebrew calendar is based on lunar calculations—it takes exactly twenty-nine and a half days for the moon to circle the earth—the new moon would become visible after twenty-nine or thirty days. The astronomical average of twenty-nine and a half days was kept by having one month of twenty-nine days balance off another of thirty days. But until the Sanhedrin or an authoritative Beth Din ruled on the basis of the visual testimony, no one could be certain whether that particular outgoing month would be one of twenty-nine or thirty days.

After the fixed calendar was introduced by Hillel II in the fourth century C.E., there ceased to be any doubt on which day Rosh Hodesh should be observed. Nor was there any doubt about the days on which the holidays would fall. According to this calendar that we still use, the months of Tishrei, Shevat, Nisan, Sivan, Av, and also Adar I in a leap year, always have thirty days. The months of Tevet, Adar, Iyar, Tamuz, and Elul always have twenty-nine days. The months of Heshvan and Kislev vary between twenty-nine and thirty.

Based on ancient tradition, Rosh Hodesh is celebrated for two days when the outgoing month has thirty days. In this case, the first day of Rosh Hodesh is really the thirtieth day of the outgoing month, while the second day of Rosh Hodesh is the first day of the new month.

Although the calendar was fixed, the information still had to be transmitted to the people. Printed calendars, of course, were not available. It was important for the people to know the day(s) of Rosh Hodesh as there was Musaf to add and Hallel to say. It was also a tradition among women to refrain from working on Rosh Hodesh (Megillah 22b, Rashi). And so, apparently during the Geonic period, it became customary to publicly announce in the synagogue the day(s) on which Rosh Hodesh would be observed. The announcement may have been simply a public service, not unlike the announcements made today concerning important coming events of interest to the community. The announcement may also have been a way of asserting the authority of the rabbis in their struggle against the Karaites, who challenged the authority of the fixed calendar and sought to restore visual testimony as the way to fix each new month.

Three short prayers are also said: two before the formal announcement of the month, and one after it. The first prayer begins with the words "Yehi ratzon" ("May it be [God's] will"). Though the prayer is an ancient one, it was introduced into the siddur only as recently as the middle of the eighteenth century. The prayer is taken from the Talmud, where it is attributed to Rav, who said it as a personal prayer after the Amidah (Berakhot 16b). (See p. 104, 197.) There it is found in the first person singular. When it was added to the announcement of the new month, it was recast in the first person plural, and a few words, "renew for us this month for good and for blessing," were added to the beginning to make it more appropriate for the occasion.

May it be Thy will, Lord our God and God of our fathers, to renew for us this month for good and for blessing. Grant us long life, a life of peace, a life of goodness, a life of blessing, a life in which we earn a livelihood, a life of physical vigor, a life that reflects reverence for God and dread of sin, a life that is free of shame and disgrace, a life of wealth and honor, a life in which a love of Torah and an awe of Heaven shall be within us, a life in which the desires of our heart shall be fulfilled for good. Amen.

In many prayer books, the words *bizekhut tefilat Rav* ("by merit of Rav's prayer"), or the words *bizekhut tefilat rabim* ("by merit of the prayers of many") appear at the end. The first phrase reflects the origin of the prayer, while the second phrase is widely regarded as a printing error. Neither is part of the prayer.

The second prayer said before announcing the new month was introduced very early, perhaps even at the same time as the announcement itself. It begins with *Mi she'asah nisim:*

He who performed miracles for our fathers, and redeemed them from slavery to freedom, may He soon redeem us and gather our dispersed from the four corners of the earth, for all Israel is united in fellowship, and let us say Amen.*

A prayer recalling God's miracles in renewing and restoring the fortunes of Israel is most apt in this context, for the moon has always been symbolic of Jewish renewal and rebirth. It wanes and disappears from view only to be reborn, to appear once again, growing steadily brighter and fuller.

In the Ḥasidic-Lubavitch rite, only *Mi she'asah nisim* is said; the first prayer, *Yehi ratzon*, is not said. Nor is it said in the Sephardic rite, where we find several short *Yehi ratzon* prayers, one of which is for the rabbis, and their disciples and families:

May it be the will of our Father in heaven to preserve among us the wise men of Israel, them, their wives, their sons and daughters, and their disciples wherever they dwell, and say Amen.

This is the same prayer that is said in Ashkenazic congregations on Monday and Thursday mornings after the Torah reading. The Sephardic tradition that links a prayer for the rabbis with this

---

* It should be noted that an eleventh-century version of the prayer contains a few additional words that could make it mean: ". . . for all Israel is united in fellowship *with Jerusalem, the Holy City,* and let us say Amen." (Maḥzor Vitry: 190). This stresses the permanent bond that exists between all Jews and the city of Jerusalem.

announcement lends support to the notion that the announcement was to be more than just a public service; it was also a means to assert the authority of the rabbinic scholars in setting the calendar.

The short prayer following the announcement is as follows:

> May the Holy One, blessed be He, renew it [the month] unto us and unto all His people, the house of Israel, for life and for peace, for gladness and for joy, for salvation and consolation; and let us say Amen.

In the Sephardic and Ḥasidic versions, and in all Israeli congregations, the continuation of the sentence following "the house of Israel" is more extensive:

> . . . for goodness and for blessings, for gladness and for joy, for salvation and consolation, for a good livelihood and sustenance, for a good and peaceful life, for good reports and tidings, for rains in their season, for complete healing and speedy redemption; and let us say Amen.

THE BLESSING ON THE MOON'S REAPPEARANCE: BIRKAT LEVANAH

Of all the heavenly bodies, the moon has always held a special fascination for the Jewish people. It was after all a very useful and reliable way by which to gauge the passage of time. One need only look up into the night sky to be able to tell fairly accurately what day of the (lunar) month it is. It thus serves as the basis of the Jewish calendar.

It is to be expected that sages who prescribed that a blessing be said when coming upon great natural scenes (such as lofty mountains, great deserts, vast oceans, a falling star or a rainbow, a blossoming tree or a bolt of lightning), should also have formulated a blessing to be recited on seeing the monthly reappearance of the moon, a phenomenon that witnessed the constancy and stability of nature. This they did, praising God for establishing the laws of nature through which He governs the universe. The Talmud is the source of the blessing; Rabbi Judah is the author.

> Blessed art Thou, Lord our God, King of the universe, who with His work created the heavens, and with the breath of His mouth, all its legions; a fixed law and set time did He prescribe for them, that they should not deviate from their function. They happily do the will of their Creator, the true Maker whose work is truth; And as for the moon, He directed it to renew itself, as a crown of glory for those [Israel] who are sustained [by God] from birth, and who are destined to be renewed like her, and to extol their Creator for His glorious kingdom. Blessed art Thou, Lord, who renews the months.
>
> (Sanhedrin 42a)

There is, however, more to this blessing than to the many other blessings that are associated with natural events. The idea behind this blessing was enough to inspire Rabbi Yoḥanan's dictum that "to bless the month at its time is like welcoming the Divine Presence". For by the moon's waning and growing fuller, by its total disappearance from view at the very end of the month and its reappearance at the beginning of the month, the people were given the feeling that there was continuity in the process of Creation, as though God were still at work renewing and "rebuilding" a moon that had temporarily disappeared. Sentiments along this line are in fact expressed daily, morning and evening, in the first blessing before the Shema. But the monthly regeneration of the moon was especially felt to be a way in which God reveals Himself anew through His creative work. By saying the blessing at the proper time, we are, so to speak, extending to Him a welcome.

There is still another element to the significance of this blessing, alluded to toward the end of the berakhah. The moon has from earliest times also been seen as a symbol of the capacity of the Jewish people to regenerate itself—even after a period of decline and seeming disappearance from view.

The Psalms is the first source to have drawn the parallel between the moon and the destiny of the Davidic dynasty. "It [David's throne] shall be established forever as the moon" (Psalms 89:38). And just as the moon, while remaining a permanent fixture in the skies, temporarily disappears from view, so might David's throne, but only eventually to reappear. The comparison was a particular source of solace after the destruction of the Temple, suggesting the hope that the Davidic throne would be re-established, and with it everything else: the ingathering of the exiles, Jewish sovereignty, rebuilding the Temple, the coming of the Messiah. Said Rabbi Simeon ben Gamliel: "Just as the new month sanctifies and renews itself in this world, so shall Israel sanctify and renew itself in the distant future" (Pirkei d'Rebbe Eliezer:51).

The parallel drawn between the moon and the Davidic dynasty inspired a code message that has become a motto and rallying cry for Jews everywhere, signifying the perpetuation of the Jewish people. The Talmud tells of how Rabbi Judah Ha-Nasi once instructed Rabbi Hiyya to go to Ein Tob, a place in Judea where the Beth Din met. He was to have them sanctify Rosh Hodesh on the thirtieth day, and send a message back to Rabbi Judah Ha-Nasi notifying him that it was done. The watchword was to be "David, King of Israel, lives and endures" (Rosh Hashanah 25a).

This motto is now included in the prayers that have been added to the basic Blessing on the Reappearance of the Moon, the *Birkat Levanah*. The symbolism conveyed by the new moon is also alluded to in yet another phrase that has become part of that service: *Siman tov u'mazal tov, yehei lanu ulekhol Yisrael, Amen* ("May it be a good sign and good fortune for us and for all of Israel, Amen").

Although the Birkat Levanah was initially meant to be said when one first sees the new moon, it could be said anytime through the fifteenth of the month. In practice, it is said no earlier than the third day of the month when the waxing crescent of the moon is clearly visible in the sky. The halakha prefers that it be said on a Saturday night which falls during the prescribed period, for then the people are still dressed in [Sabbath] clothing more appropriate for "welcoming the Divine Presence." Although it may be said from a window if necessary, the usual practice is to say it outdoors. *Going out* to welcome the Divine Presence is seen as a demonstration of greater respect (OH 426:4, MB:20–21).

COUNTING THE OMER

For a period of seven weeks each spring, the Maariv service concludes with a ritual in which the days are counted. The Torah tells
us in Leviticus (23:15–16) to count forty-nine days, beginning with
the second night of Pesaḥ, and to celebrate the fiftieth day as Shavuot
(Menaḥot 66a). The purpose of the counting beyond its agricultural
dimension is to connect the festival of Pesaḥ with the festival of
Shavuot. This may be to impress upon us that the escape from physical
bondage commemorated by Pesaḥ does not constitute genuine freedom
unless it is accompanied by the disciplines and duties symbolized by
Shavuot, which recalls the day when the Torah was given to the
Jewish people. Where law and discipline, duty and obligation, are
absent, there is no freedom, only anarchy.

The start of the counting coincided with the day on which an
omer (a certain measure) of barley was to be cut down and brought to
the Temple as a first harvest offering. The entire period of counting
thus came to be known as *Sefirat HaOmer* ("the Counting of the
Omer").

As is done when performing any mitzvah, we prefix the counting
of each day with a blessing:

בָּרוּךְ אַתָּה יהוה אֱלֹהֵינוּ מֶלֶךְ הָעוֹלָם, אֲשֶׁר
קִדְּשָׁנוּ בְּמִצְוֹתָיו וְצִוָּנוּ עַל סְפִירַת הָעֹמֶר.

Blessed art Thou, Lord our God, King of the universe, who has sanctified us with His commandments and commanded us concerning the
counting of the omer.

The prayer book then lists the precise wording to be used for
counting each of the forty-nine days. The Prayer Leader or the rabbi
recites it, followed by the congregation.

In some congregations, it is customary to say a psalm and a
special prayer after the count of the day. The counting of the omer
will be found in most prayer books either at the end of the daily

evening service or in the section devoted to the holiday prayers. The
prayer book's Table of Contents will provide the exact page.

AVINU MALKEINU: FATHER AND KING

During the Ten Days of Repentance, from Rosh Hashanah
through Yom Kippur, and on the different fast days, a moving entreaty follows the repetition of the Amidah at both Shaḥarit and
Minḥa services. The prayer consists of a series of forty-five short
verses. Each verse begins with the words *Avinu Malkeinu* ("Our
Father, Our King"). It is customary to open the Ark during its
recitation.

The origin of this prayer goes back to the second century. The
Talmud tells us that Rabbi Akiva used the opening words, Avinu
Malkeinu, while leading the congregation in prayer on a fast day.
Some of the verses we still say are attributed to him (Taanit 25b).
Other verses, with the same opening formula, were added from time
to time in response to various persecutions or hardships that the
Jewish people endured. The incorporation of this series of entreaties
into the liturgy of the High Holy Day period also inspired the inclu-
sion of several verses that entreat God to inscribe us in various "Books"
—the Books of Good Life, of Salvation, of Sustenance, of Merit, of
Forgiveness and Pardon.

At first, it was the custom for the Prayer Leader and the congregation to recite the entire prayer line by line. Now, only the
fifteenth through twenty-third verses are recited line by line. The
line-by-line recital begins with:

אָבִינוּ מַלְכֵּנוּ, הַחֲזִירֵנוּ בִּתְשׁוּבָה שְׁלֵמָה לְפָנֶיךָ.

Avinu Malkeinu, haḥazireinu biteshuvah shleimah lefanekha

Our Father, Our King, bring us back before Thee in full repentance.

It concludes with:

אָבִינוּ מַלְכֵּנוּ, כָּתְבֵנוּ בְּסֵפֶר סְלִיחָה וּמְחִילָה.

Avinu Malkeinu, kotveinu b'sefer sliḥah umehilah

Our Father, Our King, inscribe us in the Book of Forgiveness and Pardon.

Avinu Malkeinu is never said on the Sabbath. This is because the prayer contains many requests that correspond to those in the daily Amidah—the Shemoneh Esrei—and one does not pray for one's material or physical needs on the Sabbath. (See p. 109.) On Yom Kippur that falls on a Sabbath, it is said only at the very end of the Neilah service, when final judgment is imminent and so a last unrestricted plea is permitted (OH 623; MB:10).

Avinu Malkeinu emphasizes a twofold relationship to God. On the one hand, we see ourselves as God's children. We therefore address Him as our Father, and plead for a father's mercy. On the other hand, we see ourselves as His subjects. We therefore also address Him as our King and plead with Him to grant our prayers.

PIYYUT: RELIGIOUS POETRY

Apart from the prayers derived from Biblical and Talmudic sources or those composed by the Men of the Great Assembly, there began to develop, particularly from the seventh century C.E. onward, a special genre of prayers, known as "piyyut" (pl. piyyutim),* which refers to religious poetry written especially for liturgical purposes or for religious occasions. Piyyut was meant to embellish the fixed or standard prayers and was generally interspersed throughout the various parts of the service. One who wrote piyyut was called a *paitan*. The most famous names among the paitanim include Eleazar

---

* A Hebraic term derived from the Greek word for poetry.

Ha Kallir of Eretz Yisrael (seventh century c.e.), Moses and Meshullam ben Kalonymus of Germany (tenth–eleventh century c.e.), and Solomon ibn Gabirol and Yehudah Halevi of Spain (eleventh–twelfth century c.e.). The *Encyclopaedia Judaica* records the names of almost five hundred paitanim who flourished at various times from the seventh through the eighteenth centuries in Eretz Yisrael, North Africa, Italy, Spain, and Central Europe. That list is by no means exhaustive. The paitanim ranged from the brilliant, whose words have been universally accepted as liturgical masterpieces, to the mediocre, whose piyyut remained local and shortlived.

I will not dwell on the various piyyutim that are still part of the prayer service, except to explain what piyyut is and to identify those that are still said. Most of the piyyut, with certain notable exceptions, have long since fallen by the wayside and disappeared from the prayer book.

There are various types of piyyut, each with a style and pattern of its own. They also vary depending on the period during which they were written. Early piyyut was lucid, the language relatively simple to comprehend. Later piyyut became more complicated, both in its language and grammatical construction, particularly in the Ashkenazic rite. Paitanim often coined their own words or idioms and resorted to vague and obscure allusions that are often impossible to understand without a commentary. Rhyme and meter distinguish most piyyut as does the use of acrostics—where each line begins with a different letter of the alphabet. Sometimes the acrostic relied on the order of the Hebrew alphabet, sometimes on reverse alphabetical order (called "תשר״ק"), and sometimes it was effected according to an arbitrary pattern. The paitan often signed his composition by weaving his own name into it.

One form of piyyut was meant to be said during the repetition of the Amidah on the Four Special Sabbaths,* the festivals, Purim, and the fast days. These are called *kerovot*. Piyyutim meant to be said as part of the blessings before and after the morning Shema are called *yotzerot*; those meant to be said before and after the evening

---

* These Sabbaths are known as Parshat Shekalim, Parshat Zakhor, Parshat Parah, and Parshat Hahodesh. On these days, Biblical passages with these names are added to the weekly Torah reading. These Sabbaths fall out during the six-week period before Passover.

Shema are called *maarivim*. These piyyutim are said today by most congregations only on the High Holy Days. It is the addition of such piyyutim that makes the High Holy Day services markedly different from that of the Sabbath and the festival. A contributing reason for the general disappearance of this form of piyyut during other times of the year was the ongoing opposition of many of the Early and Latter-day Authorities who considered the piyyutim in these categories to be an unwarranted and improper interruption of the fixed, obligatory prayers.

Still another form of piyyut is the *selihah* (pl. *selihot*), the penitential prayer. Collections of such piyyutim are still recited either after the Amidah or before the start of the services on the fast days, and during the period that begins with the week before Rosh Hashanah and concludes with Yom Kippur. Piyyut classified as *kinot* (dirges), is recited on Tisha b'Av after the standard prayers.

The short prayers for rain and dew that are said on Shemini Atzeret and Passover respectively are piyyut selections that serve to remind the congregation that they have to begin to say the prayers for rain or dew in that Amidah. Throughout the diaspora, these two piyyutim are said during the repetition of the Musaf Amidah, but in Israeli synagogues they are said just before the silent Amidah to meet the aforementioned objections of religious authorities, and so that the announcement of the prayer can be put into effect during that very service by the worshipers.

The extensive *Hoshanot* prayers said throughout the week of Sukkot, while circling the bimah with *lulav* and *etrog*, are also piyyutim composed for a ritual that commemorates an ancient Temple practice.

A piyyut said on Shavuot as an introduction to the reading of the Torah is known as *Akdamot*. This piyyut, written in Aramaic, is of the genre known as *reshut*, which is a request for permission. A reshut was meant to preface a digression in the service. At one time, it was also customary to read on the first day of Shavuot an Aramaic translation of that day's Torah reading. This digression inspired this particular reshut. The Aramaic reading of the Torah disappeared from the synagogue service, but Akdamot remained.

Certain piyyutim have achieved great popularity and have become standard hymns in the prayer service. I refer to Adon Olam,

Yigdal, Ein Keloheinu, and An'im Zmirot (*Shir HaKavod*). Three of these hymns are discussed elsewhere in this book. (See pp. 200, 214.)

The popular hymn of Lekhah Dodi, sung at the Friday evening Kabbalat Shabbat service, is an example of a later piyyut that won for itself a permanent place in Jewish liturgy. A very early piyyut that has similarly been incorporated in the services is *El Adon,* said at the Sabbath morning service as part of the first blessing before the Shema.

But the religious poetry that achieved greatest popularity is not said in the synagogue at all. They are the Sabbath *zemirot,* the table songs sung at the Sabbath meals. These religious poems, which serve to instruct in some of the essential laws of the Sabbath and give expression to the basic convictions of Judaism, have been set to a wide and ever-increasing variety of melodies. Perhaps the most famous of all non-synagogue piyyut is *Moaz Tzur* ("Rock of Ages"), which is sung on Hanukkah.

From the mournful kinot of Tisha b'Av through the reflective penitential selihot; from the inspirational affirmations of faith in some of the High Holy Day piyyutim through the joyous zemirot celebrating the Sabbath—piyyut still provides a rich and varied addition to the standard obligatory prayers.

CHAPTER

15

~~~

The Grace After Meals:
Birkat Hamazon

PRAYERS IN THE HOME

IN JEWISH TRADITION, prayers and blessings are not confined to the synagogue or limited to the formal religious service. Though sanctuaries are built and set aside as special places for prayer, we do not believe that the Shekhinah, the Divine Presence, is restricted only to such places. God's abode is the entire universe. "Thus said the Lord: The heaven is my throne and the earth is My footstool; is there a house that you can build for Me, is there a place that can be My abode?" (Is. 66:1). If God commanded the Israelites to "make for Me a sanctuary" (Exod. 25:8), it was not for Him to dwell in *it*, but so that he could dwell *"in their midst."* The language of the Torah is very precise and revealing. The purpose of the sanctuary was not to house the Divine Presence, but to create an environment that would allow His spirit to penetrate the community and be reflected in the life of the people.

The synagogue is indeed vested with greater holiness than are other places, and the sages made it abundantly clear that they regarded it as the preferred place for prayer. Said Rabin, son of Rabbi

The Grace After Meals: Birkat Hamazon

Adda, in the name of Rabbi Isaac: "How does one know that the Holy One, blessed be He, is to be found in the synagogue? For it is said (Psalms 82:1) 'God stands in the congregation of God'" (Berakhot 6a).

While not discounting the enthusiasm shown for praying in the synagogue, the Talmud is equally clear that a prayer service may be held anywhere. The only places where prayer is forbidden are places identified with idolatry or sexual lewdness, or places that are foul-smelling or in sight of excrement. A hazardous place is also unsuitable for prayer. No one who has ever prayed in the splendid isolation of nature, where hills and valleys, forests and fields, skies and oceans provide inspirational testimony to God's handiwork, can ever again think of the synagogue as the only place suitable for prayer (see OH 90, MB:11).

But of all places outside the synagogue where Jewish prayer may take place, the home is first in importance. Like the synagogue, the Jewish home has also been described as a "small sanctuary." There too does the Divine Presence dwell. Aside from those times when one prays privately at home because one cannot be at the synagogue, there are many prayers and blessings that were from their inception intended to be said at home. The best known religious service that takes place at home is the Passover seder. The dinner meal is an integral part of that service, but without the prayers and the blessings, it is not a seder.

There is also the Kiddush recited at the dinner table every Sabbath and festival eve, and the Havdalah recited at the very end of the Sabbath and festival day. There is the lighting of candles before every Sabbath and festival and throughout the week of Ḥanukkah. There is the Shema that is said before retiring for the night. The religous ceremonies of *Brit Milah* ("Covenant of the Circumcision") and *Pidyon Ha-Ben* ("Redemption of the First-Born") often take place at home. The Seven Marriage Blessings said at dinner in the week following the wedding is a home observance. Even a regular prayer service may be conducted at home instead of at the synagogue, a practice that is routinely followed in a house of mourning during the week of shiva. But no prayers or blessings are recited at home with greater regularity than those relating to our meals. We bless God before we eat. We thank Him after we eat.

A Jewish home where prayers and blessings are heard is a home where there is an awareness of God and His teachings. There Judaism lives, and there the Divine Presence dwells.

A TORAH COMMANDMENT

Among the many blessings that we recite in the fulfillment of our religious duties, the only ones that Scripture explicitly required us to say are those that we say *after* we eat. The obligation to say all the other blessings originated with our sages, who wished to heighten our awareness of God and to strengthen our faith in Him. And though the specific wording of the Grace after Meals did not begin to take shape until the time of Ezra, the Scribe, and was not totally crystallized even by the Talmudic period, to say blessings of thanksgiving after eating was prescribed by the Torah: "When you have eaten and are satisfied, you shall bless the Lord your God for the good land that He has given you" (Deut. 8:10).

The Biblical commandment is fulfilled by reciting three blessings: 1) for the food, 2) for the land (of Eretz Yisrael), and 3) for Jerusalem with its Holy Sanctuary. The Talmudic name for the Grace after Meals is in fact *Shalosh Berakhot* ("Three Blessings"). The rabbis later ordained a fourth blessing, expressing the goodness of God (Berakhot 48b).

The Talmud tells us that a blessing for food was first articulated by Moses in gratitude for the manna that the Israelites ate in the desert. A blessing for the land was introduced by Joshua when he led the Israelites into Eretz Yisrael. And King David initiated a blessing for Jerusalem when he established it as the capital of the country. His son, King Solomon, who built the first Temple, expanded upon the blessing by adding his gratitude to God for the "great and holy Sanctuary." Shortly after the destruction of the Second Temple, the sages added a fourth blessing to the Grace after Meals, so as to emphasize the everlasting goodness of God.

Saying a blessing *before* eating is widespread among many peoples and religions. Our sages instituted such blessings too. (Their unique significance will be discussed in the next chapter.) Yet the greater obligation, the Biblical duty, is to recite a blessing *after* eating. Why? Perhaps because when people are sated, they are more likely to forget Him who is the source of their nourishment. It is easier to think of God and be grateful to Him when the food is still before us and we are hungry. It often happens that when people are able comfortably to meet their basic needs, they turn away from God. This is precisely what troubled Moses when he instructed the Israelites. Immediately following the commandment to bless God after eating, Moses expressed his concern:

> Take care lest you forget the Lord your God and fail to keep His commandments . . . lest when you will eat and be sated and will build fine houses to live in, and your herds and flocks will multiply, and your silver and gold will increase, and everything you own will prosper. Beware, lest your heart grow haughty and you then forget the Lord your God . . . and you say to yourselves "My own power and the might of my own hand have won this wealth for me." Remember that it is the Lord your God who gives you the power to acquire wealth . . . .
>
> (Deut. 8:11–18)

The after-meal grace was meant to help one resist just such tendencies. It was meant to instil, and help a person maintain, a measure of humility.

THE FOUR BLESSINGS OF BIRKAT HAMAZON

The four blessings that now make up the Grace after Meals are each devoted to a separate major theme. The first blessing speaks of God providing the food to sustain all the life that He created in the world. The second blessing speaks of Eretz Yisrael, the Torah, and the Covenant of Circumcision, all of which God gave to Israel in covenants manifested through Divine revelation. The third blessing, which originally expressed thanksgiving for Jerusalem and the Beit Hamikdash, now expresses a prayer that God rebuild Jerusalem and its Holy Temple and restore the Davidic dynasty—all elements in Israel's redemption. The fourth blessing speaks of God's eternal goodness in every thing, in every way, and in every time.

Delicately interwoven throughout the three original blessings is reference to such theological motifs as Creation, Revelation, and Redemption. (These themes are also found in the Blessings of the Shema, in the Musaf Amidah of Rosh Hashanah, and in the middle blessing of the various Sabbath Amidah prayers.) But as in a symphony, the major theme emerges in each and every one of the different blessings: God is the ultimate provider; He is the source of our food, of our sustenance, of our livelihood. A second major theme stresses the centrality of Eretz Yisrael in the life of the nation.

Rabbi Abraham Isaac HaKohen Kook regards the original three blessings of the after-meal grace as a series of spiritually ascending levels. Man's very first concern is and must be with his own physical survival. If it were his only concern, however, he would not differ from the rest of the world's creatures. Still, physical survival is an essential prerequisite for going on to higher spiritual levels. The Ethics of the Fathers phrases it succinctly: "Where there is no meal, there can be no Torah" (Avot. 3:21).

While the first blessing addresses itself to physical sustenance, the first block in building a more altruistic, meaningful, and holier existence, the second blessing moves on to a concern for the physical survival and well-being of the entire nation, of all the Jewish people. Once physical survival is assured, we can turn our attention to the attainment of spiritual aspirations, on both the personal and national levels. This is reflected in the third blessing, which is a prayer for Jerusalem, the spiritual center of the Jewish people, and for the Beit Hamikdash, which embodies the universal spiritual ideal of the nation. It was built, the Bible says: "so that all the nations of the earth may know that the Lord, He is God, there is none else" (Olat Re'iyah I, pp. 363–365).

Now let us turn to examine each of the blessings separately:

The Blessing for Food: Birkat Hazan

בָּרוּךְ אַתָּה יהוה אֱלֹהֵינוּ מֶלֶךְ הָעוֹלָם, הַזָּן
אֶת הָעוֹלָם כֻּלּוֹ בְּטוּבוֹ, בְּחֵן וּבְחֶסֶד וּבְרַחֲמִים,

הוּא נוֹתֵן לֶחֶם לְכָל בָּשָׂר, כִּי לְעוֹלָם חַסְדּוֹ.
וּבְטוּבוֹ הַגָּדוֹל תָּמִיד לֹא חָסַר־לָנוּ וְאַל יֶחְסַר
לָנוּ מָזוֹן לְעוֹלָם וָעֶד, בַּעֲבוּר שְׁמוֹ הַגָּדוֹל, כִּי
הוּא אֵל זָן וּמְפַרְנֵס לַכֹּל וּמֵטִיב לַכֹּל וּמֵכִין
מָזוֹן לְכָל בְּרִיּוֹתָיו אֲשֶׁר בָּרָא. בָּרוּךְ אַתָּה יהוה,
הַזָּן אֶת הַכֹּל.

Blessed art Thou, Lord our God, King of the universe, who in His goodness, grace, loving kindness, and mercy, nourishes the whole world. He gives food to all flesh, for His loving kindness is ever-lasting. In His great goodness, we have never lacked for food; may we never lack for food, for the sake of His great Name. For He nourishes and sustains all, He does good to all, and prepares food for all His creatures that He created. Blessed art Thou, Lord, who pro-vides food for all.

This is the oldest and the most universal of the blessings. It is the basic theme in the Grace. It acknowledges God as the world's great Provider. We thank Him for the food that we have eaten and for making it possible for every creature in the world to find its own food supply.

The commandment to bless God after eating is preceded in the Torah by a reference to the manna that God provided the Israelites in the desert in order to teach them "that man does not live by bread alone, but that man lives on whatever the Lord decrees" (Deut. 8:3).

This Biblical verse is commonly explained to mean that human beings need more than the mere gratification of a physical need. Man also needs "what the Lord decrees." In other words, man also needs spiritual fulfillment.

The explanation may be a truth unto itself, but the simple meaning of the verse, in a context that deals with the basic question of physical survival, actually teaches us an even more basic lesson. People tend to become accustomed to certain staples or basic com-modities without which they feel they cannot survive. Bread has historically been an example of one such a staple: not for naught did it come to be called the "staff of life," and this is why the word for flour, "meal," became synonymous with an entire dinner. And when people face the prospect of losing such staples, be it bread or meat or fish or whatever, they panic (as did the Israelites in the desert) and they believe that they are doomed. But the Torah teaches us that if God wants us to live, He will provide alternative forms of nourishment that may have been entirely unknown before. This was the case with the manna that neither the Israelites nor their ancestors had ever encountered before. This verse simply says to us that not only bread, but *everything*, is created "by God's decree," and that life can be physically sustained in ways other than those that we have grown accustomed to and upon which we have come to depend. The important thing is to recognize the Source of our sustenance, "to walk in His ways and revere Him."

The experience of the Israelites in the Sinai desert was intended to be a lesson in faith to all of mankind. Therefore, this blessing does not thank God for feeding only us, or only the Jewish people, and only in the present, but for feeding all the world forever.

The Blessing for the Land: Birkat Haaretz

נוֹדֶה לְּךָ, יהוה אֱלֹהֵינוּ, עַל שֶׁהִנְחַלְתָּ
לַאֲבוֹתֵינוּ אֶרֶץ חֶמְדָּה טוֹבָה וּרְחָבָה, וְעַל
שֶׁהוֹצֵאתָנוּ יהוה אֱלֹהֵינוּ מֵאֶרֶץ מִצְרַיִם, וּפְדִיתָנוּ
מִבֵּית עֲבָדִים, וְעַל בְּרִיתְךָ שֶׁחָתַמְתָּ בִּבְשָׂרֵנוּ,
וְעַל תּוֹרָתְךָ שֶׁלִּמַּדְתָּנוּ, וְעַל חֻקֶּיךָ שֶׁהוֹדַעְתָּנוּ,
וְעַל חַיִּים חֵן וָחֶסֶד שֶׁחוֹנַנְתָּנוּ, וְעַל אֲכִילַת
מָזוֹן שָׁאַתָּה זָן וּמְפַרְנֵס אוֹתָנוּ תָּמִיד, בְּכָל יוֹם
וּבְכָל עֵת וּבְכָל שָׁעָה.

וְעַל הַכֹּל יהוה אֱלֹהֵינוּ אֲנַחְנוּ מוֹדִים לָךְ
וּמְבָרְכִים אוֹתָךְ, יִתְבָּרַךְ שִׁמְךָ בְּפִי כָל חַי תָּמִיד

The Grace After Meals: Birkat Hamazon

לְעוֹלָם וָעֶד, כַּכָּתוּב : וְאָכַלְתָּ וְשָׂבָעְתָּ וּבֵרַכְתָּ
אֶת יהוה אֱלֹהֶיךָ עַל הָאָרֶץ הַטֹּבָה אֲשֶׁר נָתַן
לָךְ: בָּרוּךְ אַתָּה יהוה, עַל הָאָרֶץ וְעַל הַמָּזוֹן.

We thank Thee, Lord our God, for the desirable, good and spacious land that Thou gave our forefathers as a heritage; for having brought us out of the land of Egypt and redeemed us from slavery; for Thy covenant that Thou sealed in our flesh; for Thy Torah which Thou taught us and Thy statutes which Thou made known to us; for the life, the grace and loving kindness that Thou has bestowed on us; and for the food [we eat] with which Thou constantly feed and sustain us every day, at all times [of the day] and in every hour.*

For everything, Lord our God, we thank Thee and bless Thee; may Thy name be blessed in the mouth of every living creature at all times and for all time; as is written [in Thy Torah]: "When you have eaten and are satisfied, you shall bless the Lord your God for the good land that He has given you." Blessed art Thou, Lord, for the land and for the food.

The second blessing is the one in which we proceed to comply with the Torah requirement to also bless God "for the good land that He has given you." Although it would have made more sense if the "good land" to which the Torah refers meant any land where our food grew or where we might be living, it is clear from the context that it means Eretz Yisrael, the Land of Israel.

The wording of the Torah and the subsequent ruling of our sages that "anyone who does not mention the 'desirable, good and spacious land' when giving thanks does not satisfy the requirements of saying the Grace" (Berakhot 48b) suggests another reason for the Grace after Meals, namely to imbue the Jewish people with a love for Eretz Yisrael and to impress upon them the analogy that just as food is essential for the survival and development of the individual, so Eretz Yisrael is essential for the survival and development of the nation. The Land of Israel is capable of providing physical sustenance

* On Ḥanukkah and Purim, *Al Hanisim* (see p. 137), a prayer thanking God for the miracles and victories commemorated by these holidays, is inserted at this point.

and, of course, an endless supply of spiritual nourishment for all Jews. And while it is true that both the Jewish people and Judaism survived for centuries without the land, it is equally true that their survival was sustained by the hope of someday returning to Eretz Yisrael. Their observance of Torah kept that hope alive. They never allowed the Jewish claim to the land to lapse. Eretz Yisrael may have been conquered and settled by others, but the Jewish people never yielded title to it. And mysteriously, the land never yielded itself entirely unto its conquerors and trespassers. It remained waste and desolate for over eighteen centuries until Jewish settlers returned to work it. The Biblical prophecy that Jewish exile would be accompanied by "your land remaining desolate" turned out to be so. And if for many centuries most Jews did not live in Eretz Yisrael, it lived within them: in every prayer, in every holiday, in every ceremony, day in and day out. It remained for them "our land," for which they never ceased to offer daily thanksgiving to God.

Interestingly, the sages also required, as a condition of discharging the obligation of saying the blessing for the land, that reference be made to the Brit Milah ("Covenant of the Circumcision") and to the Torah. This only reinforces the point that in addition to food, Eretz Yisrael is a central theme of the Grace and not just a peripheral motif. If this were not so, there would be no reason to consider Brit Milah and Torah as integral parts of the blessing. Only in the context of Eretz Yisrael can their inclusion be explained, for both are intimately related to Israel's possession of the land. God made a covenant with Abraham, giving to him and to his descendants as an everlasting possession, the land that was then known as Canaan. Incumbent on them, with the acceptance of this gift, was the commandment that "every male among you be circumcised" (Genesis 17:7–10, 13) and the obligation to keep to the Torah. "All the precepts that I command upon you this day you shall keep, so that you may live and multiply and come and inherit the land that the Lord promised on oath to your fathers" (Deut. 8:1).

If loyalty to Torah was a condition for acquiring the land, it is equally a factor in retaining it. Physical possession of Eretz Yisrael and a love for the land are, in themselves, not enough to assure national survival and growth. There must be a spiritual dimension to Jewish life in the holy land. It is in this context that we can turn to the popular meaning of the verse that "man does not live by bread alone." The Divine Presence must be felt, and nothing more strikingly reflects this dimension than Jerusalem and its central sanctuary, the Beit Hamikdash. This spiritual need is the theme of the third blessing.

The Blessing for Jerusalem: Birkat Yerushalayim

רַחֶם־נָא יהוה אֱלֹהֵינוּ עַל יִשְׂרָאֵל עַמֶּךָ,
וְעַל יְרוּשָׁלַיִם עִירֶךָ וְעַל צִיּוֹן מִשְׁכַּן כְּבוֹדֶךָ
וְעַל מַלְכוּת בֵּית דָּוִד מְשִׁיחֶךָ וְעַל הַבַּיִת הַגָּדוֹל
וְהַקָּדוֹשׁ שֶׁנִּקְרָא שִׁמְךָ עָלָיו. אֱלֹהֵינוּ, אָבִינוּ,
רְעֵנוּ זוּנֵנוּ פַּרְנְסֵנוּ וְכַלְכְּלֵנוּ וְהַרְוִיחֵנוּ, וְהַרְוַח
לָנוּ יהוה אֱלֹהֵינוּ מְהֵרָה מִכָּל צָרוֹתֵינוּ, וְנָא
אַל תַּצְרִיכֵנוּ יהוה אֱלֹהֵינוּ לֹא לִידֵי מַתְּנַת בָּשָׂר
וָדָם וְלֹא לִידֵי הַלְוָאָתָם, כִּי אִם לְיָדְךָ הַמְּלֵאָה,
הַפְּתוּחָה, הַקְּדוֹשָׁה וְהָרְחָבָה, שֶׁלֹּא נֵבוֹשׁ וְלֹא
נִכָּלֵם לְעוֹלָם וָעֶד.
וּבְנֵה יְרוּשָׁלַיִם עִיר הַקֹּדֶשׁ בִּמְהֵרָה בְיָמֵינוּ.
בָּרוּךְ אַתָּה יהוה, בּוֹנֵה בְרַחֲמָיו יְרוּשָׁלָיִם. אָמֵן.

Be merciful, Lord our God, to Thy people Israel, to Thy city, Jerusalem, and to Zion, the dwelling place of Thy glory, to the royal House of David, Thine anointed, and to the great and holy Temple that was called by Thy name. Our God, our Father, tend us, feed us, sustain us, maintain us, and comfort us. Grant us speedy relief, Lord our God, from all our troubles. And please, Lord our God, let us not need other people's gifts or loans, but only Thy filled and open hand, holy and bountiful. So that we may not ever be shamed or humiliated. Rebuild Jerusalem, the holy city, soon in our days. Blessed art Thou, Lord, who in His mercy builds Jerusalem. Amen.

This was originally a blessing of thanksgiving for Jerusalem and the Temple. Only after the Temple was destroyed and the city razed, was it reworded as a prayer for their rebuilding.

With respect to this blessing the sages ruled that "one who does not mention 'the kingdom of the House of David' in the context of this blessing has not fulfilled his obligation" (Berakhot 49a). This phrase reflects the national yearning for political sovereignty as symbolized by the coming of the Messiah. The sages obviously believed that the spiritual aspirations of the Jewish people could not be dissociated from its national aspirations. Judaism blends them together. Jewish prayer reflects this.

Since the passages of Retzei (said on Sabbaths) and of Ya'aleh V'yavo (said on Rosh Ḥodesh and the festivals) not only mention the special day being celebrated, but are prayers that petition for the restoration of Jerusalem and the Beit Hamikdash, they are added to the Grace on those particular days within the context of this third blessing.

"Amen" is said upon the conclusion of the third blessing to indicate the end of the biblically-enjoined grace. This is the only time that we add "Amen" to a blessing that we recite ourselves. Otherwise, the rule is to say "Amen" only in response to a blessing that someone else recites.*

The Blessing of Goodness: Birkat Hatov V'hametiv

Maimonides notes that the fourth blessing to the Grace after Meals was prescribed by the sages of the Mishnah "soon after the destruction of the Temple" circa 70 C.E. (Maimonides, Commentary to the Mishnah, Berakhot 6:8). The blessing was at first simply: "Blessed art Thou, Lord our God, King of the universe, who is good and does good," a formula that we still use upon hearing good news.

The post-Temple period was certainly not a happy one. It was a period marked by deep despair. Feelings of depression were only intensified by a Grace that thanked God for the "good land" that now lay waste before people's very eyes, and for a Jerusalem and a Temple that now lay destroyed. The contrast between the prayer and the

---

* Some prayers conclude with V'nomar Amen ("And let us say Amen") or V'imru Amen ("And say Amen"). These are not regarded as responses made to oneself but as a call to those hearing the prayer to respond with an affirmation.

reality was too great to bear. The faith of the people was put under great strain. To restore their hope and revive their spirit, the sages deliberately stressed the goodness of God who is bound to bring redemption.

More than a half-century later, Bar Kokhba led an abortive uprising against the Romans to restore Jewish independence. In 135 C.E. the downfall of Betar, his last stronghold, marked the collapse of the rebellion. The Roman emperor, Hadrian, insisted on punishing the Jews by refusing to permit their dead at Betar to be buried. And so they lay unburied until Hadrian's successor, Antoninus Pius, came to the throne in 138 C.E. and revoked the edict. Miraculously, the bodies of the fallen had not decayed beyond recognition, inspiring the sages at Yavneh to see it as a sign that Israel, though defeated, will be preserved until such time as it will be restored to glory. And so they specifically applied the fourth blessing to this event: "God is good" for preventing the decay of the corpses, and "He does good" in making it possible to bring them to burial (Berakhot 48b; Taanit 31a; Bava Batra 121b; Olat Re'iyah I, p. 366).

This fourth blessing of Grace, *Hatov V'hametiv*, was known and recited before the events at Betar. This is clearly indicated in several other Talmudic sources. It is mentioned by Rabbi Eleazar in his view on when to say Retzei (Berakhot 48b), by Rabbi Akiva on what to say in a house of mourning (Berakhot 46b), and by Rabbi Ishmael who was of the opinion that the fourth blessing should also be regarded as biblically enjoined (Yer. Berakhot 7:1). The point is that all these sages lived before the tragedy of Betar occurred. It may, however, have been lent a new dimension of significance in the aftermath of the events of Betar. By associating the blessing of God's goodness with the events at Betar, the sages wished to stress that even when God is angry with His people, He will still show them kindness. They were not to lose hope.

בָּרוּךְ אַתָּה יהוה אֱלֹהֵינוּ מֶלֶךְ הָעוֹלָם, הָאֵל,
אָבִינוּ, מַלְכֵּנוּ, אַדִירֵנוּ, בּוֹרְאֵנוּ, גּוֹאֲלֵנוּ, יוֹצְרֵנוּ,
קְדוֹשֵׁנוּ קְדוֹשׁ יַעֲקֹב, רוֹעֵנוּ רוֹעֵה יִשְׂרָאֵל, הַמֶּלֶךְ

הַטּוֹב וְהַמֵּטִיב לַכֹּל, שֶׁבְּכָל יוֹם וָיוֹם הוּא הֵיטִיב
הוּא מֵיטִיב הוּא יֵיטִיב לָנוּ, הוּא גְמָלָנוּ הוּא
גוֹמְלֵנוּ הוּא יִגְמְלֵנוּ לָעַד לְחֵן וּלְחֶסֶד וּלְרַחֲמִים
וּלְרֶוַח, הַצָּלָה וְהַצְלָחָה, בְּרָכָה וִישׁוּעָה, נֶחָמָה,
פַּרְנָסָה וְכַלְכָּלָה, וְרַחֲמִים וְחַיִּים וְשָׁלוֹם וְכָל
טוֹב, וּמִכָּל טוּב לְעוֹלָם אַל יְחַסְּרֵנוּ.

Blessed art Thou, Lord our God, King of the universe, God our Father
our King; our Mighty One; our Creator; our Redeemer; our Maker;
our Holy One, the Holy One of Jacob; our Shepherd, the Shepherd
of Israel.
Thou art the King who is good and does good to all.
For every day He has done good to us, does good to us, and will do
good to us; it is He who has bestowed, does bestow and will always
bestow upon us grace, loving kindness, mercy and relief; rescue,
success, blessing, salvation; consolation, sustenance, and maintenance;
mercy, life, peace and all good; and of everything good, may we
never lack.

The end of the fourth blessing returns to the theme of food
and sustenance. It concludes with the words *l'olam al yeḥasreinu*,
"may we never lack." When one hears another person reciting Grace
reach this point, one responds with "Amen." This is the end of the
required text of the after-meal grace. One who says the Grace over a
cup of wine may put down the cup at this point.

THE CONCLUDING HARAḤAMAN PETITIONS

The Grace continues with a series of short petitions, some personal, some national, that were gradually added to it. It became
customary to recite them. Each now begins with the word *Haraḥaman*

("May the Merciful One . . ."). They do not form part of the obligatory after-meal blessing (AH 189:7).

On special occasions, this section of petitions is expanded. When a bride and bridegroom are present, or at a meal celebrating a Brit Milah, appropriate Haraḥaman petitions are added to suit the occasion.

The section of Haraḥaman petitions concludes with the same verse that concludes the Amidah and the Kaddish: *Oseh shalom bimromav*, ("May He who makes peace in the heavens, may He make peace for us and for all Israel, and say Amen").

Only one of the Haraḥaman petitions, the Guest's Prayer, has a basis in Talmudic literature; it may even be the one that inspired the development of the others. Or it may simply be that the sages, who were accustomed to adding personal petitions at the end of the Amidah, also did so at the end of the Birkat Hamazon.

THE GUEST'S PRAYER

The Talmud tells us that if a guest is invited to dine with us, he should be given the privilege of leading the Grace. The reason for this is that he may bless the host. The text of this blessing in the Talmud is:

> May it be God's will that our host should never be humiliated in this world nor disgraced in the world-to-come.
>
> (Berakhot 46a)

To this prayer, Rabbi Judah added more words of blessing. All of it is quoted as the Guest's Prayer in the Shulḥan Arukh (OH 201:1).

The first part is an indirect way of saying that the host should be blessed with a livelihood, for poverty was seen as a humiliating plight. The second half of the blessing is a prayer that a man's wealth should not cause him to behave in such a way or live in such a manner that will disgrace him in the afterlife. It is a blessing that one use his wealth in this world in such a way as to implement his spiritual greatness in the world-to-come.

It is not known why the Talmudic text of this prayer fell into disuse. But the text of the blessing that is now said is a prayer in general terms:

הָרַחֲמָן הוּא יְבָרֵךְ אֶת בַּעַל הַבַּיִת הַזֶּה וְאֶת בַּעֲלַת הַבַּיִת
הַבַּיִת הַזֶּה, אוֹתָם וְאֶת בֵּיתָםוְאֶת זַרְעָם וְאֶת כָּל אֲשֶׁר לָהֶם.
אוֹתָנוּ וְאֶת כָּל אֲשֶׁר לָנוּ, כְּמוֹ שֶׁנִּתְבָּרְכוּ אֲבוֹתֵינוּ אַבְרָהָם
יִצְחָק וְיַעֲקֹב בַּכֹּל מִכֹּל כֹּל, כֵּן יְבָרֵךְ אוֹתָנוּ כֻּלָּנוּ יַחַד
בִּבְרָכָה שְׁלֵמָה, וְנֹאמַר אָמֵן.

May the Merciful One bless the host and hostess and all who are seated about the table . . . just as our forefathers were blessed in every way with every manner of blessing.*

One who hears this or any one of the other Haraḥaman petitions should answer "Amen."

THE SUMMONS TO SAY GRACE: ZIMUN

When three or more males over the age of thirteen dine together at the same table, they do not say the Birkat Hamazon individually. The Talmud requires them to join together as a unit where one recites and the others respond (Berakhot 49b).

The reason for joining together to say Grace is probably based on the same considerations that favor congregational public worship over private worship. But their decision to recite the blessings so that one person elicits a response from at least two others, instead of every-

---

* The Hebrew use of the words *bakol* ("with everything"), *mikol* ("of everything"), and *kol* ("everything"), is an allusion to the comprehensiveness of the blessings bestowed upon each of the Patriarchs. These words are found in Genesi 24:1, 27:33, and 33:11. The Talmud calls these blessings "a foretaste of the world-to-come" (Bava Batra 16b–17a).

one saying it at the same time (as in the Amidah), follows a pattern found in two Biblical verses. In each verse one person is found addressing a plural (minimum of two):

> *Gadlu la'Adonai iti, uneromemah shemo yaḥdav*
>
> Exalt the Lord together with me and let us together extol His name.
>
> (Psalms 34:4)
>
> *Ki shem Adonai ekra, havu godel leiloheinu*
>
> For I proclaim the name of the Lord, give glory to our God.
>
> (Deut. 32:3)

The convening of those present for the purpose of saying Grace is called *zimun*. It also connotes an invitation to say Grace. It is done with two summonses by the one who leads the Grace. The first summons is *Rabotai, nevareikh* ("Gentlemen, let us bless"). This is simply a call to attention. With these words, the one who is to lead the Grace calls the attention of those present to the prayers that are about to be recited. One may use the word *ḥaverai* ("friends") in place of *rabotai*. It is often said in Yiddish: *Rabosai, mir velen benshen*. And it may be said in English as well.

The response of others around the table to this initial summons is:

יְהִי שֵׁם יהוה מְבֹרָךְ מֵעַתָּה וְעַד עוֹלָם:

Yehi shem Adonai mevorakh mei'atah ve'ad olam

Let the Name of the Lord be blessed from now and for ever more.

Then everyone is invited to say Grace together. The wording for this invitation was inspired by an aggadic tale told about the hospitable Abraham, who would invite passersby to stop and eat with him. When they finished eating and drinking, they would get up to thank and bless him. He would then say to them: "Did you then eat of what is mine? Thank and bless the Creator, for it is of His that you ate!" (Sotah 10b, Bereshit Rabbah 54:8). This thought is the essence of the invitation.

> *Birshut maranan verabotai.*
> *Nevareikh (Eloheinu) she'akhalnu mishelo.*

299

With the permission of those present.
Let us bless Him (our God) of whose [food] we have eaten.

The response to the formal invitation is:

בָּרוּךְ (במנין) אֱלֹהֵינוּ) שֶׁאָכַלְנוּ מִשֶּׁלּוֹ וּבְטוּבוֹ חָיִינוּ.

Barukh (Eloheinu) she'akhalnu mishelo uvetuvo ḥayinu

Blessed be He (our God) of whose [food] we have eaten and from whose goodness we live.

The one leading the Grace always repeats the response of the others before continuing.

If a minyan is present, that is, ten or more males over thirteen, *Eloheinu* ("our God"), is specifically mentioned where indicated in the parentheses. Otherwise, it is omitted.

If the one leading the Grace is a guest in someone else's home, or if his father, or rabbi, or a kohen, is present at the table, it is proper to phrase the request for permission so as to include these people. In such cases, one might insert after the word *Birshut*, one or more of the following designations: *baal habayit* ("host"), *avi mori* ("my father, my teacher"), *haRav* ("the rabbi"), *ha-kohen*, before the more general designation of *maranan verabotai*. This procedure is followed in order to show special courtesy to those who should have taken precedence or who merit special recognition. It is no different from the practice followed by speakers before they address an audience. The host has the right to determine whom he wishes to honor with the leading of the Grace. It is proper for him to give precedence to a kohen if one is present; if not, then to a scholar.

When the after-meal grace is thus convened, it is not necessary for everyone to say the Grace separately. The one leading the Grace says it aloud; the others need only respond "Amen" at the end of each of the four blessings. Today, however, it is a widespread practice for those at the table to join in reciting the entire Grace.

Three or more women dining together may and, even should, use the formula of the zimum (Berakhot 45b). The first word *rabotai* (gentlemen) is replaced by *gvirotai* ("ladies") or *ḥaverotai* ("friends").

THE INTRODUCTORY PSALMS

It is customary to recite a short psalm before Birkat Hamazon. Psalm 137, *Al Naharot Bavel* ("By the rivers of Babylon, there we sat and wept"), is said during the week. Psalm 126, *Shir HaMaalot* ("When the Lord brought back those that returned to Zion, we were like unto them that dream"), is said on Sabbaths and holidays.

In saying this introductory psalm, we achieve a double purpose. First, it serves as an ongoing memorial to the destruction of the Temple. On the Sabbath, the sorrowful Psalm 137, which contains the traditional oath of allegiance to Jerusalem, is replaced by an optimistic and joyous one that looks forward to God's salvation and redemption. Both, however, serve the same purpose of recalling Zion and Jerusalem. Second, the psalm touches upon the saying of Rabbi Simeon who taught that "If three have eaten at a table and spoke there no words of Torah, it is as if they had eaten of a sacrifice to idolatry . . . but if words of Torah were spoken, it is as though they had eaten at the table [of the All-present] that is before the Lord" (Avot 3:4). The recitation of a psalm is considered to be at least one way to have some words of Torah spoken at the table, where one is otherwise unable to engage in such talk.

WHEN THE FULL GRACE IS SAID

The Biblical commandment clearly says that Birkat Hamazon must be said only if one eats to the point of being full or sated without regard to what is being eaten. However, the sages decreed that since bread is the accepted basis of a meal, the full grace must be said only if bread is eaten. On the other hand, one does not have to reach satiety before incurring the obligation. Even if one eats an amount of bread equivalent only to the size of an olive (*kazayit*), approximately one ounce by volume, one is obligated to recite the full Birkat Hamazon. Bread as defined in the Torah is only that which is baked from the flour of one of the following five grains: wheat, spelt, barley, rye, and oats.

בָּרוּךְ אַתָּה יהוה אֱלֹהֵינוּ מֶלֶךְ הָעוֹלָם, עַל

על עונות	על יין	על פירות משבעת המינים
הַמִּחְיָה וְעַל הַכַּלְכָּלָה	הַגֶּפֶן וְעַל פְּרִי הַגָּפֶן	הָעֵץ וְעַל פְּרִי הָעֵץ

על יין ועונות יחד הַמִּחְיָה וְעַל הַכַּלְכָּלָה וְעַל הַגֶּפֶן וְעַל פְּרִי הַגָּפֶן

וְעַל תְּנוּבַת הַשָּׂדֶה וְעַל אֶרֶץ חֶמְדָּה טוֹבָה וּרְחָבָה, שֶׁרָצִיתָ וְהִנְחַלְתָּ לַאֲבוֹתֵינוּ לֶאֱכֹל מִפִּרְיָהּ וְלִשְׂבֹּעַ מִטּוּבָהּ. רַחֶם־נָא יהוה אֱלֹהֵינוּ עַל יִשְׂרָאֵל עַמֶּךָ וְעַל יְרוּשָׁלַיִם עִירֶךָ וְעַל צִיּוֹן מִשְׁכַּן כְּבוֹדֶךָ וְעַל מִזְבְּחֶךָ וְעַל הֵיכָלֶךָ. וּבְנֵה יְרוּשָׁלַיִם עִיר הַקֹּדֶשׁ בִּמְהֵרָה בְיָמֵינוּ, וְהַעֲלֵנוּ לְתוֹכָהּ וְשַׂמְּחֵנוּ בְּבִנְיָנָהּ וְנֹאכַל מִפִּרְיָהּ וְנִשְׂבַּע מִטּוּבָהּ, וּנְבָרֶכְךָ עָלֶיהָ בִּקְדֻשָּׁה וּבְטָהֳרָה.

בשבת: וּרְצֵה וְהַחֲלִיצֵנוּ בְּיוֹם הַשַּׁבָּת הַזֶּה,

בראש חודש: זָכְרֵנוּ לְטוֹבָה בְּיוֹם רֹאשׁ הַחֹדֶשׁ הַזֶּה,

בראש השנה: זָכְרֵנוּ לְטוֹבָה בְּיוֹם הַזִּכָּרוֹן הַזֶּה,

בשלש רגלים: וְשַׂמְּחֵנוּ בְּיוֹם

בפסח: חַג הַמַּצּוֹת הַזֶּה,

בשבועות: חַג הַשָּׁבוּעוֹת הַזֶּה,

בסוכות: חַג הַסֻּכּוֹת הַזֶּה,

בשמיני עצרת ובשמחת תורה: הַשְּׁמִינִי חַג הָעֲצֶרֶת הַזֶּה,

כִּי אַתָּה יהוה טוֹב וּמֵטִיב לַכֹּל וְנוֹדֶה לְּךָ עַל הָאָרֶץ

על עונות	על יין	על פירות משבעת המינים
וְעַל הַמִּחְיָה. בָּרוּךְ אַתָּה יהוה, עַל הָאָרֶץ וְעַל הַמִּחְיָה.	וְעַל פְּרִי הַגָּפֶן. בָּרוּךְ אַתָּה יהוה, עַל הָאָרֶץ וְעַל פְּרִי הַגָּפֶן.	וְעַל הַפֵּרוֹת. בָּרוּךְ אַתָּה יהוה, עַל הָאָרֶץ וְעַל הַפֵּרוֹת.

על עונות ויין ביחד

וְעַל הַמִּחְיָה וְעַל פְּרִי הַגָּפֶן. בָּרוּךְ אַתָּה יהוה, עַל הָאָרֶץ וְעַל הַמִּחְיָה וְעַל פְּרִי הַגָּפֶן.

If one partakes *only* of other kinds of food (or drink), shorter forms of grace are prescribed, even if a full meal is eaten. There are two shorter forms. One is the *Berakhah Aharonah* ("Concluding Blessing"), also known in the Talmud as "The One Blessing that Summarizes the Three" (*Berakhah Ahat M'ein Shalosh*). The other is the *Borei Nefashot* blessing.

SHORTER FORMS OF GRACE AFTER MEALS

The Berakhah Aharonah: The Concluding Blessing

The Concluding Blessing consists of a single paragraph that mentions all the central themes contained in the four blessings of Birkat Hamazon. Thanks is given for the food that was eaten and for the "desirable, good and spacious land." God's mercy is invoked on the city of Jerusalem and on Zion. We plead for its rebuilding, and He is praised as being good and doing good to all.

This condensed blessing is recited whenever one eats a minimum of one ounce by volume or drinks a minimum of three fluid ounces of any of the foods mentioned in the Torah as indigenous to the Land of Israel. They are as follows: wine, grapes, figs, pomegranates, olives, dates (the honey mentioned in the Bible); also wheat, barley, spelt, rye, and oats whenever these grains are not in the form of bread.

The beginning of the Concluding Blessing varies depending on what is eaten. For wine, the words "for the vine and the fruit of the vine" are used at the beginning. For any of the five fruits, the words "for the tree and the fruit of the tree" are used. For foods other than bread made from any of the five grains, the words "for the sustenance and nourishment" are used. The end of the blessing reflects the same variations.

The Borei Nefashot Blessing

Whenever one eats or drinks food other than bread or those foods that require the recitation of the Concluding Blessing, a very brief form of grace is prescribed:

בָּרוּךְ אַתָּה יהוה אֱלֹהֵינוּ מֶלֶךְ הָעוֹלָם,
בּוֹרֵא נְפָשׁוֹת רַבּוֹת וְחֶסְרוֹנָן, עַל כָּל מַה שֶּׁבָּרֵאתָ
לְהַחֲיוֹת בָּהֶם נֶפֶשׁ כָּל חָי. בָּרוּךְ חֵי הָעוֹלָמִים.

Blessed art Thou, Lord our God, King of the universe, who creates
many different living beings and the things they need [to survive].
For all that Thou hast created to sustain the life of every living being,
blessed [art Thou], the Life of all worlds.

An Abbreviated Version of Birkat Hamazon

Although it is not now customary to recite an abbreviated version
of Grace in lieu of the full four-blessing Grace, such versions were
used in Talmudic times for farm laborers (Berakhot 16a), and authorities have occasionally sanctioned their use under pressing circumstances. The abbreviated version now in use contains all four berakhot,
but each of the last three blessings is condensed, with only a concise
reference to the essential elements in each blessing.* The abbreviated
version can be adopted, not only for emergency situations, but as a
children's Grace after Meals.

* See *To Be a Jew*, pp. 170–172.

16

*The Blessings
Before Eating:
Birkhot Hanehenin*

THE SAGES also prescribed blessings to say before eating. It does not matter if one sits down to eat a full dinner or a casual snack. The blessings before eating or drinking are part of a broader category of berakhot, collectively known as *Birkhot Hanehenin*, ("Blessings of Enjoyment") said for things which bring one pleasure. These blessings are not only prescribed for what we eat or drink but also for fragrances we smell. Although I will discuss only the food blessings, blessings were formulated also for things we see and hear.* (In most prayer books, all these blessings are found right after the Grace after Meals.) The Birkhot Hanehenin are not blessings of thanksgiving, but of authorization.

The underlying principle of these Blessings of Enjoyment is that

---

* Meriting a blessing of thanksgiving is the sight of mountains, oceans, deserts, falling stars, or the rainbow. A blessing is also called for when seeing a person distinguished either for his Torah or secular knowledge; when hearing either good news or bad tidings; or when hearing the sounds of thunder and storm.

"man is forbidden to enjoy anything of this world without first say-ing a blessing" (Berakhot 35a, b). Judaism takes seriously the teaching of Psalms (24:1): "The earth and all it contains is the Lord's." The blessing is a way of asking for and receiving God's permission to take and enjoy that which belongs to Him. The wording of the blessings reflects this purpose. It doesn't say "thank you" to God as is done in the blessings after eating. But it does acknowledge Him as the one who "created the fruit of the tree," the one "who brings forth bread from the earth," and so forth. By acknowledging His owner-ship, we seek to obtain a permit to use His gifts.

To enjoy the things of this world without first receiving Divine authorization was compared by the sages to sacrilege, the stealing of items consecrated to God. It would be the same as taking something that doesn't belong to us without the permission of the owner.

This underlying view provides a basis for resolving the problem created by an apparently contradictory verse in Psalms (115:16) which says that "the heavens are the heavens of the Lord, but the earth He gave to mankind." This is a clear statement and would seem to oppose that "the earth and all it contains is the Lord's." Instead, it says that God turned the earth over to man, for him to use and en-joy. The sages saw no contradiction in this. Before one recites a berakhah, they said, the earth is the Lord's. After one recites it, it becomes man's to use and enjoy.

This philosophy is also the basis for the halakhic objection to reciting a blessing either before or after eating forbidden foods. One might be inclined to think that the faith and piety reflected by a blessing of thanksgiving, or one that acknowledges God's ownership of the world, mitigates the transgression. Not so, insisted the sages; it even aggravates it. The comparison they make is to a person who asks a friend's permission to eat some of the friend's food. Were his friend to say no, it would be sheer impudence and brazen contempt if he proceeded to eat it; and the "thank you" he followed it up with would only be adding insult to injury. Since a blessing for food is a formula for receiving God's permission to eat the food, and since per-mission to eat the forbidden food has already been denied by God, to go ahead and eat it and then thank Him shows only defiance and contempt. Better not to say the blessing, for in addition to the afore-mentioned objections, it is, under the circumstances, also a blessing said in vain. To such acts of "piety" the sages applied the verse from Psalms (10:13): "The thief who blessed has blasphemed the Lord" (Maim. Hil. Berakhot 1:19).

THE FOOD BLESSINGS: A CLASSIFICATION

The blessings for food are formulated according to the following classifications:

ò¦ For all food that does not grow from the earth, the blessing concludes with the words *she-hakol nih-yeh bidevaro* ("through whose Word all things were called into being").

This category includes water, meat, fish, eggs, honey, milk and milk products (cheese, creams, yogurts, ice-cream). Vegetables grown by hydroponics or in a planter also require this blessing.

This blessing is also used for food that comes from the earth or was grown on a tree but whose natural form is so altered in processing that it is no longer recognizable.

This includes fruit juices, alcoholic beverages (except grape wine), meat soups, jams, coffee, tea, sugar, fruit sauces, and candy. (See p. 308.)

This blessing is so all-inclusive and all-embracing that it can be regarded as the most useful of the blessings. If one does not know or cannot remember the proper blessing to make on any particular food, one can never go wrong by reciting this one. The obligation to recite a blessing before eating is always fulfilled by this blessing.

As different foods and beverages are rated along an increasing scale of importance, their blessings become more and more specific. (At the top of the list is bread and wine, where the blessing specifically mentions them by name.)

ò¦ For all food that grows from the earth, except for food baked from the flour of wheat, barley, oats, rye, and spelt (the five grains mentioned or alluded to in the Torah as indigenous to Eretz Yisrael), the blessing concludes with: *borei pri ha-adamah* ("who creates the fruit of the earth").

> This includes all such vegetables as tomatoes, cucumbers, carrots, peas, beans, beets, spinach, celery, eggplant, cabbage, cauliflower, corn, and potatoes.
>
> It also includes such fruits as bananas, pineapples, strawberries, watermelons, cantaloupes, as well as peanuts and sunflower seeds.

৪০ Inasmuch as greater importance was always attributed to the aforementioned grains, the sages stipulated a special blessing for food, other than bread, prepared from the flour of these grains. It concludes with: *borei minei mezonot* ("who creates various kinds of nourishment").

> This includes most cereals, cakes, cookies, pretzels, spaghetti and noodle products, pancakes and dough-covered foods. This blessing is also said for rice, though it is not one of the five major grains.

> But cakes and cereals, even bread made from the flour of other grains or vegetables, such as corn and potatoes, are not included in this category. They take the general blessing of she-hakol.

৪০ Still greater importance was attached to bread since bread has always been the basis of a meal and a major source of nourishment (the "staff of life"). Hence, bread baked from the five grains merited a blessing all its own: *hamotzi lehem min ha-aretz* ("who brings forth bread from the earth").

The specific wording used for the blessing over bread is based on a verse from Psalms 104:14, which praises God, the Creator, for providing the resources that enable man, through his toil, to bring forth bread from the earth. Though it is man who toils, it is God who makes it happen.

The blessing for bread, said at the beginning of a meal, suffices for everything eaten as part of the meal, except wine and fresh fruit, which require separate blessings (Berakhot 41b).

৪০ Tree fruit, though it comes ultimately from the earth and is technically covered by the blessing of *borei pri ha-adamah,* has its own classification. The blessing concludes with: *borei pri ha-etz* ("who creates the fruit of the tree").

This includes all such fruits as apples, oranges, grapefruits, grapes, cherries, olives, figs, dates, persimmons, plums, and apricots.

It is also said for avocados, coconuts and nuts such as walnuts, cashew nuts, almonds, and pistachios.

For the purpose of this blessing, a tree is defined as that which produces fruit from year to year. Furthermore, the tree and its branches must remain intact when the fruit is removed. This definition of a tree includes what we call bushes. If the tree trunk or its branches wither or are cut off (as with the banana or pineapple plants), or if fresh seeds must be planted annually, it is not classified as tree fruit but as "fruit of the ground."

&❧ The only fruit that merits a blessing of its own is grape juice or wine, the fermented juice of the grape. The blessing concludes with: *borei pri hagafen* ("who creates the fruit of the vine"). The fermented juice of other fruits or vegetables, even if called "wine," does not qualify for this blessing.

Like bread, wine has always enjoyed a special distinction. Wine satisfies and is a source of nourishment; it also makes a person cheerful. The Psalmist immortalized its significance: "Wine maketh glad the heart of man . . . and bread sustains the heart of man" (Psalms 104:15; Berakhot 35b).

Wine as a symbol of joy and celebration was given halakhic status when the sages required that drinking a cup of wine accompany certain prayers or ceremonies. And so a blessing for wine is added to Kiddush, Havdalah, the Rite of Circumcision, the Redemption of the First-Born, the Ceremony of Betrothal, and the Marriage Blessings. Wine, popularly referred to in halakhic literature as a "Cup of Blessing," plays a key role in the seder ritual, and is also utlized in the Grace after Meals, when said by a quorum (OH 182:1, MB:1,4).

L'ḤAYIM: THE CLASSIC JEWISH TOAST

The classical Jewish toast before drinking wine or other alcoholic beverages is well-known: *L'ḥayim* (To Life!). This is not a blessing in the traditional sense of the word, but is rather a prayer, a hope. When it is said, it should precede the berakhah said over the wine or liquor. The toast is typically Jewish, because Judaism places great stress upon life.

This toast has a Talmudic origin. It is credited to Rabbi Akiva who lived in the second century c.e. It was apparently the custom during that period to give wine to bereaved persons who were sitting in mourning (Ketubot 8b). It must have been considered an important use for the wine, to judge by the statement made by Rabbi Ḥanin that "wine was created only for the purpose of comforting mourners" (Eruvin 65a). It was then known as the "Cup of Comfort." On joyous occasions therefore, the hope was expressed that the drinking of the wine should continue to be l'ḥayim ("for life"), for reasons of joy and gladness rather than for reasons of bereavement and grief. When Rabbi Akiva once made a banquet in honor of his son Simeon, he said as he brought each glass of wine: "To the life and health of the rabbis and their disciples!" (Shabbat 67b).

THE SEVEN MARRIAGE BLESSINGS: SHEVA BERAKHOT

The Torah tells us in referring to the first couple at the dawn of human history that "God blessed them" (Genesis 1:28). Jewish tradition, in seeking to emulate the Divine example, followed suit by introducing blessings on behalf of the bride and groom. These blessings are found in the Talmud (Ketubot 8a).

As a home ritual, the Seven Marriage Blessings are said together with the Grace after Meals and so should have been part of the previous chapter. However, so as not to interrupt the continuity involved in discussing blessings related to food, the Marriage Blessings were put aside till now. Even so, there is justification for inserting these blessings into a chapter on Birkhot Hanehenin, even though the Marriage Blessings are not officially so classified. Like the blessings before eating, the Marriage Blessings—first recited as part of the wedding ceremony symbolizing the consummation of marriage—are said before partaking and enjoying. By reflecting the sanctity of the sexual relationship, these blessings, too, imply a sort of authorization for the marital relationship.

The Jewish wedding ceremony consists of two sets of blessings. The first is called the "Blessing of Betrothal" (*Birkat Eirusin*), which is a single blessing preceded by the blessing for wine. The second set is called the "Blessings of Marriage" (*Birkhot Nisuin*) and consists of six blessings preceded by the blessing for wine, making a total of seven blessings. The Talmudic name for the latter set is *Birkat Ḥatanim* ("Bridegrooms' Blessing"). Its primary purpose is to bless the couple with success, joy, and happiness. The current popular name for these marriage blessings is simply *Sheva Berakhot*, ("Seven Blessings").

These blessings are said not only during the wedding ceremony, but also after Grace following the wedding dinner and the festive meals that occur throughout the week of rejoicing.

The only difference between the Sheva Berakhot recited at the wedding ceremony and those recited at the dinner table following the Grace after Meals is that during the wedding ceremony, the blessing for the wine is said before the prescribed six blessings as is usually done in rituals where wine is used. At the dinner table however, the blessing for the wine is said after the prescribed blessings. Saying the wine blessing at the very end is a clear indication that it is also meant to encompass the Marriage Blessings and should not mistakenly be associated only with the Grace.

The Sheva Berakhot are not said during the week following the wedding ceremony if the bride and groom dine alone or in the company of family and friends who had been either to the wedding dinner or to subsequent dinners in their honor. Some authorities have ruled that the last of the Sheva Berakhot may and, indeed, should be said even then (Rashi, Ketubot 8a).

The condition permitting another complete recitation of the Sheva Berakhot during the week of celebration is the presence at the meal of at least one new face who had not been at the wedding dinner or at any of the other meals in honor of the bride and groom. The new face must be a person qualified to be part of a minyan since a prayer quorum is necessary for these blessings (Ketubot 7b).

To make it possible to recite the full Sheva Berakhot at least once each day in the week following a wedding, it has become customary in contemporary traditional circles for a different friend or relative to host a dinner each day in the couple's honor. Apart from social custom, entertaining the bride and groom in this way is regarded as praiseworthy for it gladdens them. To this dinner, the host invites one or more of his own friends who did not attend the wedding dinner. Invitations can be extended just for dessert and the blessings. One need not have been to the entire dinner in order to be a participant in the quorum needed for the blessings. The name "Sheva Berakhot" has now come to mean not only the blessings themselves, but the entire festive occasion at which these blessings are said.

The Meaning of the Marriage Blessings

The first three blessings (excepting the one for wine) relate to the theme of creation in general, and of Adam and Eve in particular, for their creation and union marked the inception of a husband-wife relationship. The theme of creation is fitting in the context of marriage, because marriage itself is seen as an element in the continuing process of creation. One of the purposes of marriage is "to be fruitful and multiply." By having children, a couple become partners with God in an act of creation, one that serves to preserve the human race that He brought into being with the first Man.

The very first blessing, however, was intended to set a tone of humility. People sometimes tend to think of everything as having been created to serve their own purposes. A marriage especially is often seen in this light—as the fulfillment of personal desires and needs. "It's only the two of us that matter" might adequately describe the feelings of young couples in love. We are therefore reminded by the blessing that marriage has a higher purpose: it serves Divine goals as well as the legitimate needs of the individual. A teaching from the very end of the Ethics of the Fathers says, "Whatever the Holy One, blessed be He, created in His world, He created it only for His own glory . . . ," that is, to serve Him. Isaiah had said it earlier: "Everyone who is called by My name, I have created, formed, and made for My glory" (Is. 43:7). The sages embodied this idea in the first blessing:

בָּרוּךְ אַתָּה יהוה אֱלֹהֵינוּ מֶלֶךְ הָעוֹלָם, שֶׁהַכֹּל בָּרָא לִכְבוֹדוֹ.

Blessed art Thou, Lord our God, King of the universe, who created everything for His glory.

The second blessing goes on to thank God for having created Man, a reminder perhaps of the couple's responsibility to perpetuate Man.

Although the Hebrew word for "Man" is "Adam,"* and Adam is identified as the male of the species, the initial Biblical use of the name "Adam" is not so specific. "Male and female, He created them; And when they were created, He blessed *them* and called *them* 'Adam'." (Gen. 5:2). Here Adam or Man is a generic reference to both sexes.

בָּרוּךְ אַתָּה יהוה אֱלֹהֵינוּ מֶלֶךְ הָעוֹלָם, יוֹצֵר הָאָדָם.

Blessed art Thou, Lord our God, King of the universe, Creator of Man.

The third blessing then alludes to the separate formation of the female, and to the fact that both sexes were fashioned in "the image of God." This is an expression that has always been understood to mean that the human being was created with qualities that make him capable of acquiring wisdom, understanding, and knowledge—which, in turn, become the basis for the exercise of free will. It is in these qualities that Man is likened unto God.

---

* He was so called because he was made from the earth (*adamah*). Man is certainly made of the same chemical elements found in the earth.

The reference to "the image of God" is a reminder of the spiritual potential inherent in the human species, and of the couple's responsibility to choose of their own free will those goals in life that reflect credit upon this status.

בָּרוּךְ אַתָּה יהוה אֱלֹהֵינוּ מֶלֶךְ הָעוֹלָם, אֲשֶׁר יָצַר אֶת הָאָדָם בְּצַלְמוֹ, בְּצֶלֶם דְּמוּת תַּבְנִיתוֹ, וְהִתְקִין לוֹ מִמֶּנּוּ בִּנְיַן עֲדֵי עַד. בָּרוּךְ אַתָּה יהוה, יוֹצֵר הָאָדָם.

Blessed art Thou, Lord our God, King of the universe, who fashioned Man in His image after His own likeness, and prepared for him [a woman] out of his very self, an everlasting structure. Blessed art Thou, Lord, Creator of Man.

The third blessing, with its reference to the very first union, would seem to be the appropriate moment to turn our attention to the new couple. But before proceeding to bless the bride and groom, which after all is the main purpose of the blessings, one more obligation remains to be discharged, and this constitutes the theme of the next blessing.

The fourth blessing is in keeping with the spirit of a Biblical passage that has become the Jewish oath of allegiance to Jerusalem. This passage avows that Jerusalem will be set above one's personal joy.

If I forget thee, O Jerusalem, let my right hand forget its cunning. Let my tongue cleave to the roof of my mouth, if I remember thee not, if I set not Jerusalem at the top of my joy.

(Psalms 137:5–6)

And so the sages introduced a blessing recalling Jerusalem, which precedes the two blessings for the happiness of the couple.

שׂוֹשׂ תָּשִׂישׂ וְתָגֵל הָעֲקָרָה בְּקִבּוּץ בָּנֶיהָ לְתוֹכָהּ

314

בְּשִׂמְחָה. בָּרוּךְ אַתָּה יהוה, מְשַׂמֵּחַ צִיּוֹן בְּבָנֶיהָ.

May she who was barren [Jerusalem] be exceedingly glad and joyful, with the ingathering of her children into her midst in joy. Blessed art Thou, Lord, who causes Zion to rejoice through her children.

This blessing prays for the return of the Jewish people to Jerusalem and for the rejoicing that will result from that homecoming. The prayer for Jerusalem is particularly appropriate for a wedding. The Prophet Isaiah used the rejoicing of the groom toward the bride as a metaphor to describe the way God will rejoice over Jerusalem when He brings the redemption.

As the bridegroom rejoices over the bride, so shall thy God rejoice over thee [Jerusalem].

(Isaiah 62:5)

The last two blessings are the heart of the Sheva Berakhot, for they are prayers on behalf of the couple being united in marriage.

שַׂמֵּחַ תְּשַׂמַּח רֵעִים הָאֲהוּבִים כְּשַׂמֵּחֲךָ יְצִירְךָ בְּגַן עֵדֶן מִקֶּדֶם. בָּרוּךְ אַתָּה יהוה, מְשַׂמֵּחַ חָתָן וְכַלָּה.

Greatly gladden these beloved ones, even as Thou gladdened Thy creation in the Garden of Eden in days of yore. Blessed art Thou, Lord, who gladdens the bridegroom and bride.

This is a prayer that God make the couple happy by providing them throughout their lives with all their material needs and with all that is good, just as He provided for Adam and Eve in the Garden of Eden. This is a prayer for the success of the couple, individually and together.

The last marriage blessing prays that the bride and groom find their happiness and joy in and with one another. This is a prayer not for material success but for the fulfillment of their mutual love. The

315

blessing enumerates many kinds of joy and many nuances of gladness, a whole series of qualities that can contribute to the happiness of the couple. In the latter half of the blessing there is another allusion to the redemption of Jerusalem, a prospect that can only increase the happiness of bride and groom.

בָּרוּךְ אַתָּה יהוה אֱלֹהֵינוּ מֶלֶךְ הָעוֹלָם, אֲשֶׁר בָּרָא שָׂשׂוֹן וְשִׂמְחָה, חָתָן וְכַלָּה, גִּילָה, רִנָּה, דִּיצָה וְחֶדְוָה, אַהֲבָה וְאַחֲוָה וְשָׁלוֹם וְרֵעוּת. מְהֵרָה יהוה אֱלֹהֵינוּ יִשָּׁמַע בְּעָרֵי יְהוּדָה וּבְחוּצוֹת יְרוּשָׁלַיִם קוֹל שָׂשׂוֹן וְקוֹל שִׂמְחָה, קוֹל חָתָן וְקוֹל כַּלָּה, קוֹל מִצְהֲלוֹת חֲתָנִים מֵחֻפָּתָם וּנְעָרִים מִמִּשְׁתֵּה נְגִינָתָם. בָּרוּךְ אַתָּה יהוה, מְשַׂמֵּחַ הֶחָתָן עִם הַכַּלָּה.

Blessed art Thou, Lord our God, King of the universe, who created joy and gladness, groom and bride, mirth and song, pleasure and delight, love, brotherhood, peace and companionship. May there soon be heard in the cities of Judea and in the streets of Jerusalem the sound of joy and happiness, the sound of groom and the sound of bride, the jubilant sound of bridegrooms from their canopies and of youths from their feasts of song. Blessed art Thou, Lord, who causes the groom to rejoice with the bride.

Mixing the Wine Cups

When Sheva Berakhot are recited at the end of a meal, two cups of wine are used in the Ashkenazic tradition. This is because two separate mitzvot are involved. One is the Grace after Meals ("Birkat Hamazon"), the other is the Marriage Blessings (the "Birkhot Nisuin"). Each is said over its own cup of wine, for each mitzvah merits its own symbol of joy. The sages disapproved of performing mitzvot in wholesale fashion, or as they metaphorically put it, "in bundles." This is the reason for the underlying Talmudic principle that "two sanctifications are not made over one cup" (Pesaḥim 102b; Sukkah 46a).

One cup of wine is held by the person leading the Birkat Hamazon. As soon as he completes the Grace, he sets it down and lifts up the second cup for the six basic marriage blessings. The same person who led in the Grace may continue to say these blessings too, or the privilege of reciting them may be divided among other people. Where this is done, the cup of wine is passed around so that the cup is always held by the person reciting the blessing.

After the six marriage blessings have thus been said or chanted, the second cup is set down alongside the first cup. The person who led the Birkat Hamazon picks up the first cup again and recites the blessing for wine, *borei pri hagafen.*

Inasmuch as the wine blessing is made for both cups of wine, the wine from the two cups is then mixed together. The one who led the Birkat Hamazon drinks from the mixed wine. Some of it is given to the groom and bride to drink. Others at the table may also drink from it.

There is nothing mysterious about the mixing and no ritual procedure governs it. The purpose is simply to drink the wine from both cups mixed together.

1. Take a third empty cup or glass (C) in advance.
2. Pour out some wine from each of the cups (A & B) into the empty cup (C).
3. Mix the wines in the now partially-filled cups A & B by pouring one into the other. An alternate way: Pour the mixed wine from cup C back into cups A and B.

Directions for Mixing the Wine from the Two Full Cups

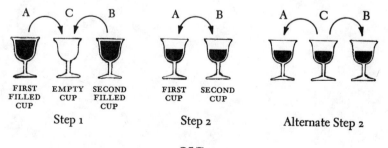

| FIRST FILLED CUP | EMPTY CUP | SECOND FILLED CUP | FIRST CUP | SECOND CUP | | | |

Step 1   Step 2   Alternate Step 2

317

There are now three partially filled cups containing mixed wine. Give one of the cups of mixed wine, it doesn't matter which one, first to the groom. He now drinks some of it and gives it to the bride to drink. The one who led the Birkat Hamazon and the immediate members of the two families partake of the other two cups.

CHAPTER

17

Home Prayers for
Sabbaths and Festivals

KIDDUSH: THE PRAYER OF SANCTIFICATION

THE FOURTH COMMANDMENT bids us to remember the Sabbath day, *lekadsho*, "to keep it holy" (Exod. 20:8). This is done by abstaining from all work. But lekadsho can also mean "to sanctify it." Jewish law therefore requires us to sanctify the Sabbath—at its beginning and at its conclusion—with an oral declaration. The prayer that does so at the start of the Sabbath is Kiddush; the prayer that does so at the conclusion of the Sabbath is Havdalah.

When Kiddush and Havdalah were first instituted by Ezra and the Men of the Great Assembly, it was not as independent rituals but as part of the Amidah prayer. These have been retained. In the Friday night Amidah, the middle blessing affirms the sanctity of the day. This is Kiddush. A passage added to the first of the middle blessings said in the weekday Amidah as the Sabbath ends, proclaims the separation of the Sabbath from the other days. This passage is Havdalah.

At a later time, when the impoverished Jewish community became more affluent and wine became plentiful, the sages ruled that Kiddush and Havdalah be said also over a cup of wine. As the symbol of joy and celebration, wine added significance to an occasion. Therefore it was reserved for special occasions and for honored guests. And what could be more special than the Sabbath and the festivals?

I might also point out that pouring wine on the altar was part of the sacrificial ritual in the Temple. It was at this point in the ceremony that the Levites sang their songs of praise to God. The Temple service may have been influential in the introduction of wine for Kiddush and Havdalah. This is hinted at in the Talmud: Rav links the kind of wine that may be used for Kiddush with the kind suitable for the altar. "Kiddush," he said, "may not be said except over wine that is worthy of being poured on the altar" (Bava Batra 97a).

After much rabbinic debate as to whether Kiddush over wine should be said in the synagogue or at home, the halakhic verdict came down in favor of the home. Actually, the decision was that it be said only *when and where one sits down to eat the Sabbath dinner.* A verse in Isaiah is interpreted as support for this ruling: "And you shall call the Sabbath a delight" (58:13). This implies that "where you call the Sabbath [i.e., recite Kiddush], there shall be your delight [i.e., eat and drink]" (Pesaḥim 101a, Tos s.v. *af yedei*).

The custom in Babylonia was also to say Kiddush over wine in the synagogue at the end of the Friday night service. This was due to the frequent presence in the synagogue of wayfarers who would remain to eat and sleep. Synagogues in ancient Babylonia had annexes serving as community hostels that provided food and lodging to travelers. It was for the benefit of these people that Kiddush was said (Pesaḥim 101a, Tos. s.v. *d'akhlu*). And though it has remained customary throughout the diaspora for Kiddush to be said in the synagogue, one's personal obligation to recite Kiddush or to hear it recited is only fulfilled at the dinner table. It should be noted that the custom of reciting Kiddush at the end of the Friday night synagogue service never arose in Eretz Yisrael, and so to this day Kiddush is not said in Israeli synagogues on Friday night (OH 269:1).

At dinner, the recitation of Kiddush not only serves to sanctify the day, but also exalts the religious significance and spiritual import of the meal itself. It was the Talmudic sage, Rava, who noted that on Sabbath day, Jews "eat and drink, but begin with the words of Torah and praise [of God]" (Megillah 12b). Kiddush provides such a beginning.

Rabbi Ḥayim David Halevy sees a Jewish religious ideal expressed in the link between Kiddush and the meal, namely, the fusion of the spiritual and material, the sacred and the secular. The intense spirituality and deep faith of the sages did not make them disown the material comforts of life or affect their appreciation for the good things in life. "Three things expand a man's spirit: a pleasing dwelling, a pleasing wife, pleasing clothing" (Berakhot 57b). The spiritual and material worlds are compatible, even good one for the other. Perfection in this world, to whatever degree this is possible, cannot be attained only through one or the other. The material must be infused with the spiritual; the sacred must be joined to the secular. As the natural wholeness of man consists of both the physical and the spiritual, so does the wholeness of the Sabbath (see Mekor Ḥayim HaShalem III: 115, pp. 76–77).

This thought underlies the rule that just as one may not sit down to eat on Friday night without first reciting Kiddush, one may not recite Kiddush without immediately afterward sitting down to eat. A person who, for whatever reason, cannot yet eat, may not therefore say Kiddush. Kiddush will have to be delayed until that person is ready to eat (OH 273:3). Although Friday evening is the principal time for Kiddush, it may under extenuating circumstances be said throughout the Sabbath day. In that case, one omits the introductory passage of *Vayekhulu*, for it relates only to the very end of the sixth day.

The general rule which exempts women from observing those mitzvot that depend upon a set time does not apply to Kiddush. Since the Sabbath rule is that everyone who is duty-bound to observe the prohibitions of the Sabbath must also say Kiddush, women are under equal obligation to say it. This being the case, it is halakhically permissible for a woman to recite Kiddush not only on her own behalf, or on behalf of other women when there is no male adult to do so, but also on behalf of males who are present (Mekor Ḥayim HaShalem III, 114:11; Yesodei Yeshurun III, p. 209).

Opinions differ as to whether Kiddush should be said while standing at the dinner table or while seated. The ancient sources are ambiguous on this point. Rabbi Moses Isserles reflects this non-resolution when he writes that "one can stand for Kiddush, but it is better to sit" (OH 271:10, Rema). This clearly implies that both ways are correct. Both practices are, in fact, widespread among Ashkenazic Jews. One should follow family tradition or the tradition of one's teachers in this matter. Sephardic tradition calls for standing during Kiddush. This was also the practice followed by Rabbi Isaac Luria and the kabbalistic school, whose ways are emulated by many Hasidic groups. The kabbalistic explanation for standing for these Sabbath blessings is that the Sabbath is compared to a bride, and the bridal blessings are said while standing.

On the other hand, some Ashkenazic scholars ruled that one should sit while saying Kiddush. If the person saying Kiddush is to discharge the ritual obligation of the others in the room, the people present must establish themselves as a group (keviut), best symbolized by sitting down together. Those whose custom is to stand for Kiddush consider the very act of gathering around the table sufficient in establishing this condition of keviut.

While Kiddush is said, it is customary that the two whole hallot on the Sabbath table remain covered.* Covering the hallah enables us to reverse the order of the blessings and to first say Kiddush over wine before the blessing for bread, since that serves as the equivalent of removing the bread from the table. This is necessary because a blessing for bread halakhically takes precedence over a blessing for wine, since wheat is mentioned ahead of the vine in the Torah (Deut. 8:8).**

If wine suitable for Kiddush is not available or if one may not drink wine, it is permissible to say Kiddush over the two whole loaves of hallah. The blessing for bread is then substituted within the Kiddush for that of wine; all else remain the same. When Kiddush is said over hallah, it is customary to place one's hands on the hallah while

---

* The Sabbath table is traditionally set with two whole unsliced Sabbath loaves known as hallah (pl. hallot). The two hallot, called lehem mishneh, represent the double portion of manna that the Israelites gathered on the sixth day (Exodus 16:22). Like the two candles, the two hallot are also said to symbolize the two forms of the Fourth Commandment: "Remember the Sabbath day . . ." (Exodus 20:8) and "Observe the Sabbath day . . ." (Deut. 5:12).

** Several non-halakhic, symbolic reasons for covering the hallot during Kiddush are suggested by the Tosephists. If bread does not appear until after the Sabbath has been sanctified in the Kiddush, this clearly demonstrates that the meal is not an ordinary one but in honor of the Sabbath. Another explanation is based on the hallah's symbolic representation of the manna. The cover over the hallah and the cloth beneath it represent the two layers of dew between which the manna is said to have fallen (Yoma 75b), protecting it from the sand below and the heat of the sun above. (Pesahim 100b, Tos. s.v. she'ein)

saying it. Furthermore, according to this reasoning, the ḥallot need not then be covered.

Kiddush consists of three parts:

1. an introductory passage from Genesis 2:1–3: Vayekhulu
2. the blessing for wine
3. the blessing of sanctification.

Vayekhulu

From about the third century c.e., it has been customary to say the Biblical passage from Genesis in the Friday night service. It was later also introduced in the home as a preface to Kiddush.

יוֹם הַשִּׁשִּׁי: וַיְכֻלּוּ הַשָּׁמַיִם וְהָאָרֶץ וְכָל צְבָאָם:
וַיְכַל אֱלֹהִים בַּיּוֹם הַשְּׁבִיעִי מְלַאכְתּוֹ אֲשֶׁר עָשָׂה,
וַיִּשְׁבֹּת בַּיּוֹם הַשְּׁבִיעִי מִכָּל מְלַאכְתּוֹ אֲשֶׁר עָשָׂה:
וַיְבָרֶךְ אֱלֹהִים אֶת־יוֹם הַשְּׁבִיעִי וַיְקַדֵּשׁ אֹתוֹ,
כִּי בוֹ שָׁבַת מִכָּל־מְלַאכְתּוֹ, אֲשֶׁר בָּרָא אֱלֹהִים
לַעֲשׂוֹת:

The sixth day. The heavens and the earth were completed and all their host. On the seventh day God finished the work that He had made; On the seventh day He rested from all the work that He had made. Then God blessed the seventh day, and sanctified it, because on it God ceased from all the work that He created to function thenceforth.

This Biblical passage expresses the main reason for the Sabbath, that is, as a memorial to Creation. It is first said in the Amidah at the Maariv service. It was added to the home Kiddush to enable members of the household, who were not in attendance at the Friday evening service at the synagogue, to say the passage or to hear it said (Shabbat 119b).

The words *yom hashishi* ("the sixth day"), are actually the last two words of the Biblical sentence that immediately precedes Vayek-

hulu, "And there was evening and there was morning, the sixth day."
The words are customarily added as a preface to the passage. Scholars
note the symbolism inherent in this custom. The first letters of these
two Hebrew words, Y (*yod*) and H (*heh*), plus the first letters of the
first two Hebrew words of Vayekhulu, V (*vov*) and H (*heh*), together
constitute the four letters that spell out the Tetragrammaton.

The Blessing for Wine

The blessing for the wine is introduced with the words *savri
maranan verabotai*, meaning either: "With the permission of those
present" or "Be attentive, those of you present." It is similar to the
formula used by the one who leads the Grace after Meals: *Birshut
maranan verabotai*. (See p. 299.) The word *birshut* is used with
bread, *savri* is used with wine. This formula is used to call the attention of those present to the fact that a blessing is about to be said
and to obtain their silent consent in having Kiddush recited on their
behalf. Each person need only listen to the blessing, and to answer
"Amen" with the intent to fulfill his or her individual obligation to
recite Kiddush.

The Blessing of Sanctification for the Sabbath

בָּרוּךְ אַתָּה יהוה אֱלֹהֵינוּ מֶלֶךְ הָעוֹלָם, אֲשֶׁר
קִדְּשָׁנוּ בְּמִצְוֹתָיו וְרָצָה בָנוּ, וְשַׁבַּת קָדְשׁוֹ בְּאַהֲבָה
וּבְרָצוֹן הִנְחִילָנוּ זִכָּרוֹן לְמַעֲשֵׂה בְרֵאשִׁית, כִּי הוּא
יוֹם תְּחִלָּה לְמִקְרָאֵי קֹדֶשׁ, זֵכֶר לִיצִיאַת מִצְרָיִם,
כִּי בָנוּ בָחַרְתָּ וְאוֹתָנוּ קִדַּשְׁתָּ מִכָּל הָעַמִּים, וְשַׁבַּת
קָדְשְׁךָ בְּאַהֲבָה וּבְרָצוֹן הִנְחַלְתָּנוּ. בָּרוּךְ אַתָּה
יהוה, מְקַדֵּשׁ הַשַּׁבָּת.

Blessed art Thou, Lord our God, King of the universe, who sanctified
us with His commandments and has taken pleasure in us. He caused

us to inherit His holy Sabbath in love and favor as a memorial to the work of creation. This day is the first of the sacred festivals, a memorial to the exodus from Egypt. For Thou hast chosen us and sanctified us above all nations, and Thy holy Sabbath did Thou bequeath to us as an inheritance in love and favor. Blessed art Thou, Lord, who sanctifies the Sabbath.

The Sabbath owes its primary distinction and sanctity to its status as a memorial to God's creation of the universe. "Therefore the Lord blessed the Sabbath day and hallowed it" (Exod. 20:11). By desisting from work on the seventh day, we show our homage to the Lord and bear witness that the world is not ours, but His. By sanctifying the day, we recognize God as the Creator and Lord of the universe.

Although the sanctity of the Sabbath day is implicit in the Creation and thus predates the Jewish faith, the Sabbath is also meant to remind Israel of its exodus from Egypt. "Remember that you were once a slave in the land of Egypt and that the Lord your God brought you out from there . . . hence [He] commanded you to observe the Sabbath day" (Deut. 5:15).

By recalling the slavery endured by our ancestors and the freedom that God won for us at the very beginning of our history as a nation, we should be better able to appreciate the freedom of mind and body that the Sabbath weekly affords to those who faithfully keep it. If keeping the Sabbath attests to our servitude to God, it simultaneously establishes our freedom from the servitude that is imposed on us by society and by the responsibilities we each bear. On the Sabbath, we heed no human taskmaster. For twenty-four hours, nothing (unless it be a matter of life or death) is permitted to interfere with rest, with tranquility of mind, with freedom from the pressures of daily affairs and the tensions of work. The Sabbath is intended to prevent us from slipping back into a slave mentality and to free us from worldly concerns.

The exodus is mentioned in the Kiddush to emphasize our faith in Divine Care, namely, that God acts in history. That He does so is inseparable from Jewish belief that He exists and is the Creator.

The Sabbath is called *tehilah l'mikra-ei kodesh* ("the first of the sacred festivals"). It is listed first in Leviticus, Chapter 23 where all the sacred days on the Jewish calendar are summarized.

The Blessing of Sanctification for the Festivals

Kiddush said for a festival differs slightly from that said for the Sabbath. If the festival coincides with a Sabbath, the Sabbath theme is incorporated into the festival Kiddush. The additional words for the Sabbath usually appear in parentheses or brackets.

בָּרוּךְ אַתָּה יהוה אֱלֹהֵינוּ מֶלֶךְ הָעוֹלָם, אֲשֶׁר
בָּחַר בָּנוּ מִכָּל עָם וְרוֹמְמָנוּ מִכָּל לָשׁוֹן וְקִדְּשָׁנוּ
בְּמִצְוֹתָיו, וַתִּתֶּן לָנוּ יהוה אֱלֹהֵינוּ בְּאַהֲבָה
(בשבת: שַׁבָּתוֹת לִמְנוּחָה וּ) מוֹעֲדִים לְשִׂמְחָה, חַגִּים
וּזְמַנִּים לְשָׂשׂוֹן, אֶת יוֹם (בשבת: הַשַּׁבָּת הַזֶּה וְאֶת יוֹם)

בפסח: חַג הַמַּצּוֹת הַזֶּה, זְמַן חֵרוּתֵנוּ,

בשבועות: חַג הַשָּׁבוּעוֹת הַזֶּה, זְמַן מַתַּן תּוֹרָתֵנוּ,

בסוכות: חַג הַסֻּכּוֹת הַזֶּה, זְמַן שִׂמְחָתֵנוּ,

בשמע״צ ובשמח״ת: הַשְּׁמִינִי חַג הָעֲצֶרֶת הַזֶּה, זְמַן שִׂמְחָתֵנוּ,

(בשבת: בְּאַהֲבָה) מִקְרָא קֹדֶשׁ זֵכֶר לִיצִיאַת מִצְרָיִם,
כִּי בָנוּ בָחַרְתָּ וְאוֹתָנוּ קִדַּשְׁתָּ מִכָּל הָעַמִּים,
(בשבת: וְשַׁבָּת) וּמוֹעֲדֵי קָדְשֶׁךָ (בשבת: בְּאַהֲבָה וּבְרָצוֹן)
בְּשִׂמְחָה וּבְשָׂשׂוֹן הִנְחַלְתָּנוּ. בָּרוּךְ אַתָּה יהוה,
מְקַדֵּשׁ (בשבת: הַשַּׁבָּת וְ) יִשְׂרָאֵל וְהַזְּמַנִּים.

Blessed art Thou, Lord our God, King of the universe, who hast chosen us above all people and exalted us above all nations and sanctified us by His commandments. Thou, Lord our God, hast given us in love [Sabbaths for rest] festivals for gladness, holidays and sacred seasons for joy: [this Sabbath day and] this: [appropriate insert]
. . . Festival of Matzot, the season of our freedom
. . . Festival of Shavuot, the season of the Giving of our Torah

... Festival of Sukkot, the season of our rejoicing
... Festival of Shemini Atzeret, the season of our rejoicing
[in love] a sacred festival commemorating the exodus from Egypt.
For Thou hast chosen us and hallowed us above all nations, and Thy
holy [Sabbath and] festivals Thou didst bequeath to us as an inheritance [with love and favor], with gladness and joy. Blessed art Thou
Lord, who sanctifies [the Sabbath], Israel, and the festive seasons.

The theme of Israel as the chosen is here also associated with the
idea that Israel was given special commandments to keep, whose
observance sanctifies Israel.

The reason why the word "love" (b'ahavah) is always added to
the festival Kiddush on the Sabbath is because of the Jewish belief that
God demonstrated special love to Israel when He gave it the Sabbath
to keep—so precious a possession is the Sabbath. Another reason for
adding this particular word on the Sabbath is based on a tradition
that the Sabbath was given to the children of Israel while they were
still at Marah, before they ever reached Mt. Sinai and heard the Ten
Commandments proclaimed (Sanhedrin 56b). It was at Marah,
midrash tells us, that they first accepted the Sabbath *of their own free
will* and *with great love*. This contrasts with the other Torah commandments, including the festivals, that were given to them later at
Mt. Sinai, where according to one tradition, their acceptance was
accompanied by a measure of Divine coercion (Shabbat 88a).

On the two nights of Rosh Hashanah, the Kiddush is similar to
that of the festival Kiddush, except for several small variations that
venture on the theme of Rosh Hashanah as a Day of Remembrance,
a Day of Blowing the Shofar. (Consult a siddur or maḥzor for the
exact text.)

When the night of a festival coincides with the end of a Sabbath
day, a blessing for light and a blessing of havdalah (see pp. 333–334)
are added to the Kiddush. A Havdalah candle, however, is not lit,
since the candles that were lit for the festival satisfy the basic requirement for the blessing for light.

בָּרוּךְ אַתָּה יהוה אֱלֹהֵינוּ מֶלֶךְ הָעוֹלָם, הַמַּבְדִּיל בֵּין
קֹדֶשׁ לְחֹל, בֵּין אוֹר לְחֹשֶׁךְ, בֵּין יִשְׂרָאֵל לָעַמִּים, בֵּין יוֹם

הַשְּׁבִיעִי לְשֵׁשֶׁת יְמֵי הַמַּעֲשֶׂה. בֵּין קְדֻשַּׁת שַׁבָּת לִקְדֻשַּׁת יוֹם טוֹב הִבְדַּלְתָּ, וְאֶת יוֹם הַשְּׁבִיעִי מִשֵּׁשֶׁת יְמֵי הַמַּעֲשֶׂה קִדַּשְׁתָּ, הִבְדַּלְתָּ וְקִדַּשְׁתָּ אֶת עַמְּךָ יִשְׂרָאֵל בִּקְדֻשָּׁתֶךָ. בָּרוּךְ אַתָּה יהוה, הַמַּבְדִּיל בֵּין קֹדֶשׁ לְקֹדֶשׁ.

Except for the last day(s) of Pesaḥ, the festival Kiddush is always concluded with the blessing of she'heḥeyanu:

בָּרוּךְ אַתָּה יהוה אֱלֹהֵינוּ מֶלֶךְ הָעוֹלָם, שֶׁהֶחֱיָנוּ וְקִיְּמָנוּ וְהִגִּיעָנוּ לַזְּמַן הַזֶּה.

Blessed art Thou, Lord our God, King of the universe, who hast kept us in life, and hast preserved us and hast enabled us to reach this season.

HAVDALAH: THE PRAYER OF SEPARATION

The ending of the Sabbath calls for a special declaration (Havdalah), which identifies the Sabbath as a day distinct from the rest of the week. It is said twice, once during the Saturday night Amidah and once again over a cup of wine (The Havdalah that is said in the Amidah is explained in chapter 5). The sages attached great significance to also saying Havdalah again over a cup of wine. (Berakhot 33a; Shabbat 150b).

In Babylonia where wine was scarce, Havdalah, like Kiddush, was said over wine only in the synagogue, the intent being to discharge the obligation of all those present. Havdalah is still said in the synagogue at the end of the Maariv service. Like Kiddush, Havdalah became a familiar home ceremony. It is said at home to discharge the obligation of the entire household. Although wine is the preferred beverage for the ceremony, Havdalah may be said over other "important liquids (*ḥamar medinah*). In the view of many authorities, this includes beer, milk, coffee, tea, and fruit juice.

Although it is the view of some authorities that Havdalah, like Kiddush, should be said while seated and for the same reason (see p. 321) the majority opinion prefers standing for Havdalah. Just as courtesy demands that one rise when an honored guest takes leave, so we should stand as we bid farewell to the Sabbath. Both practices are correct and both have their adherents (OH 296:6).

The Havdalah ritual contains the following components: a) introductory verses, b) a blessing for wine, c) a blessing for spices, d) a blessing for light, and e) the Havdalah blessing, which is the basic prayer of the ritual.

The Introductory Verses

It is now customary to recite several verses from Isaiah, Psalms, and the Scroll of Esther before the Havdalah ritual. These verses are not an obligatory part of Havdalah. As late as the sixteenth century, Rabbi Moses Isserles lists only three of the eight verses that we today recite (OH 296:1, Rema). The verses all express trust in God and hope for the days ahead. Their recitation is regarded as a "good sign" (*siman tov*). The "salvation" referred to in these verses is the deliverance from immediate troubles or dangers. The verses are as follows:

הִנֵּה אֵל יְשׁוּעָתִי, אֶבְטַח וְלֹא אֶפְחָד, כִּי עָזִּי וְזִמְרָת יָהּ יהוה, וַיְהִי לִי לִישׁוּעָה: וּשְׁאַבְתֶּם מַיִם בְּשָׂשׂוֹן, מִמַּעַיְנֵי הַיְשׁוּעָה: לַיהוה הַיְשׁוּעָה, עַל עַמְּךָ בִרְכָתֶךָ סֶּלָה: יהוה צְבָאוֹת עִמָּנוּ, מִשְׂגָּב לָנוּ אֱלֹהֵי יַעֲקֹב סֶלָה: יהוה צְבָאוֹת אַשְׁרֵי אָדָם בֹּטֵחַ בָּךְ: יהוה הוֹשִׁיעָה, הַמֶּלֶךְ יַעֲנֵנוּ בְיוֹם קָרְאֵנוּ: לַיְהוּדִים הָיְתָה אוֹרָה וְשִׂמְחָה וְשָׂשׂוֹן וִיקָר: כֵּן תִּהְיֶה לָּנוּ. כּוֹס יְשׁוּעוֹת אֶשָּׂא וּבְשֵׁם יהוה אֶקְרָא:

TO PRAY AS A JEW

Behold, I will trust in the God of my salvation; and will not fear; for God, the Lord is my strength and song; He has been to me a salvation. (Is. 12:2)

With joy shall you draw water out of the wells of salvation.
(Is. 12:3)

Salvation belongs to the Lord; Thy blessing be upon Thy people, Selah. (Psalms 3:9)

The Lord of hosts is with us; the God of Jacob is our refuge, Selah.
(Psalms 46:12)

Lord of hosts, happy is the person who trusts in Thee.
(Psalms 84:13)

Lord, save us; the King will answer us on the day we call.
(Psalms 20:10)

The Jews had light and joy, gladness and honor. (Esth. 8:16) So be it with us.

I will lift the cup of salvation, and call upon the name of the Lord.
(Psalms 116:13)

The quotation from the Scroll of Esther is the only place in the entire prayer book where the name *Yehudim* ("Jews") is used as a reference to the Jewish people. Throughout the Bible and siddur, only the name *Yisrael* ("Israel") is used. It is customary for everyone present to join in saying this verse from Esther and the parenthetical hope that "so be it with us."

The Blessing for Wine

The introductory verses lead into the blessing for wine, which is the obligatory beginning of Havdalah. It is customary to fill the Havdalah wine cup to overflowing. A basis for this custom is an aggadic interpretation of the Biblical verse that God "will bless your bread and your water" (Exod. 23:25). A household where wine flows *like water* is regarded as within the framework of this Divine blessing (Eruvin 65a). Hence the overflowing cup, symbolizing good fortune and our share in the Divine blessing.

The Blessings for Spices and Light

Fragrant spices and light used in connection with the Havdalah ritual began around the second century B.C.E. It was then customary for the sages to extend their third Sabbath meal, usually eaten on

Sabbath afternoons, well past nightfall. Toward the end of this meal, fire (which could not be made on the Sabbath) and incense (which, since it had to be heated, could not be prepared on the Sabbath) would be brought in. These two items and the blessings associated with their use eventually became an integral part of the Havdalah ritual.

The two blessings are as follows:

בָּרוּךְ אַתָּה יהוה אֱלֹהֵינוּ מֶלֶךְ הָעוֹלָם, בּוֹרֵא מִינֵי בְשָׂמִים.

בָּרוּךְ אַתָּה יהוה אֱלֹהֵינוּ מֶלֶךְ הָעוֹלָם, בּוֹרֵא מְאוֹרֵי הָאֵשׁ.

Blessed art Thou, Lord our God, King of the universe, who creates various kinds of fragrant spices.

Blessed art Thou, Lord our God, King of the universe, who creates the lights of the fire.

The blessing for spices is a blessing of enjoyment (Birkat Hanehenin); it is in the same category as the blessings said for food and drink. Whenever one enjoys the fragrance of spices, one must recite a blessing.

A reason that is given for the use of fragrant spices at the end of the Sabbath day is that a Jew is saddened by the departure of the Sabbath. The lift provided by the fragrance is supposed to compensate somewhat for the resultant gloom. The sages had taught that "three things restore a man's good spirits: [beautiful] sounds, sights, and smells (Berakhot 57b). Fragrant spices serve to refresh and revive the spirit (Maim. Hil. Shabbat 29:29).

A similar reason offered is to compensate for the departure of the additional soul (*neshamah yeteirah*) that every Sabbath-observant Jew acquires on the Sabbath. The additional soul is defined as the restful, content feeling that comes to a person on the Sabbath (Rashi, Beitzah 16a). The loss of this spiritual serenity is somewhat replaced by the refreshing fragrance (Beitzah 33b, Tos. s.v. *ki*). To compensate for a "lost soul" by the use of fragrant spices was plausible to the rabbis because they regarded a pleasant odor to be the delight of the soul rather than of the body (Berakhot 43b). The Hebrew word for breathing (*nashom*) stems from the same root as the word for soul (*neshamah*).

The blessing for light or fire is not in the same category as the blessing for spices. It is not classified as a blessing of enjoyment, which is why we do not have to say the blessing when deriving the benefit of fire, either as light to see by, as heat to be warmed by, or as flames to cook with. The Birkhot Hanehenin were prescribed only for benefits or pleasures that are directly absorbed by the body (Pesaḥim 53b, Tos. s.v. *ein*).

The blessing for light on Saturday night is to commemorate man's discovery of fire. The Talmud tells us that God provided Adam with the knowledge to take two stones and strike them together, bringing forth fire (light) and that this discovery took place on the first Saturday night (Pesaḥim 54a). Furthermore, since it is forbidden to light a fire on the Sabbath, it is as though fire was renewed for us and so we thank God for it.

The Talmudic aggaddah may also be a subtle rejoinder to the ancient Greek legend that fire was given to man by Prometheus, who stole it from heaven. When Zeus, the king of the gods, discovered the theft, he ordered Prometheus chained and tortured. Jewish legend, by contrast, teaches us that God Himself taught man about fire. Ours is a God who wants to help man discover the way to progress. For this heavenly gift, the blessing expresses thanks. The sages deliberately chose the plural "lights of the fire" to emphasize that God gave man the wisdom to fashion many kinds of illumination. We credit God with being the source of all light, even that developed by man.

A braided multiwick candle is used for Havdalah since a "torch" that sheds a greater light is regarded as the choicest way to perform the mitzvah (Pesaḥim 103b). If one does not have such a candle, one may use two ordinary candles if they are held together so that their flames merge together. This qualifies as a "torch" (OH 298:2, Rema). In the absence of candles, the blessing may be said by the light of two matches or even by the light of an electric bulb.

While saying the blessing for light, it is customary to spread one or both hands toward the flame and momentarily to examine the palms of the hand or the nails of the fingers. This is done to derive some use from the light over which the blessing is recited. The candle itself is usually held by a member of the household. It is a favorite assignment among the children.

Only the wine blessing and the basic Havdalah blessing are said at the end of any festival that does not fall on Saturday night. Neither the introductory verses, nor the blessings for light and spices are said. The religious symbolism of the latter two blessings applies only to the end of the Sabbath day.

If the end of the Sabbath coincides with the *onset* of a festival, the blessing for spices is omitted. The festival, or yom tov, has more than enough "fragrance" to compensate for the departure of the Sabbath (Pesaḥim 102b s.v. *rav*).

The Havdalah Blessing

בָּרוּךְ אַתָּה יהוה אֱלֹהֵינוּ מֶלֶךְ הָעוֹלָם,
הַמַּבְדִּיל בֵּין קֹדֶשׁ לְחֹל, בֵּין אוֹר לְחֹשֶׁךְ, בֵּין
יִשְׂרָאֵל לָעַמִּים, בֵּין יוֹם הַשְּׁבִיעִי לְשֵׁשֶׁת יְמֵי
הַמַּעֲשֶׂה. בָּרוּךְ אַתָּה יהוה, הַמַּבְדִּיל בֵּין קֹדֶשׁ
לְחֹל.

Blessed are Thou, Lord our God, King of the universe, who separates between the holy and the everyday, between light and darkness, between Israel and the other nations, between the seventh day and the six days of work. Blessed art Thou, Lord, who separates the holy from the everyday.

The text of the Havdalah blessing found in the Talmud (Pesaḥim 103b) is based on various separations (*havdalot*) mentioned in Scripture:

"Between the holy and everyday" comes from Leviticus 10:10.
"Between light and darkness" comes from Genesis 1:4.

"Between Israel and the nations" comes from Leviticus 20:26.

The "separations" imply different levels of holiness established by the Holy One, blessed be He. (See pp. 125–126 for a fuller discussion.)

The Havdalah, said as part of a festival Kiddush, further distinguishes the greater holiness of the Sabbath from that of the incoming festival (Ḥulin 26b). The festival is of a lesser holiness for it is permissible on these days to cook and bake.

In making use of all the senses: touching the cup, tasting the wine, smelling the fragrance, seeing the light, hearing the blessing, and applying the mind to understand the separations Havdalah speaks of, we may look upon this blessing as a consecration of all our senses to God at the very start of each new week.

THE BLESSINGS FOR LIGHTING CANDLES

From earliest Talmudic sources we learn that the lighting of lights for the Sabbath was an essential element in preparing for the Sabbath. Midrashic sources give as the reason for the practice the greater delight that this adds to the Sabbath and in keeping with the requirement that "You call the Sabbath a delight." (Tanḥuma, Noah). To sit in the dark on the night of Shabbat, a practice followed by sects who rejected the authority of the Oral Torah, would have meant a diminishing of the Sabbath joy. While the sages may have debated about which kinds of oils and wicks were suitable for use as Sabbath lights, there was unanimity about the practice itself. It is customary to light two candles to symbolize the two forms of the fourth commandment: "Remember (Zakhor) the Sabbath day to keep it holy" (Exod. 20:8) and "Observe (Shamor) the Sabbath day to keep it holy" (Deut. 5:12).

Home Prayers for Sabbaths and Festivals

The lighting of Sabbath lights is one of seven ritual mitzvot that the sages legislated (Shabbat 25b).* The blessing itself employs the standard formula of all berakhot said before doing a mitzvah:

בָּרוּךְ אַתָּה יהוה אֱלֹהֵינוּ מֶלֶךְ הָעוֹלָם, אֲשֶׁר
קִדְּשָׁנוּ בְּמִצְוֹתָיו וְצִוָּנוּ ...

Barukh atah Adonai eloheinu melekh ha-olam, asher kidshanu b'mitzvotav, v'tzivanu ...

Blessed art Thou, Lord our God, King of the universe, who sanctified us by His commandments and commanded us to ...

The blessing concludes with: *lehadlik ner shel Shabbat* ("to kindle the Sabbath light"). On the festivals, the conclusion is: *lehadlik ner shel Yom Tov* ("to kindle the festival lights"). On Yom Kippur, it is: *lehadlik ner shel Yom Hakippurim.* For lighting the Ḥanukkah candles, the conclusion is: *lehadlik ner shel Ḥanukkah.*

The question may well arise how one can say a blessing to God "who commanded us to light the (Ḥanukkah, Sabbath, festival, etc.) lights," when this mitzvah was prescribed by the rabbis. The Talmudic sages themselves asked that same question: "Where indeed were we commanded to light the Ḥanukkah lights?" This question also applies to the Sabbath lights. Rabbinic authority for ordaining this mitzvah rests on the commandment of the Torah to act "in accordance with the instructions that they [the religious leaders of each generation] give you and the rulings they hand down to you; deviating ... neither to the right nor to the left" (Deut. 17:11). This Biblical commandment embraces the rabbinically-prescribed mitzvot and justifies the words of the blessing (Shabbat 23a).

---

* The other six are: 1) to light candles on Ḥanukkah, 2) to say Hallel at certain times, 3) to read the Scroll of Esther on Purim, 4) to wash the hands before eating and upon arising, 5) to say an appropriate blessing before deriving various satisfactions and (6) to set up an eruv where necessary. A blessing is said in conjunction with these observances.

The duty to light candles for the Sabbath and to have them burning in one's dwelling place falls equally on men and women. In a family setting, the carrying out of this mitzvah is the woman's responsibility. Because she is normally found at home and involved in the work of the house, it is easier for her to meet this obligation (Maim. Hil. Shabbat 5:3). If there is no woman at home to light the candles, it becomes the man's responsibility to do so.

To be on the safe side, Sabbath candles are lit twenty minutes before sundown. Sundown is the actual deadline. The kindling of a fire thereafter, even for Sabbath candles, is forbidden.

Since the recitation of the blessing means the immediate acceptance of the Sabbath for the woman lighting the candles (see pp. 256–257), the usual practice of reciting the berakhah before performing the mitzvah is reversed in this instance. First the candles are lit, then the blessing is said (OH 263:5 Rema).

The moments after the blessing have become sanctified to most Jewish women as a time to add a personal prayer, in the quiet privacy shared by her lips and her heart.

18

*Rules Relating to
the Prayer Service*

THE TIMES FOR PRAYER

WHEN Ezra the Scribe and the Men of the Great Assembly prescribed the number of prayer services for each day, they also fixed the time framework in which to say them. The official time for the various services was set to correspond to the time that the daily communal offerings were brought in the Temple.

These periods still provide the framework within which these various prayers may be recited. The opinion of local rabbinic authority should, however, be sought to pinpoint the proper times in any given community, since both the latitude and the season of the year are factors that must be taken into account when determining the length of time between dawn and sunrise, and between sunset and nightfall. Furthermore, differences of opinion do exist among religious authorities on how to determine the length of these twilight periods.

An Explanation of the "Variable Hour" (Sha-ah Zemanit)

In order to understand how the exact time parameters of the daily services are fixed, one must begin by knowing that wherever the

Mishnah or later halakhic sources referred to the time of the day, they were not referring to a fixed hour, nor, when they used the term "hour" did they mean our constant interval of sixty minutes. They were referring to a certain fraction of the day, and the hour they had in mind is a "variable hour" or "seasonal hour" (*sha-ah zemanit*) whose length is determined by the length of the day measured from sunrise to sunset, which in turn changes with the seasons. The one constant thing about the "variable hour" is that it is always one-twelfth of the day. The fourth "hour," for example, always means a third of the day; the sixth "hour" means midday (Igrot Moshe OH:24). If we were dealing with a day that has twelve daylight hours beginning at 6 A.M. and ending at 6 P.M. this would mean 10 A.M. and 12 noon respectively. But days are not so perfectly fixed. They are longer or shorter; they begin and end earlier or later.

Let us consider a hypothetical exact fifteen-hour summer day beginning at precisely 5 A.M. A third of the day is five hours after sunrise; in this instance, 10 A.M. remains the fourth "hour." The sixth "hour," midday, however, is seven and one-half hours after sunrise or 12:30 P.M. Or let us consider a hypothetical nine-hour winter day beginning at precisely 7 A.M. A third of the day is three hours after sunrise; here too, 10 A.M. is the fourth "hour." But the sixth "hour" or midday is four and one-half hours after sunrise or 11:30 A.M.*

If one knows the exact time of sunrise and sunset of any given day, the length of the variable hour is easily calculated. Once this is established, it is easy to determine the time of the fourth "hour" or the sixth "hour" or the exact time on the clock that corresponds to two and one-half or one and one-quarter "hours" before sundown.

Some authorities choose to follow different coordinates, basing their calculations of the "variable hour" not on sunrise and sunset, but on dawn and nightfall. This has the effect of advancing the "hours" to an earlier time. This view is sometimes followed only in determin-

---

* To figure out the length of the "variable hour" on any given day even when dealing with minutes, divide the number of daylight hours and minutes into twelve equal parts. Each part is one variable hour. A fifteen-hour and twenty-four minute summer day, for example, is 15 × 6 minutes plus 24 or 924 minutes long. One-twelfth of that day (924 ÷ 12) is 77 minutes. This is the length of the "variable hour." The end of the fourth "hour" on this day is therefore 4 × 77 minutes after sunrise.

ing the deadline for eating ḥametz on the morning before Passover (OH 233:1, Rema, MB:4).

The Time for Shaḥarit

The time frame within which Shaḥarit should be recited begins at sunrise and lasts until the end of the fourth "hour", which is equivalent to one-third of the day (OH 443, MB:8).

Since the daily morning offering could be brought at dawn, one may if necessary begin the Amidah as early as the crack of dawn. Although the "proper time" requirement is not met if one prays after the fourth-"hour" deadline, Shaḥarit may be said through the sixth-"hour", and the requirement of prayer will still be regarded as having been fulfilled. After midday. Shaḥarit may no longer be said.

The Time for Minḥa

The preferred time for saying Minḥa begins nine and a half "hours" into the day and lasts till sundown, for it is during this interval that the Minḥa offering was brought. When said during this period, the service is called *Minḥa Ketanah* (the short Minḥa) because the time period during which it is said (two and a half "hours") is relatively short.

One may, however, say Minḥa as early as six and a half "hours" into the day. The precedent for this originates with the practice of advancing the Minḥa offering to the sixth and one half "hour" on a Passover eve that fell on a Friday. This was done to allow sufficient time to process the Paschal offering before the onset of the Sabbath. When said during the earlier part of the afternoon, the prayer is called *Minḥa Gedolah* (the long Minḥa) because the time until sundown is quite long.

The period between sundown and nightfall, is called *bein hashemashot* ("between the suns") and is regarded as "doubtful night." By halakhic definition, night begins when no fewer than three medium-sized stars become visible in the skies (*tzeit hakokhavim*). This is approximately thirty-five or forty minutes after sundown along the latitude of New York. In Israel, it is about eighteen minutes after sundown. Today we consult a calendar to determine the exact moment of nightfall, but it can also be done visually.

The view of one of the Talmudic sages, Rabbi Judah, is that Minḥa should be said no later than one and one quarter "hours" before sundown. Since the standard Minḥa period begins at two and a half "hours" before sunset, Rabbi Judah's deadline for Minḥa is called *pelag ha-Minḥa*, which means "half Minḥa", for it is the half-way mark in that period (Berakhot 4:1).

The pelag ha-Minḥa was not an arbitrary time; it had some significance in the Temple ritual. It marked the time when the afternoon sacrificial offering had to be completed; the rest of the afternoon was taken up with other aspects of the ritual, such as the burning of the incense and the libation of the wine.

The halakha gives us the option of following either the view of Rabbi Judah or that of the other sages.

The Time for Maariv

The time for Maariv begins when the time for Minḥa ends. Those who follow the opinion of Rabbi Judah and consistently say Minḥa before pelag ha-Minḥa, may say Maariv immediately after pelag ha-Minḥa. This means that Maariv can begin as early as one and a quarter "hours" before sundown. This is the opinion relied upon when the Sabbath evening service is conducted before sundown so as to "add to the holy" (OH 293:3, MB:9). During the summer months when many communities welcome the Sabbath and say Maariv long before sundown, the ruling of Rabbi Judah sets the earliest possible time for Maariv.

Those who regularly say Minḥa until sundown may say Maariv right after sundown, which is within the range of Maariv's "proper time." Still, the generally preferred practice is to wait until night is halakhically definite before saying Maariv, in order to coordinate it with the proper time for saying the Shema.

Throughout the centuries, many congregations followed the practice of saying Maariv immediately upon the conclusion of Minḥa even though it was still before sundown. Since people dispersed after Minḥa and found it difficult to reassemble for Maariv, this procedure was permitted by the rabbis so that persons should not miss a communal prayer service and so that the less pious, who might not pray privately, would have this chance to recite the evening prayer (OH 233:1, MB:11; OH235:1, MB:8).

The procedure of saying the two services back-to-back is still followed in many congregations, but with Minḥa just before sundown and Maariv just after sundown. Where it is not burdensome upon a congregation, and a minyan for both services is assured, most authorities agree that it is preferable to wait till nightfall to say Maariv. This procedure permits the Shema to be recited at its proper time. Maariv may, under extenuating circumstances, be said all night until dawn. However, it is preferable to say it before midnight.

The Time for Musaf

Musaf always follows Shaḥarit, inasmuch as the Musaf offering on Sabbaths and festivals always followed the daily Shaḥarit offering. It should not be delayed beyond the end of the seventh "hour" (OH 286:1).

The Time for Shema

The proper time framework for reciting Shema is independent of that for the prayers. In this case, it was not prescribed by the sages in terms of the Temple offerings but to conform to the Biblical stipulation that it be said, "When you lie down and when you rise up."

To discharge one's religious duty, the evening Shema must be said no earlier than nightfall. If one does say it earlier, as part of a Maariv service that is conducted before nightfall, then the Shema must be repeated after nightfall (OH 235:1).

Where a congregation conducts the Maariv service earlier than nightfall, it is preferable to say Maariv with the congregation rather than saying it privately after nightfall, even if it means having to repeat Shema privately later.

Shema is said until midnight, a deadline established by the sages to discourage procrastination and inadvertent forgetfulness. If a delay nevertheless does occur, one may say Shema throughout the night until dawn.

The morning Shema may be said as soon as there is enough natural light "to recognize an acquaintance at a distance of four cubits" (approximately six feet). This is supposed to occur at about thirty-five minutes before sunrise. It may be said until the end of the third "hour", which is equivalent to one-fourth of the day. Where necessary, the Shema may be recited as early as dawn, but it should not be delayed beyond the third "hour" after sunrise (OH 58:1, 3, 4).

WHEN COMING IN LATE: HOW TO JOIN IN THE SERVICE

It is best to come to the synagogue at the start of the service and to participate unhurriedly in the entire service. But if one does arrive after a service has begun, what should one do? Does one start at the beginning and rush to catch up? Or does one simply skip everything that has already been said by the congregation and join them at whatever page they happen to be reading? There are clear-cut guidelines for what ought to be done.

Rule One: The highest priority must be given to reciting the Amidah at the same time that the congregation recites it. This is the essence of *tefilah betzibbur* ("public worship"). The "favorable time" for God to listen to one's prayers is when the congregation is praying. The latecomer should therefore arrange his prayers in such a way that he is able to fulfill this first basic requirement, even if it involves omitting preliminary parts of the service. One must estimate how much time it will take the congregation to reach the Amidah, and on that basis decide how to proceed.

Rule Two: A second rule to bear in mind is that the Shema and its Blessings constitute a unit from which no paragraph is to be omitted.

Rule Three: A third rule relates to the first two. At the Shaḥarit service, the Shema and its Blessings should immediately precede the Amidah and must not be separated from it. The flexibility that we have therefore affects mostly the two preliminary sections of the service.

Rule Four: A fourth rule to remember is that certain blessings should always be said before the Shema and Amidah; they should not be omitted. They are:

Rules Relating to the Prayer Service

1. the blessing for washing hands, *al netilat yadayim,*
2. the Torah blessings,
3. the blessing of Elohai neshamah.

If these blessings are omitted at the beginning of the service, they cannot be made up at the end of the service.

Let us now suppose that one arrives for morning services just about the time that Shema is being recited and there is not enough time to comply with Rules Three and Four and still say the Amidah with the congregation. One has no choice but to forfeit the religious merit involved in praying with the congregation. One should then begin at the start of the service and privately say the prayers in their proper order.

But suppose the congregation is about to say or has just said Borkhu. One should then say the three short blessings listed under Rule Four and proceed at once to the Shema and its Blessings. By doing so, the latecomer is able to say the Amidah with the congregation. (At the end of the service, one can fill in what had been omitted from the preliminary sections. The blessings of Barukh She'amar and Yishtabaḥ, however, are not said at the end of the service.)

Suppose one arrives shortly before Borkhu. There is time to say more prayers in addition to those mentioned under Rule Four. These should be Barukh She'amar, Ashrei, Yishtabaḥ—and Nishmat (on Sabbaths and festivals). These will be found respectively at the beginning, in the middle, and at the end of the section known as Pesukei d'Zimra ("Verses of Song"). The omitted passages may be said at the end of the service.

Depending upon the amount of time available, certain prayers have priority over others. After the ones already mentioned in the preceding paragraph, the following prayers are listed in descending order of importance:

1. *Halleluyah, Hallelu El B'kodsho* (Psalm 150).
2. *Halleluyah, Hallelu et Adonai* (Psalm 148).
3. The other psalms after Ashrei that begin with *Halleluyah* (Psalms 146, 147, 149).
4. The first half of *Vayevarekh David* (through *l'shem tifartekha*).
5. The first half of *Hodu* (through *ki kadosh Adonai Eloheinu*).
6. Psalm 92, "The Psalm for the Sabbath Day," (*Mizmor Shir*

L'yom HaShabbat), followed by Psalm 136, "the Great Hallel" (*Hodu l'Adonai ki tov*), said only on the Sabbath and the festivals.

If there is ample time to say more than these prayers, one doesn't need this outline. One can start at the beginning and easily catch up with the congregation.

If one arrives late for Minḥa, after the congregation has already begun the silent Amidah, one has to make a quick judgment. If it seems that they have only just begun, and it is possible to start the Amidah and conclude it in time to join in the recitation of the Kedushah (during the repetition), then one should do so. The Ashrei prayer, which normally precedes the Amidah, may be omitted and said later (OH 109:1).

If it appears that the congregation is almost through with the Amidah, then one should first say Ashrei, stop—and wait until the Prayer Leader begins the repetition. Say the Amidah quietly along with the Prayer Leader, join the congregation in saying Kedushah, complete the blessing of Ha-El Hakadosh with the Prayer Leader, and proceed to complete the Amidah.

If one arrives at Minḥa after the Prayer Leader has just begun the repetition of the Amidah, one should wait to say Kedushah with the congregation, and then say the entire Amidah privately.

Let us now suppose that one arrives late for evening services. The rule here is somewhat different from that at Shaḥarit. The Shema and its Blessings may be recited here independently of the Amidah. If one therefore feels that he cannot catch up in time to recite the Amidah with the congregation, one should not begin the Shema and its Blessings but first say *Vehu Raḥum*, the introductory verse to the weekday Maariv, and then join the congregation in saying the Amidah. The Shema and its Blessings may be said after the Amidah.

RULES PERTAINING TO THE REPETITION OF THE AMIDAH

There are several rules that should guide a Prayer Leader and the congregation in the repetition of the Amidah.

ৡ Before the Prayer Leader begins the Amidah aloud, he should first say the short verse that usually appears in very small print just before the Amidah: *Adonai sefatai tiftah ufi yagid tehilatekha* ("Lord, open Thou my lips and my mouth will declare Thy praise").

ৡ No fewer than nine worshipers must listen and respond to the Prayer Leader. Otherwise the blessings are considered to be said in vain. If exactly ten people are present, the Prayer Leader should wait for everyone to finish before beginning the repetition of the Amidah (Igrot Moshe, OH 28–30).

ৡ At least six of the ten who make up the minyan must be individuals who have not as yet said their prayers and are still obliged to do so. If there are less than six such obligatory participants in the minyan, there is no repetition of the entire Amidah (Igrot Moshe, OH 30).

ৡ In this case, the Prayer Leader first recites the Amidah aloud only through the third blessing. This enables everyone present to join in saying Kedushah. The Prayer Leader then continues to say the remainder of the Amidah quietly. The other worshipers do likewise but from the beginning of the Amidah. This procedure is referred to in Yiddish as *a heiche Kedushah*, which means "a loud Kedushah" said in the context of a silent Amidah.

ৡ The procedure of a heiche Kedushah is sometimes adopted for a Minha service if the hour is late and there is not enough time to finish Minha before sundown.

ৡ When the Prayer Leader reaches the blessing of Modim, the custom is to say only the first three words of the passage aloud, and then say the greater part of Modim quietly to himself (while the congregation says the Modim d'Rabbanan). He resumes reciting aloud only the last dozen words, beginning with *hatov ki lo khalu*. Some authorities, however, insist that the Prayer Leader say the entire passage aloud.

&» Whenever the verses of the Priestly Blessing are read by the Prayer Leader—which he does at every Shaḥarit and Musaf Amidah—the congregation should respond to these verses with: *kein yehi ratzon* ("So may His will be"). The response of "Amen" is used only during the rite of the Priestly Blessing.

&» When he concludes the last blessing of the Amidah (*Sim Shalom* or *Shalom Rav*), the Prayer Leader should add the verse: *Yihyu l'ratzon imrei fi v'hegyon libi lefanekha, Adonai tzuri v'goali* ("May the words of my mouth and the meditation of my heart be acceptable to Thee, O Lord, my Strength and my Redeemer").

&» A worshiper who prays more slowly than the rest of the congregation and does not complete the silent Amidah before the Prayer Leader reaches Kedushah, should simply stop and listen attentively while the congregation says Kedushah, and then resume his own prayer after Kedushah. Unless one finishes the second blessing at the same time as the Prayer Leader, one does not interrupt the silent Amidah in order to say Kedushah. (See pp. 129–130.)

The repetition of the Amidah requires the congregation to be attentive and to respond "Amen" after each blessing. One may not engage in idle talk or turn one's attention to other matters, even to studying Torah or reading from other sacred texts (OH 124:4, MB: 17, 18, AH 124:9, 12).

WHAT TO DO IF ONE FORGETS TO SAY . . .

Depending on the time of the year, there are words or passages that are either added to or deleted from the Amidah. Worshipers, who say the Amidah so frequently that the words begin to roll off their tongues, are apt to slip up if they momentarily forget the occasion or if their concentration momentarily lapses.

One should be aware of the relative seriousness of these errors, and know which ones require going back to a certain point and which do not, which require the Amidah to be repeated and which do not. They do not all carry the same weight.

Errors at Year-Round Services

Before listing the possible slips that may occur on special occasions, let me set forth some general rules which apply to errors in the standard text of the Amidah.

· An error in any of the first three blessings requires one to go back to the beginning of the Amidah;

· An error in any one of the intermediate blessings requires one to go back only to the beginning of the blessing where the mistake occurred;

· An error in any of the last three blessings requires one to go back to *Retzei* (the first of the last three blessings), if one becomes aware of the error before concluding the Amidah. If one only becomes aware of it after completely finishing the Amidah, then the Amidah must be repeated from the beginning.

From Rosh Hashanah through Yom Kippur

During the Ten Days of Repentance, several short passages are added to the Amidah to reflect the theme of the period. If one forgets to say any one of these passages, the following general rules apply:

If one forgets to substitute *hamelekh hakadosh* for *ha-el hakadosh* in the third blessing, and does not immediately correct himself, it is necessary to begin the Amidah from the start. But if one forgets to substitute *hamelekh hamishpat* for *melekh oheiv tzedakah umishpat* (in the eleventh blessing of the weekday Amidah), it is *not* necessary to go back or repeat the blessing. It is also not necessary to repeat the blessing if one forgets to say *zokhreinu l'hayim* or *mi kamokha* (in the first and second blessings), or *ukhtov l'hayim tovim* or *b'sefer hayim berakhah* (in the last two blessings).

During the Winter and Summer Seasons

From Shemini Atzeret until the first day of Passover (the winter season), the phrase *mashiv haruah u'mori hageshem* is added to the second blessing of the Amidah. These words are essential to the blessing. If one forgets to say them but remembers the omission before concluding the second blessing, one simply adds those words before the end of the blessing. If one does not become aware of the omission until after concluding the second blessing, then one must start the Amidah over again.

If the phrase was inadvertently added to the Amidah during the summer and spring months, the following rules apply: If one becomes aware of the error before concluding the blessing, one goes back and repeats the second blessing from the beginning. If one does not become aware of the error until after concluding the second blessing, the Amidah must be repeated from the beginning.

During most of the winter season, the phrase *v'tein tal umatar livrakhah* ("give dew and rain for a blessing") is inserted into Birkat Hashanim, the ninth blessing of the weekday Amidah.* (See p. 86.) If one forgets to say it but remembers the omission before concluding the blessing, one may say it immediately and continue on.

If one remembers the omission only after concluding the blessing, one may wait to insert the entire phrase in the Shema Koleinu blessing, just before the words *ki atah shomei'a tefilah.*

If one remains unaware of the omission until after completing the blessing of Shema Koleinu, one should go back to the beginning of the blessing of Birkat Hashanim and say the Amidah over from there. If one completes the entire Amidah before becoming aware of the omission, it should be said over again.

Similarly, if *tal umatar* is said needlessly during the summer months, and one becomes aware of the error before concluding the Amidah, one starts over from the beginning of the Birkat Hashanim blessing. If not, the entire Amidah is repeated.

On the Festivals

On the three festivals of Pesaḥ, Shavuot, and Sukkot, and on Rosh Ḥodesh, the prayer of Yaaleh V'yavo is added to the blessing of Retzei in every Amidah except Musaf. If one forgets it and becomes aware of the omission before concluding the Amidah, one goes back only to Retzei and repeats from there. If not, the entire Amidah must

---

* A tourist who is in Israel at any time between the seventh of Heshvan, which falls in October, and the fourth of December adds this prayer as does everyone else in Israel. Upon his return to the diaspora, he continues to say it even if it is still before December 4.

be repeated. It is not necessary to repeat the Amidah if the error was made in the Maariv service of Rosh Hodesh.

On Hanukkah and Purim, Al Hanisim is added to the blessing of Modim. If one forgets to add this prayer, but remembers the omission before concluding the blessing, one merely goes back to Al Hanisim and continues on from there. If the error is caught *after* finishing the blessing of Modim, it is not necessary to go back to Retzei nor to repeat the Amidah.

According to Early Authorities, the obligation to repeat the Amidah in the face of certain omissions or errors is intended only for a person when he is praying privately. Latter-day Authorities recommend repeating the Amidah, when the rule calls for doing so, even if one is praying with a congregation (OH 124:10, MB:40). But if it is the Prayer Leader himself who has erred while praying silently, opinion is unanimous that he need not repeat the Amidah again. So as not to unduly impose upon the congregation, he may depend on his own repetition aloud to fulfill his personal prayer obligation.

THE ORDER OF PRECEDENCE FOR GETTING AN ALIYAH

It is a long-established tradition that a person celebrating certain occasions is entitled to certain synagogue honors, most specifically that of being given an aliyah. (See pp. 49–50.) The number of people to whom this honor can be extended at any given time is limited. And since at times the number of honors that must be distributed may exceed the number of aliyot available, it has become necessary to dictate a schedule of priorities. Otherwise a certain amount of ill-will could be fostered in a congregation. By establishing certain guidelines, the potential for bias among synagogue leaders is eliminated, resentment among worshipers is reduced, and dissension is avoided.

Although I now offer a set of traditional guidelines dealing with aliyah distribution and with resolving the problem of what to do when there is a conflict of several equal priorities, it should be remembered that the elimination of dissension is the paramount consideration. It is possible that in any given community, the leadership will deem it to be in the interest of the community to follow a policy other than the one presented here. It is their prerogative to do so, provided that the guidelines are made known and are consistently adhered to.

In general, precedence in the distribution of aliyot is as follows: The first two aliyot are always reserved for a kohen and a Levite. From the third aliyah onward, from which a kohen or a Levite is excluded, the following priorities customarily prevail:

1. a bridegroom on the Sabbath *before* his wedding
2. a boy who has turned thirteen years of age (Bar-Mitzvah)
3. the father of a newborn infant, male or female, on the first Sabbath that the mother appears in the synagogue
4. a bridegroom on the Sabbath after his wedding
5. the father of a baby girl who has to be named
6. one observing yahrzeit for one's parents on that day
7. the father of a baby to be circumcised on that day or during the coming week
8. one observing yahrzeit for one's parents during the coming week
9. one who has to recite the blessing of gomel
10. one who is about to leave on a long journey or has just returned from such a journey
11. a distinguished guest in the community
12. one who is or will be observing yahrzeit for someone other than parents is not among those to whom an aliyah must be given, but some congregations try to accommodate such persons where possible.

[OH 136, Biur Halakha]

If there are two or more people at services observing the same occasion and therefore enjoying equal priority, the following set of considerations come into play:

1. a regular worshiper has priority over one who comes infrequently
2. a member of the congregation over a nonmember
3. a resident in the community who belongs to no other synagogue*

* In some communities, a failure to belong to some local synagogue may result in the denial of all ritual privileges and honors to any person who thus dissociates himself from the organized Jewish community. The right to impose such sanctions is within the prerogative of synagogue leadership.

4. an out-of-town visitor
5. a resident in the community who belongs to another local synagogue.

It is not customary to give consecutive aliyot to two brothers, to a father and son, or to a grandfather and grandson. The reason for this is in order to avoid having the two honorees become the object of "jealous glances." Jewish law, however, permits such consecutive aliyot where necessary.

If there is no kohen who can be called up, a Levite or an Israelite may be called in his stead for the first aliyah. When such a substitute is called, the gabbai should be certain to add the words *Yisrael bimkom kohen* "an Israelite in place of the kohen," or *Levi bimkom kohen*, "a Levite in place of the kohen." In this way, the person called for the first aliyah will not be mistaken for a kohen by those present in the synagogue (OH 135:6, Rema).

When a Levite is called up for the first aliyah in the absence of a kohen, only Israelites can be called from the second aliyah onward. Should an Israelite be called up for the first aliyah, a Levite is not given his second aliyah. Only Israelites receive the remaining aliyot.

If a kohen is called up for the first aliyah, and there is no Levite present for the second aliyah, that kohen is given a double aliyah, and he recites both Torah blessings twice. Neither an Israelite nor a second kohen may be called up (OH 135:8, MB:28).

If more than seven aliyot are distributed on a Sabbath, a kohen or a Levite may be called up for the very last aliyah. Each one may also be given the honor of Maftir.

If a kohen offers to decline in favor of an Israelite on a weekday, he may do so. This is sometimes helpful at a weekday service when only three aliyot are distributed and there are several non-kohanim present who should receive aliyot. It is not necessary for the kohen to step out of the synagogue in order to permit the calling up of an Israelite for the first aliyah. The gabbai should, however, preface his call with the words *birshut kohen* ("with the permission of the kohen") (Igrot Moshe OH II:34).

THE ORDER OF PRECEDENCE FOR LEADING THE SERVICE

It has always been regarded as an act of great religious merit to lead a service. It was never the exclusive domain of a professional. Every Jew has the privilege of doing so, and many exercise that privilege. The only requirement is that one be able to do so properly. The minimum prerequisite is the ability to read the Hebrew prayers correctly and fluently.

When it comes to choosing one of the worshipers to lead a weekday service, preference is always given to those in mourning, because, as in the case of Kaddish, the religious merit involved benefits the deceased. It is, in fact, seen as a mourner's obligation to lead the service if he is capable of it. But since only one person may serve in this capacity at a time, tradition dictates the order of precedence should there be more than one mourner present at services. It is as follows:

1. during the week of shiva
2. when observing a yahrzeit
3. during the period of *shloshim* (from the end of shiva through the thirtieth day of mourning)
4. on the last day of saying Kaddish, at the end of the eleventh month
5. from the end of shloshim through the end of the eleventh month of mourning.

If two or more mourners have equal priority and both are capable and desirous of leading the service, a second set of considerations comes into effect: those listed on pp. 350–351 in connection with aliyot also apply here.

If there are two or more mourners with equal priority in all respects, then an equitable arrangement in which they alternate should be worked out. It is possible to divide the weekday Shaharit service between two mourners. The second person takes over following the Amidah, before the Ashrei prayer. One mourner can lead Minha, the other Maariv.

A mourner does not lead the service on a Sabbath or a festival (including the intermediate days), unless there is no one else qualified to do so. If a mourner is the official Ḥazzan, or the regular Ba'al Tefilah of a congregation (who led the services regularly even before he became a mourner), he may continue to do so even on Sabbaths and festivals.

On Rosh Ḥodesh, Ḥanukkah, and Purim, a mourner may lead the Minḥa and Maariv services, and also the Shaḥarit service until Hallel. In some communities, however, the custom is that a mourner does not lead any of the services on these days.

A person observing yahrzeit on a Sabbath or a festival may lead the service on such days. However, if the synagogue has an official Ḥazzan or Ba'al Tefilah who regularly leads these services, the person observing yahrzeit does not supplant him.

WHEN A SERVICE IS CONDUCTED IN A HOUSE OF MOURNING

One of the most widely observed customs that relate to mourning is conducting daily services during the week of shiva in the house of the deceased or where the mourners are "sitting shiva." This is done to accommodate the mourners, who are confined to their home during the week, and also out of respect for the deceased. The convening of a communal prayer service in the home of a deceased person is an act of great loving kindness to his or her memory. The practice is a very ancient one. Its origin is found in the Talmudic story about ten men who were assembled each day by Rabbi Judah to sit in the home of a deceased man for whom there were no mourners. After the seven-day period, the dead man appeared in a dream to Rabbi Judah and said to him: "May your mind be at rest, for you have set my mind at rest" (Shabbat 152a–b).

When a service is conducted in a house of mourning, a number of changes in the services are made.

ৡৄ In the repetition of the Amidah, the Prayer Leader omits the passage containing the Priestly Blessing. This is because the ritual of the Priestly Blessing is not performed in a house of mourning; it is a blessing that must always be said in a context of joy. (See p. 136.)

&» *Tahanun*, the prayer of supplication, is omitted. Although Tahanun speaks of suffering and misfortune and would therefore seem to be appropriate for a house of mourning, the rabbis were sensitive to the mourner's feelings and did not wish to add to his grief. (See pp. 208–209.)

&» Lamenatzei-ah (Psalm 20), following Ashrei, is omitted.

&» The second sentence in the prayer, *U'va L'tziyon*, which follows Psalm 20 is omitted. That sentence begins with *Va'ani zot briti otam* ("And as for me, said the Lord, this is My covenant with them."). It is omitted to avoid any suggestion at such a time that what befell the mourner might be the result of God's covenant with us, that the deceased transgressed the covenant and was therefore punished through Divine providence.

&» Hallel is omitted on Rosh Hodesh and Hanukkah. Since Hallel is a prayer of joy, it is not to be said by mourners. How could they identify with the heart of the Hallel, which declares: "This is the day that the Lord had made; let us rejoice and be glad thereon"? Another reason for omitting Hallel is because it contains the verse: "The dead cannot praise the Lord." To recite such a verse in a house of mourning where the spirit of the deceased is, so to speak, to be found, seems like "mocking the poor and helpless" (the dead are included in the latter category), which Jewish law considers an ethical transgression. Some communities follow the custom of asking mourners to leave the room while the rest of the worshipers recite the Hallel. While this procedure may comply with the first reason for not saying Hallel, it does not resolve the problem raised by the second reason.

&» Worshipers who attend a service at a house of mourning during Hanukkah and do not say Hallel there must do so privately, later in the day as the prayer remains an obligatory one for them. This is not necessary on Rosh Hodesh.

&» It is a widespread custom for the Prayer Leader not to say the verse beginning with *titkabal* ("Accept our prayers") in the whole Kaddish after U'va L'tziyon. Many authorities, however, have ruled that it should indeed be said. The halakha requires the omission of this line from the whole Kaddish only on Tisha b'Av and not in a house of mourning. Indeed, even then it is omitted not on account of Tisha b'Av being a day of mourning but only to dissociate the verse *titkabal* from the *kinot* that precede it (Yesodei Yeshurun I p. 240).

ð Psalm 49 (*Lamenatzei-ah livnei Korah*) is added to the end of the Shaharit and Maariv services. On days when Tahanun would ordinarily not be said (such as Rosh Hodesh and Hanukkah) Psalm 16 (Mikhtam l'David) is substituted. Neither of these psalms is added on Purim.

ð A Torah scroll is not brought to a house of mourning, unless a minimum of three services at which the Torah is read will be held.

ð It is proper for one of the mourners, particularly a son, to conduct the service if he is capable of doing so.

ð A mourner during the week of shiva, may not be called to the Torah for an aliyah in the house of mourning or in the synagogue. This is because a mourner may not study Torah, for Torah is a source of spiritual delight. This is so even on the Sabbath day when one does not publicly observe shiva practices. But if the mourner is a kohen or a Levite and there is no other kohen or Levite to call up to the Torah, then it is permissible for him to be given an aliyah in the synagogue on the Sabbath.

ð A mourner may go up for hagbah and glilah during the week of shiva. He may open the Ark to take out or return a Torah scroll.

ð A mourner who recites Havdalah in a house of mourning at the end of the Sabbath should omit the introductory paragraph (*Hinei el yeshuati*) and start with the blessing for wine.

ð Care should be taken when praying in a private home not to inadvertently face mirrors, portraits, or sculptures. One may not stand before them during prayer .

ð A mourner, though he goes to synagogue on Friday evening, does not say the Kabbalat Shabbat service. He omits everything from *Lekhu neranenah* through *Lekhah Dodi*. He begins with the Psalm for the

Sabbath Day (*Mizmor Shir l'Yom HaShabbat*). In some communities, he steps out of the synagogue for Kabbalat Shabbat and comes in only after Lekhah Dodi, when the congregation turns to him to extend a greeting of comfort: *Hamakom yenahem otkha b'tokh she'ar aveilei Tziyon vi'yerushalayim* ("May God comfort you together with all the mourners of Zion and Jerusalem").

The Ethical Dimension of Jewish Prayer

WHAT HAS ETHICS to do with prayer? The answer that Judaism gives is—everything! In Judaism, the two are inextricable. The union of ethics and prayer can be discerned in the regulations that govern the formal procedure of prayer, in the contents of prayer, and in the theology of prayer.

Ethics is about the way we relate to other people and to the world in which we live. Prayer, on the other hand, appears to be concerned only with our relationship to God and to a world that is beyond the one we experientially know. There are people who view the world of ethics and the world of prayer as two separate and independent domains. But Judaism very clearly demands a linkage between them. If the popular image of a religious personality is that of a person who prays, Judaism insists that this should not be the sole criterion by which to gauge the religious personality. Although prayer is one way in which a righteous and saintly person expresses his faith, it is by no means the litmus test of being a devout person. Unless prayer is also accompanied by the traits of character and ethical behavior that Judaism demands, prayer is no indication of piety at all. One need only stop to consider that in real life, evil men pray too. So it has been throughout history. Unscrupulous people seek out God not in order to abide by His will, nor to purify their own hearts and deeds, but in the hope that God will respond to their selfish demands. Judaism regards such prayer as a sacrilege. Instead of being an act that reflects reverence for God, such prayer is seen as an act of contempt for God and a desecration of the Divine Name (*hilul ha-Shem*).

The linking of religious devotion to ethical behavior was imbued in the very fiber of Judaism from its inception. The Psalmist equated the prayer of a thief with blasphemy (Psalms 10:3). The Prophet Isaiah was even more blunt. Although the Torah sets forth elaborate regulations concerning pilgrimages to the Temple and the bringing of various offerings to God, the prophet boldly proclaimed in the name of God: "Who asked you to trample in My courtyards? Do not continue to bring Me false offerings and incense, they are an abomination to Me . . . and when you spread out your hands [in prayer], I will turn My eyes from you; even if you multiply your prayers, I will not listen, for your hands are filled with blood " (Isaiah 1:12–15).

The prophet was not any more opposed to sacrifices than to prayer. What he opposed and condemned equally were prayers and sacrifices that were offered against the background of immoral and unethical practices that he saw all around him. "Remove the evil of your deeds . . . learn to do good, seek justice," he said. This, not prayer, was the real test and criterion of man's loyalty to God. Coming from those who passed the test, prayers and offerings were no abomination.

The wording used by the Midrash to teach us that God wants human beings to pray to Him is illuminating: "God longs for the prayers of the righteous (*shel tzadikim*)" (Yevamot 64a). This pointedly excludes the prayers of the wicked and the unjust. The Psalmist put it this way: "Who may ascend the mountain of the Lord and who may stand in His holy place; he who has clean hands and a pure heart . . ." (Psalms 24:3, 4; Exodus Rabbah 22).

Prayer that follows in the wake of wrongdoing is regarded as desirable only when it is associated with teshuvah, with a person's attempt to improve himself, spiritually, morally, and ethically, by repenting from that wrongdoing and returning to the "ways of the

The Ethical Dimension of Jewish Prayer

Lord." In the popular piyyut said on the High Holy Days (*Vekhol Ma'aminim*), we express our faith that God "opens the gates to those who knock with repentance" and that "He waits for the wicked, desirous of their return to righteousness."

Indeed, all prayer should be seen as a way of helping a person strengthen himself against the temptation to do wrong; it is a means of self-purification. In the Jewish concept of things, prayer is not a way of life, but a way station in life—a moment when one stops to self-evaluate, to consolidate spiritual gains, and to make them a lasting, durable part of oneself (Olat Re'iyah I, p. 262). For worship of God manifests itself not only in ritual, but also in the ethical and moral standards by which one lives.

Jewish prayer, based as it is on the assumption that the human soul is basically good and possesses the capacity to improve itself, is essentially a reflection of Jewish ethics. This is what accounts for the optimistic and hopeful tone of Jewish prayer. Our prayers may relate to many troubles, but except for the kinot of Tisha b'Av, they are not sad or somber.

The Torah study passages that were selected for the early morning preliminary prayers are Talmudic passage that dwell on highly specific ethical obligations. (See pp. 188–190.) Charity to the poor, honor to parents, deeds of loving kindness, hospitality, visiting the sick, providing the bride with a dowry, bringing harmony and peace between people—one is daily reminded of these duties before going on to the prayers that dwell on man's relationship to his Creator.

The long confessional known as *Al Het*, said twice at each of four Yom Kippur services, concentrates exclusively on every possible wrongdoing that one person can commit against another, in thought and in deed.

The very fact that most Jewish prayers are in the first person plural rather than in the first person singular is itself an expression of Jewish ethical concern. Not only do we pray *with others* in congregational worship, we also pray *on behalf of others*. Our concerns must not be selfish.

The siddur yields impressive evidence of this interrelationship. Between the covers of the Jewish prayer book, following the section on the Sabbath afternoon service, is found the entire tractate of the Mishnah, known as Pirkei Avot, the Ethics of the Fathers. This book goes beyond Law, and points to higher ethical goals. And it has always been a favorite for popular study. It became traditional to study one chapter of Avot every Sabbath afternoon between Pesaḥ and Shavuot. This has now been extended to a five-month period ending on the Sabbath before Rosh Hashanah.

Some editions of the siddur contain excerpts from ethical writings of saintly Jewish personalities of later periods. Such selections will be found in the Daily Prayer Book, edited by the late Chief Rabbi of Great Britain, Joseph H. Hertz (pp. 260–263, 722–724, 1112–1115). These excerpts reveal how the siddur was used to develop character, refine behavior, and improve morality. Obviously, our religious teachers did not deem it sufficient for people just to pray.

Ethical considerations also played a role in the laws of prayer and in synagogue practice. It is often the main consideration in halakhic rulings regarding prayer procedure. Take, for example, the halakhic decision to omit portions of the Hallel prayer during the last days of Passover. It is to symbolize the tempering of our joy in compliance with the ethical teaching inherent in the verse from Proverbs (24:17): "Do not rejoice over the fall of your enemy." (Avot 4:19.) Another ethical precept holds that the public humiliation of a person is the equivalent of murder (Bava Metzia, 58b; Sotah 10b). One who transgresses this commandment is said to have "no share in the world to come" (Maim. Hil. Teshuvah 3:14). This precept influenced the prayer ritual in many ways. For instance, once he is called up for an aliyah, a person may not be sent back to his seat. This holds true even if it is discovered that he was called up in error, lest the congregation get the impression that he was disqualified from his aliyah because of some personal flaw. Likewise, the drastic innovation in the Torah reading service, in which one person reads the Torah on behalf of all who are called up for an aliyah—replacing the older practice where each person read his own portion. This was instituted to avoid embarrassing those who could not read from the Torah. For the same reason, that is, to help those who do not know the Torah blessings by heart or who become easily flustered when performing in public, synagogues should clearly display the blessings before *everyone* called up for an aliyah.

To impose unnecessarily upon a congregation is also regarded as an ethical breach (*tirḥah d'tzibura*). Thus, courtesy does not demand that the Prayer Leader wait for those who take an extraordinarily long time to complete the Amidah before beginning the repetition, even if these people are leading members of the community. It is now customary to wait only until the rabbi of the community finishes the Amidah. Also, the congregation need not wait for the late arrival of some important dignitary expected at any moment (OH 124:3; Rema).

A similar concern is the reason why the reading of a Haftarah is confined only to the Sabbath and festivals. It would lengthen the service on days when people must rush off to work (Megillah 21a, Rashi; Yesodei Yeshurun IV: p. 408).

The principle of equal treatment for all, regardless of social status, has also had an impact on the laws of prayer. The Talmud rules that the Shema must be recited "upon arising"; it then goes on to list the hours it was customary for the different social classes to arise. The common laborer arose the earliest at "the first hour." But since the king's household would not generally arise until the third "hour" of the day, that "hour" was fixed as the standard for everyone and was set as the deadline for the recitation of the Shema for *all* the people. One underlying principle is that before God "all Israel are children of royalty" (Shabbat 128a) and the requirement for the commoner should be no different from that of royalty.

The synagogue was, in fact, the great democratizer of Jewish society. Communal prayer, by its very nature, took into consideration the needs and religious sensitivity of the most unlearned sectors. Every male adult Jew, be he a poor laborer or a wealthy prince, counted equally in constituting a prayer quorum. Anyone could lead a prayer service. He did not have to be a scholar or a priest. He just needed to possess the minimum knowledge for doing so and the faith to make him a suitable emissary of the congregation.

A straightforward reminder of the ethical dimension of Jewish prayer is to be found in a short passage at the very beginning of old prayer books of the Sephardic rite, one that should perhaps now be restored or introduced into our liturgy. (See OH 46:1, MA) The passage is a typical declaration of our readiness to perform a mitzvah, such as is found in the Passover Hagaddah before saying the blessing for each of the four cups of wine. It starts out with *Hineni mukhan umezuman* ("I am hereby ready and prepared to fulfill the mitzvah of . . . .").

One would think that such a declaration, said before one begins to pray, should address itself to "the mitzvah of worshiping God." And so it does, but the passage surprisingly goes on to include still another mitzvah, this one meant to be the outcome of engaging in prayer. That mitzvah, from Leviticus 19 is "Love thy neighbor as thyself."

APPENDIX

~~~~~~

TABLE OF TORAH AND HAFTARAH READINGS
FOR THE FESTIVALS AND
OTHER SPECIAL OCCASIONS

Day	Torah Reading	Maftir	Haftorah Readiı
Pesaḥ			
First day	Exodus 12:21–51	Numbers 28:16–25	Joshua 5:2–6:1
Second day	Leviticus 22:26–23:44	Numbers 28:16–25	Kings II 23:1–9, 21–25
Third day	Exodus 13:1–16	Numbers 28:19–25	
Fourth day	Exodus 22:24–23:19	Numbers 28:19–25	
Fifth day	Exodus 34:1–26	Numbers 28:19–25	
Sixth day	Numbers 9:1–14	Numbers 28:19–25	
Sabbath of hol hamoed	Exodus 33:12–34:26*	Numbers 28:19–25	Ezekiel 37:1–14
Seventh day	Exodus 13:17–22, 14:1–13, 15:1–26.	Numbers 28:19–25	Samuel II 22:1–51
Last day Pesaḥ	Deuteronomy 15:19–16:17**	Numbers 28:19–25	Isaiah 10:32–12:6
Shavuot			
First day	Exodus 19:1–20:23	Numbers 28:26–31	Ezekiel 1:1–28, 3:1
Second day	Deuteronomy 15:19–16:17***	Numbers 28:26–31	Ḥabakkuk 3:1–19

* If the Sabbath of hol hamoed falls on the third day of Pesaḥ, then the readings for the th
fourth, and fifth days are moved ahead.

** If the last day of Pesaḥ falls on a Sabbath, the reading is Deuteronomy 14:22–16:17.

*** If the second day of Shavuot falls on a Sabbath, the reading begins with 14:22.

Day	Torah Reading	Maftir	Haftorah Reading
Rosh Hashanah			
First day	Genesis 21:1–34	Numbers 29:1–6	Samuel I 1:1–2:10
Second day	Genesis 22:1–24	Numbers 29:1–6	Jeremiah 31:1–19
Yom Kippur			
Morning	Leviticus 16:1–34	Numbers 29:7–11	Isaiah 57:14–58:14
Afternoon	Leviticus 18:1–30		Book of Jonah
			Micah 7:18–20
Sukkot			
First day	Leviticus 22:26–23:44	Numbers 29:12–16	Zachariah 14:1–21
Second day	Leviticus 22:26–23:44	Numbers 29:12–16	Kings I 8:2–21
Third day	Numbers 29:17–25		
Fourth day	Numbers 29:20–28		
Fifth day	Numbers 29:23:31		
Sixth day	Numbers 29:26:34		
Seventh day	Numbers 29:26		
Sabbath of hol hamoed	Exodus 33:12–34:26	Numbers 29	Ezekiel 38:18–39:16
Shemini Atzeret	Deuteronomy 14:22–16:17	Numbers 29:35–30:1	Kings I 8:54–66
Simhat Torah	Deuteronomy 33:1–34:12,	Numbers 29:35–30:1	Joshua 1:1–18
	Genesis 1:1–2:3	Numbers 29:35–30:1	
Rosh Hodesh	Numbers 28:1–15		
Sabbath of Rosh Hodesh	regular portion	Numbers 28:9–15	Isaiah 66:1–24
Fast day	Exodus 32:11–14, 34:1–10		Isaiah 55:6–56:8 (only at Minha service)
Tisha b'Av (Shaharit)	Deuteronomy 4:25–40		Jeremiah 8:13–9:23
(Minha)	as on any other fast day		
Purim	Exodus 17:8–16		
Hanukkah			
First day	Numbers 7:1–17		
Second– Seventh days	the two passages that refer to that day of Hanukkah and the next		
Eighth day	Numbers 7:54–8:4		
Sabbath	regular portion	The Torah reading for that day of Hanukkah is read as the maftir.	Zachariah 2:14–4:7 Kings I 7:40–50 (Only on the Second Sabbath of Hanukkah)

APPENDIX

Day	Torah Reading	Maftir	Haftorah Reading
Special Sabbaths			
Shekolim	regular	Exodus 30:11–16	Kings II, 12:1–17
Zakhor	regular	Deuteronomy 25: 17–19	Samuel I, 15:2–34
Parah	regular	Numbers 19:1–22	Ezekiel 36:16–38
Haḥodesh	regular	Exodus 12:1–20	Ezekiel 45:16–46:18
Shabbat HaGadol	regular		Malachi 3:4–24

INDEX TO JEWISH
VALUES AND
PRINCIPLES OF FAITH

INDEX

369